Reaching Your Potential

Personal and Professional Development

Third Edition

Join us on the web at

careersuccess.delmar.com

Reaching Your Potential

Potential

Personal and Professional Development

Third Edition

ROBERT K. THROOP
MARION B. CASTELLUCCI

THOMSON

DELMAR LEARNING

Australia Canada Mexico Singapore Spain United Kingdom United States

Reaching Your Potential: Personal and Professional Development, 3rd edition

Robert K. Throop and Marion B. Castellucci

Vice President, Career Education Strategic Business Unit:
Dawn Gerrain

Director of Editorial:
Sherry Gomoll

Acquisitions Editor:
Martine Edwards

Developmental Editors:
Patricia Gillivan
Shelley Esposito

Editorial Assistant:
Paul Carmon

Director of Production:
Wendy A. Troeger

Production Editor:
Kathryn B. Kucharek

Technology Project Manager:
Joseph Saba

Director of Marketing:
Donna J. Lewis

Channel Manager:
Wendy E. Mapstone

Cover Images:
Getty One

Cover Design:
David Arsenault

For permission to use material from the text or product, contact us by

Tel.   (800) 730-2214
Fax   (800) 730-2215

http://www.thomsonrights.com

Library of Congress Cataloging-in-Publication Data

Throop, Robert K.
  Reaching your potential : personal and professional development / Robert K. Throop, Marion B. Castellucci.—3rd ed.
     p. cm.
Includes bibliographical references and index.
  ISBN 1-4018-2016-6
  1. College students—Conduct of life.   2. Success.   I. Castellucci, Marion.   II. Title

BJ1661.T48 2004
158—dc22   2003061820

NOTICE TO THE READER

This is for my father, Ken, who lives within me;
for my mother, Joie, who always made me feel unique;
for my wife, Joyce, who provides me with unconditional love;
and for my daughters, Tracey, Wendee, and Bethany,
who fill me with resounding joy.
—Robert K. Throop

•

For my mother, Agatha Eken Bonney.
—Marion B. Castellucci

Contents

Preface

Self-belief is the foundation of success in all personal, educational, and professional endeavors. In order to succeed, students must deal with personal, economic, and societal problems and make a commitment to work to achieve their goals. A solid sense of who they are and who they might become is the springboard for overcoming obstacles and succeeding in school and all other areas of life.

Reaching Your Potential is designed to help students take control of their lives and improve their self-belief. The text provides a blend of concepts and applications to help students discover their emotional, intellectual, physical, and social potential. Through a process of learning and self-examination, students discover their values, increase their commitment to personal goals, and challenge themselves to grow and learn. While gaining practical knowledge and skills, students will discover their emotional, intellectual, physical, and social resources. They will learn that they can improve their lives by changing the way they think about themselves—and then acting accordingly.

Coverage   *Reaching Your Potential,* Third Edition, is divided into five units and fifteen chapters. Unit 1, "Developing Your Emotional Potential," discusses the fundamentals—values, self-belief, commitment, and goal setting. Unit 2, "Dveloping Your Intellectual Potential," explores the thinking skills, creativity, and study skills needed for school and professional success. Unit 3, "Developing Your Physical Potential," discusses how good nutrition, exercise, and rest contribute to well-being and provides information on overcoming substance abuse and preventing the spread of sexually transmitted diseases. Unit 4, "Developing Your Social Potential," stresses the importance in today's diverse society of good communications and human relations skills, including avoiding miscommunication, active listening, speaking, ethical conduct, conflict resolution, group interaction, and leadership. The fifth and final unit, "Developing Your Action Plan," provides suggestions for dealing with stress and change, managing time and money, and choosing and pursuing a career.

How to Use this Book

Reaching Your **Potential**
Personal and Professional Development
Third Edition

ROBERT K. THROOP
MARION B. CASTELLUCCI

Because people learn best from their own experiences, *Reaching Your Potential* offers a unique format that involves students in active learning. Before they begin, students fill in a self-assessment questionnaire— a benchmark against which they will measure their progress.

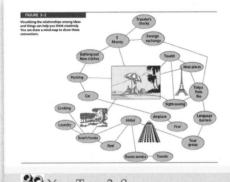

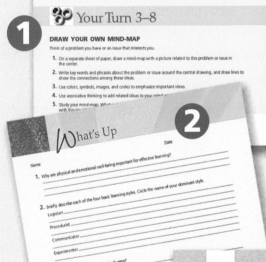

1 As students work through the text, they apply the concepts they learn to their own situations in the "**Your Turn**" activities that are interspersed throughout each chapter. Through these activities, students participate in a process of self-discovery, which engages and holds their interest.

2 At the end of each chapter, students test their comprehension by answering "**What's Up**" questions.

3 Students also test their comprehension with the **case studies** presented in each chapter. They can use their critical thinking skills to solve the problems.

4 Each chapter ends with a **journal activity** in which students reflect on the contents of the chapter as it pertains to their lives and their futures.

Finally, when students finish the text, they reassess themselves and the progress they have made toward reaching their potential.

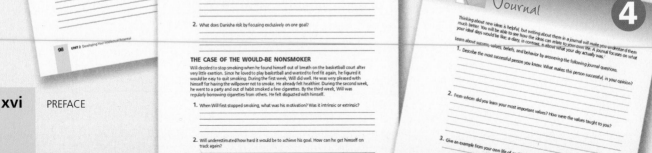

Additional features make the text attractive to students. Its format and concise coverage make the book easy to read and comprehend.

5 Full color **photos, illustrations,** and **tables** provide visual interest as well as reinforce concepts.

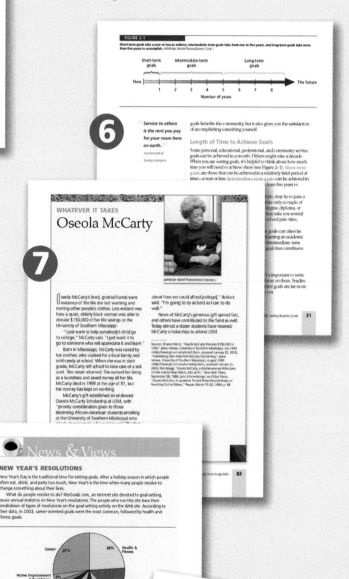

6 **Quotations** from great leaders and role models serve to inspire students to succeed.

7 A diverse array of people who have overcome challenges and succeeded in life are profiled in "**Whatever It Takes**," providing motivation for students to do the same.

8 "**News & Views**" highlight trends, topics, or issues of particular interest to students.

9 "**The Information Highway**" provides suggestions for using the Internet to supplement text coverage.

New to the Third Edition

To improve the effectiveness of the text, we have made changes in the third edition's pedagogy. First, to prompt students to reflect on their lives and to set challenging goals for themselves, we have added a journal activity at the end of each chapter. Students are prompted to review the content of the chapter as a whole and to analyze its relevance to their present and future. These "Chapter Journals" build on and reinforce the "Your Turn" activities in each chapter. Second, we have revised many of the "What's Up" questions at the end of each chapter so that answering them requires critical thinking skills. And third, we have revised several of the "Your Turn" activities to draw on the student's own experience rather than on a hypothetical case.

Our second goal in undertaking this revision was to make the text up to date in terms of the Internet. Although the Internet played a large role in our lives when the second edition was published, its use and influence are even more pervasive today. We have, therefore, written or updated sections on:

- using the Internet, including e-mail, search engines, and newsgroups (Chapter 1)
- doing research on the World Wide Web and evaluating Web sites (Chapter 4)
- doing research in on-line databases available to libraries by subscription (Chapter 4)
- using good e-mail etiquette (Chapter 7)
- preparing a resume in the proper format for posting to on-line resume databases or for sending over the Internet (Chapter 15)
- using Internet resources for career guidance and job searches (Chapter 15)

In addition, we have checked and updated all the Web site references in "Getting Up to Speed on the Information Highway." These Web sites provide students with a starting point for supplementing the content of each chapter via the Internet.

Finally, our third goal was to revise and update the instructional content to make it useful to students and relevant to their needs.

- In Chapter 3, a new approach to problem solving, called PrOACT, gives students a framework for assessing alternatives and making good decisions.

- In Chapter 5, the treatment of the USDA Dietary Guidelines and Food Guide Pyramid was completely overhauled in view of new knowledge about the role of complex carbohydrates in diet and a clearer understanding of how the pyramid has been used and should be used. In addition, the approach to weight was modernized, using body mass index as an indication of healthy weight rather than traditional height and weight charts.

- In Chapter 6, a new section on so-called club drugs was added to the material on drug abuse to reflect the growing use of such substances among young adults.

- In Chapter 9, a new section on cell phone do's and don'ts brings the treatment of telephone etiquette into the 21st century.

- In Chapter 11, a section on the norms of classroom behavior was added as an example of group norms with which students should be familiar.

- In Chapter 12, new material on coping with stress through lifestyle changes helps focus the chapter on effective ways to deal with stress.

- In Chapter 14, a new section on debit cards explains their uses, advantages, and disadvantages.

- Much of Chapter 15 was revised and updated. The importance of networking in getting a job was given greater emphasis. The resume section was completely overhauled, reflecting technology-driven changes. The need for both plain text, scannable resumes, and formatted resumes is explained, and both types of resumes are illustrated. E-mail cover letters are discussed and illustrated as well. A new section on preparing a career portfolio was added, since these often play a role in getting a job. Finally, the typical sequence of employment interviews is outlined, and the basic types of questions job applicants can expect are presented, with examples.

- Throughout the text, there are many new News & Views features: positive psychology, a branch of psychology that focuses on strength and coping skills rather than pathology (Chapter 1); the nun study, a long-term examination of why some nuns fare better than others as they age (Chapter 3); ethnic food guide pyramids, variations on the basic pyramid for different cuisines (Chapter 5); and where the jobs will be in 2010 (Chapter 15). Other News & Views features have been expanded and updated.

- Most of the Whatever It Takes profiles have been replaced with new profiles of people from all backgrounds and walks of life. Others have been updated.

- Photos have been updated in all chapters. As in the previous edition, we have tried to show a wide range of people of all races, ethnicities, and ages to reflect our diverse society.

Complete Learning and Instructional Package

Student Resources

WebTUTOR™

Designed to complement the text, WebTUTOR™ is a content-rich, web-based teaching and learning aid that reinforces and clarifies concepts. The WebCT™ and Blackboard™ platforms provide rich communication tools to instructors and students, including a course calendar, chat, e-mail, and threaded discussions.

WebTUTOR™ on WebCT™	(ISBN 1-4018-4916-4)
WebTUTOR™ on Blackboard™	(ISBN 1-4018-4917-2)
Text Bundled with WebTUTOR™ on WebCT™	(ISBN 1-4018-4914-8)
Text Bundled with WebTUTOR™ on Blackboard™	(ISBN 1-4018-4915-6)

Online Companion

An online companion is available to accompany the text. It includes additional articles and success profiles, helpful links to resources on the Web, video clips of appropriate interview techniques, printable forms, and additional quizzes for further student self-assessment. To access the companion, go to <http://www.delmarlearning.com/companions/> and search by author (Throop) or title (*Reaching Your Potential*).

Instructor Resources

The instructor's manual offers teaching suggestions, transparency masters, tests, answer keys, and additional activities and resources.

Instructor's Manual   (ISBN 1-4018-2018-2)

Because so many of the improvements in this text have come from your suggestions, we always welcome comments. Send us your thoughts care of Delmar Learning, 5 Maxwell Drive, Clifton Park, NY 12065-2919, ATTN: Career Success, or e-mail us at rkthroop@worldnet.att.net or marioncast@aol.com

Robert K. Troop

Marion B. Castellucci

Acknowledgments

We would like to acknowledge all the students who have proven that education—both through teaching and writing—is the ultimate profession, and that there could not have been a better path for us to have traveled.

Delmar Learning and the authors thank the following instructors, who reviewed the second edition and the manuscript for the third edition and provided valuable suggestions for improving the third edition:

Tricia Berry
Hamilton College
Urbandale, Iowa

Marianne Fitzpatrick
Bauder College
Atlanta, Georgia

Nancy Gleason
Hamilton College
Urbandale, Iowa

Carolyn Hagaman
Western Kentucky University
Bowling Green, Kentucky

Aleyenne Johnson-Jonas
Maric College
Vista, California

Susan Klemm
Lincoln School of Commerce
Lincoln, Nebraska

Maris Roze
DeVry Institute
Oakbrook Terrace, Illinois

Louise Sundermeier
Lynn University
Boca Raton, Florida

Diana Wyatt
Danville Area Community College
Danville, Illinois

Delmar Learning and the authors are also indebted to the following instructors, who reviewed the first edition and the manuscript for the second edition and made many helpful suggestions.

Thomas Bledsaw
ITT Technical Institute
Arlington, Texas

Sally Combs
Atlanta Technical Institute
Atlanta, Georgia

Joann Driggers
Mt. San Antonio College
Walnut, California

Martha Hannah
Valdosta Technical Institute
Valdosta, Georgia

Jonathan Hayward
ITT Technical Institute
West Covina, California

Lisa Hoover
ITT Technical Institute
Pittsburgh, Pennsylvania

Herman Kuminkoski
ITT Technical Institute
Pittsburgh, Pennsylvania

Thom Perrino
City College
Lauderhill, Florida

To the Lifelong Learner

Your values, beliefs, and thoughts make you the person you are today. They influence your current and future behaviors. But if you are like most people, perhaps you feel that you could be more than you are today. Perhaps your values, beliefs, and thoughts are limiting your ability to make the most of the present and grow toward a better future. To improve your life, you must change the way you think about yourself and your potential.

Reaching Your Potential is based on the simple idea that you can be what you want to be. Through a process of self-examination and self-discovery, you can change your life. But to change, you must understand the various aspects of yourself and how they interrelate to form the whole you.

Each of us has four areas of potential growth. We have:

- **emotional potential**: how we feel and what we want
- **intellectual potential**: how we think and learn
- **physical potential**: how we maintain our body's well-being
- **social potential**: how we relate to other people

Each of these four potentials will be discussed in this book separately so you can develop insight into that aspect of your own character and life. But it is important to remember—and we will keep reminding you—that these areas are interrelated and are simply parts of the whole you. It is vital that you develop all these potentials as an ensemble.

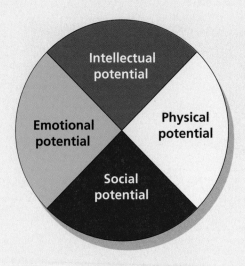

Each person has emotional, intellectual, physical, and social areas of potential.

How can you develop to your fullest potential? You must change the way you think about yourself and create a mindshift—a new way of looking at things. And the way to do this is through learning. Learning is the critical key to achieving success:

> Through learning we re-create ourselves. Through learning we become able to do something we were never able to do. Through learning we reperceive the world and our relationship to it. Through learning we extend our capacity to create, to be part of the . . . process of life.[1]

This type of learning is not passive. You cannot simply soak up information. Instead, to learn you must continually question your beliefs, values, and goals. You must apply what you learn to your own life in order to change and grow. *Reaching Your Potential* will help you do this.

The process of reaching your potential takes place in stages. Each stage builds upon the previous stage to expand your ability to create your own success.

Stage 1. Developing Your Self-Belief   Self-belief is the foundation of success. It is your knowledge of and confidence in your own abilities. Self-belief underlies all your actions, both good and bad. You develop your self-belief little by little, by succeeding in small ways that eventually build up into a solid foundation.

Stage 2. Reframing Your Thoughts   By changing your beliefs and values, you can change the way you perceive and act. An example of reframing is the ugly duckling who was transformed into a beautiful swan. The ugly duckling's situation did not change, but he perceived it completely differently and acted accordingly. Another example of reframing is a student who gets an F on a math exam. At first, she perceives herself as a math "dummy," but then she reframes that F: She decides the failing grade is really a wake-up call and she gets help from a math tutor. In order to change your behavior, you have to reframe your thoughts.

Stage 3. Setting Goals   Goals are the targets that we try to achieve. Without goals, we are aimless and confused. To establish goals, you must define your values and beliefs and examine the world around you in a realistic way. It's no good to be unrealistic about yourself or the world when you set goals. That's simply a way to excuse inaction and failure: *If there's no problem, I don't have to solve anything. If my parents were rich, I wouldn't be behind in my car payments. If I were smarter, I would pass that course.* Instead, goals should be realistic and achievable in a series of small steps.

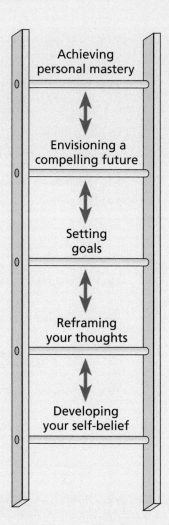

The success model: Achieving personal mastery is an ongoing process.

Stage 4. Envisioning a Compelling Future   Envisioning a compelling future means you have a vivid picture of what the future can be. This creates a driving force that helps you move from your current reality toward your future reality. The gap between the present and the future creates the tension necessary to motivate you to act. If you take no action toward achieving a compelling future, the gap between the present and your vision of the future remains.

Stage 5. Achieving Personal Mastery   The final stage in reaching your potential is achieving personal mastery. When you achieve this, you are able to get consistent results from your actions. You have a thorough understanding of yourself, the ability to reframe your thoughts when necessary, realistic and achievable goals, and a vision of the future.

Note that progress toward personal mastery is not a straight, unbroken line. Instead, we may achieve personal mastery in an area but then fall back to a previous stage. One way to think of the five stages is to compare them to the method used by mountain climbers to scale a high peak like Mt. Everest.[2] Climbers don't make straight for the top. Instead, they establish a base camp where plans and supplies are stored and where the climb begins. From the base camp they climb a few thousand feet and establish a second camp, and so on up the mountain. During the ascent the climbers sometimes run into problems at a certain height and have to return to the base camp or a lower campsite for supplies, rest, or help before they resume the climb and reach the top. Similarly, in our quest for personal mastery we go from stage to stage, but when we get stuck we return to a previous stage and start again.

So the process of reaching your potential and achieving personal mastery does not end when you finish this book. Instead, it is a lifelong process. As you grow and change, your visions of a compelling future and your goals will also change. What you will get from working through *Reaching Your Potential* are the knowledge and skills you need to keep up the habits of self-examination, self-discovery, and self-management that will serve you all your life.

Take a few minutes to assess yourself at this point in time, before you begin reading Chapter 1. Respond to the statements in the survey "Before You Begin: Self-Assessment." Later, when you have finished the book, you will reassess yourself by retaking the survey "After You're Done: Self-Assessment." We are confident that when you compare the two assessments, you will find that you have made real progress toward reaching your potential.

Before You Begin:
Self-Assessment

Read each of the following statements. Then circle *yes, maybe,* or *no* to indicate whether the statement is true of you at this time.

To the Lifelong Learner

1. I can name and describe the four areas of potential that each of us has.	Yes	Maybe	No
2. I have good self-belief, the foundation of success.	Yes	Maybe	No
3. I can learn new things and change my beliefs to change my behavior.	Yes	Maybe	No
4. I can set, pursue, and achieve realistic goals.	Yes	Maybe	No
5. I can envision a compelling future for myself.	Yes	Maybe	No
6. I have achieved personal mastery over at least some aspects of my life.	Yes	Maybe	No

UNIT 1 Developing Your Emotional Potential

Chapter 1 The Power of Self-Belief

7. I can explain my most important values and beliefs to another person.	Yes	Maybe	No
8. I usually think about things in a positive way.	Yes	Maybe	No
9. I recognize my good qualities and always make the most of them.	Yes	Maybe	No

Chapter 2 Setting Realistic Goals

10. I have a dream for my future.	Yes	Maybe	No
11. I have written personal, educational, professional, and community service goals.	Yes	Maybe	No
12. I have action plans for achieving my goals.	Yes	Maybe	No
13. I have the motivation needed to achieve my goals.	Yes	Maybe	No

UNIT 2   Developing Your Intellectual Potential

Chapter 3   Improving Your Thinking Skills

14. I use techniques to improve my memory.   Yes   Maybe   No
15. I am able to think critically.   Yes   Maybe   No
16. I try to solve problems in a
    systematic way.   Yes   Maybe   No
17. I use techniques to improve my
    creative thinking.   Yes   Maybe   No

Chapter 4   Improving Your Study Skills

18. I know my learning style and try to use it
    whenever possible.   Yes   Maybe   No
19. I have good study skills.   Yes   Maybe   No
20. I use special reading techniques
    when I read to learn.   Yes   Maybe   No
21. I take good notes on my readings
    and in class.   Yes   Maybe   No
22. I have good test-taking skills.   Yes   Maybe   No
23. I know how to use the resources
    of a library.   Yes   Maybe   No

UNIT 3   Developing Your Physical Potential

Chapter 5   Eating Well

24. I can list the basic nutrients and
    their food sources.   Yes   Maybe   No
25. I eat a balanced diet.   Yes   Maybe   No

Chapter 6   Staying Healthy

26. I am physically fit because I
    exercise regularly.   Yes   Maybe   No
27. I do not abuse drugs, including
    alcohol and tobacco.   Yes   Maybe   No
28. I understand how to prevent the spread
    of sexually transmitted diseases.   Yes   Maybe   No

UNIT 4   Developing Your Social Potential

Chapter 7   Communicating Effectively

29. I can explain the basic elements
    of communication.   Yes   Maybe   No

30. I know what my own communication style is.	Yes	Maybe	No
31. I use techniques to improve my communication with others.	Yes	Maybe	No

Chapter 8   Improving Your Listening Skills

32. I am an active listener, with respect for the speaker and comprehension of the message.	Yes	Maybe	No

Chapter 9   Improving Your Speaking Skills

33. I am a good speaker, with good voice qualities and a good command of standard English.	Yes	Maybe	No
34. I am good at conversing with another person.	Yes	Maybe	No
35. I have good telephone skills.	Yes	Maybe	No
36. I can prepare and deliver an oral presentation.	Yes	Maybe	No

Chapter 10   Getting Along with Others

37. I am assertive without being aggressive.	Yes	Maybe	No
38. I have ethical values that I try to live by.	Yes	Maybe	No
39. I am good at understanding the needs of other people.	Yes	Maybe	No
40. I give feedback tactfully and receive feedback openly.	Yes	Maybe	No
41. I use conflict resolution techniques to defuse angry situations.	Yes	Maybe	No

Chapter 11   Functioning in Groups

42. I can describe the basics of group dynamics.	Yes	Maybe	No
43. I function well as a member of a team or group.	Yes	Maybe	No
44. I can use different leadership styles in different situations.	Yes	Maybe	No

UNIT 5   Developing Your Action Plan

Chapter 12   Handling Change and Stress

45. I understand the relationship between change and stress.	Yes	Maybe	No

46. I know the signs of stress and watch out for them.	Yes	Maybe	No
47. I can reduce my feelings of stress by using coping techniques.	Yes	Maybe	No

Chapter 13 Managing Time

48. I perform tasks in a timely manner and I am punctual.	Yes	Maybe	No
49. I set priorities on the things I need to do.	Yes	Maybe	No
50. I use a planner and "to do" list to organize my time.	Yes	Maybe	No

Chapter 14 Managing Money

51. I know my values and goals and base short- and long-term financial decisions upon them.	Yes	Maybe	No
52. I have a written budget.	Yes	Maybe	No
53. I understand and use savings institutions, debit, credit, and insurance wisely.	Yes	Maybe	No
54. I know the factors that influence whether I should rent or buy a home.	Yes	Maybe	No
55. I invest now for large future expenses such as retirement.	Yes	Maybe	No

Chapter 15 Preparing for Your Career

56. I can match my skills and interests to one or more suitable occupations by using career resources.	Yes	Maybe	No
57. I have a good resume and can write a good cover letter.	Yes	Maybe	No
58. I know how to use various job-hunting resources.	Yes	Maybe	No
59. I am good at preparing for and undergoing employment interviews.	Yes	Maybe	No
60. I can evaluate whether a job fits into my long-term professional goals.	Yes	Maybe	No

Look over your self-assessment. Underline the statements to which you replied *maybe* or *no*. These statements reflect areas in which you may not yet have reached your potential. Pay particular attention to the chapters that cover these areas as you work through the book.

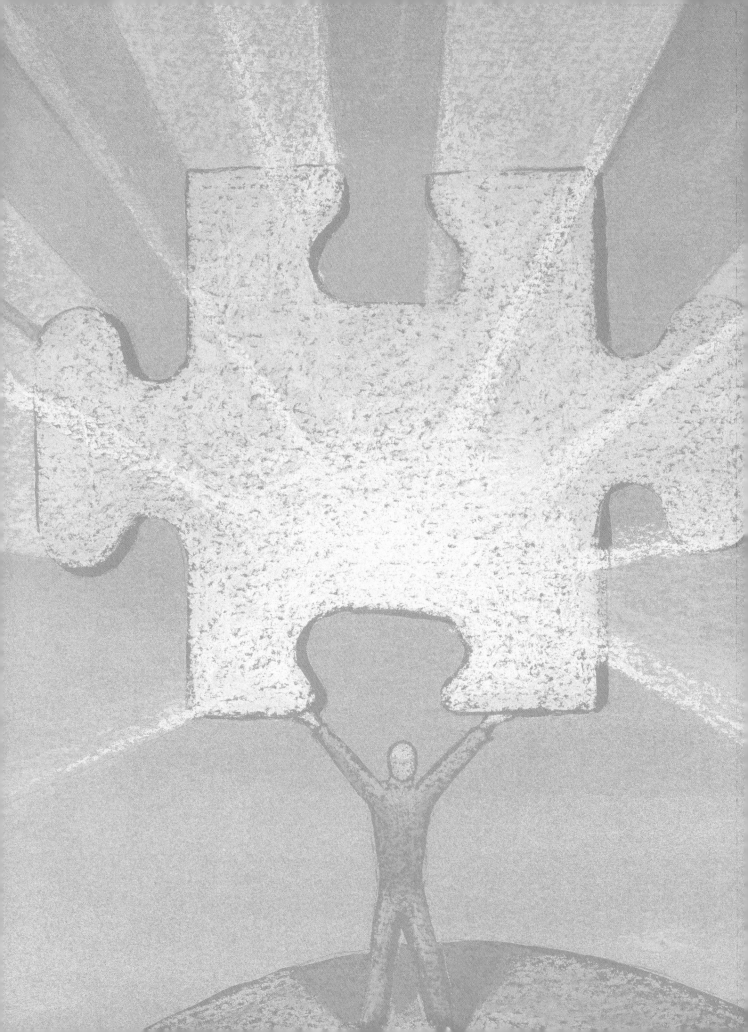

Developing Your Emotional Potential

Everything you think and do is colored by feelings and values, including setting your goals. In this unit you will explore your values and your self-belief. You will use your values and self-belief as the foundation for your goals.

Success requires self-knowledge, motivation, and hard work. Erik Weihenmayer climbed many mountains before tackling Mt. Everest.
(©Didrik Johnck/Corbis.)

Chapter 1

The Power of Self-Belief

After Erik Weihenmayer climbed Mt. Everest, he was hailed as the first blind person to reach the top of the world's tallest peak. His achievement was featured in newspapers and magazines and on TV. Weihenmayer was personally congratulated by President Bush in the Oval Office.

Weihenmayer's success in climbing Mt. Everest was not an overnight accomplishment. Blinded at age 13, Erik began climbing when he was 16, using his hands and feet to find places to hold on to the rock. Over the years, he climbed several of the world's highest mountains, in North America, South America, and Antarctica. Still, climbing Mt. Everest was a lifelong goal.

During the Everest climb, Weihenmayer kept reminding himself to stay focused and not let fear and frustration stand in his way. The hardest part of the climb was crossing the Khumbu Icefall. The icefall is 2,000 feet of broken blocks of ice and crevasses so treacherous that climbers can fall to their deaths. Weihenmayer made his way very slowly. He followed directions from the climber ahead of him, who wore a bell on his jacket as a guide.

Weihenmayer doesn't climb mountains to prove that blind people can do amazing things. To him, that's a side benefit of climbing. Rather, he climbs because he loves it. "It's a lot of hard work," says Weihenmayer, "but there are some really beautiful moments."[1]

Weihenmayer's achievements have gained him a great deal of publicity. Yet there are many people whose success occurs in more private ways. These people—whether successful in athletics, personal relationships, business, community affairs, or other areas—share several characteristics. Successful people know who they are and what they want. In addition, they are committed to achieving their best.

The foundation of success is a belief in yourself and your abilities. This is called **self-belief**. In this chapter, you will start developing your personal self-belief by exploring yourself, your values, and your beliefs. You will learn how beliefs can affect behavior, and you will use this knowledge to change your beliefs and behavior. Finally, you will discover how you can further develop a positive self-belief.

WHAT IS SUCCESS?

Let's take a moment to think about success. In the United States, success is often equated with glamor, fame, and riches. Or it is thought of as a single achievement—winning an election or getting a good job. Yet leading a successful life is an ongoing process.

For example, Jimmy Carter was president of the United States, surely one of the peaks of success. But when he returned to Georgia after his presidency, he explored new tasks. Carter's work with Habitat for Humanity, a volunteer organization that helps build and renovate low-income housing, helped that organization grow. He represented the United States on a number of diplomatic missions over the years. In 2002 Carter was awarded the Nobel Prize for Peace primarily for his work *after* he was U.S. president.

Fame and awards are not the only marks of a successful life. A feeling of worth and good relationships with others are often the basis of a successful life. As golf champion Chi Chi Rodriguez said, "The most successful human being I know was my dad and he never had anything financially."

So people who are truly successful are always trying to fulfill their **potential**. They focus on possibilities and work to turn them into realities. Furthermore, they see their potential as wide-ranging, from emotional to intellectual, from social to physical. They also see that their potential continues to change and grow as they gain experience. People who are trying to reach their potential know that the pursuit of success is a lifelong process.

VALUES

People who lead successful lives live by certain values. **Values** are your deepest feelings and thoughts about yourself and life. Values have three parts: (1) what you think, (2) how you feel, and (3) how you act, based

Success doesn't come to you . . . you go to it.

marva collins,

american educator

If we did all the things we are capable of doing, we would literally astonish ourselves.

thomas a. edison,

inventor

Your Turn 1–1

WHO ARE YOU?

Successful people usually have a clear sense of who they are and what they want from life. Take a few minutes to think about yourself and your life. Then answer these questions.

1. I like:

a._____

_____

b._____

_____

c._____

_____

2. I appreciate:

a._____

_____

b._____

_____

c._____

_____

3. I am good at:

a._____

_____

b._____

_____

c._____

_____

4. Someday I would like to:

a._____

_____

b._____

_____

c._____

_____

It can be hard for families to teach their children what they value. Children learn values from many sources outside the family. Ratings systems help parents decide what movies, TV shows, CDs, and video games are appropriate for their children. *(©Keith Dannemiller/Corbis.)*

on what you think and feel. For example, one of your values might be honesty. You think that telling a lie is wrong (thought). If someone you trust lies to you, you feel betrayed (feeling). When you make a mistake, you admit it rather than try to cover up or blame someone else (action).

Sometimes the three aspects of values do not always work in harmony. Let's take the value of honesty again. Even though you think telling a lie is wrong, there are times when you feel or act as though lying is okay. If someone asks you to do something you don't want to do, you might lie and say you're busy. Lying makes you feel uncomfortable because your actions and thoughts contradict one another. People are most comfortable in situations in which the thinking, feeling, and acting aspects of their values are working together.

Where Do Values Come From?

You weren't born with a set of values. Rather, as you grew up, you were influenced by your family, friends, religion, culture, school, and society at large. For example, if your family expected each member to pitch in with chores, you may have learned the values of cooperation and helpfulness. When your friends became more of an influence, you may have learned the value of friendship.

Xernona Clayton, a broadcasting executive, says her basic values come from lessons her father taught her. Her father, a minister in a small Oklahoma town, often worked with people of various races and backgrounds. As a child, Xernona saw Native Americans, whites, and blacks like herself consulting with her father. Her father's example taught her to look beyond race to see a person's inner qualities. He taught her to be kind to all people, regardless of race, and to focus on inner qualities and strength, not on outward appearances.

Our Society's Values

Although Americans come from many national, ethnic, and racial groups, we share many values. Polls have shown that adult Americans value honesty, ambition, responsibility, and broad-mindedness. We value peace, family security, and freedom. We may not always behave according to our values, but they are the standard against which we judge ourselves. Rank your values in Your Turn 1–2.

It's interesting to see how a large group of technical and business school graduates ranked the same values you ranked. Look at this list to find out:

1. Competent (capable)
2. Self-controlled (committed)

Your Turn 1–2

WHAT DO YOU VALUE?

Here is a list of 15 values arranged in alphabetical order. Study the list carefully. Then place a 1 next to the value most important to you, a 2 next to the value that is second in importance, and so on. The value that is least important to you should be ranked 15.

When you have completed ranking the values, check your list. Feel free to make changes. Take all the time you need so that the end result truly reflects your values.

Value	Rank	Value	Rank
Affectionate	___	Honest	___
Ambitious	___	Logical	___
Brave	___	Neat	___
Cheerful	___	Obedient (dutiful, respectful)	___
Competent (capable)	___		
Courteous (well-mannered)	___	Open-minded	___
Forgiving	___	Responsible	___
Helpful (working for others' welfare)	___	Self-controlled (committed)	___

> **The only place that success comes before work is in the dictionary.**
>
> *vidal sassoon,*
>
> *salon professional*

3. Ambitious
4. Open-minded
5. Honest
6. Neat
7. Forgiving
8. Helpful (working for others' welfare)
9. Affectionate
10. Cheerful
11. Courteous (well-mannered)
12. Responsible
13. Brave
14. Obedient (dutiful, respectful)
15. Logical

Apparently, these technical and business school graduates feel that being competent or capable (number 1), and self-controlled or committed (number 2) were of greatest importance. They believe that competence and commitment are necessary for a successful life.

Research has supported the conclusions of these graduates. A five-year study to determine what 120 of the nation's top artists, athletes, and scholars had in common came up with surprising results. Researcher Benjamin Bloom, professor of education at the University

Your Turn 1–3

EXAMINE YOUR VALUES

Answer the following questions about the 15 values you ranked.

1. Why is your top-ranked value so important to you?

_____

_____

2. Describe a situation in which your top-ranked value influenced your behavior.

_____

_____

_____

_____

3. How did your ranking of the values differ from those of the students who ranked them?

_____

_____

4. Now that you know how others ranked the values, how would you change your rankings, if at all?

_____

_____

of Chicago, said, "We expected to find tales of great natural gifts. We didn't find that at all. Their mothers often said it was their other child who had the greater gift." The study concluded that the key element common to these successful people was not talent but commitment.[2]

Changing Values

Our values can change as a result of experience. For example, after the terrorist attacks on the United States on September 11, 2001, a shift took place in Americans' values. According to a CBS News/*New York Times* poll taken a year later, 14 percent of Americans reevaluated their lives as a result of the attack. Although many felt the country had not changed, 17 percent thought that communities had become stronger, and 7 percent felt that Americans were more patriotic, had more pride in their country, and were nicer to one another than they had been before.[3]

Values can also change because of personal experience. A young woman overcame a drug abuse problem with the help of her church's

BENJAMIN FRANKLIN'S VALUES

Throughout history, people have been concerned about figuring out their values and trying to live by them. Benjamin Franklin, the 18th-century American printer, author, diplomat, and scientist, was one of the writers of the Declaration of Independence. He also helped draft the U.S. Constitution. In his *Autobiography,* Franklin explains how he tried to change his behavior by describing and then trying to live by his values, which he called "virtues." How many of Franklin's values are still important today? Which of Franklin's values do you share?

The Thirteen Virtues

1. Temperance: Eat not to dullness. Drink not to elevation.
2. Silence: Speak not but what may benefit others or yourself. Avoid trifling conversation.
3. Order: Let all your things have their places. Let each part of your business have its time.
4. Resolution: Resolve to perform what you ought. Perform without fail what you resolve.
5. Frugality: Make no expense but to do good to others or yourself, i.e., waste nothing.
6. Industry: Lose no time. Be always employed in something useful. Cut off all unnecessary actions.
7. Sincerity: Use no hurtful deceit. Think innocently and justly; if you speak, speak accordingly.
8. Justice: Wrong none by doing injuries or omitting the benefits that are your duty.
9. Moderation: Avoid extremes. Forbear resenting injuries so much as you think they deserve.
10. Cleanliness: Tolerate no uncleanliness in body, clothes, or habitation.
11. Tranquility: Be not disturbed at trifles or at accidents common or unavoidable.
12. Chastity: Rarely use venery* but for health or offspring—never to dullness, weakness, or the injury of your own or another's peace or reputation.
13. Humility: Imitate Jesus and Socrates.[†]

Source: Franklin, Benjamin, *The Autobiography of Benjamin Franklin and Selections from His Other Writings*. New York: Random House, 1994, pp. 93–95.
*Sexual activity.
[†]Ancient Greek philosopher who taught about virtue and justice.

music director. As a result, she became aware of the importance of helping others. Today she is studying to become a psychotherapist so she can help others.

BELIEFS

While values are your most deeply held general thoughts and feelings, beliefs are the specific opinions you have about yourself and particular people, situations, things, or ideas. In other words, beliefs are the specific attitudes that arise from your values. For example, if one of your values is ambition, you may have the belief that further education is important for success. If you value helpfulness, you may believe that you should do volunteer work in your community.

The Effects of Beliefs

Psychologists have shown that beliefs have a tremendous influence on behavior, and in turn, behavior can affect beliefs. Aesop's fable about the fox and the grapes shows how this can happen. When the fox first sees the grapes, he thinks they look delicious. This belief influences his behavior. He leaps up again and again, trying to reach the grapes. But the bunch of grapes is too high for him, and he gives up. Frustrated, the fox changes his belief: He decides the grapes must be sour.

This type of interplay between beliefs and behavior goes on all the time. Most of the time, you may not even be aware that it is happening. Yet your beliefs and other people's beliefs about you—both positive and negative—have a powerful influence on how you behave.

Negative Beliefs   Each person has the potential to live a successful and happy life. Yet most of us fall short of that ideal because we are carrying a bag of mental "garbage" that weighs us down. This garbage is negative beliefs about ourselves. Some examples of negative beliefs are:

"I can't do algebra."

"I'm not smart enough to do that."

"Nobody cares about me."

"I'll never find a job."

Unfortunately, negative beliefs like these influence our behavior. The person who says she can't learn algebra in fact can't. The person who says he can't find a job doesn't find a job. Why? Because they don't try very hard. They think they will fail and so they do fail. A belief that comes true because it is believed is called a **self-fulfilling prophecy**.

Positive Beliefs   Self-fulfilling prophecies need not be negative, however. Sometimes they are positive; they enable you to take action and make progress. Some positive, or enabling, beliefs are:

"I will find the money to go to school."

"I will speak up even though I'm nervous."

"I'm going to start my own business in five years."

"I will learn to swim."

The power of enabling beliefs is that they often come true. They come true not because of wishful thinking, however. Rather, enabling beliefs help you focus on what you need to do to accomplish something. They give you the self-confidence to persist and succeed.

> **They cannot take away our self-respect if we do not give it to them.**
>
> *gandhi, indian political and spiritual leader*

Beliefs can transform behavior. Jaime Escalante's students didn't believe they could learn calculus, much less pass a national calculus exam. Yet because he believed they could, they mastered calculus. *(AP/Wide World Photos.)*

Others Affect Your Beliefs Your beliefs about yourself, both positive and negative, are influenced by the people around you. Family, friends, coworkers, and acquaintances all affect your beliefs. For example, many studies have shown the effect of teachers' beliefs on students' performance. In one experiment, 60 preschoolers were taught symbols. One group was taught by instructors who were told to expect good symbol learning. The other group was taught by instructors told to expect poor learning. The results? Nearly 77 percent of the first group of children learned five or more symbols. Only 13 percent of the second group of children learned five or more symbols.[4]

The power of other people's beliefs was dramatized in the movie *Stand and Deliver*, based on a Los Angeles mathematics teacher named Jaime Escalante. Escalante believed that his underachieving inner-city high school students could learn calculus. He also believed they could pass a national standardized calculus exam. After a year of intense effort on his part and theirs, *all* the students passed the exam. Such outstanding results were so unusual that the testing authority had the students retake the test. They passed again. Without the power of Escalante's belief in them and their belief in themselves, these students probably would not have learned calculus.

> **I am somebody!
> If my mind can
> conceive it, and
> my heart can
> believe it, I know
> I can achieve it!**
>
> *the reverend jesse jackson,*
>
> *civil rights activist and*
>
> *political leader*

Victims and Nonvictims If you allow yourself to be persuaded by negative beliefs, you will soon view yourself as a victim. Victims operate from a position of weakness. They feel that they are not smart enough or strong enough to take charge of their own lives. They live from day to day, allowing things to happen to them and others to control them.

Nonvictims, on the other hand, understand that negative beliefs can be crippling. Nonvictims have the ability to resist the negative beliefs of others because they believe in their own strengths. Because they have positive views of their abilities and goals, nonvictims often succeed where victims fail. The Reverend Jesse Jackson, for example, grew up in poverty and went on to become a political leader and Democratic presidential candidate. "My mother was a teenaged mother and her mother was a teenaged mother. With scholarships and other help, I managed to get an education. Success to me is being born in a poor or disadvantaged family and making something of yourself."

Your Turn 1–4

THE POWER OF OTHER PEOPLE'S BELIEFS

Think about a time when another person's opinion of you influenced your thoughts or actions. Then recall a time when your opinion of someone else changed what that person thought or did.

1. Describe a time when someone's opinion of you influenced your thoughts or actions.

_____

_____

_____

2. Describe a time when your opinion of someone changed that person's thoughts or actions.

_____

_____

_____

> *No one can persuade another to change. Each of us guards a gate of change that can only be opened from the inside.*
>
> marilyn ferguson

Changing Your Beliefs

We all suffer the effects of negative beliefs, some of us more than others. Sometimes events don't happen the way we expect. Or we fall into a pattern of negative behavior toward the people around us. Or a stressful event or change in our lives throws us off balance. When these situations happen, it's time to pay attention to your beliefs. If your beliefs are contributing to your difficulties, you can change them—and change your life for the better.

Why should you drop negative beliefs and adopt beliefs that will enable you to succeed? Because it works. You must:

1. understand the power that beliefs have in your life
2. realize that continuing to think in a negative way will harm the quality of your life
3. change your beliefs and how you feel about yourself

If you change your beliefs, you will change your behavior. If you change your behavior, you will change your life.

WHATEVER IT TAKES

Linda Pauwels

(*Courtesy of Nick Koon,* The Orange County Register)

You may have seen her on CNN, Fox, or Telemundo—Captain Linda Pauwels, the only female spokesperson for the Allied Pilots Association. In 2000, at the age of 37, Captain Pauwels became the first Hispanic woman to captain a jet for American Airlines. She has another "first" to her credit. According to the International Society of Women Airline Pilots, Pauwels became the world's youngest female jet captain at age 25.

Nothing in Pauwels's childhood hinted at her future success in aviation. When she was 6, she came to Miami from Argentina with her mother and younger brother. Her mother worked two jobs, and when she could not care for the children, she sent them back to Argentina to stay with family. Pauwels and her brother went back and forth between Miami and Argentina as they grew up.

At age 16, Pauwels returned to the United States for good and earned her GED. She took a job at an aviation company and fell in love with flying. At 17, she earned her private pilot's license. Soon she was test-flying small planes. When she was 22, she went to work for Southern Air Transport—the first female pilot they ever hired.

Today Pauwels wants to establish a foundation to help young Hispanics become pilots. "I want to identify . . . children of character, competent, who you can see are going to make it," explains Pauwels. "I always had people help me." She's also gone back to school for a bachelor of science degree in aeronautics.

Sources: Julia Bencomo Lobaco, "Capt. Linda Pauwels: Flying Sky High," *Hispanic,* June 2002, pp. 20, 32; "Pauwels Named *Hispanic Business* 100 Most Influential Hispanics," APA Pilot Perspective, Oct. 14, 2002, p. 2; "Other Notable Firsts," International Society of Women Airline Pilots Web site, <http://www.iswap.org/firsts/other.html>, accessed January 21, 2003.

Using Positive Self-Talk   That negative inner voice that tells you how bad things are and how bad they always will be has to be silenced. Talking back to that negative voice can help you change your beliefs, attitudes, and behavior.

To change your beliefs and behavior, you needn't talk out loud in public, but you can use positive self-talk. Positive self-talk has three characteristics:

1. Positive self-talk consists of "I" statements. "I" statements show that you are taking charge of your life.

2. Positive self-talk uses the present tense. Using the present tense shows you are ready for action.

3. Positive self-talk is positive and enthusiastic. It focuses on *what is* rather than *what is not*.

For example, suppose that Jessica's longtime boyfriend Brian has broken off their relationship. Jessica wants to meet new people, but she makes no effort to do so. Instead, she gets more depressed and lonely. Jessica thinks, "Brian broke up with me so I must be boring and unattractive. Why should anyone want to go out with me?" It would be far more helpful if Jessica used positive self-talk. She could tell herself, "I am an interesting and attractive person. I am looking for chances to meet new people and form new relationships."[5]

Your Turn 1–5

USE POSITIVE SELF-TALK

Each of the following is a negative belief. Rewrite each so that it is positive self-talk.

1. I'll never pass that exam. I missed too many classes.

_____

_____

2. That computer is too hard to operate.

_____

_____

3. I'll be ____ years old before I get my diploma (or degree or certificate).

_____

_____

Answer the following questions.

4. Describe a situation about which you had negative thoughts and feelings.

_____

_____

5. How could you have used positive self-talk to change your beliefs and behavior?

_____

_____

POSITIVE PSYCHOLOGY

After World War II, many psychologists concentrated on researching and treating mental illness. Since then, there have been many breakthroughs in the treatment of mental disorders. At least 14 can now be cured or their symptoms relieved. However, the field of psychology lost sight of making the lives of all people better and encouraging exceptional achievement.

In response, positive psychology is a new branch of psychology that studies the positive aspects of human experience. It focuses on people's strengths instead of their weaknesses. It is concerned with mental health rather than mental illness.

At the level of the individual, positive psychology focuses on positive traits: the ability to love and work, courage, interpersonal skill, appreciation for beauty, perseverance, forgiveness, originality, future-mindedness, spirituality, talent, and wisdom. At the community level, positive psychology is about civics and citizenship: responsibility to the group, nurturance, generosity, civility, moderation, tolerance, and work ethic.

One aspect of positive psychology is prevention. How can problems like depression, substance abuse, and violence be prevented when society contributes to these problems? According to positive psychologists, improvements in prevention have come from building competencies in people, not from treating their weaknesses. There are human qualities that help prevent mental illness and antisocial behavior. Optimism, courage, hope, and perseverance are just a few.

People who are optimistic tend to interpret their troubles as passing, controllable, and specific to one situation. In contrast, pessimistic people believe that troubles last forever, undermine everything that they do, and can't be controlled. Positive psychologists think that people can be taught to be more optimistic. Pessimistic people can distract and distance themselves from negative beliefs and reactions to failure. They can argue with themselves about the failure and discover it is not as bad as it could have been. By doing this, people can learn to turn pessimistic thought patterns into optimistic thought patterns. They can increase their sense of well-being.

Sources: Martin E. P. Seligman, *Authentic Happiness: Using the New Positive Psychology to Realize Your Potential for Lasting Fulfillment,* New York: Free Press, 2002; Martin E. P. Seligman and Mihaly Csikszentmihalyi, "Positive Psychology: An Introduction," *American Psychologist,* millennial issue, 2000, at <http://www.psych.upenn.edu/seligman/apintro.htm>, accessed February 17, 2003; Martin E. P. Seligman, *Learned Optimism: How to Change Your Mind and Your Life,* New York: Simon & Schuster, 1990, p. 219.

The Seven Beliefs of Successful People

Positive beliefs will empower you to use all your emotional, intellectual, physical, and social potential to make things happen your way. People who consistently succeed can commit all their resources to achieving their goals. Let's examine seven beliefs that many successful people live by.[6]

1. **Everything happens for a reason and a purpose.** People have both good and bad experiences. Instead of dwelling on the bad, successful people think in terms of future possibilities.

2. **There is no such thing as failure.** Rather, there are only results. If the result is not desirable, successful people change their actions and produce new results.

3. **Whatever happens, take responsibility.** Successful people don't blame others when something goes wrong. Taking responsibility is one of the best measures of a person's maturity.

4. **It's not necessary to understand everything in order to use everything.** Successful people don't get bogged down in every detail. They learn what they need to know and don't dwell on the rest.

5. **After yourself, people are your greatest resource.** Successful people have a tremendous respect and appreciation for other people. They understand that good relationships are one of the foundations of a successful life.

6. **Work is play.** No one succeeds by doing something they hate to do. Work should be exciting, challenging, interesting. It should be fun.

7. **There's no lasting success without commitment.** Successful people are persistent. They keep doing their best.

SELF-BELIEF

The net effect of your values and beliefs is your self-belief. Self-belief is your confidence in and respect for your own abilities. Self-belief is the part of us that is resilient in the face of difficulties. Bad things may happen and hurt us—physically, emotionally, or economically—but our positive self-belief does not need to be harmed. People with positive self-belief understand that outward circumstances do not change this inner belief.

WHAT'S YOUR SELF-BELIEF?

Self-belief involves the way you think and feel about yourself. Use the following list of personality traits to describe your current self-belief.

aggressive	dishonest	irresponsible	quiet
ambitious	dumb	lonely	reserved
assertive	eager	loyal	responsible
bossy	fair	mature	sensitive
capable	funny	motivated	shy
caring	goal-oriented	neat	sincere
cheerful	gloomy	negative	sweet
confident	healthy	nervous	trusting
considerate	honest	open	unambitious
creative	humble	outgoing	understanding
daring	indecisive	passive	unhealthy
decisive	insensitive	polite	unmotivated
determined	intelligent	positive	warm

1. Current self-belief: I see myself as

_____

_____

_____

_____

_____

Now imagine that you are at a banquet. Your family, friends, and colleagues are there to praise you. What qualities do you hope they talk about?

2. Future self-belief: I will be

_____

_____

_____

_____

_____

_____

Improving Your Self-Belief

Have you decided that your self-belief is not all it could be? There are ways to improve your self-belief.

1. **Accept yourself.** Recognize your own good qualities and don't expect to be perfect. Everyone has special talents and abilities. Work to discover and develop yours.

2. **Pay attention to yourself.** Try to discover what gives you inner satisfaction, and do things that give you pleasure. Successful people do what they enjoy.

3. **Use positive self-talk.** Encourage yourself to make the most of your abilities by developing a positive mental attitude. People who succeed tell themselves that they will succeed.

4. **Don't be afraid to try new things.** Remember that there is no such thing as failure—only results. If you don't try new things, you won't reach your potential.

5. **Remember that you are special.** No one else has your set of capabilities and talents. Your values, beliefs, and emotions, and the way you act upon them, make up your unique personality.

The Foundation of Success

Positive self-belief is the foundation of success. When you believe in yourself, you can accomplish what you set your mind to. Self-belief allows you to use your emotional, intellectual, social, and physical potential to take action. Taking action means making progress toward achieving your dreams and goals. When you act, you get results. When you get results, your self-belief improves because you've succeeded at something. Improved self-belief gives you the confidence to take further action. The process of building self-belief is cyclical, as shown in Figure 1–1, page 20. The more you try, the more you accomplish and the greater your self-belief. Self-belief with commitment can create miracles.

Take the example of Mahatma Gandhi, a man with many exceptional traits, one of which was a strong belief in himself and his abilities. While the Indian power elites were trying to break England's colonial rule with speeches and infighting, Gandhi was out in the countryside working alone with the poor. Gradually he gathered overwhelming support and trust from the ordinary people of India. With no political office or military capability, he and his followers eventually defeated England. India won its independence as a nation.

> **If you want a quality, act as if you already had it.**
>
> *william james,*
> *psychologist and philosopher*

> **If you want to succeed in life . . . you . . . need to know what you believe in. . . . Then you have to have the courage to act on those beliefs.**
>
> *rudolph giuliani,*
> *former mayor*
> *of New York City*

FIGURE 1–1

Self-belief increases your potential; you act, and you get good results. Good results improve your self-belief, and the cycle starts again. *(Reprinted with the permission of Simon & Schuster Adult Publishing Group, from* Unlimited Power *by Anthony Robbins. Copyright © 1986 by Robbins Research Institute.)*

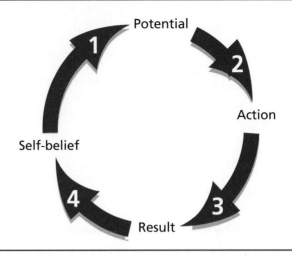

Although Gandhi was clearly an exceptional person, successful people share some of his characteristics. They are willing to do whatever it takes to reach their potential without harming others. They are not necessarily the "best" or the "brightest," but they have positive self-belief and a strong commitment to their goals. You can be one of them.

The Information Highway

GETTING UP TO SPEED

To use the Internet, you must have a computer with a modem that connects you to the network via phone lines, cable lines, or a wireless connection. You also must have an Internet service provider, such as America Online or earthlink.net. If you don't have these things yourself, you can find them elsewhere. Your school library and computer labs, public libraries, and Internet cafes now make Internet access available to students and the public.

WHAT'S ON THE INTERNET?

Once you are on line, take time to learn your way around. The Internet is huge and growing daily. It is somewhat disorganized. It has many elements, some of which you may use all the time; others you may never use. Here is a brief overview of some aspects of the Internet.

1. **The World Wide Web.** The World Wide Web consists of millions of Web pages— interlinked documents containing text, pictures, sounds, and movies. When you click on a

continues

link, which usually appears as underlined text or a picture, you are taken to a related Web page. **Surfing the Net** refers to the process of clicking on links to go from one page to another, following topics that interest you. A collection of related Web pages maintained by an individual or group is called a **Web site**. The World Wide Web is the largest and fastest growing portion of the Internet.

2. **E-mail. E-mail** allows you to exchange messages via computer with anyone else who has an e-mail address, anywhere in the world. You can attach files with documents, sounds, pictures, or software to your e-mail messages. You can also use e-mail to subscribe to a **discussion list**, a special interest discussion group. Once you join, you will receive copies of messages that are distributed to all list subscribers. If you don't have an e-mail address, you can get one through Web sites such as <http://www.hotmail.com> or <http://www.yahoo.com>. You may also be able to get an e-mail address through your school.

3. **Usenet Discussion Forums.** There are a huge number of discussion forums, or groups, on almost any subject you can think of, from horror movies to college to entrepreneurs. These forums are global bulletin boards where you can read and post messages. Keep in mind that in most groups no one is keeping an eye on the content or the users. You may find silly, boring, repetitive, or obscene material. On the other hand, you may also find something useful or brilliant.

FINDING INFORMATION ON THE INTERNET

There are two main ways of finding information on the Internet: by its address and by using a search engine.

If you know the Internet address of what you are looking for, you can use it to locate the information. Different types of Internet addresses look different:

Type	Example
World Wide Web	http://www.delmarlearning.com
Usenet	news.announce.newusers
E-mail	Jsmith@abc.com

If you do not know the Internet address, you can use a **search engine**, which is a computerized index such as Google <http://www.google.com>, Yahoo <http://www.yahoo.com>, or Alta Vista <http://www.altavista.com>. These are accessed through your Internet service provider. Once you have accessed a search engine, you enter a **key word** or words, and the search engine provides a list of Internet locations where they appear. The more specific you can be, the better the results of your search.

For example, using Google we did a search on "Benjamin Franklin" and got more than a million "hits," or Web pages, with a reference to Benjamin Franklin. To narrow the search, we added the word *values* to "Benjamin Franklin." This time we got 67,000 hits. To narrow it even further, we added a fourth word, *virtues,* and got 4,000 hits. So, the more specific the key words, the fewer the results and the more on-target they are.

continues

Try finding some information related to the topics in Chapter 1. First, you can visit a Web site:

■ Self-Improvement Online, Inc., has information on personal growth, including links to other sites and newsgroups <http://www.selfgrowth.com>.

Second, if you have e-mail, send a message to one of the authors. We'd love to get your suggestions and comments.

■ rkthroop@worldnet.att.net
■ MarionCast@aol.com

Third, find a Usenet group on a particular topic, such as success. You can search in the Groups section of Google or ask this group:

■ http://www.faqs.org

Last, use a search engine and try searching for these key words: *Erik Weihenmayer, American Success Institute, American values, positive psychology, Benjamin Franklin,* and *Linda Pauwels.*

Evaluating What You Find

Remember that anyone can post anything on the Web. The quality of the material you will find ranges from the full text of authoritative encyclopedias to "get rich quick" schemes to biased opinions. Be very skeptical of what you find. Ask yourself, Who is running this Web site? What is its purpose? Is it a commercial, educational, nonprofit, or government site? How credible is the site? We'll give you further suggestions for evaluating Web sites when we discuss doing research on the Internet in Chapter 4.

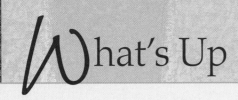

What's Up

Name _____   Date _____

1. What are values?
_____

2. List the three aspects of values.
_____
_____
_____

3. What are beliefs?
_____

4. How do negative beliefs affect you?
_____
_____

5. How do other people's beliefs affect you?
_____

6. How can positive self-talk be used to change your beliefs?
_____
_____

7. What are the three characteristics of positive self-talk?
_____
_____
_____

8. What effect does changing your beliefs have?
_____

9. What is self-belief?
_____

10. Why is self-belief important?
_____
_____

Case Studies

THE CASE OF THE NEW ROOMMATE

Elisa was discovering that her new roommate Pam had some unsettling habits. Although they had agreed to share chores, even listing who would do each task, Elisa felt that Pam was not doing her share. For example, when it was Pam's turn to clean, the apartment stayed messy for days. When Pam finally did clean up, Elisa thought she didn't do a thorough job. Elisa was very uncomfortable living in a dirty, disorderly apartment. She was starting to think she had made a mistake when she had asked Pam to share the apartment. Yet Elisa liked Pam because she was a cheerful, pleasant person.

1. Why is Elisa uncomfortable with her new roommate?

_____

_____

2. What does Elisa value?

_____

3. Does Pam share these values? Explain.

_____

_____

4. What might Elisa do to improve the situation with her roommate?

_____

_____

THE CASE OF THE GLOOMY COWORKER

Lee and Dave were technicians who serviced computers for home-based and small businesses. Their boss was going to take a week's vacation, and she asked Lee to fill in for her. Instead of repairing systems in the field, Lee would have to take customer calls, assign field technicians to particular jobs, and make sure everything went smoothly. He was looking forward to the challenge. When Dave heard about Lee's temporary assignment, he began to discourage Lee. He told him all the things that could go wrong—angry customers, not enough technicians, systems that couldn't be fixed. Finally, Dave told Lee that Lee wouldn't get through the week without a major catastrophe. Lee started to feel very nervous about the assignment.

1. What was the effect of Dave's negative beliefs on Lee's attitude toward substituting for his boss?

_____

_____

2. What should Lee do to counteract the effect of Dave's beliefs?

_____

_____

_____

Journal

Thinking about new ideas is helpful, but writing about them in a journal will help you understand them much better. You will be able to see how the ideas can relate to your own life. This journal focuses on what your ideal days would be like; a diary, in contrast, is about what your day actually was.[7]

Learn about success, values, beliefs, and behavior by answering the following journal questions.

1. Describe the most successful person you know. What makes this person successful, in your opinion?

   _____
   _____
   _____
   _____
   _____

2. From whom did you learn your most important values? How were the values taught to you?

   _____
   _____
   _____
   _____
   _____

3. Give a personal example of positive thoughts or beliefs that influenced your actions.

   _____
   _____
   _____
   _____
   _____

4. Describe (a) a behavior that you would like to change and (b) how you might use positive self-talk to help you change the behavior.

   _____
   _____
   _____
   _____
   _____

Extraordinary accomplishments often start with a dream. Steve Fossett dreamed of being the first person to circle the world alone in a balloon. In 2002, on his sixth attempt, he finally accomplished his goal. *(AP/Wide World Photos.)*

Chapter 2

Setting Realistic Goals

Did you ever set out on a weekend afternoon for a walk or drive with no clear destination in mind? You changed direction at random, perhaps saw some interesting things, perhaps not. When you got home, you couldn't really say whether you had accomplished anything or not.

Wandering around might be a fine way to spend an afternoon, but it won't really do for a lifetime. Yet many people live their lives this way— reacting to chance events, letting things happen to them, drifting from one thing to another. In 20, 40, or 60 years, they may realize that they've used up a lot of their time on earth and have little to show for it.

People who can point to achievements and successes generally are those who take charge of their lives. They realize that they are responsible for themselves. They understand their own values and abilities. They decide what they want, and they go after it.

If you are not like this, you may envy people who are. Everyone knows a few people who from an early age knew exactly what they wanted of life— to be a model or a mechanic or a nurse, for example. Having such clear goals helped these people focus their efforts and achieve what they wanted.

You too can take charge of your life and determine its direction. You have already started this process in Chapter 1.

The previous chapter prompted you to think about your values, beliefs, and self-beliefs. By now, you should have a good idea about who you are and what you do well. With this in mind, you can start thinking about what you want to accomplish. In this chapter, you will identify and state your goals, create an action plan for three goals, and learn some techniques for getting started on your goals. Finally, you will learn how to keep yourself motivated to succeed—not always an easy task!

> ## Life is a journey: if you don't have a map and a plan and a timetable, you will get lost.
>
> *phillip c. mcgraw,*
>
> *author of* life strategies

IDENTIFYING YOUR GOALS

A good way to start identifying your goals is to think about your deepest wishes and dreams. Perhaps you've always longed to be a dancer, visit China, or own your own home. Maybe you want to have three children, be governor of your state, or start your own business.

Perhaps you haven't thought about your dreams in a long time. If that's the case, try asking yourself these questions: If you had only one year left to live, what would you do? If you were granted three wishes, what would they be? If you were guaranteed success in anything you chose to do, what would you do?[1]

Goals: Challenging and Realistic

Your dreams can be the source of many of your goals. People whose achievements are extraordinary often started with dreams that may have seemed out of their reach. By focusing on their dreams, they were able to concentrate their energies on achieving them, one step at a time.

> ## People are not lazy. They simply have limited goals—that is, goals that do not inspire them.
>
> *anthony robbins,*
>
> *motivational writer*

However, it's important to be realistic. Suppose, for example, that Jon loves cars and wants to become a mechanic. Yet Jon has little aptitude for taking things apart and putting them together. He has trouble visualizing how things work. Jon's dream is not realistic. He can use up all his energy trying to become a master mechanic, or he can revise his dream. Perhaps another career involving cars would make better use of Jon's talents.

Being realistic doesn't necessarily mean giving up dreams that appear to be long shots. Your goals should be realistic, taking into account your unique talents and abilities. Yet they should also be challenging and require effort to achieve. If your goals are too easily achieved, you are not realizing your full potential. You can do more.

Your Turn 2–1

WHAT ARE YOUR DREAMS?

Take a few minutes to write down what you've always dreamed of doing.

_____

_____

_____

_____

_____

_____

_____

_____

_____

_____

> **Education is not preparation for life; education is life itself.**
>
> *john dewey,*
>
> *philosopher and educator*

Types of Goals

Do you have dreams and goals for each aspect of your life? Goals can be thought of as personal, educational, professional, and community service.

Personal Goals   Personal goals relate to your family or private life. You may want to increase your strength, lose 10 pounds, get along better with your spouse, or learn to play the electric guitar. Improving your relationships with family and friends and improving yourself in personal ways are the general objectives of personal goals.

Educational Goals   Educational goals relate to your efforts to learn more and improve your educational credentials. They may take the form of learning about something new, for example, learning how to use a spreadsheet program. Or the goals may relate to certificates, diplomas, and degrees that you want to earn or schools you want to attend.

Professional Goals   Your objectives for your work life are *professional goals*. Professional goals may be broad, for example, becoming a salesperson or earning $50,000 a year. Or the goals may be more specific. You may want to pass a licensing exam in a particular field or get a job at a specific company.

Community Service Goals   *Community service goals* are related to improving conditions in your neighborhood, town, or city. Examples are helping homeless people, giving kids the opportunity to play team sports, participating in a parent–teacher organization, and bringing meals to housebound people. Achieving community service

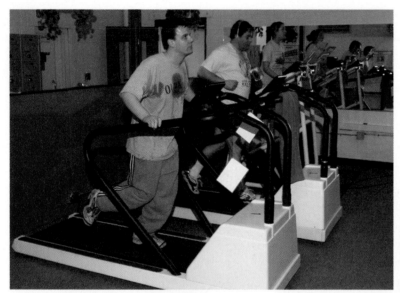

People have goals in many areas of life. Exercising to lose weight, getting a college degree, becoming a health care worker, and helping to clean up the community are examples of personal, educational, professional, and community service goals. *(Top photos courtesy of Tom Stock; photo bottom left courtesy of PhotoDisc; photo bottom right courtesy of Anreal Vohra/Index Stock.)*

FIGURE 2–1

Short-term goals take a year or less to achieve, intermediate-term goals take from one to five years, and long-term goals take more than five years to accomplish. *(AP/Wide World Photos/Dennis Cook.)*

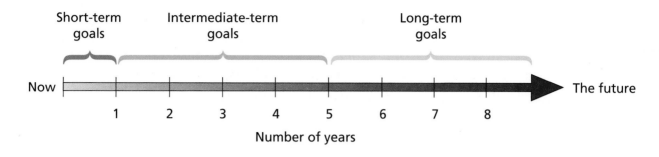

> *Service to others is the rent you pay for your room here on earth.*
>
> muhammad ali,
>
> boxing champion

> *If you are planning for a year, sow rice; if you are planning for a decade, plant trees; if you are planning for a lifetime, educate people.*
>
> chinese proverb

goals benefits the community, but it also gives you the satisfaction of accomplishing something yourself.

Length of Time to Achieve Goals

Some personal, educational, professional, and community service goals can be achieved in a month. Others might take a decade. When you are setting goals, it's helpful to think about how much time you will need to achieve them (see Figure 2–1). **Short-term goals** are those that can be achieved in a relatively brief period of time—a year or less. **Intermediate-term goals** can be achieved in one to five years. **Long-term goals** take at least five years to accomplish.

One of your short-term goals, for example, may be to pass a particular course. Achieving this goal will take only a couple of months. On the other hand, earning your degree, diploma, or certificate is an intermediate-term goal. It may take you several years to accomplish. For people who go to school part-time, earning a degree may be a long-term goal.

Note that long- and intermediate-term goals can often be thought of as a series of short-term goals. Earning an academic degree, diploma, or certificate is a long- or intermediate-term goal; each course you pass is a short-term goal that contributes to your objective.

Six Rules for Stating Goals

Thinking about your goals is not enough. It's important to write them down. Stating your goals helps you focus on them. Studies have shown that people who write down their goals are far more likely to achieve them than people who do not.

When you state your goals, you should keep the following six rules in mind:

1. **Express your goals in positive language.** For example, "I will change my eating habits to maintain a weight of 120 pounds," rather than "I will not eat candy or cookies." Or "I will get at least a C in English," rather than "I won't get a D or F in English." When writing goals, you will find that positive language has the same beneficial effects as positive self-talk.

2. **Make your goals as specific as possible.** Avoid vague, general language like "I would like to travel." Instead, be specific and say something like "I will vacation in Aruba." Making goals specific helps you focus your efforts on achieving them.

3. **Make your goals measurable.** For example, suppose you want to save some money. How will you know whether you've reached your goal? When you've saved $100? $1,000? You have to have some way to measure whether you've achieved your goal. If you say you want to save $1,000 of your part-time earnings, you have a measurable goal. When you state a goal, ask yourself, "What do I want to accomplish? How will I know that I have accomplished it?" Your goal will be measurable if you can respond to these questions.

4. **Set yourself a deadline.** When do you want to achieve this goal? In two months? In two years? Whatever the answer, commit yourself to a time frame. Decide when you will start and when you will be done.

5. **Have a variety of goals.** It's important not to channel your efforts toward only one goal or one type of goal. If all your goals are professional, for example, you will find yourself neglecting other aspects of your life. Try to achieve a balance of personal, educational, professional, community service, short-term, and long-term goals.

6. **Make your goals your own.** Having others set goals for you, even well-meaning people like parents, spouses, and friends, means that the goals are not truly your own. Your goals must be just that—yours. That way, you'll be committed to achieving them. Accomplishing your goals ought to give *you* pleasure and satisfaction.

> *A numerical goal without a method is nonsense.*
>
> *w. edwards deming,*
>
> *statistician and*
>
> *quality-control expert*

CREATING AN ACTION PLAN

If you wanted to reach a specific place in downtown Kansas City, a street map of the city or directions from mapquest.com would be very helpful. But suppose you used the wrong map or no directions at all. You'd probably get lost and become very frustrated.

WHAT ARE YOUR GOALS?

Use the chart below to record your personal, educational, professional, and community service goals. Remember to classify goals as either short-term (one year or less to accomplish), intermediate-term (one to five years), or long-term (more than five years to achieve). You may have more than one goal or no goals in a particular category.

Personal Goals

Short-term: _____
_____
_____

Intermediate-term: _____
_____
_____

Long-term: _____
_____
_____

Educational Goals

Short-term: _____
_____
_____

Intermediate-term: _____
_____
_____

Long-term: _____
_____
_____

Professional Goals

Short-term: _____
_____
_____

Intermediate-term: _____
_____
_____

Long-term: _____
_____
_____

Community Service Goals

Short-term: _____
_____
_____

Intermediate-term: _____
_____
_____

Long-term: _____
_____
_____

NEW YEAR'S RESOLUTIONS

New Year's Day is the traditional time for setting goals. After a holiday season in which people often eat, drink, and party too much, New Year's is the time when many people resolve to change something about their lives.

What do people resolve to do? MyGoals.com, an Internet site devoted to goal-setting, issues annual statistics on New Year's resolutions. The people who run this site base their breakdown of types of resolutions on the goal-setting activity on the Web site. According to their data, in 2003, career-oriented goals were the most common, followed by health and fitness goals.

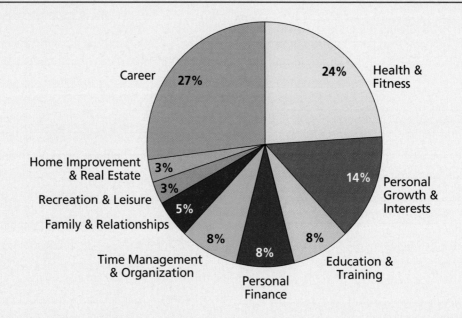

Source: myGoals.com annual survey

"Jobs are what's on everybody's mind, period," said Greg Helmstetter, chief executive officer of myGoals.com. "The dramatic increase in work-related goals is not just about getting jobs but, in particular, doing well at current jobs," said Helmstetter. "People are focusing on acquiring new skills. . . . It's a real sign of the times."

Source: "New Trends for 2003 New Year's Resolutions," <http://www.myGoals.com/about/pressRelease010.html>, accessed January 23, 2003.

Your Turn 2–3

PREPARE AN ACTION PLAN

Refer to your goals statement on page 33 and select three of your most important intermediate- or long-term goals. Using the Action Plan form below, create an action plan for these goals.

ACTION PLAN: INTERMEDIATE- OR LONG-TERM GOALS

1. Intermediate- or long-term goal:

To be accomplished by: _____

Step 1: _____

  Results needed: _____

  _____

  To be accomplished by: _____

Step 2: _____

  Results needed: _____

  _____

  To be accomplished by: _____

Step 3: _____

  Results needed: _____

  _____

  To be accomplished by: _____

Step 4: _____

  Results needed: _____

  _____

  To be accomplished by: _____

2. Intermediate- or long-term goal:

To be accomplished by: _____

Step 1: _____

  _____

  Results needed: _____

  _____

  To be accomplished by: _____

Step 2: _____

  Results needed: _____

  _____

  To be accomplished by: _____

Step 3: _____

  Results needed: _____

  _____

  To be accomplished by: _____

Step 4: _____

  Results needed: _____

  _____

  To be accomplished by: _____

3. Intermediate- or long-term goal:

To be accomplished by: _____

Step 1: _____

  Results needed: _____

  _____

  To be accomplished by: _____

Step 2: _____

  Results needed: _____

  _____

  To be accomplished by: _____

Step 3: _____

  Results needed: _____

  _____

  To be accomplished by: _____

Step 4: _____

  Results needed: _____

  _____

  To be accomplished by: _____

Running a marathon is an intermediate-term goal that requires a step-by-step action plan. Over the course of a year or more, these runners gradually increase the distance they can cover. (©S. Carmona/Corbis.)

In the same way, once you've decided on your goals—your destination—you need to plan how you'll reach them. A written action plan will help you focus your efforts and reach your goals without getting lost along the way.

When preparing an action plan, think about your long-term goals first. In other words, start by knowing where you want to wind up. Let's say, for example, that Elena wants to open her own specialty clothing shop. First she decides that she wants to accomplish this within seven years. With that target in mind, Elena plans the steps she must take to open the shop. First she plans to work in a large clothing store for five years to get experience. At the same time, she will take courses at night in fashion merchandising, accounting, and other business subjects. She will also save 10 percent of her income each year toward the expense of starting a business. At the end of five years, Elena plans to look for a job in a small specialty shop in order to get more experience. During the two years before she opens the shop, she will save 15 percent of her income.

Elena has created an action plan for one of her long-term goals. Essentially, the steps she took were:

1. stating a long-term goal in specific terms and giving it a time frame
2. breaking down the goal into short-term goals, or steps, that will lead to achieving the long-term goal
3. indicating specific results of the short-term goals in order to monitor progress
4. setting deadlines for the short-term goals

If you follow these steps for each of your intermediate- or long-term goals, you will have an action plan for each goal. A plan for a short-term goal would skip step 2. The plan should be written so you can monitor your progress toward achieving your goals.

REACHING YOUR GOALS

Light tomorrow with today.

elizabeth barrett browning,

19th-century british poet

Making an action plan to achieve your goals is an important step. But to make progress, you will have to work hard, keep your goals in view, and persevere, even when you run into problems. Some people have trouble taking the first step toward a goal, and others make progress and then give up when they reach a plateau. Some people need to supplement their inner motivation with help from family, friends, and support groups. Some people must come to grips

WHATEVER IT TAKES
Doug Blevins

(Courtesy of AP/Worldwide Photos.)

It is not unusual for a child to dream of a career in professional sports. Although few children grow up to achieve this dream, Doug Blevins did. Blevins, the kicking coach for the Miami Dolphins, has achieved his childhood goal despite having a disabling disease, cerebral palsy.

As a boy in Abingdon, Virginia, Blevins told his skeptical family and friends that one day he would be in the National Football League. Although he was on crutches at the time, he got involved in peewee football. When he was in junior high, he watched films of the local high school team's games and thought he saw problems with their kicking game. Blevins wrote to the kicking coach of the Dallas Cowboys, Ben Agajanian, asking for advice. Agajanian sent him coaching notes and tapes to study.

Thus Blevins's coaching career was launched. His first job was in high school as assistant student coach for the football team. Later, he got an athletic scholarship and part-time job as a student coach at Emory & Henry College and Tennessee State University. After graduating, he taught kicking skills from his wheelchair to a wide range of players from high school teams to the World Football League. "Not having actually kicked has helped me, because I don't bring a lot of bad mechanics or techniques to the game," says Blevins.

Finally, in 1994, Blevins achieved his dream: he was hired as a kicking consultant for an NFL team, the New York Jets. Later, he worked with players from the New England Patriots. In 1997, Blevins joined the Miami Dolphins as a full-time kicking coach.

During his years with the Miami Dolphins, Blevins has coached kicker Olindo Mare, whose career field goal accuracy is now 84.5 percent—the second best in NFL history.

"A lot of people see Doug for the first time and wonder, 'How can this guy know anything about kicking?'" says Mare. "But what they don't know is how much film he has watched, how much he has studied about kicking, and how much experience he has in the business."

During off-seasons, Blevins speaks to the disabled, telling them to follow their dreams. "Don't listen to what everyone else says," Blevins advises. "You've got to follow your heart and do what you are capable of doing."

Sources: Metzger's *Miami Dolphin News,* June 4, 1997; "Blevins tutors kickers from wheelchair," Associated Press, August 3, 1997; Allison Burke, "Willing and able: Cerebral palsy couldn't keep Doug Blevins from a place in pro football," *People,* September 8, 1997; Bethany Broadwell, "Blevins coaches his way toward goal," iCan News Service, November 22, 2001, at <http://www.ican.com/news>, accessed January 23, 2003; "Coaching staff profile," Miami Dolphins Web site, <http://www.miamidolphins.com/lockerroom/coachingstaff/coachingstaff_blevins_d.asp, accessed January 23, 2003.

with their feelings about failure and success. Others lack the flexibility to change and adapt to new situations. Finally, all of us can learn to improve our chances for success from naturally optimistic people.

Taking the First Step

Old habits and ways of living are powerful forces. Taking the first step toward a major goal can be hard. But procrastinating, or postponing a task that ought to be done now, is the sure way to fail to reach a goal. People who procrastinate usually have a "good" reason. Danielle may say, for example, that she will start studying for a course as soon as pressure eases up at work. In fact, Danielle knows she should start studying now, but she gives herself an excuse not to start.

Postponing a task will not make it easier. Rather, when you are tempted to put off something important, you should carefully think about what is holding you back. You may be feeling shy, indecisive, fearful, negative, or bad about yourself. You feel you can't do something, so you don't do it. The result is inaction.

To overcome procrastination, you can change your beliefs and you can change your behavior. We've already discussed the power of positive self-talk in improving your self-belief. If you are a procrastinator, now is the time for some serious conversation with yourself. Danielle, for example, should be telling herself, "Studying is important. I want to study to pass the course. I can start now despite pressures at work. When I'm at home I'll study from 8 to 10 each evening."

Another technique you can use is visualization. Visualization means imagining what it would be like to have already reached the goal. What scene do you picture? What sounds do you hear? How are the people around you reacting to you? Imagining the future can compel us to do things now, in order to create the kind of future we want. Visualizing your success gives you a powerful mental boost to get started.

Tips for Getting Started Another approach for people who procrastinate is to start by doing a little bit. There are several techniques you can use to get yourself started on a task:

- Set a deadline for getting started. By focusing on a starting date, you will find the energy to begin because you have made a commitment to yourself.
- List small tasks—that will take only a minute or two—that can get you started. Then do the first one.
- Do anything in connection with the goal. If you have to write letters and can't get started, then ease into the task by looking up the addresses or preparing the envelopes first.

- Assign a short period of time during which you will work on the goal. For example, tell yourself that for the next five minutes you will do things that relate to the goal.

- Do the worst thing first. Sometimes tackling the hardest part and getting it done opens up the way to achieving the goal.

Any one of these approaches, in combination with positive self-talk and visualization, can help you get started.

Using the Mastery Approach

Many people get off to a good start when they try to work on their goals, and then they get bogged down and give up. They experience a short burst of progress, followed by a period of being on a plateau, during which nothing seems to happen. A perfect example of this is a man whose goal is to learn a new sport. At first, he makes rapid progress. But then, instead of continuing to improve, he reaches a plateau. For weeks or even months, his skill level remains the same. Finally, another burst of progress occurs, and his mastery of the sport increases.

The secret of the mastery approach is to expect and accept that you will reach plateaus and stop progressing. When this happens, don't give up! Instead, persist, understanding that plateauing is natural and that you will eventually make more progress.

Motivating Yourself

How do you keep yourself moving toward a goal even when you've reached a plateau? How can you motivate yourself to act in ways that will keep you striving and trying?

Motivation is having the energy to work toward a goal. It is made up of the needs and incentives that make us act in particular ways. Motivation can be complex, but we will consider two aspects that are particularly relevant to achievement.

First, motivation that comes from within is called **intrinsic motivation**. When you are intrinsically motivated, you do something because you want to and you enjoy it. Let's say you like to do aerobic exercises. They make you feel good. You are intrinsically motivated to exercise.

You may have a friend, however, who knows she should exercise but thinks it's boring. You want your friend to take an aerobics class with you. To persuade her, you think of some **extrinsic motivation**, which is an outside

Praise is a very effective form of extrinsic motivation. Receiving the approval and good wishes of others increases a person's intrinsic motivation to do well. *(Courtesy of Tom Stock.)*

reward for behavior. You offer your friend an exercise outfit and a ride to class. These extrinsic motivations may be enough to get your friend to come with you, at least for a while. Over time, though, the value of extrinsic motivation decreases. After a few weeks the extrinsic rewards may lose their power to get your friend to aerobics. However, if your friend has discovered that aerobics is fun and makes her feel and look great, then she will have acquired intrinsic motivation to exercise. Your rewards will no longer be necessary because your friend is motivated from within to continue exercising.

In most situations, people have a combination of intrinsic and extrinsic motivations. Meg may enjoy learning how to use a computer (intrinsic) but she is also doing it to earn course credits (extrinsic). Psychologists have found that the best form of extrinsic motivation is praise. Unlike other extrinsic rewards, praise tends to increase a person's intrinsic motivation to do well.

If you are intrinsically motivated to achieve a goal, your chances of achieving it are good. Working on the goal is something you enjoy, so you don't look for excuses to stop. If your intrinsic motivation needs a boost, you can use positive self-talk and visualization to keep your energy high. Congratulate yourself on what you've accomplished so far, and imagine what it's going to be like when you reach your goal.

If you need some extrinsic motivation to keep you going, you can do two things:

- Set up a system of rewards for yourself. For example, when you accomplish one step toward a goal, reward yourself with something you enjoy. Just be careful not to let the reward become more important than doing the task.
- Enlist the support of your family or friends. If you communicate your goals and successes, the pride that others feel in your accomplishments will provide powerful motivation for you to persevere.

Overcoming Fears

Fear often stands in the way of action. People are hampered by fear of many things. The two most important fears that can interfere with reaching a goal are fear of failure and fear of success.

You may think that fearing failure makes perfect sense. In a way, it does. No one likes to look stupid, incompetent, or ridiculous. Actually, it's our perception of failure that causes fear. Instead of seeing failure as a poor result or a temporary setback, we see failure as defeat and shame. If we remember that everyone fails at times, we can start putting failure in perspective. Out of failure can come valuable lessons for success.

> *Fame or one's own self, which matters to one most? One's own self or things bought, which should count most?*
>
> lao-tzu,
>
> ancient chinese philosopher

> *A failure is not always a mistake; it may simply be the best one can do under the circumstances. The real mistake is to stop trying.*
>
> b. f. skinner, psychologist

Your Turn 2–4

WHAT MOTIVATES YOU?

What motivates you to achieve your goals? Consider the three goals for which you prepared action plans. What will motivate you to accomplish these goals?

1. Goal 1:

Your intrinsic motivation: _____

_____

Sources of extrinsic motivation: _____

_____

2. Goal 2:

Your intrinsic motivation: _____

_____

Sources of extrinsic motivation: _____

_____

3. Goal 3:

Your intrinsic motivation: _____

_____

Sources of extrinsic motivation: _____

_____

However odd it sounds, people often fear success also. People who fear success are seldom aware of it. Yet they put obstacles in the way of achieving their goals. Why? They fear that success will bring new situations and new responsibilities they can't handle. Some may believe that they don't deserve to succeed. In fact, they probably can succeed. Most people tend to underestimate their abilities.

If fear is preventing you from achieving your goals, tell yourself this: "Fear is natural. I feel afraid, but I'm going to do this anyway."

Being Flexible

Life means change, and people who don't change their goals accordingly run into trouble. Suppose your family moves to another

Your Turn 2–5

ARE YOU A PERFECTIONIST?

Read the following pairs of sentences, and circle the letter of the sentence in each pair that is most like you.

1. a. I make mistakes occasionally.

b. When I make a mistake, it's someone else's fault.

2. a. I do the best I can.

b. It's hard, but I try.

3. a. My goals are pleasing to me.

b. My goals are pleasing to my family and friends.

4. a. I take my time in getting things done.

b. I'm always in a hurry to finish.

5. a. I'm open to sharing my feelings.

b. I'd rather appear strong than show weakness.

If you circled three or more b's, you tend to be a perfectionist. Try to be easier on yourself!

state or you become interested in another career. It would be foolish to persist in trying to reach goals that are no longer relevant to you. Goals and action plans are not carved in stone. When your situation changes, be flexible and change your goals and action plans to suit your new circumstances.

Being Less Than Perfect

People who are perfectionists often get bogged down in trying to reach their goals. They demand perfection of themselves. Nothing they do is ever good enough. They are always in a hurry. Most important, perfectionists can't acknowledge that they can make mistakes. They must appear to be strong at all times.

> **The man who makes no mistakes does not usually make anything.**
>
> *edward john phelps,*
>
> *19th-century lawyer*
>
> *and diplomat*

On the other hand, people who reach their goals tend to be more relaxed about themselves. They acknowledge that they are human and have faults. They make mistakes, but they do as well as they can. They realize the importance of pleasing themselves. They are flexible and relaxed and open to new situations and people. These are the people who have the inner resources to succeed.

The Importance of Hope

Psychologists are finding that hope plays an important role in achieving success in life.

A study of 3,920 college freshmen showed that the level of hope at the start of school was a better predictor of their college

The Information Highway

GETTING UP TO SPEED

The Internet has several Web sites that provide good goal-setting guidance and advice:

- MyGoals.com is one of the Internet's leading goal-setting sites. According to the Web site, "MyGoals.com walks you through a comprehensive, step-by-step goal-setting process for any goal, whether it's short-term or long-term, easy or difficult, practical or lofty."

- Mind Tools Ltd. is a British company that sells software to help people think more productively. Their Web site offers solid general advice on goal setting and tips for achieving goals <http://www.mindtools.com/mtsite/index.html>. They also offer goal-setting software.

- College Net and College Opportunities On-Line can help you to set or achieve educational goals by providing a search tool for information about colleges <http://www.collegenet.com> and <http://nces.ed.gov>.

- If your educational goals include attending a community college, you can check out two sites that provide information on community colleges throughout the United States <http://www.mcli.dist.maricopa.edu/> and <http://www.sp.utoledo.edu>.

Instead of going to a specific Internet address such as these, you can do a search using the key word *goal-setting* or key words having to do with your specific goals. For example, you can do a search on a particular career, a specific type of volunteer work, or the name of a school you're interested in attending.

grades than previous performance on standardized tests or their high school grade-point average. Dr. Charles R. Snyder, a psychologist at the University of Kansas, says, "Students with high hope set themselves higher goals and know how to work to attain them."[3]

To Dr. Snyder, hope is more than the feeling that everything will be okay. Rather, he defines having hope as believing that you have both the will and the way to accomplish your goals. In other words, people with commitment and self-belief are hopeful people.

People who are naturally hopeful are fortunate. But others can learn hopeful ways of thinking. To imitate the mental habits of hopeful people, you can:

- turn to friends for help in achieving your goals
- use positive self-talk
- believe that things will get better
- be flexible enough to change your action plans when necessary
- be flexible enough to change your goals when necessary
- focus on the short-term goals you need to achieve in order to reach your long-term goal

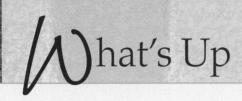

What's Up

Name _____ Date_____

1. Why is it important to have realistic goals?

_____

_____

2. Why should goals be challenging?

_____

_____

Match the specific goal in the second column to the type of goal in the first column. Write the letter of the goal in the space provided.

Type of Goal	**Specific Goal**
3. ____ personal	a. earning a degree, diploma, or certificate
4. ____ educational	b. becoming a supervisor
5. ____ professional	c. running five miles
6. ____ community service	d. becoming a hospital volunteer

7. List the six rules for stating goals.

_____

_____

_____

8. What is the purpose of a written action plan?

_____

_____

9. What are two techniques that can be used to get started on a task?

_____

_____

10. Describe the difference between intrinsic and extrinsic motivation.

_____

_____

Case Studies

THE CASE OF TWO FRIENDS AND THEIR GOALS

At lunch one day, Danisha and Vicki were talking about what they wanted out of life. Danisha wanted to get married and have three children. She didn't care much about school or jobs because she thought she'd be busy raising her kids. Vicki, on the other hand, wanted to get an associate's degree, work with children for a couple of years and save money, then go back to school to become a social worker. Vicki also wanted to get married and have children someday, but she thought she'd try to have a profession as well.

1. Whose goals are more balanced? Why?

_____

_____

_____

_____

2. What does Danisha risk by focusing exclusively on one goal?

_____

_____

_____

_____

THE CASE OF THE WOULD-BE NONSMOKER

Will decided to stop smoking when he found himself out of breath on the basketball court after very little exertion. Since he loved to play basketball and wanted to feel fit again, he figured it would be easy to quit smoking. During the first week, Will did well. He was very pleased with himself for having the willpower not to smoke. He already felt healthier. During the second week, he went to a party and out of habit smoked a few cigarettes. By the third week, Will was regularly borrowing cigarettes from others. He felt disgusted with himself.

1. When Will first stopped smoking, what was his motivation? Was it intrinsic or extrinsic?

_____

_____

_____

_____

2. Will underestimated how hard it would be to achieve his goal. How can he get himself on track again?

_____

_____

_____

_____

Journal

Answer the following journal questions.

1. In Your Turn 2–2 (page 33), you listed your personal, professional, educational, and community service goals. Of all the goals you listed, which is most important to you? Why?

_____

_____

_____

_____

_____

2. Visualize yourself when you achieve your most important goal. Describe what your life will be like.

_____

_____

_____

_____

_____

3. What is the biggest obstacle you think you will face in achieving this goal? How can you overcome this obstacle?

_____

_____

_____

_____

_____

4. List people who can help or support your effort to reach this goal.

_____

_____

_____

_____

_____

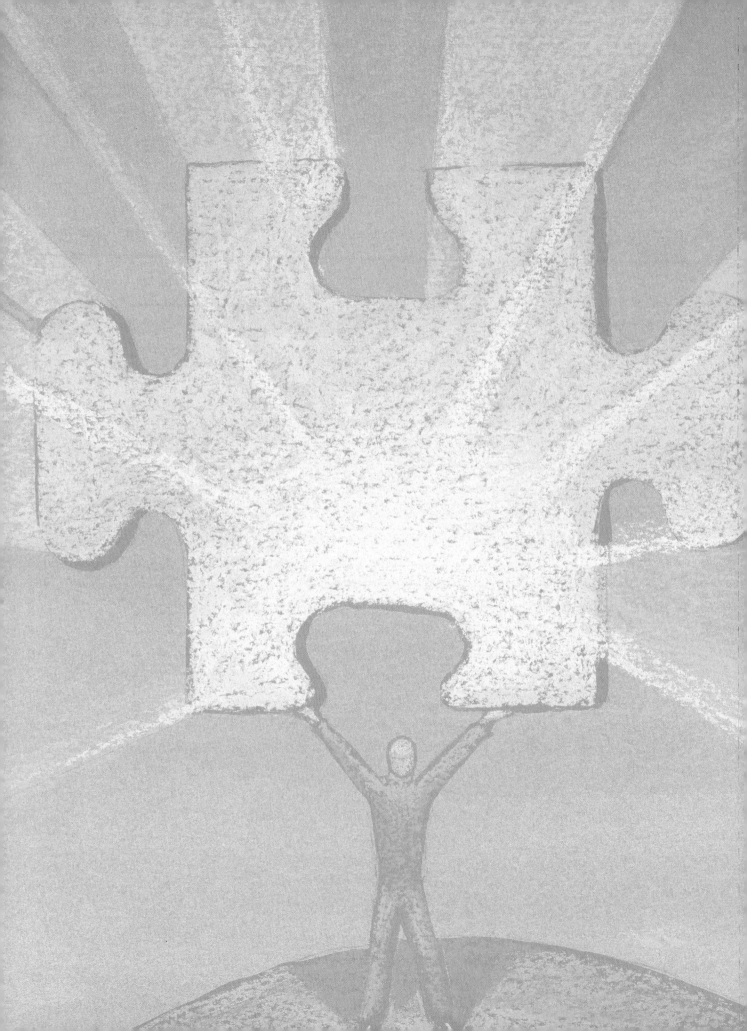

Developing Your Intellectual Potential

The human brain is a powerful tool that helps us

master our environment. In this unit, you will learn

techniques to use your brain to its full potential.

You will learn thinking and study skills to help you

in school and in all areas of life.

People in all walks of life solve problems and think creatively. Astronauts Ellen Ochoa and Donald McMonagle use their education and NASA training to meet the challenges of space flight.

Chapter 3

Improving Your Thinking Skills

Have you ever done poorly on an exam because you had a cold? Have you ever been unable to solve a problem because you were too anxious about it? These common experiences show that our ability to think is affected by our physical and emotional well-being. When we feel good about ourselves, both emotionally and physically, our ability to think improves.

Studies have shown that all of us have far more brain power than we use. We can improve our ability to think by tapping into some of that unused power. If we understand how the brain works, we can sharpen our thinking skills. In this chapter, you will learn about the brain and you will improve your ability to remember, think critically, solve problems, and think creatively.

THE BRAIN

Make two fists and place them together with your thumbs on top and your arms touching from wrist to elbow. You have just made a crude model of the human brain. The brain, a three-pound organ, is the complex director of all of your body's activities. It regulates basic life support systems such as breathing, controls all your movements, interprets your environment, and feels, remembers, thinks, reasons, and creates.

How does the brain do all this? Basically, the brain is made of billions of tiny cells called neurons. In fact, they are so tiny that 30,000 neurons would fit on the head of a pin. Neurons are shaped like trees, with roots, trunk, and branches. Networks of neurons provide communications pathways through the brain. Chemicals called neurotransmitters pass from one neuron to another, activating electrical impulses. The activation of a particular group of neurons produces a perception, feeling, thought, or memory. Each neuron's branches can make contact with between 5,000 and 50,000 other neurons, so you can imagine that billions of complex connections are possible. When you learn something new, you are making new connections among your neurons.

The human brain's ability to deal with complex perceptions, thoughts, and feelings is the key to our success as a species. We cannot run as fast as a cheetah or see our prey with eyes as sharp as an eagle's, but we use our brains to make up for our physical limitations. Humans survive because our brains are constantly filtering the information coming in from the environment. The brain tells us what is safe to ignore—most of what's around us. It tells us what we must pay attention to. Every encounter with something new means that the brain must try to fit the new information into an existing pattern of neurons or else change the pattern to make room for the new thing. Because humans learn and remember, we have thrived.

However, your brain can pay attention to only one train of conscious thought at a time. It is always getting rid of excess information through the process of forgetting. What does the brain pay attention to? It pays attention to things that have meaning to you (information that connects to an existing network of neurons) or things that arouse feelings (information that makes you afraid, happy, or angry).

We can use this very basic understanding of how the human brain works to improve our ability to remember, think logically, solve problems, and think creatively.

> *I will stuff your head with brains. I cannot tell you how to use them, however; you must find that out for yourself.* *(The Wizard of Oz to the Scarecrow, who asked for brains.)*
>
> l. frank baum,
>
> american writer

REMEMBERING

One of the most basic functions of the brain is to remember. Without memory, other learning and thinking skills would be impossible. Imagine trying to solve a problem if you couldn't even remember what it was! Your brain stores a vast amount of information in memory. This ranges from important information such as a friend's appearance to trivial information like the sound of the doorbell in your last apartment or house.

How does memory work? And why do we remember some things and not others? With the answers to these questions, we can actually improve our ability to remember.

How Does Memory Work?

Most psychologists think of memory as having three stages: (1) sensory memory, (2) short-term memory, and (3) long-term memory. Figure 3–1 is a diagram of the three-stage model of memory.[1]

Before you can remember anything, you have to **perceive** it. That means you must see, hear, smell, or become aware of it through some other sense. Everything you perceive is registered in **sensory memory**, the first stage of memory. The material in sensory memory lasts less than a couple of seconds while your brain processes it, looking for what's important. Then most of it disappears.

Some material in sensory memory reaches the second stage, **short-term memory**, where it lasts about 20 seconds. To make it into short-term memory, the new material is matched with information you already have stored, and a meaningful association or pattern is made. For example, when you see a T, you immediately recognize it as the letter *T*. You would recognize it whether it was a lowercase t,

FIGURE 3–1

The three stages of memory are sensory memory, short-term memory, and long-term memory. Our five senses perceive information from our environment, which is processed in sensory memory. Only the important information is sent on to short-term memory. There it is processed and used. Then the information is either forgotten or sent to long-term memory for storage. When the information is needed, it is retrieved from long-term memory, if it can be found.

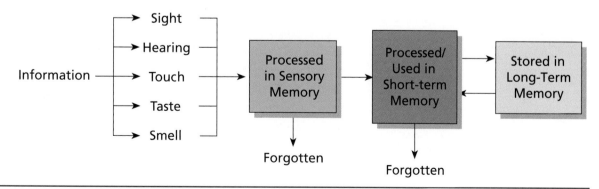

an italic *t*, an uppercase T, or a handwritten T. If you did not have these associations for the letter *T*, you would have much more difficulty placing it in short-term memory.

The material in short-term memory is the information we are currently using. The capacity of short-term memory is small—on average, about seven meaningful units of information. And short-term memory usually doesn't last more than 20 seconds. To make it last longer, repetition helps. For example, if you are lost and someone is giving you directions, you should repeat them to fix them in your memory. But if someone interrupts you, you will probably confuse or forget the directions.

Some material in short-term memory makes it into the third stage, long-term memory, which lasts much longer than short-term memory. Long-term memories are those we don't need at the moment but have stored. In fact, long-term memory is often compared to a complicated filing system, index, or database. The way memories are stored affects the ease with which we can retrieve them. In general, we store new memories by associating them with old memories. For example, if we see a new shade of blue we may associate it with other shades of blue we know or with a blue object.

The capacity of long-term memory seems limitless. Even after a full life of remembering, people have room to store more information in long-term memory. Much of what we "forget" is still actually in long-term memory, but we have trouble getting it out.

Improving Your Memory

> **The true art of memory is the art of attention.**
>
> *samuel johnson,*
> *18th-century english author*

There are several techniques you can use to improve your short-term and long-term memory. Of course, one time-honored way to improve your memory is to write yourself lists and notes. However, you can learn other purely mental aids to memory that take advantage of how the brain works. These include repetition, organization, and mnemonics.

Repetition   Repetition is an effective way to improve your short-term memory. Going over something again and again in your head—or even better, out loud—will help you keep it in short-term memory long enough to use it.

Organization   Organizing material can help both your short-term and long-term memory. To help keep something in short-term memory, you can organize it into seven or fewer chunks. A grocery list of 20 items, for instance, can be "chunked" into produce, dairy, deli, meats, packaged foods, paper products, and cleaning products.

The way you organize material for long-term storage will help you when you need to retrieve it. One way is to make meaningful associations between the new information you are memorizing and

Your Turn 3–1

HOW SOON WE FORGET . . .

Try this experiment on yourself to test your memory.

1. Look at the number below just once, cover it up, and then do something distracting such as singing a song.

8519472

Now write the number here: _____

a. If you got the number right, which level of memory was it in?

_____

b. If you got the number wrong, which level of memory was it in?

_____

2. Now look at the number below for a few seconds and repeat it to yourself several times. Then cover it up.

851-9472

Now write the number here: _____

a. If you got the number right, which level of memory was it in?

_____

b. If you got the number wrong, which level of memory was it in?

_____

c. Why was this number easier to remember than the number in the first item?

_____

_____

other information you already know. For example, if you are trying to remember to buy fish at the supermarket, you can associate it with the meal you're planning to cook. Associations need not involve only words. You can associate new information with music, sounds, images, places, people, and so on.

Another way to organize information for long-term memory is by rearranging or categorizing it. You can categorize by meaning, sound, familiarity, alphabetic order, size, or any other pattern that makes sense to you.

THE NUN STUDY: THE IMPORTANCE OF MENTAL EXERCISE

"Use it or lose it" is a familiar saying that may turn out to be true in regard to the brain. A study of 678 nuns has provided insights about why some people live to a great age with their minds lively and intact, while others suffer from Alzheimer's disease or other forms of dementia.

The School Sisters of Notre Dame are a good group to study from a scientific point of view. They do not smoke, drink very little, and get good health care. In addition, they live in similar communities all their lives. The sisters keep mentally and physically active well into old age. The Nun Study, as it is known, is conducted by Dr. David Snowdon of the University of Kentucky.

Each year, Dr. Snowdon and his colleagues test the nuns' memory, concentration, and language ability. For example, the nuns are asked to recall words they have seen on flash cards and to name as many items in a category as they can in one minute.

Dr. Snowdon also analyzed essays the nuns wrote decades earlier when they entered the convent. These autobiographies provided evidence of the young sisters' thinking and language abilities. The researchers measured the "idea density"—the number of ideas in 10 written words—and the grammatical complexity of the essays. They also looked for words that indicated a positive or a negative mental outlook. The essays gave Dr. Snowdon a way to compare the nuns' mental skills in their youth and in old age.

Much to his surprise, Dr. Snowdon found that the sisters who had shown a positive outlook in their essays lived longer than those whose essays showed a negative outlook. Furthermore, those whose essays had high idea density and grammatical complexity were far less likely than the others to develop symptoms of Alzheimer's disease in old age.

The results of the study suggest that people who exercise their minds may protect themselves from declining mental function as they age. Sisters who had taught school, for example, showed better mental health in old age than those who cooked and cleaned in the convent. Of course, Alzheimer's disease is partially caused by genetic factors, so in many cases it may not be possible to prevent the disease. Still, the educated nuns whose lives had been mentally active may have developed extra brain capacity—more connections among neurons. These extra connections gave them a surplus they could draw on, even as Alzheimer's disease may have been developing.

This suggests that the average person should choose new and stimulating things to do or study throughout life. A personal trainer could take up painting. A computer technician might learn a new language. Even simple activities like brain teasers, crossword puzzles, and jigsaw puzzles can help expand the brain's capacity.

Sources: Michael D. Lemonick and Alice Park, "The Nun Study: How One Scientist and 678 Sisters Are Helping Unlock the Secrets of Alzheimer's Disease, *Time Pacific*, May 14, 2001, <http://www.time.com/tim/pacific/magazine/20010514/cover1.html>; Jay Copp, "This Is for the Benefit of Those Who Come after Us," *Our Sunday Visitor*, June 17, 2001, <http://www.osv.com/periodicals/show-article.asp?pid=313>; "Creative Challenges," 1998, Creative Thinking Web site, <http://www.sunmoments.com/DT/vlil>, all accessed January 28, 2003.

Repetition is a memory technique used by actors and actresses when they are memorizing their parts. *(Courtesy of Comstock Images.)*

Mnemonics   "I before E except after C and when it sounds like A, as in *neighbor* or in *weigh*" has helped children learn one of the rules of English spelling for years. Devices that help people remember are called **mnemonics**. Mnemonics can be poems, like this example, or they can be acronyms—the first letter of each item to be memorized. If you have ever studied music, you probably remember the acronym FACE, which stands for the notes associated with the spaces in the treble clef.

In addition to rhymes and acronyms, there are mnemonic systems that can be used to help memorize information. One system, called the **pegword method**, involves learning a jingle that contains words corresponding to the numbers 1 through 10:

1 is a bun; 2 is a shoe; 3 is a tree; 4 is a door; 5 is a hive; 6 is sticks; 7 is heaven; 8 is a gate; 9 is swine; 10 is a hen.

After repeating this jingle a few times, you will be able to count to 10 by pegwords: bun, shoe, tree, door, and so on. Then you can visually associate items you need to remember with the pegwords. For example, if the first item on your list is a notebook, you can imagine a notebook sandwiched on a bun. Later, when you need to remember the list, the 10 pegwords will serve as clues to the items. The numbers will help you keep track of how many items you must remember.

Another mnemonic system that makes use of images is the **method of loci**. In this system, you associate items on a list with images of places along a route. (*Loci* means "places" in Latin.) First you must develop the stops along your route. You can use the path from your front door to the kitchen, from your home to school, or any other familiar route. When you want to memorize a list, you create an image of the item at the corresponding stop along your route. For example, if you must remember notebook, you could picture a notebook hanging on your front door. When you want to remember the list, you take a mental walk along your route, remembering the scene at each stop.

THINKING CRITICALLY

Memory is one form of thought, or **cognition**, as psychologists refer to mental processes. Another is critical thinking. When you think critically, you are evaluating what's true and making judgments. To do this, you must be able to reason, or think logically. You must also be able to distinguish fact from opinion.

Take time to think. . . .
It is the source of power.

Your Turn 3–2

DO YOU REMEMBER?

Practice using the pegword method or the method of loci to memorize a list.

1. Make a list of the items you are carrying with you. There should be at least ten items on your list.

_____
_____
_____
_____
_____
_____
_____
_____
_____
_____

2. Describe or sketch your mental image for each item. Go over it a few times. Then cover the list and proceed to the next question.

_____
_____
_____
_____
_____
_____
_____
_____
_____
_____
_____

3. Without referring to the original list, recall your mental images and write the ten items here:

_____
_____
_____
_____
_____
_____
_____
_____
_____
_____

Logic

Whether you are aware of it or not, you use logic hundreds of times a day. When you are hungry, you decide to eat. When you need to know the time, you look at a clock. When it's chilly, you put on a jacket. In all these cases, you have used a logical sequence of steps in thinking.

One type of logical thinking is called **deductive reasoning**. In deductive reasoning, the conclusion that is reached is true if the information it is based on, called the **premises**, is true. Let's consider an example of deductive reasoning:

Premise   When it rains, the street gets wet.
Premise   It is raining.
Conclusion The street is wet.

You can see from this example that you use deductive reasoning all the time without even being aware of it. When you make a decision, however, you are often aware of your thought process. Let's say you must decide whether your car needs servicing. You might follow this train of thought:

Premise   If the car leaks oil, it needs servicing.
Premise   The car leaks oil.
Conclusion The car needs servicing.

The conclusion in deductive reasoning is always true if the premises are true.

A type of thinking in which the conclusion is not always true is called **inductive reasoning**. In inductive reasoning, the conclusion drawn is probably true. Here's an example of inductive reasoning:

Premise   Coworkers Francine and Bill have the same last name.
Premise   Francine and Bill leave the office together every day.
Conclusion Francine and Bill are married.

While it is possible that Francine and Bill are married, this conclusion may not be true. Francine and Bill may be sister and brother, mother and son, daughter and father, or cousins. In fact, Francine and Bill may not be related at all—they may simply have the same last name.

Fact or Opinion?

An important part of critical thinking is the ability to distinguish between fact and opinion. A **fact** is something that can be shown to be true. The premises and conclusions of sound deductive reasoning are generally facts. **Opinions**, on the other hand, are beliefs based on values and assumptions. Opinions may or may not be true.

Your Turn 3–3

DRAW YOUR OWN CONCLUSIONS

Read each set of premises. If you can reach a logical or probable conclusion, write it down. Indicate whether you used deductive or inductive reasoning.

1. If a hurricane is predicted, the barrier islands are evacuated.
A hurricane is predicted.

Conclusion: _____

Type of reasoning: _____

2. When I'm in love, I'm happy.
I'm happy.

Conclusion: _____

Type of reasoning: _____

3. Dexter uses his computer to surf the Internet.
Dexter used his computer yesterday.

Conclusion: _____

Type of reasoning: _____

> **It is the mark of an educated mind to be able to entertain a thought without accepting it.**
>
> *aristotle,*
>
> *ancient greek philosopher*

To distinguish between fact and opinion, think logically. Evaluate the material and sort out the reasonable from the emotional or illogical. Look for inconsistencies and evidence. Above all, trust your own ability to distinguish logical facts and ideas from opinions and assumptions. One area in which Americans have had a lot of practice in sorting fact from opinion is advertising. Think of your favorite commercial and try to sort out the facts from the assumptions.

SOLVING PROBLEMS

Problem solving is another important thinking skill. To be a good problem solver, you must be able to think critically. In addition, recognize that problems often have an emotional component that affects your ability to deal with them.

Your Turn 3–4

WHAT DO YOU THINK?

Indicate whether each of the following is a fact or opinion by writing *fact* or *opinion* in the space provided.

1. Living in the suburbs is better than living in the city. _____

2. Mixing blue and yellow yields green. _____

3. On average, women live longer than men._____

4. Modern fashions look better than those of 50 years ago. _____

5. Swimming is good exercise. _____

Proactive versus Reactive Attitudes

Let's consider Steve, who is having trouble getting along with a coworker. Steve thinks, "It's unfair that I have to deal with him. He shouldn't be my problem. Anyway, it's his fault. I don't have the time to work things out." With this attitude, how likely is it that Steve will be able to solve the problem?

Now Steve pulls himself together and tells himself that he will take full responsibility for this problem. He will do what's necessary to solve it. Steve will even enlist the help of others, if necessary. Steve imagines that he has worked out the problem with his coworker. Since he believes that he can solve the problem, his chances of success are increased.

These two attitudes toward problem solving can be characterized as reactive or proactive. A reactive approach is essentially negative. A person with a reactive attitude feels incapable of solving the problem and tries to blame someone else. In contrast, a person with a proactive attitude takes responsibility and is committed to solving the problem.[2]

So before we undertake the steps involved in thinking through and solving a problem, it's important to have a proactive attitude.

WHATEVER IT TAKES

Lonnie G. Johnson

(AP/Wide World Photos/John Bazemore.)

You may never have heard of a flow-actuated pulsator, but you certainly know it by its more common name—the Super Soaker. Invented in 1982 by engineer Lonnie G. Johnson, the high-powered water gun has become one of the most popular summer toys ever made.

Johnson, who grew up in Mobile, Alabama, was the third of six children. Even though he was told he didn't have what it takes to become an engineer, Johnson persevered. When he was a high school senior, his science project, a remote-controlled robot, won first place at a University of Alabama science fair. "Back then, robots were unheard of, so I was one of only a few kids in the country who had his own robot," said Johnson. Johnson went to college on math and military scholarships. He earned a bachelor's degree in mechanical engineering and a master's degree in nuclear engineering.

Johnson worked for NASA's Jet Propulsion Laboratory, helping to fit an atomic battery into the space probe *Galileo*. He also worked on the stealth bomber for the Air Force. In his free time, Johnson fooled around with things at home. While trying to invent a cooling system that didn't use Freon gas, Johnson rigged up some tubing and a nozzle in his bathroom. When he pressed the nozzle, a blast of water shot into the bathtub. Johnson thought, "This would make a great water gun."

The Super Soaker sold so well that in 1991 Johnson was able to form his own company, Johnson Research and Development. When asked what the key to success is, Johnson said, "Perseverance! There is no short, easy route to success." And when asked why he invented things, he replied, "I have these ideas, and they keep on coming."

Sources: Tracie Newton, "Inventor Encourages Audience to Persevere in Quest for Dreams, Holds Up Own Life as Example," *Athens Online,* February 28, 1999, <http://www.onlineathens.com/stories/022899/new_0228990002.shtml>, accessed January 13, 2003; Susan Fineman, "Sometimes It Does Take a Rocket Scientist," Associated Press, February 13, 1999, <http://www.invention-express.com/lonniejohnson.html>, accessed January 13, 2003; William J. Broad, "Rocket Science, Served Up Soggy," *New York Times,* July 31, 2001, pp. D1, D7.

Your Turn 3–5

APPROACH PROBLEMS PROACTIVELY

Think of a problem you have—personal, school-related, or job-related—and answer the following questions.

1. Describe your problem in one sentence.

_____
_____

2. Write down all the reasons why you can't solve this problem.

_____
_____
_____

3. Now imagine that you can successfully solve the problem. Write down all the factors that are driving you to solve this problem.

_____
_____
_____
_____

4. Write a positive message to yourself about your commitment to solving the problem.

_____
_____
_____
_____

The PrOACT Approach to Problem Solving

Now that we've decided on a proactive attitude to problem solving, let's consider the elements involved in solving a problem or making a decision. Many people approach problem solving by using the trial-and-error method. This means they try out solutions at random and use the first one that works. It's not very efficient, and the results are often poor.

A better approach has been devised by three business professors and decision-making consultants.[3] Essentially, they advise breaking down a problem and considering it one step at a time: **Pr**oblem, **O**bjectives, **A**lternatives, **C**onsequences, and **T**rade-offs. The acronym for these—PrOACT—serves as a reminder that the best attitude to problem solving is *proactive*.

In the PrOACT approach, you break a problem into the five PrOACT elements and think about each one separately. Then you put your thoughts back together and make a smart choice.

1. **Problem.** First, you have to figure out just what the problem is. Your ability to solve a problem depends on how you define it. For example, is your problem deciding whether or not to buy a car, or deciding which car to buy?

2. **Objectives.** Solving a problem or making a decision should bring you closer to achieving your goals. In a problem-solving situation, therefore, you need to know what your objectives are. For example, your objective could be to buy a vehicle that has room for your family of six, is reasonably priced, and gets good gas mileage.

3. **Alternatives.** What different courses of action can you think of? What solutions are there to your problem? Think of as many possible alternatives as you can.

4. **Consequences.** For each reasonable alternative you come up with, think through the possible consequences, or results. Which alternatives have consequences that match your objectives?

5. **Trade-offs.** Whatever solution you choose, there will be pros and cons. You need to evaluate the pros and cons and decide what trade-offs are acceptable. There is no perfect solution to a problem; even the best alternative has drawbacks.

Constructing a decision matrix, or grid, such as the one in Table 3–1, can help you frame the problem, explore alternatives, and make a good decision. Which car would be best for the family of six?

TABLE 3–1 Decision Matrix for Buying a Family Car

Objectives	Alternatives		
	Sedan	Minivan	SUV
Seating	5	7	6
Approximate cost	$20,000	$20,000	$30,000
Gas mileage	28 mpg	25 mpg	13 mpg

THINKING CREATIVELY

You may think of creativity as a characteristic of artists and writers rather than of ordinary people. Yet psychologists define creativity as the ability to see things in a new way and to come up with unusual and effective solutions to problems. When we use this definition of creativity, it's apparent that anyone can be creative. A secretary who works out a new and efficient office procedure and a parent who helps a child overcome a problem are both being creative.

To raise new questions, new possibilities, to regard old problems from a new angle requires creative imagination. . . .

albert einstein, physicist

SOLVE A PROBLEM

Ramon has a problem. He volunteered to buy T-shirts for his son's baseball team. The shirts will cost about $100. Ramon doesn't have $100 to spare for the T-shirts. What should Ramon do? Use the PrOACT approach to solve Ramon's problem.

1. Problem. Define Ramon's problem.

_____

_____

2. Objectives. What objective(s) does Ramon need to achieve?

_____

3. Alternatives. What alternative solutions are there to Ramon's problem?

_____

_____

_____

4. Consequences. What are the consequences of the different alternatives?

_____

_____

_____

5. Trade-offs. List any trade-offs Ramon needs to make.

_____

_____

6. In your opinion, what is the best solution to Ramon's problem?

_____

_____

What makes people creative? Intelligence, you may be surprised to learn, has little relation to creativity. Many highly intelligent people do not think creatively. Rather, creative people tend to be those who are intrinsically motivated. They *choose* to do what they do. Often they live or work in an environment that is stimulating and brings them into contact with other creative people. Creative people perform tasks without fear of being judged foolish. They are not afraid to make mistakes.

TEST YOUR CREATIVITY

This is an ordinary brick. How many uses for a brick can you think of? Write these uses below.

_____

_____

_____

_____

_____

_____

_____

_____

Improving Your Creativity

Creativity does not depend on talent or intelligence. Rather, creativity depends on how we use our brains. Most of the techniques associated with improving creativity are based on using neglected modes of thinking. Since analytic, verbal, and sequential modes of thinking dominate in our society, creative breakthroughs often come about when people tap into other modes of thinking. The techniques described here have one thing in common: They all focus on getting us to change our routine thought processes.

Associative Thinking   One thinking process that helps give you a jump start on creativity is associative thinking. Associative thinking is a method in which you let your mind wander from one thing to another, even seemingly unrelated matters, in order to get fresh insight on a problem. If you have ever used the Internet, wandering from Web site to Web site with the links provided, you have a good idea of how associative thinking works.

To use associative thinking, start with the problem or issue and think of a couple of key words. For example, if you must decide whether to go to school full-time or part-time, your key words might be *school* and *time*. Starting with those words, let your mind wander, and jot down words and thoughts as they come to you. Sometimes associative thinking triggers useful new connections in your mind.

Backburner Thinking   Occasionally, when you think too much about a problem, you get stuck. No matter how you rack your brain, nothing useful occurs to you. So you put the problem out of your mind. Some time later, as if from nowhere, you have a great insight. The problem is solved.

What has happened? Essentially, although you've stopped thinking about the problem on a conscious level, your brain continues to work on it. You've put the problem on a "back burner." Backburner thinking involves knowing when to stop thinking about a problem and let your unconscious mind take over.

You can improve the chances that backburner thinking will help you solve a problem by following these tips:

- Think about your problem, but if you are getting nowhere, stop.
- Do something else, preferably something relaxing. If it's night, go to sleep.
- Return to the problem after the break.

When you start thinking about the problem again, you may have gained a new perspective.

Mind-Mapping   Mind-mapping is a creative technique that draws on the visual, intuitive thought processes that we often neglect when trying to solve a problem. In mind-mapping, you sketch your problem or topic and the thoughts that come to mind. The result is a drawing that represents your ideas (see Figure 3–2).

To draw a mind-map, follow these steps:

- Draw a picture of the problem or issue in the center of a piece of paper.
- Print key words and ideas, and connect these to the central drawing.
- Use colors, images, symbols, and codes to emphasize important points.
- Use associative thinking to come up with more ideas, and connect them with other parts of the mind-map.

FIGURE 3–2

Visualizing the relationships among ideas and things can help you think creatively. You can draw a mind-map to show these connections.

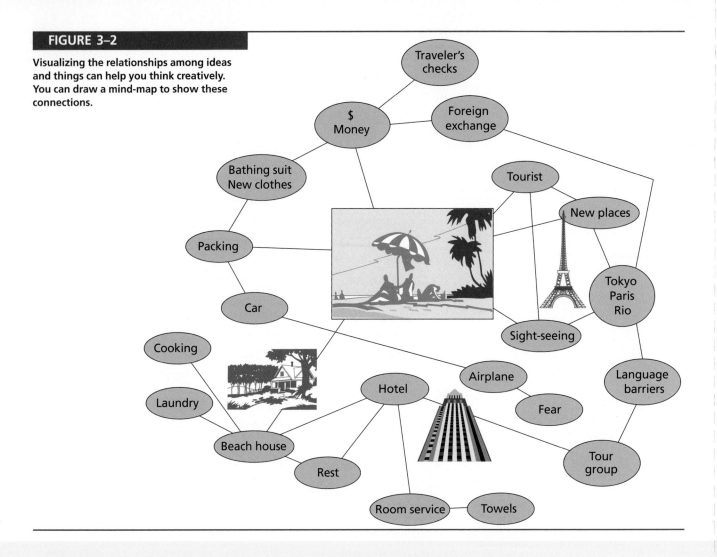

Your Turn 3–8

DRAW YOUR OWN MIND-MAP

Think of a problem you have or an issue that interests you.

1. On a separate sheet of paper, draw a mind-map with a picture related to this problem or issue in the center.

2. Write key words and phrases about the problem or issue around the central drawing, and draw lines to show the connections among these ideas.

3. Use colors, symbols, images, and codes to emphasize important ideas.

4. Use associative thinking to add related ideas to your mind-map.

5. Study your mind-map. What patterns or ideas might help you with solving this problem or dealing with this issue?

Your Turn 3–9

HAVE A BRAINSTORMING SESSION

With four or five other people in your class, have a five-minute brainstorming session on this issue: looking for a job in the computer industry.

One person should take notes on the ideas that come up. When the session is done, answer the following questions:

1. What did the group decide was important to do when looking for a job in the computer industry?

_____

_____

_____

_____

2. Did everyone contribute an idea? If not, why not?

_____

_____

_____

_____

3. Did you contribute an idea inspired by something someone else said?

_____

_____

_____

_____

4. Would you have come up with the same ideas the group did if you were thinking about this matter on your own? Explain.

_____

_____

_____

_____

When your mind-map is done, you can study it to find new relationships, insights, and ideas. Perhaps a pattern will emerge that can help you with the problem.

Brainstorming   Someone once said that two heads are better than one. Taking this idea even further, brainstorming allows a group of people—preferably five to eight—to come up with as many ideas about a problem or issue as they can. To brainstorm effectively, people must not be critical of one another's ideas. Any idea, however far-fetched, is considered. Evaluating and judging will come later. Brainstorming can be used effectively in business situations where groups of people share problems and goals.

Mindstorming Mindstorming is similar to brainstorming, but you do it alone. Take a piece of paper, and at the top write your problem or issue of great concern. Then list 20 ways you can solve the problem or approach the issue. The first 10 ideas will probably come easily and seem obvious. However, don't judge your ideas yet. Let your imagination take over and write down 10 more ideas, however odd, that come to mind. Then review the list and choose the ideas that are most likely to solve your problem.[4]

The Information Highway

GETTING UP TO SPEED

Here are Web sites that have information on thinking skills, including memory and creative thinking:

- Mind Tools Ltd. sells software to help people think more productively. Their Web site offers free information on improving thinking and memory skills <http://www.mindtools.com/>.
- For an overview of how the brain works, visit the How Stuff Works Web site <http://howstuffworks.com/brain>.

Try the following key words to search for information on thinking skills: memory techniques, mnemonics, critical thinking, problem solving, creativity.

In addition, if you need help in solving a particular problem or thinking about a topic, search for the specific problem or topic that concerns you.

Last, do a search on any topic that interests you, and follow the links from one Web site to another. The links between sites are examples of associative thinking!

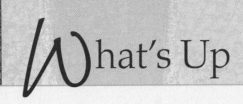

What's Up

Name _____   Date_____

1. How has the brain contributed to our success as a species?

_____

2. Describe the three stages of memory.

_____

_____

_____

3. What are two mnemonic systems that are used to memorize lists of information?

_____

_____

4. What is the difference between deductive and inductive reasoning?

_____

_____

5. Describe the PrOACT approach to solving a problem.

_____

_____

_____

_____

6. Why are there no perfect solutions to problems?

_____

7. How do psychologists define creativity?

_____

_____

8. What happens during associative thinking?

_____

9. Describe what happens in backburner thinking.

_____

10. In what situations is brainstorming particularly useful?

_____

_____

Case Studies

THE CASE OF THE FORGETFUL COUNSELOR

Anita was a counselor at the day camp run by her local YMCA. Every two weeks, she met a new group of ten campers for whom she was responsible. Anita found that she was terrible at remembering the campers' names. As soon as they introduced themselves, their names would vanish into thin air. Often she didn't get the kids in the group straight until the end of the two-week session. Then those kids left and she had to learn who was who in a new set of campers.

1. Why was Anita having trouble remembering the names of the kids in her group?

_____

_____

_____

_____

2. What suggestions do you have for Anita that would help her remember the campers' names?

_____

_____

_____

_____

THE CASE OF THE UNSOLD BIKE

Arlen wanted to sell his old bike so he could buy a new, better model. He placed an ad on the Internet auction site eBay. Arlen wanted at least $300 for his bike, but the bids he got were $150 or less. Arlen was discouraged. He can't afford a new bike unless he sells the old one.

1. Using the PrOACT problem-solving method, indicate how Arlen might solve his problem.

_____

_____

_____

_____

2. Use associative thinking to help solve Arlen's problem. Write your associations in the space below.

_____

_____

_____

_____

Journal

Answer the following journal questions.

1. What is your earliest memory of school? Why do you think you remember this event or thing?

_____
_____
_____
_____
_____

2. If your memory was better, how would this affect your studies? Your job?

_____
_____
_____
_____
_____

3. In Your Turn 3–5, you wrote about a problem you have. Describe how you might use the PrOACT approach to solve this problem.

_____
_____
_____
_____
_____

4. Describe the most creative person you know. What makes this person creative, in your opinion?

_____
_____
_____
_____
_____

A library is one of a school or community's greatest resources. During the Great Depression of the 1930s, the Pack Horse Library Project provided reading materials to residents of eastern Kentucky. Librarians riding horses or mules traveled 50 to 80 miles a week up rocky creek beds, along muddy footpaths, and among cliffs to deliver books and magazines to the most remote homes and schools in the mountains.
(Courtesy of WPA Photo Collection, Public Records Division, Kentucky Department for Libraries and Archives.)

Chapter 4

Improving Your Study Skills

In Chapter 3 we learned that the brain is capable of far more than most people realize. Regardless of your age, sex, or cultural background, your brain can remember phenomenal amounts of information, detect patterns, analyze information, and think creatively. These processes have a physiological basis in the structures of the brain. Therefore, your physical well-being can affect your ability to think and learn. We've all had the experience of performing poorly when we're feeling ill or tired.

In addition, your brain does not separate emotion from thinking. How you feel colors how you think. We saw a powerful example of this in self-belief, the connection between what you believe (thought) and how you feel about yourself (emotion). Your self-belief affects everything you do. More specific feelings have more specific effects. The feeling of stage fright can make an actress forget her lines. Someone who is in love may be unable to think logically about his loved one.

In effect, physical and emotional well-being is the foundation upon which you can build specific learning skills. In this chapter, you will identify your learning style preferences and discover what makes a good place and time for studying. You will learn a technique for reading assigned books and articles that will help you remember what you read. You will improve your note-taking and test-taking skills. Finally, you will discover the wealth of resources, both print and computer based, that school and community libraries provide to support your lifelong learning.

75

LEARNING STYLES

Just as no two people look alike, no two people learn in the same way. Some people like to get the big picture first and then fill in the details. Others prefer to start with examples and details, and from them develop an overarching concept. Many people are comfortable learning from books, and others prefer to participate in discussions. People have preferences for facts or feelings, analysis or intuition.

Have you ever thought about how you prefer to learn? The chances are you will recognize yourself in the description of one or two of the four basic learning styles. These styles can be called the Logician, the Procedurist, the Communicator, and the Experimenter.[1]

The Logician

The Logician feels comfortable with facts and thinks they are of utmost importance. When learning a new subject, the Logician prefers to build on a base of solid information. Only when the Logician has the facts straight does he or she come up with theories to explain them.

The Procedurist

The Procedurist loves order. When learning, the Procedurist feels most comfortable knowing that an expert has laid out the subject in the best sequence. The Procedurist doesn't want to waste time or effort. He or she wants a well-planned curriculum to work through.

Some people prefer to learn from lectures or textbooks. Logicians like to have a solid foundation of facts when they are studying something new. *(Courtesy of PhotoDisc.)*

What happens in the body can affect the brain and what happens in the brain can affect the body. Hope, purpose, and determination are not merely mental states. They have electro-chemical connections that play a large part in the working of . . . the human organism.

norman cousins, editor and writer

The Communicator

Communication among people is the Communicator's ideal way to learn. The Communicator likes to talk to other people about the subject he or she is learning. The Communicator also wants to know what other people think the subject means. A good discussion or cooperative learning activity is the Communicator's favorite way to learn.

The Experimenter

The Experimenter wants to understand the underlying essence of a subject. He or she feels that learning is meaningful only when you understand the basic feeling or vision. The Experimenter doesn't accept information as given. Rather, the Experimenter likes to look at things in an entirely new way.

Tailoring Learning to Your Style

Each of the four learning style preferences does best with different teaching techniques.

- Logicians are comfortable with textbook reading assignments, lectures, slides, and instructional tapes.
- Procedurists find it easier to learn from workbooks, lab manuals, step-by-step demonstrations, and interactive computer programs.
- Communicators learn best from class discussions, seminars, team projects, audiotapes, movies, television, and Internet discussion groups.
- Experimenters favor games, simulations, independent study, problem-solving activities, and searching the Internet when they learn.

If you think back on your education, you probably will conclude that most of the learning you did was in the Logician or Procedurist style, whether or not those are your preferences. That's because classroom teaching is often heavily dependent on lectures, textbooks, and workbooks.

If you favor the Logician or Procedurist styles, you have a head start on learning in most school situations. But what can you do to improve your ability to learn if you favor the Communicator or Experimenter styles? You can try to set up more suitable learning situations on your own, and you can enlist the help of your instructors.

Procedurists learn best when facts and ideas are presented step by step. They often benefit from demonstrations and interactive computer programs. *(Courtesy of Scott T. Baxter/Getty Images, Inc.)*

> *Whatever is received is received according to the nature of the recipient.*
>
> st. thomas aquinas,
>
> 13th-century italian philosopher

Interaction with others helps some people learn. Communicators learn best when they share ideas through discussion. *(Courtesy of PhotoDisc.)*

Your Turn 4–1

WHAT IS YOUR LEARNING STYLE?

You can identify your learning style preferences by ranking each set of words in the following list. Think about a subject that you recently learned. Give a 4 to the word that best describes you, a 3 to the word that is next most descriptive, 2 to the word that is third most descriptive, and a 1 to the word that is least like you.

Example:

_4_ outgoing	_2_ reserved	_3_ friendly	_1_ shy
1. ___ precise	___ orderly	___ moody	___ playful
2. ___ analytic	___ to the point	___ sensitive	___ questioning
3. ___ concrete	___ stable	___ aware	___ visualize
4. ___ facts	___ sequence	___ feelings	___ possibilities
5. ___ rational	___ responsible	___ intense	___ perceptive
6. ___ choosy	___ practical	___ involved	___ observant
7. ___ intelligent	___ competent	___ open	___ spiritual
8. ___ conceptual	___ hands-on	___ responsive	___ imaginative
9. ___ concentrate	___ process	___ listen	___ test
10. ___ focus	___ plan	___ empathize	___ experiment

Totals

___ Logician   ___ Procedurist   ___ Communicator   ___ Experimenter

Add your rankings for each column. The column with the most points represents your preferred learning style. If you score nearly the same in two categories, that's because you have a blend of learning styles, not a clear preference for one.[2]

Some people prefer to learn by doing. Experimenters like to get to the basics of a subject through projects, games, and other hands-on activities. *(Courtesy of Tom Stock.)*

Communicators can try to sign up for small classes, in which discussions are likely to take place, rather than lecture courses. If this is not possible, Communicators can try to set up small study groups or participate in Internet discussion groups to talk about what's being learned in class. In addition, Communicators can ask their instructors for videotapes to supplement classroom work. If there are term papers or special projects, Communicators can set up people-oriented rather than library-oriented research.

Experimenters have several options to supplement traditional classroom work. They can enlist the help of their instructors to get additional reading assignments, plan independent study projects, search the Internet for information, and find subject-related games or simulations. In addition, Experimenters can choose problem-solving activities for term papers and special projects.

PREPARING TO STUDY

No matter what your learning style, you must set the stage for studying in order to learn productively. Establish a study area you can call your own, a study schedule that takes advantage of your peak learning times, and clear learning goals to focus your efforts.

Set Up a Study Area

The word *study* refers to the process of learning as well as the place where learning occurs. Many great learners have set up ideal spaces in which they can work and think. A good study area is a place where you can concentrate and learn with few distractions.

Setting aside space to study sends a message to yourself and others that you take studying seriously and have made a commitment to succeed. In addition, studying in the same place helps people learn. Psychologists have found that learning is often **state specific**. That means that what we learn is connected with the state and place in which we learn. The environment in which learning takes place provides cues associated with the learning, making things easier to recall when you're in the same location. That's why students who take a class and final exam in the same room generally do better than those who are tested in a different room.

You may be thinking that a good study area requires both space and cash. True, you can do a lot with these two resources. However, a study area can be set up in the corner of a bedroom or living room or on the kitchen table after dinner. If your home has too many distractions, you can find a quiet, temporary, portable study area in your school or local library. The most important consideration is that you find a study area, however small, that works for you.

Here's a list of questions to help you plan your ideal study or work area:

- Where will the study be located?
- What kind of furniture, if any, will you need?
- How will you decorate the area to make it functional, pleasant, and inspiring? What light, color, sound, pictures, and objects will you use?
- What equipment and supplies will you need? Will you need a computer or can you use a computer lab when necessary?
- What other resources will you need (for example, dictionaries, manuals, and calculators)?

Once you've got your study area set up, no doubt you will run into problems that will interfere with your ability to learn. Instead of thinking of these problems as inevitable, try making changes to improve your study environment. Some common problems include:

- **Too much noise from the environment.** People who need silence to concentrate can try earplugs to block out noise.
- **Too little noise from the environment.** Some people work better with background sounds. Use a portable cassette or CD player and headphones for background music that won't disturb others.
- **Visual distractions.** Set up the work area so your back is to the source of distractions. You can also screen off the study area.
- **Interruptions.** Ask people around you not to disturb you when you're studying. To avoid phone interruptions, you can use an answering machine. To avoid instant message (IM) interruptions when you are working on line, post an "away" message. That way, friends and family will know you are not currently available for IMs.
- **Discomfort.** If you are uncomfortable, try adjusting your posture, chair, or work surface height.

Schedule Study Time

Once your study area is set up, plan a study schedule. In other words, studying should be part of your everyday routine, not be left for occasional marathon sessions before exams.

Regular studying is much more effective than cramming because it takes advantage of the way your memory works. As you recall from Chapter 3, repetition and organization are two ways to improve your ability to remember. When you study each day, you organize what you've learned in class and from reading assignments. By reviewing this material, you commit it to your long-term memory.

FIGURE 4–1

People learn best at different times of day. This person's peak study time is clearly the morning.

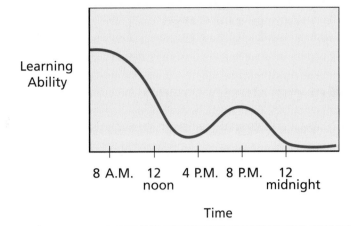

If you think you are too busy to study every day, think again about your daily schedule. Can you study while commuting or between classes? Perhaps you have time after work or after dinner. You should plan your study time as carefully as you plan your work or class schedule. (We'll discuss scheduling your time more thoroughly in Chapter 13.) You can improve the effectiveness of your studying by taking advantage of your peak learning times. (See Figure 4–1.) Different people are mentally alert and motivated at different times of the day. Some people wake up early full of energy and purpose; others would sleep until noon each day if given the chance. If you can schedule studying for your peak times, you will learn faster and more easily.

Set Study Goals

Do you remember the educational and professional goals you set in Chapter 2? If you don't, now is a good time to review them. Keep your educational and professional goals in mind, because studying is part of any action plan to accomplish them. If you commit yourself to studying, you are committing yourself to doing well in your courses. Focusing on a short-term goal like studying helps you progress toward your intermediate- and long-term goals.

READING BOOKS AND ARTICLES

One of the key study skills is the ability to read. When you were in elementary school, you learned how to read by reading stories. You may still enjoy reading novels and other books for your own pleasure. But reading in order to learn is a different process. It involves special techniques to help you understand and remember what you read. The basic steps in reading for information are (1) previewing, (2) questioning while reading, and (3) reviewing. This method is sometimes called the P.Q.R. system.

Your Turn 4–2

EARLY BIRD OR NIGHT OWL?

For each of the following statements, answer *true* or *false* to get a better sense of when your peak studying time occurs.

1. I would wake up early even if my alarm didn't go off. _____

2. When I have something to do that requires concentration, I do it first thing in the morning. _____

3. If I stay up late to get something done, I often fall asleep over it. _____

4. It usually takes all morning for me to get started. _____

5. I would rather go to school or work in the afternoon instead of the morning. _____

6. When I have to concentrate on something, it's best if I work on it after lunch. _____

7. I could stay up all night. _____

8. I usually start tasks that require concentration after dinner. _____

9. I wish I could relax during the day and go to work or school at night. _____

Here's how to figure out your peak learning time:
  If you answered true to items 1–3, your best time is the morning.
  If you answered true to items 4–6, your best time is the afternoon.
  If you answered true to items 7–9, your best time is the evening.

> *Tell me, I'll forget.*
> *Show me, I may*
> *remember.*
> *But involve me and*
> *I'll understand.*
>
> chinese proverb

Previewing

When you first turn to a reading assignment, do you start at the first word and proceed until you get to the last? If you take this approach, you aren't getting as much out of the assignment as you could.

Experienced readers preview the material, before they start reading. **Previewing** means scanning the selection, looking for main points, and discovering how the material is organized. Previewing is like standing back from a new item of clothing and getting an idea of its style and fit rather than closely examining each button, thread, zipper, and piece of fabric.

Oseola McCarty

(AP/Wide World Photos/Steve Coleman.)

Oseola McCarty's lined, gnarled hands were evidence of the life she led: washing and ironing other people's clothes. Less evident was how a quiet, elderly black woman was able to donate $150,000 of her life savings to the University of Southern Mississippi.

"I just want to help somebody's child go to college," McCarty said. "I just want it to go to someone who will appreciate it and learn."

Born in Mississippi, McCarty was raised by her mother, who cooked for a local family and sold candy at school. When she was in sixth grade, McCarty left school to take care of a sick aunt. She never returned. She earned her living as a laundress and saved money all her life. McCarty died in 1999 at the age of 91, but her money has kept on working.

McCarty's gift established an endowed Oseola McCarty Scholarship at USM, with "priority consideration given to those deserving African-American students enrolling at the University of Southern Mississippi who clearly demonstrate a financial need." The first scholarship winner, Stephanie Bullock, was thrilled to have been chosen. "I was worried about how we could afford [college]," Bullock said. "I'm going to try as hard as I can to do well."

News of McCarty's generous gift spread fast, and others have contributed to the fund as well. Today almost a dozen students have received McCarty scholarships to attend USM.

Sources: Sharon Wertz, "Oseola McCarty Donates $150,000 to USM," press release, University of Southern Mississippi, July 1995 <http://www.pr.usm.edu/oola1.htm>, accessed January 30, 2003; "Hattiesburg Teen Gets First McCarty Scholarship," press release, University of Southern Mississippi, August 1995 <http://www.pr.usm.edu/oo1astep.htm>, accessed January 30, 2003; Rick Bragg, "Oseola McCarty, a Washerwoman Who Gave All She Had to Help Others, Dies at 91," *New York Times*, September 28, 1999; Lynn Schnurnberger and Ellise Pierce, "Oseola McCarty: A Laundress Turned Philanthropist Keeps on Reaching Out to Others," *People*, March 15–22, 1999, p. 68.

Previewing a Book   To preview a book, you should look at the pages at the front. Skim the preface, which is a short essay that often summarizes the author's point of view. Then turn to the table of contents and examine it. The table of contents is an outline of the main ideas of the book and how they relate to one another. Finally, page through the book to get a feel for it.

Previewing a Chapter   To preview a chapter from a text, skim it first, looking at the headings. Like the table of contents, the headings provide an outline of the material. Many textbooks have other features to help you preview. These may include a list of what you will learn by reading the chapter and a chapter summary. Read these first to get an idea of the chapter's content and organization.

Previewing an Article   When previewing an article, scan any headings and look at charts, graphs, or other illustrations. These often highlight key ideas in the article. If the article has a summary, read it. If not, read the first and last paragraphs to get a general idea of what it is about.

Questioning While Reading

Only after you have previewed a reading assignment are you ready to start reading. To understand what you are reading, you must be an active reader. Take a questioning approach to the material. Ask yourself, Why am I reading this? How will this material meet my needs? What do I already know about this topic? By doing so, you will begin to make associations between the new material and what you already know.

As you are reading, continue to question yourself, using the words *who, what, where, when, why,* and *how*. One way to do this is to turn every heading into a question that you must answer. For example, if the heading in an accounting text is "Balance Sheet," ask yourself, What is a balance sheet? Then read the section with your question in mind. If you own the book, after you read a section you can underline or highlight key ideas and words that help answer the question. Asking and answering questions as you read helps you master the material and commit it to your long-term memory.

When you read to learn, you should take notes. By taking notes, you repeat the important material, making it easier to remember. *(Courtesy of Tom Stock.)*

Your Turn 4–3

READING TO LEARN

Practice using the P.Q.R. method on the next main section of this chapter, Taking Notes, on pages 86–89.

1. Preview the section. In one sentence, describe what this section is about.

_____

_____

2. Question yourself while reading:

a. What do you expect to learn by reading this section?

_____

_____

b. What do you already know about this topic?

_____

_____

c. Write down questions you ask yourself as you read:

_____

_____

_____

_____

_____

_____

3. Review.

a. **See** the material—go over the section again.

b. **Say** the answers to your questions out loud.

c. On a separate sheet of paper, **write** brief answers to the questions you posed in item 2c.

Reviewing: Seeing, Saying, Writing

When you are studying, reading something once is not enough. You must review what you read to fix it in your long-term memory. You do this by using three processes: seeing, saying, and writing.

First, go back over the material, skimming each section of the chapter or article. As you *see* the material, *say* the main points out loud. Then *write* brief study notes that outline the main ideas. This review method helps you remember by organizing and repeating the material using three different processes: seeing, saying, and writing.

TAKING NOTES

When you are learning a subject, it's important to take notes during class sessions and reading assignments for two reasons. First, taking notes forces you to be an active learner. Writing down important facts and ideas helps you understand and remember them. Second, a good set of notes provides you with a concise summary of the course content—a valuable resource when you're preparing for an exam.

You should use a spiral notebook or loose-leaf binder with ruled paper for your notes. Set up sections or separate notebooks for each course. When you go to class, make sure you have the right notebook and a couple of pens with you.

If you prefer to take notes on a laptop computer, be sure the battery is charged. Set up a note-taking document template that you can use in all your classes. Bring a notebook, too. You may need to draw sketches, diagrams, or flowcharts as part of your note taking.

Choose a seat near the front of the room so you will be able to see and hear clearly. You'll find that taking classroom notes is easier if you keep up with reading assignments and come to class prepared.

Taking good notes on your readings is less difficult than taking good classroom notes. If you miss something in class, you can't go back over it to fill it in. You have to wait until the class is over and ask your instructor or another student for help. On the other hand, when you miss something in a reading, you can reread it as many times as you need to in order to understand it.

Several techniques can help you get the most out of note taking. Formatting your notes, outlining, and diagramming are basic techniques. In addition, there are special techniques you can use for building your vocabulary.

Using a Two-Column Format

Many students find that a two-column format, with one narrow and one wide column, is the best setup for notes (see Figure 4–2). The narrow column is used for **recall words**, important words that provide cues for the main ideas. These are filled in when you review your notes, not when you first take them. The wide column is used for main ideas and important facts.

Outlining and Diagramming

When you take notes, you should not be writing every word the instructor says or copying a whole reading. Rather, you should write main ideas and important facts. Generally, definitions, lists, formulas, and solutions are important enough to write down. To save time, use phrases and abbreviations rather than full sentences.

FIGURE 4–2

These notes were taken using a two-column format and outlining. Note the recall words in the narrow column.

	Evaluating Software	Oct. 10
Hardware requirements	Check that computer system matches hardware requirements:	
	• PC or Macintosh	
	• processor speed needed	
	• which operating system?	
	• amount of memory needed to run the program (RAM)	
	• amount of free space on hard drive	
	• CD-ROM or Internet download	
Documentation	"How to" manual (documentation) and/or help system	
	• complete	
	• well-organized	
	• easy to find what you need (good index)	
	• tech. support available	
Installation	Installation	
	• clear instructions	
	• fast & easy	
	Easy to learn	
	Does what it's supposed to	
	Cost	

Using an outline format will help you take down the important material and organize it at the same time. In an outline, indentions are used to show the relationship of main ideas to secondary ideas or supporting details. For example:

I. Three stages of memory

    A. Sensory memory—perceptions of senses

    B. Short-term memory—information brain is using

    C. Long-term memory—permanent storage

Your outline need not be numbered. More important than letters and numbers are the indentions that show the relation of one idea to another.

In addition to outlining your notes, you should use diagrams and drawings whenever possible to simplify the ideas (see Figure 4–3).

FIGURE 4–3

Diagrams and drawings can be helpful when you are taking notes. An image can summarize facts and ideas that would take many words to describe.

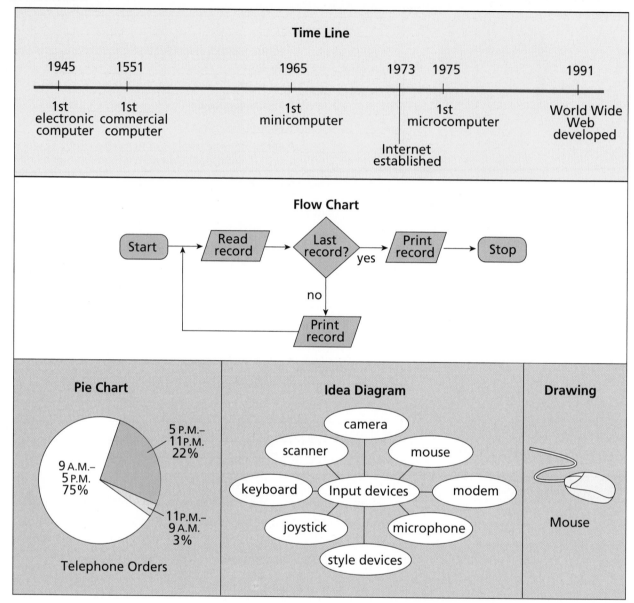

- **Time lines** are good for showing the sequence of historical events.
- **Flowcharts** can be used to show the steps in a process or procedure.
- **Pie charts** show the relationship of parts to a whole.
- An **idea diagram** is like a mind-map; it shows the relationship of secondary ideas to a main idea and to one another.
- A **drawing** gives an instant description of something visual.

Your Turn 4–4

TAKE NOTES ON THIS CHAPTER

Use the techniques described in the sections on reading and taking notes to prepare notes on this chapter. Use your own notebook or laptop.

laser printer

a printer that uses laser light to make an image on a rotating drum before transferring the image to paper using toner

Building Your Vocabulary

You may hear words you don't understand from your instructor and find unfamiliar words in your textbooks. Don't skip over them! Building a good vocabulary is important for educational and professional success. Particularly important are the specialized words, called jargon, that are used in every field.

When you hear an unfamiliar word in class, write it down as best you can and look it up in a dictionary after class. In your readings, you will find that many words are defined for you in the text or at the end of the book in a glossary (see page 397). When you look up a new word, write it down, along with its definition. Some students prefer to record vocabulary words for each course on a separate page in their course notebook. They write the word in the narrow column and the definition in the wide column. Other students prefer to make flash cards with the word on one side and the definition on the other (see Figure 4–4).

Having written notes of all new vocabulary words associated with a subject will help you master the subject and prepare for exams.

TAKING TESTS

Many students think that a long cramming session—even an "all nighter"— is the best way to prepare for an exam. Unfortunately, this method doesn't work well. Learning is more effective when done in short sessions of no more than two hours. Longer study sessions are tiring, and a tired brain doesn't think, memorize, or recall things effectively.

The keys to doing well on exams are good study habits; preparation, both mental and physical; and an understanding of some basic test-taking techniques.

ARE THERE MANY TYPES OF INTELLIGENCE?

Scientists have struggled for centuries to define the idea of intelligence. Psychologist Howard Gardner proposed that intelligence is not one ability; instead, there are many forms of intelligence that people have in varying degrees. Gardner's ideas have influenced educators, because people benefit from being taught in ways that develop their particular combinations of intelligences. Here, briefly, is Gardner's theory of multiple intelligences.

The first two types of intelligence that Gardner proposes are those stressed in most schools and by most standardized tests such as IQ tests, MATs, and SATs. People who are strong in these types of intelligence tend to do well in school.

- **Linguistic intelligence** is the ability to use language well. Writers and journalists possess a high degree of this type of intelligence.
- **Logical-mathematical intelligence** is the ability to think logically, mathematically, and scientifically. Scientists, mathematicians, computer programmers, financial analysts, accountants, and others whose work involves logic and numbers have a high degree of this type of intelligence.

The next types of intelligence involve abilities to understand and use aspects of the environment.

- **Spatial intelligence** is the ability to form and use a mental model of a three-dimensional world. Sailors, engineers, mechanics, artists, architects, drafters, and surgeons have a high degree of spatial intelligence.
- **Musical intelligence** is the ability to hear musical sounds and make music. Singers, conductors, and other musicians have lots of musical intelligence.
- **Bodily-kinesthetic intelligence** is the ability to solve problems or make things using your body, or parts of your body. Athletes, dancers, and crafts people have high degrees of bodily-kinesthetic intelligence.

The last two types of intelligence that Gardner proposes are personal. Although they are not usually thought of as forms of intelligence, they are very important because they influence how well people do in life.

- **Interpersonal intelligence** is the ability to understand other people and to work cooperatively with them. Good salespeople, teachers, therapists, politicians, and parents possess this ability in a high degree.
- **Intrapersonal intelligence** is the ability to assess and understand yourself and use the knowledge to live an effective life. People with good self-belief and appropriate goals have considerable intrapersonal intelligence.

Looking at intelligence as a variety of different abilities opens up the way we evaluate ourselves and others. Each of us possesses some degree of each of these abilities, but most people have more of some than of others. What is your intelligence profile? How might it influence what you like to learn, the way you learn, and your professional goals?

Sources: Howard Gardner, *Multiple Intelligences: The Theory in Practice,* New York: Basic Books, 1993; Howard Gardner, *Frames of Mind: The Theory of Multiple Intelligences,* New York: Basic Books, 1983.

Studying for Tests

You will never need to pull an "all nighter" if you have made studying a regular part of your routine. If you attend class regularly, take class notes, read your assignments, and take notes on your readings, you will have absorbed a good part of the course content. Studying for a test will mean reviewing what you have already learned, not learning it from scratch.

Your notes are your primary resource when you are preparing for an exam. A complete set of course notes, on class discussions and readings, provides an outline of the course content. By studying your notes, you can refresh your memory.

Now is the time that the two-column format for note taking will pay off. If you have not already done so, *read* the material in the wide column and *write* corresponding recall words and questions in the narrow column. Then cover the wide column with a sheet of paper and answer *out loud* the questions you have written in the narrow column. Lift the sheet of paper up to check each answer. If you did not answer correctly, review the material and ask yourself the question again. This time *write* your answer and check it. Repeat this process until you have mastered the material.

You can use the memory techniques discussed in Chapter 3 to help you remember. Repeating material, organizing facts and ideas into small groups, and using associations, acronyms, rhymes, the pegword method, and the method of loci are useful ways to improve your ability to recall what you are studying.

Preparing to Take a Test

If you have studied thoroughly, you have done 90 percent of the preparation needed for taking an exam. But don't stop now—the other 10 percent is also important.

First, check your emotional state. Are you feeling prepared, relaxed, and capable? Do you feel you will do well on the exam? Or do you feel uneasy, anxious, and sure to fail? A certain amount of anxiety is normal; it will even sharpen your performance. But excessive anxiety can cause you to "blank out" during an exam. If you tend to be anxious before exams, don't tank up on coffee or cola. The caffeine in these beverages will make you feel even more stressed. Instead, have a carbohydrate snack (grains, fruits, or vegetables) to calm yourself and help you focus.

If you are feeling very anxious, ask yourself whether you have studied enough. Perhaps you need to review your notes one more time. Or perhaps you need a positive self-talk session to boost your confidence. Tell yourself it's normal to feel anxious but that you are prepared and will do well anyway. Remember, a positive attitude will improve your performance.

Test taking can be stressful. Thoroughly prepared students who are well rested and have good test-taking habits generally do well. *(Courtesy of Getty Images, Inc.)*

Your Turn 4–5

HOW GOOD ARE YOUR STUDY HABITS?

Use the following checklist to evaluate your study habits.

	Yes	No
1. I have a separate notebook, section, or computer file for each class.	☐	☐
2. I attend class regularly.	☐	☐
3. When I miss class, I borrow another student's notes to learn what was covered.	☐	☐
4. I take notes on class lectures and discussions.	☐	☐
5. I keep up with reading assignments and special projects.	☐	☐
6. I take notes on readings.	☐	☐
7. I review my notes regularly.	☐	☐
8. I use my notes to study for exams.	☐	☐

If you answered *yes* to all these items, congratulations! You have excellent study habits.
If you answered *no* to any items, you should concentrate on improving these aspects of your study routine.

You can give your feelings of preparedness a boost by making sure that you are physically ready—not just mentally and emotionally ready. Gather all the materials you will need to take the exam—pens, pencils, calculator, watch, books, and so on—and pack them the night before. Then get a good night's sleep and eat breakfast so you will be well rested and have plenty of energy.

Basic Test-Taking Techniques

Successful students also improve their test-taking performance by using some basic test-taking techniques. Of course, no technique can substitute for thorough preparation. But understanding the best way to approach a test can improve your score. Here are some suggestions:

■ **Skim the whole test first.** Just as you preview a reading to get an idea of what it's about, you should preview the test to see what's on it.

- **Pace yourself.** Know how much each question is worth and budget your time accordingly. For example, if the test is an hour, don't spend half an hour on a question worth only 10 points. Check your watch or a clock every few minutes to make sure you are not wasting time.

- **Answer the easy questions first.** Put a check in the margin next to difficult questions, and return to these questions last. That way you won't spend too much time trying to answer the hard questions and miss answering the easy ones.

- **Make sure you understand each question.** Underline key words and ideas. If you think a question is vague or unclear, ask your instructor for help.

- **Look for clues to the answer in the question itself.** For example, if you get stuck on a multiple-choice item, eliminate the choices that are clearly wrong, then choose from the two or three remaining possibilities. When answering true-false questions, look for the words *always* or *never*. These words often signal a false statement.

Approaching test taking in this methodical way will help you minimize feelings of anxiety.

USING THE LIBRARY

He who asks is a fool for five minutes, but he who does not ask remains a fool forever.

chinese proverb

Your school and community libraries are among the most useful resources to which you have access. Not only do libraries provide material when you need to prepare a research paper or project for school but also they have information that can help you in your professional and personal life. It pays, therefore, to become acquainted with your libraries, because as a lifelong learner, you can benefit from these resources over the years. If you have never used a particular library before, sign up for an orientation session, if these are given. Otherwise, take a tour on your own or ask a librarian to give you an overview of the library's resources.

A modern library may have books, periodicals, reference works, on-line or CD-ROM indexes and reference materials, and Internet access. Doing research in such a library can be confusing because there are so many possible sources of information. When you are looking for information, it helps to narrow the topic you need to research; the more specific you can be, the better the quality of information you will find. It also helps to know what type of source material is likely to have the information you need, whether books, magazines, newspapers, academic journals, or Web sites. Above all, do not hesitate to ask a librarian for help if you get stuck. Librarians, because they know where to find different types of information, are still the most valuable resource of the library.

Using the On-line Catalog

You can find books, and nonbook items such as tapes and DVDs, by searching the library's catalog. The catalog used to be a collection of alphabetized index cards, but now most library catalogs are on line. You access the catalog through a computer terminal at the library. Some library catalogs can be accessed from any computer, anywhere. You may need a password to do this.

You can search the on-line catalog in three main ways: by the author's last name, the title, and the subject. If you are looking for a specific book or item, look under the author's name or the title. If you are looking for books on a particular topic, look under the subject. Once you find an item that interests you, copy its **call number**, an identification number that shows where it is shelved in the library.

Some on-line catalogs offer even more information. In addition to searching by general subject headings, you may be able to search an on-line catalog by specific key words. Once you find material that looks promising, you can find related works with a keystroke. An on-line catalog may also tell you whether the item is checked out and, if so, when it is due back. It may tell you which other libraries in your area have the item.

Specific methods for using on-line catalogs vary from library to library. You'll need to learn how to use your own library catalog by direct experience. Ask a librarian for help if you need it.

Using Reference Works

Most libraries have collections of basic reference works that cannot be borrowed. Reference works include dictionaries, encyclopedias, atlases, biographical directories, indexes, handbooks, telephone books, and almanacs. Most of these are in book form, but an increasing number are published on CD-ROM or in an on-line database and are accessed from a computer terminal.

In addition, many school libraries put copies of texts and other course readings in the reference collection during the term so that students can use them in the library.

Finding Articles in On-line Databases

Periodicals are publications that appear at regular intervals, such as newspapers, magazines, and scholarly journals. Newspapers and magazines contain articles geared to the general public. Scholarly journals contain articles written by experts and geared to students, teachers, and professionals in a particular field. Since the information in periodicals is more up to date than the information in books, you may need to consult periodicals when doing research.

Articles are not indexed in the library's main on-line catalog. Instead, you must search for articles in on-line databases compiled by various companies.

- *EBSCOhost.* A database covering most academic subject areas and containing full-text articles from more than 3,000 periodicals.
- *ProQuest.* A database covering many academic areas, as well as articles from newspapers.
- *ERIC.* A specialized database that contains articles from education journals.
- *Medline.* A specialized database that covers health-related and medical journals.

You can access on-line databases at a computer terminal in the library or from home by using a password. Note that these databases of periodical articles cannot be searched by Web search engines like Google or Yahoo. Your library must subscribe to a particular database for you to access it.

Each database has its own search engine. You can search the articles by author, title, subject, key words, date, type of periodical, and other characteristics. The database usually contains citation information as well as an abstract, or summary, of each article. In many cases it also contains the full text of the article (but usually no illustrations). You can download the article, print it, or e-mail it to yourself.

The database also tells you whether the library owns a paper copy of the periodical in which the article appears. If it does, you should locate the paper copy, even if it seems easier just to download the article's text from the database. That's because seeing the paper copy will give you a better idea of what type of publication the article appears in. The paper copy also includes illustrations, which may be very important in your research.

Evaluating Information You Find on the World Wide Web

In addition to their other computerized services, libraries also offer access to the World Wide Web portion of the Internet. (See Chapter 1, pages 20–22, for an overview of the Internet and Internet search engines.) The Internet can be a powerful research tool, providing access by address or by key word searches to Web sites maintained by different types of groups. You can tell what type of group runs a Web site by its domain abbreviation:

- companies (.com)
- nonprofit organizations (.org)

Your Turn 4–6

CHECK OUT YOUR LIBRARY

Get to know your library better by taking a tour and answering the following questions. Use your school or local library.

1. What types of searches can you do on the on-line catalog?

_____

2. List four books in the library's reference section.

_____

_____

_____

3. What periodicals' databases does your library subscribe to? Which of them is used for general searches?

_____

_____

4. How can you get back issues of periodicals?

_____

_____

5. What Internet search engines does your librarian recommend?

_____

_____

■ government departments and agencies (.gov)

■ the armed services (.mil)

■ schools (.edu)

■ individuals (who often have a ~ in their URLs)[3]

When you are doing research for school, you have to be skeptical about what you find on the Internet. Company Web sites (.com) seek to promote the best image they can. Many organization sites, like those of environmental groups or the National Rifle Association (.org), have a point of view that influences the information they post. Other Web sites may be maintained by individuals with lots of opinions and very little data to back them up (~). Government sites, on the other hand, often contain valuable information and statistics (.gov). For example, the U.S. Census Bureau posts reams of population data for anyone to use <http://www.census.gov>.

When you evaluate a Web site, ask yourself:

1. Is the author or sponsor clearly identified? Does the site have a mission statement and contact information?
2. What is the purpose of the site? Does the site have a point of view?
3. Is the site well organized with solid content?
4. Does the site indicate where its information comes from? Can you check its data against other sources?
5. Is the site up to date?[4]

If you are in doubt about the credibility of information on a Web site, ask your librarian or instructor for help in evaluating it.

 # The Information Highway

GETTING UP TO SPEED

There are many Web sites with information on learning styles and study skills, including reading techniques, note-taking, and test-taking tips. Here are a few:

- The study habits section of the academics channel of the I Am Next Web site, a site for college students, provides tips on improving study skills <http://www.iamnext.com>.
- Suggestions for improving study skills, from working in groups to writing essays to taking math tests, can be found on the University of St. Thomas Web site <http://www.iss.stthomas.edu>.
- Checklists for evaluating different types of Web sites can be found on the Wolfgram Memorial Library section of the Widener University Web site <http://muse.widener.edu>.

In addition, you will find many other study skills and library resource sites and discussion groups by searching with these key words: *learning styles, Howard Gardner, multiple intelligences, study skills, reading techniques, note-taking skills, test-taking skills,* and *library resources*.

Finally, check whether your own school library has a Web site. Many college libraries maintain Web sites with useful information, including library maps, links to databases and other sources of information, and a link to the on-line catalog.

What's Up

Name _____ Date _____

1. Why are physical and emotional well-being important for effective learning?

_____

_____

_____

2. Briefly describe each of the four basic learning styles. Circle the name of your dominant style.

Logician _____

_____

Procedurist _____

_____

Communicator _____

_____

Experimenter _____

_____

3. Why it is important to have a study area?

_____

_____

_____

4. How can you take advantage of your peak learning times?

_____

_____

_____

_____

5. Describe each step in the P.Q.R. system of reading.

_____

_____

_____

_____

_____

_____

_____

_____

continues

Name _____ Date_____

6. Give two reasons for taking notes on class sessions and readings.

_____

_____

7. Why should you outline and diagram your notes?

_____

_____

_____

8. How can the two-column format for note taking be used when you are studying for an exam?

_____

_____

9. Describe two techniques for taking tests.

_____

_____

_____

_____

10. How would you find each of the following items in your school library?

(a) a book by Colin Powell, secretary of state for President George W. Bush

_____

(b) an article in an education journal about methods of teaching freshman composition

_____

(c) current financial aid guidelines from the U.S. Department of Education

_____

Case Studies

THE CASE OF THE UNHAPPY LEARNER

When Arianne transferred from a small rural school to a large urban school, she found her studies suffering. In the country, classes had been small and group discussions encouraged. Arianne had done very well and had always enjoyed her courses. Now Arianne found herself in large classes in which instructors lectured and assigned readings and other solo activities. The subjects were not harder, but Arianne's marks were slipping and she wasn't happy about her studies.

1. What learning style does Arianne prefer? Why?

_____

_____

_____

_____

2. How can Arianne make up for the fact that her new school does not offer instruction tailored to her preferred learning style?

_____

_____

_____

_____

THE CASE OF THE DISORGANIZED STUDENT

Michael had always managed to get by on the strength of his cleverness, but when he got to college he found that cleverness was not enough. He had several hard courses and lots of reading to do for each one. In addition, there were quizzes plus midterms and finals. Michael liked the freedom of college, and often he skipped class. Since no one checked whether he was keeping up with the readings, he let them slide. Michael had always depended on cramming to pass exams. When he tried this during his first semester, he was dismayed to find he had failed two of his midterms.

1. What poor study habits has Michael fallen into?

_____

_____

_____

_____

2. What can Michael do to improve his school performance?

_____

_____

_____

Journal

Answer the following journal questions.

1. Now that you understand your own learning style preferences, what will you do to change the way you study and learn?

_____
_____
_____
_____
_____

2. Describe your ideal study location.

_____
_____
_____
_____
_____

3. If you suffer from anxiety before tests, what can you do to reduce this? How can you improve your approach to taking tests?

_____
_____
_____
_____
_____

4. What do you use the Internet for? If you don't regularly use the Internet now, what uses might it have for you in the future?

_____
_____
_____
_____
_____

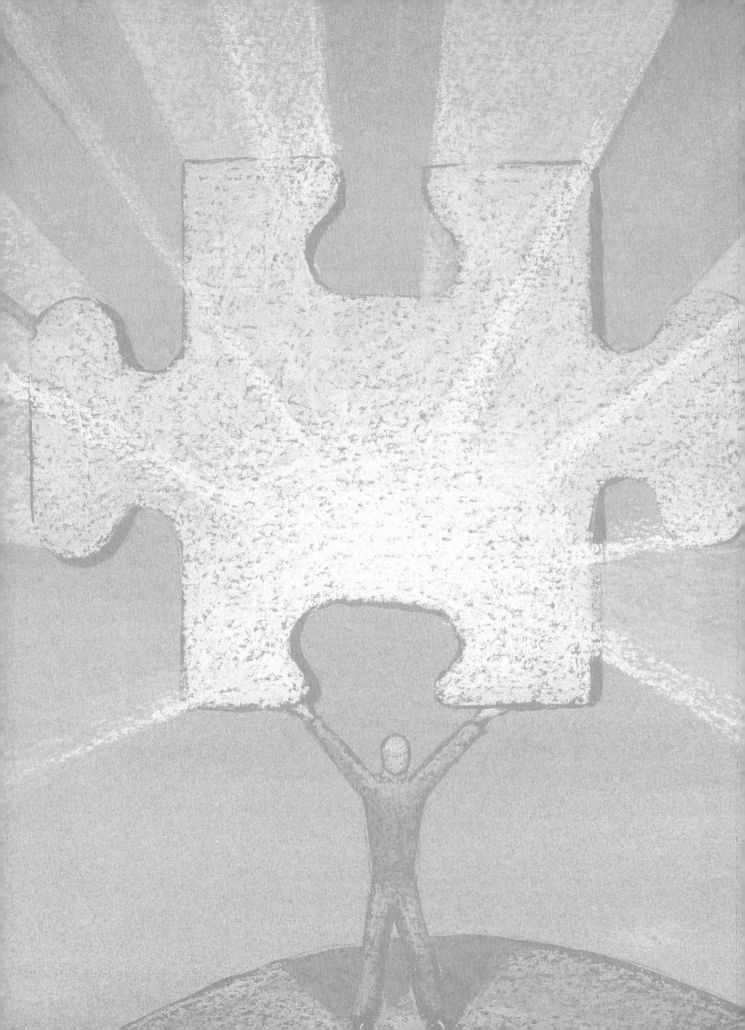

Developing Your Physical Potential

A strong and healthy body provides the foundation for all your activities—as well as your state of mind. A feeling of well-being will help you reach your potential in all areas of your life. In this unit, you will learn how to eat well and stay healthy.

One of the keys to a healthy diet is plenty of fruits and vegetables. Chef Curtis Aikens got his start hanging out in the produce section of his local supermarket. After learning to read at the age of 26, he began writing cookbooks and hosting TV shows like *Pick of the Day* and *From My Garden*. *(Courtesy of Curtis Aikens.)*

Chapter 5

Eating Well

In the last 30 years, Americans have been warned against eating too much salt, sugar, and fat, smoking cigarettes, drinking alcoholic beverages, failing to exercise, practicing unsafe sex—the list goes on and on. As the headlines come and go, people try to adjust their habits to the latest round of advice. The result is often confusion about what's healthy and what's not.

Anyone who has been ill doesn't doubt the value of good health. People who don't feel well simply don't perform up to their potential. As we've seen, our ability to reach our potential as human beings depends on our emotional and intellectual well-being. Add physical well-being to that list, and you have the foundation for all your achievements. The better your physical condition, the greater your chances of reaching your potential.

You may think you're in great physical condition, and perhaps you are. Yet studies have shown that most Americans have poor eating habits, don't get enough exercise and rest, and abuse their bodies with substances like alcohol and tobacco. These people may think they feel well, but in reality they are functioning below their potential.

On the other hand, people who take care of their bodies are rewarded by increased well-being and self-confidence. To reach your physical potential, you must have a well-balanced approach to maintaining good health.

In this chapter, the focus is on eating a healthy, well-balanced diet. You will learn about the major nutrients and how they affect your health. You will learn how to classify foods into the basic five food groups and how to eat a balanced diet. Last, you will figure out your body mass index to see if your weight is healthy.

NUTRIENTS

Food provides nutrients, the substances your body uses for growth, maintenance, and repair, as well as for energy. Diets with too much or too little of a nutrient can be harmful to your health. In addition, the nutrients in foods affect your mind, mood, and energy level. To look, feel, and act your best, you have to eat your best, and that means a diet with the proper balance of nutrients.

All foods contain one or more nutrients. The major types of nutrients are protein, carbohydrates, fats, water, vitamins, and minerals. Table 5–1 shows the major nutrients, their functions in the body, and their food sources. The key to making sure you get all the necessary nutrients is to eat a wide variety of healthy foods.

Protein

Protein is a chemical substance that is part of all body cells. It has many functions, including growth and the maintenance and repair of tissue. Meat, fish, poultry, eggs, dairy products, nuts, and tofu are all sources of protein. In addition, beans can be sources of protein if they are eaten with grains.

Carbohydrates

Sugar, corn syrup, and other sweets are simple carbohydrates. Starches and grains are complex carbohydrates. Starches and grains also contain dietary fiber that aids digestion. In general, the more a complex carbohydrate food has been processed, the less fiber it has. So, for example, white bread has less fiber than whole wheat bread. Flour, cereal, bread, rice, noodles, grits, fruits, and vegetables all contain carbohydrates and varying amounts of dietary fiber.

Fats

Fats provide concentrated storage of energy for the body. They also provide insulation and dissolve certain vitamins. There are two main types of fat:

- Saturated fats are those that are solid at room temperature; they are found in meat and dairy products and palm and coconut oils. Saturated fats increase the body's own production of cholesterol.

TABLE 5–1 Nutrients and Their Sources

Nutrients	Major Functions	Major Sources
Protein	Growth, maintenance of tissue, enzymes, and hormones to regulate body processes	Meat, fish, poultry, beans, eggs, nuts, dairy products, tofu
Carbohydrates	Primary sources of energy	Bread, cereal, rice, pasta, and other grain products; fruits, vegetables, potatoes; sweets
Dietary fiber	Indigestible roughage that helps digestion	Raw barley, bulgur wheat, beans, prunes, peas, lentils, whole-grain wheat flour, oat bran. Also present in other grains, fruits, and vegetables.
Fats	Concentrated storage of energy; insulation, dissolves certain vitamins	Meats, fish, poultry, and dairy products; oils, lard, margarine; fried foods
Water	Present in all cells. Transports nutrients and wastes, takes part in many chemical reactions, cushions, regulates body temperature	All beverages. Also present to a degree in all foods
Vitamin A	Growth, healthy skin, bones and teeth, good vision	Meat, egg yolk, dairy products, dark green leafy and deep-yellow vegetables
Thiamin (Vitamin B_1)	Helps use carbohydrates for energy, maintains healthy nervous system	Whole-grain products, enriched breads and cereals, meat, poultry, fish, beans, nuts, egg yolk
Riboflavin (Vitamin B_2)	Contributes to use of proteins, carbohydrates, and fats for energy; healthy skin	Dairy products, organ meat, green leafy vegetables, enriched breads and cereals
Niacin (Vitamin B_3)	Healthy nervous system, skin, digestion	Poultry, meat, fish, beans, nuts, dark green leafy vegetables, potatoes, whole-grain or enriched breads and cereals
Ascorbic acid (Vitamin C)	Helps hold cells together; healthy teeth, gums, and blood vessels; helps body resist infection and heal wounds	Citrus fruits and their juices, tomatoes, broccoli, raw green vegetables
Vitamin D	Needed to absorb calcium and phosphorus, healthy bones and teeth	Milk, egg yolk, liver, herring, sardines, tuna, salmon (body can make this vitamin with direct sunlight on the skin)
Vitamin E	Protects cells from oxidation (antioxidant)	Vegetable oils, margarine, wheat germ, nuts
Calcium	Needed for structure of healthy bones and teeth, healthy muscles and nerves	Dairy products, broccoli, turnips, collards, kale, mustard greens, oysters, shrimp, salmon, clams, tofu
Iodide	Prevents goiter, needed to manufacture enzyme thyroxine	Iodized salt, small amounts in seafood
Iron	Needed for healthy blood and formation of many enzymes	Liver, meat, poultry, shellfish, egg yolk, green leafy vegetables, nuts, enriched cereals and breads
Potassium	Helps in synthesis of protein, fluid balance, healthy nerves and muscles	Citrus fruits, bananas, apricots, meat, fish, and cereal
Sodium (salt)	Helps maintain fluid balance, absorb other nutrients	Table salt; processed food, especially meats and salty snacks

Source: Adapted from U.S. Department of Agriculture, *Home and Garden Bulletin No. 1*, 1978, and U.S. Department of Agriculture, Agricultural Research Service 2002, USDA National Nutrient Database for Standard Reference, Release 15. Nutrient Data Laboratory Home Page <http://www.nal.usda.gov/fnic/foodcomp>.

- **Unsaturated fats** are liquid at room temperature. **Polyunsaturated fats** are found in corn, safflower, and soybean oil. **Monounsaturated fats** are found in peanut and olive oils.

In addition, cholesterol, a fatty acid, is found in animal products like meat, cheese, shellfish, and eggs.

Fats and cholesterol have been the focus of much attention in recent years. Studies have linked diets high in fat, especially saturated fat and cholesterol, with increased risk of heart disease, stroke, and certain cancers, as well as with obesity. Nutritionists have been urging Americans to cut down their fat and cholesterol intake—in other words, to eat less meat, cheese, and other fatty foods—to protect their health.

There is one type of fat that most Americans don't get enough of. Omega-3, a fatty acid needed for proper brain functioning, is found in fish such as tuna, salmon, trout, and sardines. Fish also has the benefit of being low in saturated and unsaturated fats. More fish and less meat would provide a better balance and quantity of fats in the diets of most people.

Water

Water is an extremely important nutrient; it is found in every cell of the body. It transports nutrients throughout the body and removes waste products. Water cushions and lubricates parts of the body, and it is an essential part of many chemical reactions. It also helps regulate the body's temperature. Water is present in most foods, as well as in the liquids we drink. Nutritionists recommend drinking 64 ounces (8 glasses) of water a day.

Vitamins and Minerals

Protein, carbohydrates, fats, and water are the major nutrients by weight in most food. However, foods also contain trace amounts of other chemicals, called vitamins and minerals, that are essential for life and growth. Each vitamin and mineral has specific functions in the body. Table 5–1 summarizes the functions and sources of the major vitamins and minerals.

Nutrition Information

How can you tell what nutrients are in the foods you eat? You can look up the foods you eat in a chart such as Table 5–1, which will give you a very general idea of which nutrients the foods contain. You can buy or borrow a booklet containing tables of nutrition information, or check the Internet for such tables (see page 124). For all packaged foods, you can check the Nutrition Facts chart on the label (see Figure 5–1). This

FIGURE 5–1

All packaged foods must have a Nutrition Facts chart showing the nutrients in one serving. This chart is from a package of macaroni and cheese. (*Source: U.S. Department of Agriculture and U.S. Department of Health and Human Services,* Dietary Guidelines for Americans, *2000, p. 18.*)

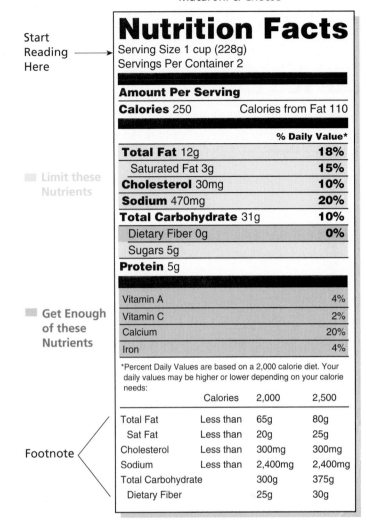

Macaroni & Cheese

Nutrition Facts

Serving Size 1 cup (228g)
Servings Per Container 2

Amount Per Serving

Calories 250	Calories from Fat 110

	% Daily Value*
Total Fat 12g	**18%**
Saturated Fat 3g	**15%**
Cholesterol 30mg	**10%**
Sodium 470mg	**20%**
Total Carbohydrate 31g	**10%**
Dietary Fiber 0g	**0%**
Sugars 5g	
Protein 5g	

Vitamin A	4%
Vitamin C	2%
Calcium	20%
Iron	4%

*Percent Daily Values are based on a 2,000 calorie diet. Your daily values may be higher or lower depending on your calorie needs:

	Calories	2,000	2,500
Total Fat	Less than	65g	80g
Sat Fat	Less than	20g	25g
Cholesterol	Less than	300mg	300mg
Sodium	Less than	2,400mg	2,400mg
Total Carbohydrate		300g	375g
Dietary Fiber		25g	30g

Start Reading Here

Limit these Nutrients

Get Enough of these Nutrients

Footnote

chart, which is required by law on all packaged foods, tells you the amount of each nutrient a serving of that food contains. It also tells you what percentage of the daily requirement for that nutrient one serving contains. If you make a habit of checking the Nutrition Facts charts on the foods you eat, you will have a pretty good idea of the nutrient content of your diet. You may be surprised to discover how much fat, salt (sodium), and sugars most packaged foods contain.

Nutrients and Health

In the early 1900s, scientists discovered that many vitamins and minerals are essential to prevent certain diseases. For example, rickets, a disease that affects bone development in children, can be prevented with vitamin D and calcium, both found in fortified milk. Goiter, an enlargement of the thyroid gland, can be prevented with iodine, a mineral in iodized salt.

Your Turn 5–1

WHAT ARE YOU EATING?

Use the Food Diary on page 111 to keep track of what you eat or drink for three days. Be honest! Then review your diet. Use the information in Table 5–1 and the Nutrition Facts charts on the foods you've eaten to answer the following questions:

1. What foods were your major sources of protein?

_____

_____

2. What foods were your major sources of carbohydrates?

_____

_____

_____

3. What foods were your major sources of fat?

_____

_____

4. During the three days, did you eat food that provides all the vitamins and minerals listed in Table 5–1?

_____

If not, what vitamins and minerals did you miss?

_____

_____

What should you eat to make sure you get the missing vitamin(s) and mineral(s)?

_____

_____

_____

_____

5. What types of food would you like to cut down on? What types of food do you think you need to eat more of?

_____

_____

_____

_____

The relationship between diet and health in these types of disease is clear-cut. Today, nutritionists and other scientists are studying the health risks or value of other nutrients. As we've already mentioned, fat, cholesterol, and salt have been found to play a role in ailments such as high blood pressure, heart disease, and cancer. Although fat, cholesterol, and salt are not the only causes of these diseases, nutritionists recommend that people adjust their diets to reduce the risk to their health. For most Americans, a healthier diet means eating more fruits, vegetables, whole-grain products, and fish and less meat, dairy products, sweets, and salty snacks. Even young people, who may not yet be at risk for heart disease and cancer, should change their eating habits while young to prevent the development of disease in the future.

Three-Day Food Diary			
Meal	**Day 1**	**Day 2**	**Day 3**
Breakfast			
Lunch			
Dinner			
Snacks			
Beverages			

FAT AND CHOLESTEROL QUIZ

How aware are you of the health risk or value of fat and cholesterol? The following questions were included in a survey conducted by the Food and Drug Administration to measure public awareness of these factors.[1] After you answer the questions, check your answers and see how well you did, compared with the survey respondents.

1. If a food is labeled cholesterol-free, it is also:
   a. low in saturated fat
   b. high in saturated fat
   c. could be either high or low
   d. not sure

2. Which kind of fat is more likely to raise cholesterol level?
   a. saturated fat
   b. polyunsaturated fat
   c. both of them
   d. neither of them
   e. not sure

3. Cholesterol is usually found in:
   a. vegetables and vegetable oils
   b. animal products like meat and dairy foods
   c. all foods containing fat and oil
   d. not sure

4. Saturated fats are usually found in:
   a. vegetables and vegetable oils
   b. animal products like meat and dairy foods
   c. not sure

5. Polyunsaturated fats are usually found in:
   a. vegetables and vegetable oils
   b. animal products like meat and dairy foods
   c. not sure

Here are the answers, followed by the percent of survey respondents who answered correctly:

1. c (35 percent answered correctly)
2. a (56 percent)
3. b (33 percent)
4. b (62 percent)
5. a (55 percent)

This is a favorite meal for many people: hamburger, french fries, and soft drink. Unfortunately, it is full of fat, cholesterol, processed grains, and sugar. *(Courtesy of Tom Stock.)*

WHAT IS A BALANCED DIET?

As our understanding of nutrition has improved, the advice of nutritionists has changed. This process is continuing today. Nutritionists even disagree among themselves about what makes up a healthy diet.

Nutritionists and scientists at the U.S. Department of Agriculture and the U.S. Department of Health and Human Services periodically issue *Dietary Guidelines for Americans*.[2] Their basic diet model is a high-carbohydrate diet. Their advice is to:

Aim for Fitness

- ■ Aim for a healthy weight.
- ■ Be physically active each day.

Build a Healthy Base

- ■ Let the Food Guide Pyramid guide your food choices (see page 115).
- ■ Choose a variety of grains daily, especially whole grains.
- ■ Choose a variety of fruits and vegetables daily.
- ■ Keep food safe to eat.

Choose Sensibly

- ■ Choose a diet that is low in saturated fat and cholesterol and moderate in total fat.
- ■ Choose beverages and foods to moderate your intake of sugars.
- ■ Choose and prepare foods with less salt.
- ■ If you drink alcoholic beverages, do so in moderation.

To make sure you get a healthy variety of food, think of your diet in terms of the five food groups. Another way to make sure you get a balanced diet is to use the Food Guide Pyramid.

Five Food Groups

The basic five food groups include:

1. **Grains.** Whole-grain breads, cereals, tortillas, brown rice, and pasta are the healthiest of the grain products because they contain complex carbohydrates and dietary fiber. Processed grain products are white rice, muffins, waffles, sweetened cereals, doughnuts, pastry, and stuffing. These contain less fiber and sugars, salt, or fats that make them less desirable.

The five major food groups are grains; vegetables; meat, poultry, fish, eggs, beans, and nuts; fruits; and dairy products. *(Courtesy of PhotoDisc.)*

2. **Vegetables.** Most vegetables are extremely good for you, and you can eat as much of them as you wish. There are some exceptions, however. Canned vegetables, french fries, and pickles all contain added sugars, salt, or fats that make them less healthy choices.

3. **Fruits.** Fresh fruit is good for you, but canned fruit often contains added sugar. Dried fruit has a lot of calories.

4. **Dairy products.** Skim and 1 percent milk products and nonfat yogurt have the least fat of the dairy products. Ice milk, frozen low-fat yogurt, and 2 percent milk have moderate amounts of fat. Highest in fat are whole milk, cream and sour cream, cheeses, and ice cream. People who do not eat dairy products can find the nutrients they provide in other foods, such as meat, leafy greens, and tofu.

5. **Meat, poultry, fish, eggs, beans, and nuts.** In this group, the choices with the least fat and salt are most fish, poultry without the skin, lean cuts of beef and pork, egg whites, and beans, peas, and lentils. Oil-packed tuna, poultry with skin, most red meat, tofu, peanut butter, nuts, processed meats (cold cuts and hot dogs), and whole eggs have more fat.

The Food Guide Pyramid

The basic five food groups give you an idea of how to achieve variety in your diet. However, they do not give you a sense of how to achieve moderation as well. For that reason, in the early 1990s the USDA came up with a model of a well-balanced diet called the Food Guide Pyramid (see Figure 5–2). The pyramid is a diagram that shows the number of servings per day that should be eaten from each of the five food groups. At the base of the pyramid are foods that can be eaten in quantity—primarily grain products. As the pyramid narrows, the amount of food that should be eaten decreases, with fats and sweets at the top.

FIGURE 5–2

The USDA Food Guide Pyramid shows how much to eat from each of the food groups. The bigger the section of the pyramid, the more of that food group should be eaten. As you can see, this is a high-carbohydrate diet. Grains make up much more of the pyramid than the other food groups do. *(Source: U.S. Department of Agriculture and U.S. Department of Health and Human Services,* Dietary Guidelines for Americans, *2000, p. 15.)*

Food Guide Pyramid

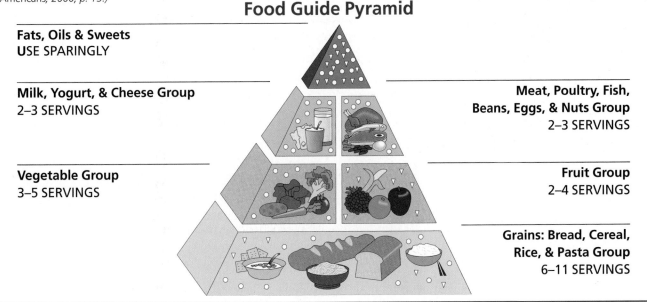

Fats, Oils & Sweets
USE SPARINGLY

Milk, Yogurt, & Cheese Group
2–3 SERVINGS

Vegetable Group
3–5 SERVINGS

Meat, Poultry, Fish, Beans, Eggs, & Nuts Group
2–3 SERVINGS

Fruit Group
2–4 SERVINGS

Grains: Bread, Cereal, Rice, & Pasta Group
6–11 SERVINGS

The number of servings recommended by the USDA depends on your age, sex, size, and level of activity:

- ■ Children age 2 to 6, inactive women, and some older adults require the fewest servings per day of each group, about 1,600 calories total.
- ■ Older children, teenage girls, active women, and most men require an average number of servings per day from each group, about 2,200 calories total.
- ■ Teenage boys and active men need the maximum number of servings per day, about 2,800 calories total.

Problems with the Food Guide Pyramid   The Food Guide Pyramid is based on a high-carbohydrate diet with lots of grains. High-carbohydrate diets can be healthy as long as most of the carbohydrates are whole-grain products. The first problem with the pyramid arose because the grains group does not distinguish between unprocessed complex carbohydrates (whole grains) and processed grains. So, many people who followed the pyramid ate too much processed grain, such as white rice, white bread, and most noodles and pasta. Processed grains are easily digested, so when you eat them, you are soon hungry again.

Second, the serving sizes in the pyramid are smaller than those found on Nutrition Facts charts and in most meal portions. For example, a serving of meat is 2 to 3 ounces, and a serving of cooked pasta is half a cup. So again, people following the pyramid were eating too much. Some nutritionists think that the increase in obesity among Americans during the 1990s was partially caused by the Food Guide Pyramid.[3]

A third problem with the pyramid is that it is based on a traditional Western diet. Many Americans who normally eat an ethnic cuisine found that the pyramid could not easily be applied to their diets (see News & Views, page 118).

The U.S. Department of Agriculture and the Department of Health and Human Services recognized these problems with the pyramid. The *Dietary Guidelines* offer further guidance on eating a balanced diet while using the pyramid. They emphasize eating whole grains rather than processed grains, cutting the intake of sugars, and decreasing portion size.

CHANGING YOUR EATING HABITS

If your diet is less than satisfactory, you can change it. The first step is to keep a food diary of what you eat for a few days, as you are doing (or did) in Your Turn 5–1. Once you've done that, you can analyze your eating habits and decide what changes are necessary.

FIGURE 5–3

These are the USDA recommendations for the daily percentage of calories from protein, carbohydrates, and fats. However, many nutritionists disagree with these percentages.

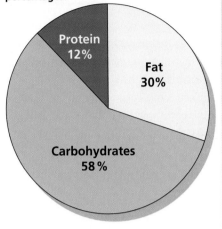

Protein 12%

Fat 30%

Carbohydrates 58%

In addition to reviewing what you eat to see whether your diet has an adequate variety of foods, you can also compare the quantities you eat with the recommendations shown on the Food Guide Pyramid. Remember that the serving sizes on the pyramid are often smaller than those found on Nutrition Facts charts or than typical portion sizes. For example, one slice of bread equals one serving of grain. That means a sandwich has two servings of grain.

If you are like most Americans, you will find you need to cut down on fats, sweets, and processed grains and eat more whole grains, fruits, and vegetables.

In general, the USDA recommends that no more than 30 percent of our calories come from fat, 58 percent from carbohydrates, and 12 percent from protein (see Figure 5–3). The "% Daily Value" information on packaged foods is based on these percentages (see again Figure 5–1). However, there is disagreement among nutritionists about the percentages. Some nutritionists think less fat is better. Other nutritionists favor increasing the percentage of protein and cutting the percentage of carbohydrates, along the lines of the high-protein Atkins diet.

After you've thought about what you eat and how much you eat, you should also consider your eating habits. For example, do you skip breakfast? That's a bad habit, because breakfast fuels the start of your day and helps spread your eating into smaller meals. Studies have shown that eating several small meals each day rather than one or two large meals helps prevent the storage of fat. Think about your snacking habits. Do you always eat a high-calorie sweet when doing a particular activity like studying? If you do, try to substitute a healthy snack like fruit. And consider the number of restaurant meals you eat. It's much harder to control what you eat when you dine out. First, portion sizes in restaurants are often very large. Second, you may have to look hard to find restaurants whose foods are not full of fat, cream, salt, and sugar.

Last, consider your weight. If you have a healthy weight, changing your eating habits may simply mean adjusting your diet so it has a better balance of foods. If you need to lose or gain weight, you will have to make further changes to increase or decrease the number of calories you take in every day.

HEALTHY WEIGHTS

> **Eat to live, and not live to eat.**
>
> benjamin franklin,
>
> 18th-century statesman,
>
> scientist, and writer

More than half of Americans are overweight or obese.[4] Being overweight or underweight is not simply an appearance issue. It's a health issue. Overweight people have a higher risk of developing high blood pressure, heart disease, stroke, certain types of diabetes, and some cancers. Underweight people have a higher risk of health problems as well. Underweight women have a greater chance of developing

THE OTHER FOOD GUIDE PYRAMIDS

When the Food Guide Pyramid came out, many Americans looked at it and asked, "Where is the food I eat?" Ethnic Americans wondered where were tortillas, grits, cornbread, couscous, guava, and other foods they loved. Lactose-intolerant Americans, who cannot digest milk products, wondered what to do about the dairy products group. And vegetarians knew the pyramid didn't fit their diet at all.

The U.S. Department of Agriculture heard these points, but they maintained that the pyramid is just a general guide based on the meat- and dairy-based diet most Americans eat. So nutritionists around the country began adapting the pyramid to the cuisines of different ethnic and special groups.

- The Soul Food Pyramid, based on the traditional African American diet, added grits and cornbread to the grains group, black-eyed peas to the meats group, and chitterlings to the fats, oils, and sweets group.

- The Asian Diet Pyramid, based on Chinese and other East Asian cuisines, added millet to the grains group and moved meat all the way to the top.

- The Mexican Food Pyramid added lard and avocados to the fats, oils, and sweets group, salsa and chilies to the vegetable group, and tortillas to the grain group.

- The Mediterranean Diet Pyramid, based on Italian, Spanish, Greek, and other Mediterranean cuisines, added polenta and couscous to the grains group and moved olive oil from the top to right above fruits and vegetables.

And these are just a few of the pyramids that have been developed since the USDA pyramid was published. Others pyramids are based on Arab, Chinese, Cuban, Indian, Italian, Japanese, Native American, Portuguese, Russian, Spanish, Thai, and vegetarian diets. Even though the USDA does not endorse these special pyramids, they do provide a Web page with links to all of them. Visit the Food and Nutrition Information Center of the USDA Web site to check them out <http://www.nal.usda.gov/fnic/etext/00023.html>.

Sources: "Ethnic/Cultural and Special Audience Food Guide Pyramids," U.S. Department of Agriculture, Food and Nutrition Information Center <http://www.nal.usda./gov/fnic/>, accessed February 6, 2003; Jenny Deam, "Rebuilding the Food Pyramid: Critics Charge USDA's Guides Fail Ethnic Test," *Denver Post*, July 25, 2000, pp. 1E, 8E.

osteoporosis, a bone disease, and underweight men and women, on average, do not live as long as people whose weight is healthy.

Finding Out Your Body Mass Index

Is your weight healthy? Your **body mass index (BMI)** will tell you. BMI is a measure of weight in relation to height. In the BMI chart shown in Figure 5–4, find your weight along the horizontal axis. Go straight up from that point to the line that matches your height. Then look to see which BMI group you fall into.

FIGURE 5–4

This chart shows the BMI ranges for healthy, overweight, and obese people. A healthy BMI ranges from 18.5 to 25.

(Source: U.S. Department of Agriculture and U.S. Department of Health and Human Services, Dietary Guidelines for Americans, 2000, p. 7.)

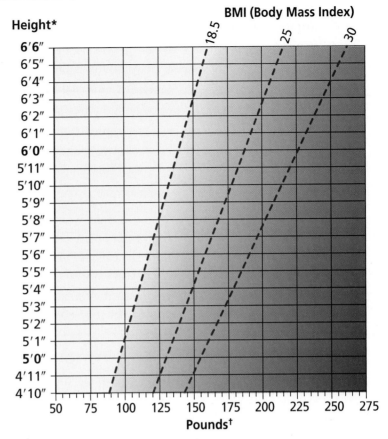

BMI (Body Mass Index)

Healthy Weight BMI from 18.5 up to 25 refers to healthy weight.

Overweight BMI from 25 up to 30 refers to overweight.

Obese BMI 30 or higher refers to obesity. Obese persons are also overweight.

*Without shoes
†Without clothes

BMI	Weight Category
18.5 to 25	Healthy weight
25 to 30	Overweight
Over 30	Obese

Counting Calories

It's easier to control your weight if you understand what a calorie is. A **calorie** is the amount of heat needed to raise the temperature of one kilogram of water one degree Centigrade. Think of a calorie as a unit of energy. If you are active, the calorie is used to produce energy. If you are inactive, the calorie is stored as fat.

The number of calories you need each day just to maintain your present weight varies according to your sex, age, and activity level.

A rough idea of how many calories you need each day to maintain your present weight can be figured as follows:

- If you are very inactive, you need about 10 calories per pound. (For example, if you weigh 125 pounds, you'll need 10×125, or 1,250 calories a day.)
- If you take part in light activity, you need about 13 calories per pound.
- If you're moderately active, you need about 18 calories per pound.
- If you're very active, you need about 20 calories per pound.

Of course, women who are pregnant or breast-feeding need more than their normal number of calories and are advised to consult with their doctors before changing their diets.

If you want to lose weight, you will have to consume fewer calories and increase your level of activity. If you want to gain weight, you will have to consume more calories.

Losing Weight

Most Americans who are overweight weigh too much because of their lifestyles. Today, we drive instead of walk, watch television instead of exercise, and eat too much food. Losing weight means changing this lifestyle with two goals in mind: (1) to cut the number of calories you eat each day and (2) to increase your activity level to burn more calories. For most people, these changes result in gradual weight loss.

To maintain the weight loss, you must change the way you live—not simply diet for a month or two and then resume your old habits. You must get in the habit of cutting down on foods and beverages rich in calories. You must get used to eating lean meat, fruits, vegetables, and whole grains. And you must exercise regularly. An exercise program is an important part of any serious plan to maintain a healthy weight.

For people whose weight problem has a genetic or medical cause, weight loss is more difficult and needs to be medically supervised. And for those who are inclined to try quick weight-loss diet programs, fads, and pills, a word of warning: Diets that rely on eating one food—like grapefruit—or on fewer than 1,000 calories a day are dangerous to your health. That's because one food—or too little food—cannot possibly provide the range of nutrients your body needs to function. Losing weight rapidly is hazardous; it can cause faintness, changes in blood pressure, and heart trouble, as well as malnutrition. In addition, avoid diet pills unless you are using them under a doctor's supervision. These can cause nausea, rapid heartbeat, nervousness, irritability, sleeplessness, and more serious side effects.

Your Turn 5–3

CALCULATE THE DAILY CALORIE INTAKE TO MAINTAIN YOUR WEIGHT

Follow these steps to calculate the number of calories per day you need to eat to maintain your current weight.

1. What is your weight in pounds? _____

2. What is your activity level? Check one.

☐ Inactive (10 calories)   ☐ Light activity (13 calories)

☐ Moderate activity (18 calories)   ☐ High activity (20 calories)

3. Multiply your weight by the number of calories for your activity level. This is your daily calorie intake to stay at your present weight.

Weight _____ × _____ calories

for activity level = _____ number of calories per day to maintain weight.

Neither diet fads nor diet pills get at the root of most people's weight problem—changing eating and exercising habits over the long term. If you need support to change your diet permanently, consider joining a diet club or group such as Weight Watchers.

Gaining Weight

If you are underweight, you must increase your intake of calories to gain weight. You can do this by eating larger portions or by adding some rich foods to your diet. It's not recommended that you cut your level of exercise unless it is extremely high. Remember, as you get older and your level of activity decreases, it's easier to put on weight and keep it on.

WHATEVER IT TAKES

Michele Hoskins

(Courtesy of Michele Hoskins, Michele's Foods.)

In 1983, Michele Hoskins was a recently divorced mother of three with no business experience. However, she did have determination—and a secret recipe for honey crème syrup passed down from her great-great-grandmother America, who was a slave, through the third daughter of each generation.

When Hoskins got the recipe from her mother, she served the syrup, a blend of honey, churned butter, and cream, at Sunday family breakfasts. Rather than passing down the recipe to her own daughter, she decided to pass down a business instead.

To finance the business, Hoskins sold everything she owned and moved into her parents' attic to save on living expenses. She and her daughters bottled syrup by hand in the basement. It took them an hour to fill 12 bottles, and their feet stuck to the spilled syrup on the floor.

At first, Hoskins made some bad deals and lost money. She and her girls moved to a public housing project and went on welfare for 18 months. But she continued to make and sell syrup. First she sold syrup to neighborhood grocers in Chicago. Then she sold syrup to local and regional grocery and restaurant chains. She added butter pecan and maple crème syrups to her inventory. Finally, in 1993, Hoskins got her big break. She landed a $3 million contract with Denny's, the national restaurant chain. How did she do that? She phoned them to promote her syrup every Monday morning for two years.

Today, Hoskins's business, Michele's Foods Inc., makes syrup in a large plant in Illinois and sells it in 30 states. To help others achieve the success she has, Hoskins started Recipes to Retail, a group that mentors women who want to start food service businesses.

Sources: Ting Yu and Barbara Sandler, "Topping o' the Morning: Ex-Welfare Mom Michele Hoskins Finds a Rich New Life in a Family Recipe," *People,* July 29, 2000, pp. 121–122; "The History of Michele's Foods," on the Michele's Foods Inc. Web site, <http://www.michelefoods.com>, accessed February 7, 2003; Charlotte Mulhern, "Through Thick and Thin: Cashing In on an Age-Old Family Recipe," *Entrepreneur,* June 1998.

Eating Disorders

"You can never be too rich or too thin." So said the Duchess of Windsor, but she was wrong. You *can* be too thin if you suffer from an eating disorder.

In anorexia nervosa, a person loses weight until she is 15 percent or more under her ideal weight. In spite of being thin, she thinks she is fat and continues to eat very little. Some people with anorexia nervosa are so worried about food intake that they won't even lick a postage stamp because the glue may have a fraction of a calorie. Between 5 and 10 percent of individuals with anorexia nervosa die of starvation or complications of severe weight loss.

Another eating disorder is bulimia. A person with bulimia secretly binges, eating huge amounts of high-calorie foods, and then purges, either by vomiting or by using laxatives. People with bulimia may or may not be underweight. Because they binge and purge in private, their condition is easy to hide.

Both anorexia nervosa and bulimia are disorders whose victims are almost all adolescent girls and young women. Some people with the disorders may have a genetic predisposition to the disorders. However, the incidence of these disorders is highest in weight-conscious cultures such as those of the United States and Europe. In these cultures, the ideal of female beauty is the ultra-thin high-fashion model. Images of thin, glamorous women are everywhere. Adolescent girls, especially those with low self-belief, feel enormous pressure to look like the ideal. As a result, many go on diets. Eventually, some lose control of their diets and develop anorexia nervosa or bulimia.

It's important to realize that people who have eating disorders cannot consciously control their eating habits. Instead, they need professional help. Both psychotherapy and drugs are used to treat the disorders.

Actress Tracey Gold described her long struggle with anorexia and her victory in her book, *Room to Grow*. Today, in addition to acting, she lectures about eating disorders on college campuses. *(Courtesy of Getty News/Sports.)*

The Information Highway

GETTING UP TO SPEED

The Internet is full of Web sites and discussion groups about food and nutrition. Three of the best sites on nutrition are:

■ Government advice on healthy eating can be found on the Food and Nutrition Information Center of the U.S. Department of Agriculture Web site. You can download several publications, including the *Dietary Guidelines for Americans,* which includes the Food Guide Pyramid. You can also click on links to other food and nutrition resources on the Web <http://www.nal.usda.gov>.

■ The American Dietetic Association provides lots of information on food and nutrition, plus links to other nutrition sites <http://www.eatright.org>.

■ The Tufts University Nutrition Navigator provides links to high-quality nutrition information on the Internet <http://navigator.tufts.edu>.

In addition, you can find resources by searching with these key words: *nutrition, Food Guide Pyramid, dietary guidelines, body mass index, eating disorders, anorexia nervosa, bulimia.* There are even Web sites and discussion groups devoted to particular foods. Try searching for your favorite.

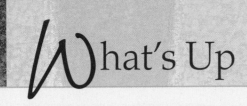

What's Up

Name _____ Date_____

Match the letter of the nutrient with the food that provides the *best* source of the nutrient.

1. Milk   a. Vitamin C

2. Oranges   b. Fat

3. Chicken   c. Carbohydrates

4. Bread   d. Protein

5. Vegetable oil   e. Vitamin D

Answer the following questions in the space provided.

6. Name the five basic food groups and give an example of a food from each.

_____

_____

_____

_____

_____

7. Sketch the Food Guide Pyramid and fill in the food groups in the appropriate locations.

8. What types of foods do nutritionists think Americans should eat more of?

_____

9. What types of foods do nutritionists think Americans should eat less of?

_____

10. What two lifestyle changes would enable most Americans to lose weight?

_____

_____

Case Studies

THE CASE OF THE MAN WHO DINED OUT

Since his work demands that he travel, Matt dines out regularly. When given a choice between a bagel and scrambled eggs for breakfast, Matt chooses the eggs. At lunchtime, he orders a sandwich with cheese and cold cuts instead of a salad. In the evening, he often chooses a steak and french fries instead of pasta with tomato sauce. Since he does not snack between meals, Matt can't understand why he is putting on weight.

1. What is wrong with Matt's diet?

_____
_____
_____

2. What can Matt do to lose the weight he has gained?

_____
_____
_____
_____

THE CASE OF THE DINNERLESS DIET

Louisa wanted to lose about five pounds, and she decided the best way to do it was to skip dinner every day. For breakfast she had a doughnut or muffin, and for lunch she ate a salad with dressing. At dinnertime she fed her family but did not eat. By 8 or 9 P.M., however, Louisa was so hungry that she had a snack of microwave popcorn or chips. Louisa maintained her level of physical activity—she went dancing one evening a week. After a month, she found she had lost only one pound. Even worse, she didn't feel very well.

1. What is wrong with Louisa's diet?

_____
_____
_____

2. How can Louisa lose five pounds and still feel well?

_____
_____
_____

Journal

Answer the following journal questions.

1. What does food mean to you and your family? What foods reflect your family's heritage?

_____

_____

_____

_____

_____

2. How would you change the Food Guide Pyramid to reflect your family's diet?

_____

_____

_____

_____

_____

3. Describe a food or beverage you love that's not very healthy. How can you enjoy this food and still have a healthy diet?

_____

_____

_____

_____

_____

4. What changes do you plan to make to your diet after reading this chapter?

_____

_____

_____

_____

_____

At 24, champion cyclist Lance Armstrong learned he had cancer that had spread to his lungs and brain. His physical well-being, which he had always taken for granted, was threatened. After treatment, Armstrong slowly returned to cycling. Eventually, he won the Tour de France, the world championship of bicycling, several times. Today the Lance Armstrong Foundation helps people manage and survive cancer. *(AP/Wide World Photos/Todd Warshaw.)*

Staying Healthy

Take a look in a mirror. Do you see a healthy person with bright clear eyes and skin, fit and attractive, with lots of energy? If you do, you are probably already working hard at reaching your physical potential. But if that person in the mirror looks less than glowing, don't worry! There are many things you can do to improve your health and feel better mentally as well as physically.

If you have ever felt sick, you know the value of good health. When you are not feeling healthy, all aspects of your life suffer. You become unable to live up to your emotional, intellectual, and social potential. All of you suffers—not just your body.

What does it take to feel healthy and energetic? You have already learned about the importance of eating a balanced diet in preventing disease and maintaining good health (see Chapter 5). In this chapter the focus shifts to other aspects of health. First, you will learn about physical benefits of different types of exercise. You will assess your current activity level and make an exercise plan to improve it. Second, you will learn about the importance of adequate and regular sleep to your physical and mental well-being. Third, you will discover that some drugs may produce pleasurable effects, but that abusing drugs—whether legal (like nicotine) or illegal (like cocaine)—has negative physical, emotional, and intellectual consequences. And fourth, you will learn about preventing and treating sexually transmitted diseases.

129

EXERCISE

Modern life, with cars, office work, computers, and TV, tends to make "couch potatoes" of us all. For most of us, physical activity is not a natural part of the daily routine. To be active, we must make a conscious decision to exercise or play sports.

Why take the time to exercise? First, exercise increases the number of calories we burn and helps us keep our weight under control. People who exercise regularly look better because they have more muscle than fat. They are stronger, more energetic, and more flexible. And perhaps most important, people who are fit feel better about themselves, both physically and mentally.

Becoming Fit

What is physical fitness? The President's Council on Physical Fitness and Sports suggests that **physical fitness** is the ability to carry out daily tasks without tiring and with enough energy left to enjoy leisure activities and to handle an emergency requiring physical exertion. Your own level of fitness is determined to a great extent by your daily routine—your work or schooling, your sports activities, and how much you walk in the course of the day. To improve your normal level of fitness, you must add exercise or sports to your regular routine.

There are several aspects to physical fitness. A woman who jogs regularly may have a heart and lungs in great condition, but she's not strong enough to carry a heavy suitcase more than five feet. That's because she lacks muscular strength and endurance in her upper body. A person who is truly physically fit has good:

- **cardiorespiratory endurance**—the ability to do moderately strenuous activity over a period of time without overtaxing the heart and lungs
- **muscular strength**—the ability to exert force in a single try
- **muscular endurance**—the ability to repeat movements or to hold a position for a long time without tiring
- **flexibility**—the ability to move a joint through its full range of motion
- **body composition**—the proportion of the body made of muscle compared with fat

Different types of physical activities improve different aspects of fitness. In general, aerobic activities such as running, basketball, step training, and tennis are best for cardiorespiratory endurance and body composition.

There are many benefits to exercise: maintaining a good weight, feeling fit, and looking good.
(Courtesy of Tom Stock.)

Your Turn 6–1

RATE YOUR LEVEL OF ACTIVITY

You can check your level of physical activity by rating how hard, how long, and how often you exercise. Circle your score for each question.

1. How hard do you exercise in a typical session?

	Score
no change in pulse	0
little change in heart rate (slow walking, bowling, yoga)	1
small increase in heart rate and breathing (table tennis, active golf)	2
moderate increase in heart rate and breathing (rapid walking, dancing, easy swimming)	3
occasional heavy breathing and sweating (tennis, basketball, squash)	4
sustained heavy breathing and sweating (jogging, aerobic dance)	5

2. How long do you exercise at one session?

	Score
less than 5 minutes	0
5 to 14 minutes	1
15 to 29 minutes	2
30 to 44 minutes	3
45 to 59 minutes	4
60 minutes or more	5

3. How often do you exercise?

	Score
less than once a week	0
once a week	1
2 times a week	2
3 times a week	3
4 times a week	4
5 or more times a week	5

4. Now take your scores from each question above and multiply them:

_____ × _____ × _____ = Activity level

Rate your activity level as follows:

Score	Activity Level
less than 15	inactive
15–24	somewhat active
25–40	moderately active
41–60	active
over 60	very active

If your score is 41 or higher, you are active enough to enjoy a wide variety of physical activities. If your score is less than 41, you should approach a change in your physical fitness program gradually and with caution. Anyone who is starting a new or increased fitness program should check with his or her doctor first.

Aerobic exercise strengthens the heart and lungs. An aerobics class is a good place to work out, but walking, running, swimming, and biking are also good aerobic exercises. *(Courtesy of PhotoDisc.)*

Activities such as calisthenics, weight training, karate, yoga, and stretching improve strength, endurance, and flexibility.

Aerobic Exercises Exercises that improve cardiorespiratory endurance are called **aerobic exercise**. Aerobic exercises work by gradually increasing the ability of the heart and lungs to supply the body's increased need for oxygen during the activity. When you first start doing aerobic exercise, you may find yourself out of breath and unable to continue. However, if you keep exercising, gradually your body will adapt and your heart will become stronger, increasing the oxygen supply without greater effort. Aerobic exercises, because they use large parts of the body, have the added advantage of turning fat to muscle, which improves body composition.

Any type of exercise that involves continuous movement is aerobic.

- Aerobic dance is 20 or more minutes of running, skipping, hopping, jumping, sliding, stretching, and bending set to music. Low-impact aerobics are designed for people who need to minimize jarring their joints. Aerobic dance can be done in exercise classes or at home using videos or DVDs.

- Step training involves stepping on and off a low bench while doing arm movements. It is a low-impact aerobic activity that offers the same benefits as jogging with fewer risks of injury.

- Walking at a brisk pace is an excellent aerobic activity. It has the advantage of requiring no special equipment or skill, and it can be done almost anywhere.

- Jogging is a very popular aerobic exercise requiring just a pair of good jogging sneakers. Joggers sometimes develop leg problems because jogging is a high-impact activity.

- Swimming is often considered the best aerobic activity because it exercises all the major muscle groups in an environment— water—that cushions impact.

- Bicycling has aerobic benefits when done at a brisk pace for long distances. In addition, it provides good exercise for the lower body.

- Cross-country skiing provides excellent aerobic benefits. It is ideal for those who live in areas with lots of snow for several months a year.

- Rowing a rowboat, paddling a canoe, or kayaking at a steady, brisk speed provides good aerobic benefits.

- Jumping rope for extended periods is an excellent aerobic activity, although it can be hard on the joints.

Strength, Endurance, and Flexibility Exercises   Although aerobic exercise improves cardiorespiratory endurance and body composition, it is not enough to promote all-around fitness. To improve muscle strength, endurance, and flexibility, you need to do other forms of exercise as well. Weight training and calisthenics are good for increasing muscle strength, endurance, and flexibility, and yoga and stretching are good for flexibility.

Weight training is an exercise program in which you use weights or resistance machines to improve strength, endurance, and flexibility. As your body becomes stronger, you gradually increase the number of pounds you are using and the number of repetitions. Weight training improves muscle tone, bone density, and appearance. Older women, who are at risk for osteoporosis, a weakening of the bones, can benefit from the increased bone strength that results from weight lifting. And contrary to popular belief, women can do weight training without developing "bulging" muscles. (The muscles of male weight trainers and weight lifters are the result primarily of a male hormone.) Weight training can be done with barbells, dumbbells, or household objects such as canned foods. Many fitness centers have exercise machines that can be used for weight training.

Calisthenics—exercises such as pushups and situps—are especially good for increasing muscular endurance. Because the exercises are repeated many times, the muscles become more able to hold a position for a length of time or to repeat the same motion many times. Calisthenics can be done at home or in an exercise class.

Weight training improves the strength of muscles. It also strengthens bones, an important benefit for women, who lose bone mass as they age. *(Courtesy of PhotoDisc.)*

For those seeking to promote flexibility, yoga is ideal. The movements of yoga are slow and emphasize joint flexibility and stretching, as well as mental relaxation. Yoga can be done at home once the movements are learned or in an exercise class under an instructor's guidance.

Sports and Recreational Activities

For those who can't bring themselves to exercise regularly—and for others as well—many sports and recreational activities provide fitness benefits. And sports and recreational activities have additional advantages. We play them because they are fun. Many activities involve interacting with people who share our interest. So the social advantages of sports and activities can be as great as the fitness advantages.

When you select a sport or activity, keep two things in mind. First, choose activities you will enjoy and to which you have easy access. And second, choose activities that will give you a range of fitness benefits. For example, bowling and golf may be fun, but they won't improve your physical fitness. On the other hand, continuous-action sports like racquetball and handball provide excellent aerobic benefits.

Sticking to an Exercise Program

Many people start an exercise program with the best intentions, and within several months they quit. To avoid this fate and to make physical activity part of your routine, follow these guidelines:

1. Choose a friend or relative, and make an agreement with them to exercise. Be sure to write it down.
2. Be specific. Write down the days you will exercise, what you will do, and the number of months you will do it.
3. Include rewards and punishments. Specify what you'll do to earn a reward and what will result in punishment—doing an unpleasant chore, for example.
4. Get the person with whom you made the agreement to support you. This will make it harder to skip sessions or quit.

For people who think exercise is boring or too much work, playing recreational sports is a way to stay fit. *(Courtesy of PhotoDisc.)*

He who has health, has hope; and he who has hope, has everything.

arabian proverb

MAKE AN EXERCISE AGREEMENT

Use the four exercise program guidelines to draw up an exercise agreement with a friend or relative.

REST

> **The sleep of a laboring man is sweet.**
>
> *ecclesiastes,*
>
> *a book of the bible*

Eating well and exercising are two components of maintaining good health. A third essential component is adequate rest. More than a hundred years ago, Thomas Edison invented the lightbulb and radically changed people's sleeping habits. Whereas people used to sleep at night because doing anything else was impractical, now it's possible to ignore the body's natural rhythms and stay awake. The result? We sometimes get less rest than we need.

Scientists have found that our bodies operate according to **circadian rhythms**, an inner time clock that roughly matches the 24-hour cycle of night and day. Left to their own devices, most people go to sleep when their body temperature is falling and sleep seven to eight hours. If you go to bed when your body temperature is at its peak, you tend to sleep much longer—as much as 15 hours. So the time of day you go to sleep, not how long you've been awake, generally determines how long you sleep.

As a consequence, people with irregular schedules often suffer from sleep problems. Airline pilots, for example, who work long shifts and cross time zones, often suffer fatigue. People whose sleep is irregular tend to be fatigued, less efficient, and irritable.

To feel good and perform at your peak, regular sleep habits are essential. If you are a poor sleeper, consider these suggestions to improve your sleep habits:

- Follow a regular schedule for sleeping and waking up, even on weekends.

Sleeping at different times of the day can make people tired and irritable. Shift workers with irregular schedules often have sleep problems. *(Courtesy of Tom Stock.)*

- Exercise regularly.

- Don't eat or drink anything with caffeine after midday. Caffeine, a stimulant found in coffee, tea, chocolate, and cola drinks, can keep you awake.

- Before bedtime, do whatever relaxes you. Read, watch TV, listen to music, or take a hot bath.

News & Views

AEROBIC EXERCISE AND MOOD

Aerobic exercise certainly strengthens the heart and lungs, but can it improve your mood? The answer seems to be yes.

Many studies indicate that aerobic exercise can reduce feelings of stress, anxiety, and depression. In fact, a single session of aerobic exercise can decrease anxiety for more than two hours. Regular aerobic exercise over the long term decreases depression. People who exercise regularly cope better with stressful events, have better self-belief, and are depressed less often than other people.

How long do you need to exercise before your mood improves? Not long at all. A study of 14 college women showed that only 10 minutes of pedaling an exercise bike was enough to improve their mood. This held true for the women who were fit as well as for those who were not.

Why does aerobic exercise improve your mood? Some of the physical benefits of aerobic exercise, like a stronger heart and lower blood pressure, also have mental health benefits. For example, when you feel stress, your blood pressure rises, but if you are aerobically fit, it rises less. Thus you feel less stressed.

Aerobic exercise also boosts the levels of certain neurotransmitters in the brain. These chemicals are responsible for the "runner's high," the feeling of euphoria that some runners experience after 30 minutes of exercise. In lesser amounts, these neurotransmitters simply improve mood.

Some people think that aerobic exercise improves mood by giving you a "time-out" from the stresses of the day. By distracting you from your troubles, exercise helps you cope with renewed energy.

Think about your own response to exercise. During periods when you exercise regularly, do you feel less anxious and depressed? How do you feel when you stop exercising for a few weeks or months? If you haven't noticed any changes in your mood, perhaps you haven't been paying close attention. If you keep track of exercise and stress, you'll probably find a relationship between the two.

Sources: C. J. Hansen, L. C. Stevens, and R. J. Coast, "Exercise Duration and Mood State: How Much Is Enough to Feel Better?" *Health Psychology,* Vol. 20, 2001, pp. 267–275; Prevention index survey by *Prevention* magazine, summarized by the Associated Press, March 6, 1995; D. L. Roth and D. S. Holmes, "Influence of aerobic exercise training and relaxation training on physical and psychological health following stressful life events," *Psychosomatic Medicine,* Vol. 49, 1987, pp. 355–365.

> **_I never take a nap after dinner but when I have had a bad night, and then the nap takes me._**
>
> samuel johnson,
>
> 18th-century english author

- Avoid alcoholic beverages before bed. They may help you fall asleep, but they interfere with your staying asleep.

- Don't worry about not sleeping. If you can't sleep, get up and do something boring until you feel sleepy.

DRUG ABUSE

In this unit, we've discussed things that help maintain your health: good food, exercise, and rest, all of which contribute to your physical and mental well-being. Unfortunately, many Americans also use **drugs**, which are chemical substances that create a physical, mental, emotional, or behavioral change in the user. Some drugs, of course, are used properly as prescription medicines under the care of a doctor. But others, such as alcohol, nicotine, and cocaine, are misused. **Drug abuse** is the nonmedicinal use of a drug, which results in physical, emotional, or mental harm to the user.

Your Turn 6–3

WHAT KIND OF SLEEPER ARE YOU?

People have different sleep patterns. Answer the following questions to establish your sleep profile.

1. How long do you normally sleep each night? _____

If you regularly sleep less than six hours a night, you are a short sleeper. If you regularly sleep more than nine hours a night, you're a long sleeper. People who sleep between six and nine hours a night are average sleepers.

2. Some people need different amounts of sleep for weeks at a time during different periods of their lives. Moving, ending a love affair, other stressful events, illness, or pregnancy may cause them to sleep more. Do you need more sleep at different periods in your life? _____

If you answered yes, you are variable sleeper.

3. Do you sleep through disturbances such as loud music, thunderstorms, babies crying, car alarms, and slammed doors? _____

If you said yes, you are a sound sleeper. If you said no, you are a light sleeper.

Why do people take drugs? People try drugs for the pleasure they bring, to feel better, to escape from problems, to experience something new, or to be sociable. The reasons people try a drug are usually very different from the reasons they continue to use it. Most drug abusers suffer from poor self-belief and lack of confidence. They use drugs to bolster their feelings about themselves. Unfortunately, drug abusers become dependent on the drugs they take. The dependence may be physical: The body needs the drug to function. Or it may be psychological: The user believes he or she needs the drug to function or even to survive. Often the dependence is both physical and psychological, and breaking the habit is extremely difficult.

Unfortunately, the harm done by drug abusers is not limited to themselves. Because of their inability to function properly, drug abusers often damage their relationships with family, friends, coworkers, and employers. Drug abuse does social and economic harm, as well as physical and psychological harm.

You may think of drug abusers as those who use illegal drugs. But many drug abusers misuse legal substances such as nicotine (in cigarettes), alcohol, and prescription drugs.

Nicotine

Cigarettes, cigars, and other forms of tobacco contain **nicotine**, a stimulant. A **stimulant** is a drug that increases brain activity and other body functions. Stimulants (like nicotine and caffeine) make the user feel more awake. Nicotine stimulates the heart and nervous system, raising blood pressure and making the heart beat faster. People who smoke become addicted to nicotine. Studies have shown that, on average, teenage girls become addicted in about three weeks; teenage boys in less than six months. Adults who have not previously smoked become addicted in about two years.[1] When smokers try to give it up, they experience irritability, headache, anxiety, depression, and nicotine cravings.

People who smoke for years may experience even worse effects. The life expectancy of smokers is shorter than that of nonsmokers. On average, women who smoke live 14.5 fewer years than women who don't smoke. Men who smoke live 13 fewer years than men who don't smoke. Smoking is the major cause of death from cancer of the lungs, throat, and mouth. It contributes to heart disease and respiratory problems. And breathing the smoke of others can affect the health of nonsmokers. According to the Centers for Disease Control and Prevention, about 440,000 Americans die from smoking-related causes each year.[2]

Most drugs that are abused fall into one of the groups shown on this poster. *(Courtesy of R. L. Allen Industries.)*

The health risks associated with smoking have caused a gradual change in the public's attitude toward smoking. Smoking was once widely accepted socially and considered to be a mark of adulthood. In fact, about 42 percent of Americans smoked in 1965. Today, smoking is banned in many government buildings, business offices, schools, and airplanes. Restaurants often ban smoking altogether or have smoking sections to accommodate smokers. As a result, smoking is on the decline, except among teenagers, although about 22 percent of Americans still smoke.[3]

Most people who quit smoking do it on their own. Others try counseling, behavior modification programs like Smoke Enders, nicotine patches, or hypnosis. The success rate of such programs is low. Health professionals emphasize that not starting to smoke is far easier than stopping.

Alcohol

One of the most abused drugs in the United States is alcohol. Almost 8 percent of American adults characterize themselves as heavy drinkers. More than 30 percent admit to binge drinking—having five or more drinks in a row, four or more for women—at least once in the previous year.[4] Among college students, binge drinking is even more widespread—44 percent of college students overall.[5]

Alcohol is a depressant, a drug that decreases brain activity and lowers blood pressure. The effects of alcohol vary. Some people become outgoing, silly, or aggressive. Others become quiet. But large amounts of alcohol dull sensation and harm judgment, memory, and coordination, eventually causing unconsciousness and sometimes death.

Alcohol becomes a problem when it interferes with a person's functioning in school, on the job, or in relationships. Problem drinkers become physically and psychologically addicted to alcohol. When alcohol is taken in large quantities or mixed with other drugs, it can be deadly. In addition, heavy alcohol use is associated with other problems: death and injury from drunk driving, sexual assaults, unplanned and unsafe sex, academic failure, and vandalism.

The Dragon Slayers

(Courtesy of Aniak High School, Aniak, Alaska.)

If you break a bone near Aniak, Alaska, don't be surprised if the EMTs who come to your rescue are teenaged girls. In Aniak, a village 320 miles west of Anchorage, teenagers serve as the community's emergency medical team, the Dragon Slayers.

The Dragon Slayers were formed in 1993 by Pete Brown, the volunteer fire chief of Aniak. Brown didn't have any adults available to respond to daytime emergency calls, so he got his daughter Mariah and several other teens to help. The first group of Dragon Slayers were mostly children of firefighters, and most were boys. But as time went on, the boys preferred hunting and snowboarding to attending the Tuesday night training meetings. The group eventually became an all-girl team.

To join the Dragon Slayers, local teens must be passing their high school courses. They also must complete emergency trauma training, the American Red Cross advanced first aid course, and the American Heart Association's CPR training.

The teenagers wear beepers, and even their teachers at school have learned to let them go gracefully when the beeper goes off. Some calls are close by; in 2000, they saved the life of the school principal, a diabetic. But many calls are distant, since the Aniak volunteers serve a rural area the size of Maryland. Traveling by snowmobile, four-wheel drive vehicles, and boat, the teens respond to 450 calls a year. They have set bones, resuscitated heart attack victims, rescued injured snowmobilers, and delivered babies.

With their experience, it's no surprise that many of the first Dragon Slayers are training for related careers. Mariah Brown joined the Navy to become a rescue swimmer. Another is taking medical courses on line and hopes to become a doctor. A third is a flight paramedic. And one Dragon Slayer has stayed in Aniak and become an adult volunteer firefighter. As the Dragon Slayers grow up and move on, another group is behind them—the Lizard Killers, preteens in EMT training.

Sources: Dina Blair, "Snow Angels," WGN TV, November 10, 2002 <http://wgntv.trb.com/templates/misc/printstory.jsp?slug=wgntv%2D111002medicalwatch>, accessed February 14, 2003; Christina Cheakalos and Lyndon Stambler, "Snow Angels," *People,* June 3, 2002; Danielle Wolffe, "Young Women Meet Emergency Services Need in Aniak," *Kenai Peninsula Online,* September 30, 2001, <http://peninsulaclarion.com/stories/093001/ala_093001ala0140001.shtml>, accessed January 16, 2003.

Alcohol is a leading cause of traffic accidents and deaths. A police officer is giving a driver a Breathalyzer test to see whether he has more than the legal limit of alcohol in his blood. *(Courtesy of PhotoDisc.)*

Considering all these dangers, why do people drink? In part, the answer is that the use of alcohol is deeply ingrained in our society. Alcohol has been part of many cultures and religions for years. It is served at social occasions, and many people can enjoy it in moderation. Since alcohol is everywhere, each of us needs to monitor our own consumption. Some people should not drink at all, and everyone should be moderate.

Alcohol abusers who have tried to stop drinking have found the most success with support groups like Alcoholics Anonymous. AA, as it is known, gets drinkers to focus on their problems, abstain totally from alcohol, and draw on the support of other recovering alcoholics, using a 12-step program.

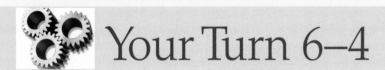 Your Turn 6–4

ARE YOU A PROBLEM DRINKER?

You can take this self-test to see if you have a problem with alcohol.

1. Do you drink when you feel depressed or anxious? _____

2. Must you drink at certain times, for example, before a meal? _____

3. When sober, are you sorry about what you've done or said while drinking? _____

4. Do you often drink alone? _____

5. Do your drinking sessions last for several days at a time? _____

6. Do you sometimes feel shaky and drink to stop the feeling? _____

If you answered *yes* to any of these questions, you should try to overcome your dependence on alcohol. A *yes* answer to two or more questions indicates a need for counseling or other help in overcoming alcohol addiction.

Other Drugs

Misusing any drug, including prescription and over-the-counter drugs, can cause problems. For example, a side effect of antihistamines is sleepiness; driving a car or operating machinery while taking antihistamines is dangerous. Prescription medicines and over-the-counter preparations should be taken as directed.

When you take illegal drugs, your exposure to risk increases. First, you don't know what you're actually buying when you buy drugs on the street. Second, you are subject to arrest for possession of illegal substances. And third, the long-term effects of some drugs are still unknown. Some of the more common abused drugs are briefly discussed here.

Marijuana   Marijuana slows thinking and reaction time, distorts perceptions, and upsets balance and coordination. Its use creates mild feelings of pleasure. In some states, it is legal for doctors to prescribe marijuana to relieve symptoms such as the nausea of chemotherapy. However, the medicinal use of marijuana is highly controversial.

Marijuana has many negative effects. Like alcohol, it harms the coordination and reaction time needed to drive a car or operate machinery. Because it is usually smoked, it harms the lungs. Marijuana interferes with the process of forming memories, an effect that continues beyond the period of smoking. Therefore, using marijuana interferes with a person's ability to learn.

Amphetamines   Amphetamines, known popularly as "uppers" or "speed," are stimulants. They help people stay awake and gather energy for tasks.

Abuse of amphetamines can cause weight loss, malnutrition, pain, and unconsciousness. Heavy users are prone to violence and aggression.

Barbiturates and Benzodiazepines   Barbiturates (barbs, reds, and yellows) and benzodiazepines (tranquilizers, tranks, downers, sleeping pills, Valium) are depressants. They slow the activity of the nervous and cardiovascular systems, making people calm down and feel relaxed and sleepy. These drugs are often abused by amphetamine users, who take them to counteract the effects of speed. When barbiturates and tranquilizers are taken with alcohol, they can cause death.

Different types of barbiturates and benzodiazepines create different levels of physical and psychological dependence. Users who stop taking them experience tremors, nausea, cramps, and vomiting.

Club Drugs   The phrase **club drugs** refers to a wide variety of drugs used by young adults at parties, dance clubs, raves, and bars. The most common club drugs are MDMA (ecstasy, X); GHB (G, Georgia home boy); Rohypnol (forget-me pill, roofies); ketamine (K, special K, vitamin K); and methamphetamine (chalk, ice, meth). These drugs have a variety of effects, which are summarized in Table 6–1. The club drugs are even more harmful when taken in combination with alcohol.

Some club drugs are colorless, odorless, and tasteless. They can easily be slipped into a drink in order to intoxicate or sedate other people. In recent years there have been reports of club drugs being used to commit sexual assaults. Women should get their own drinks at parties and keep an eye on them so they can't be tampered with.

Cocaine   **Cocaine**, a stimulant, acts on the brain to produce a brief rush of happiness and excitement. As the dose wears off, feelings of panic, depression, and anxiety set in. Cocaine can be sniffed, injected, or smoked. **Crack**, a powerful form of cocaine, is smoked, so it enters the bloodstream quickly and in higher concentrations. Since it is difficult to estimate a dose of crack, users sometimes overdose, suffering convulsions, cardiac arrest, coma, and death.

Users of cocaine become extremely dependent on it. Some experts call it the most addictive drug of all. The long-term use of cocaine often leads to emotional disturbances, paranoia, fear, nervousness, insomnia, and weight loss. Many people become unable to function normally at work or with their families. Their lives are focused on getting and using the drug.

The use of crack and other forms of cocaine peaked in the 1980s and began to decrease in the 1990s. Use declined partly because of increased awareness of cocaine's dangers. However, much of the decrease comes from the poverty, jailing, and deaths of so many crack cocaine users. Still, a 1998 survey showed that 1.7 million Americans were users of cocaine.

Steroids   **Anabolic steroid** is a synthetic form of the male hormone, testosterone. Because the drug increases the body's ability to turn protein into muscle, steroids are popular among athletes and others who wish to improve their athletic performance and appearance. Recently, steroids were in the news when baseball players were revealed as using them.

Experts say that steroid users face side effects and risks that are not fully understood. Women risk changes in their sexual characteristics, including shrinking of the breasts, growth of body hair, baldness, and a deepened voice. Some men suffer high blood pressure, lowered sperm counts, and acute acne. In addition, steroids seem to be as addictive as alcohol or nicotine.

Table 6-1   The Most Common Club Drugs

Drug	Form	Short-Term Effects	Potential Health Effects
MDMA *Ecstasy, XTC, Adam, clarity, lover's speed*	Tablet or capsule	• Stimulant: increased heart rate, blood pressure; feelings of alertness and energy; mild hallucinogenic effects • In high doses, can lead to high body temperature, dehydration, and death	Depression, sleep problems, anxiety, impaired memory and learning
GHB *Grievous bodily harm, G, liquid ecstasy, Georgia home boy*	• Clear liquid, white powder, tablet, or capsule • Often made in home laboratories	• Depressant: reduced heart rate, blood pressure; reduced pain and anxiety; feeling of relaxation and well-being; reduced inhibitions • In high doses, can lead to drowsiness, loss of consciousness, coma, and death • Has been used in sexual assaults.	Unknown
Ketamine *Special K, K, vitamin K, cat Valiums*	• Liquid for injection, powder for snorting or smoking • Used legally as an anesthetic, usually for animals	• Increased heart rate and blood pressure; poor coordination • In high doses, can cause delirium, amnesia, depression, respiratory problems, and death	Memory loss; numbness; nausea and vomiting
Rohypnol *Roofies, rophies, roche, forget-me pill*	• Pill • Used legally in Europe as a sleeping pill	• Depressant: reduced heart rate, blood pressure; reduced pain and anxiety; feeling of relaxation and well-being; reduced inhibitions • Visual and digestive disturbances; urine retention • Has been used in sexual assaults	Loss of memory for period while under the effects of the drug
Methamphetamine *Speed, ice, chalk, meth, crystal, crank, fire, glass*	Many forms; can be smoked, snorted, injected, or taken orally	• Stimulant: increased heart rate, blood pressure; feelings of alertness and energy • Agitation, excited speech, decreased appetite, aggression, violence, and psychotic behavior	Memory loss, heart damage, nervous system damage

Heroin   Heroin is a depressant that makes its user feel happy, safe, and peaceful. It is physically addictive, and users need greater amounts of it as they become tolerant of its effects. An overdose of heroin is deadly. In addition, since addicts inject the drug, they are at risk of contracting diseases such as hepatitis and HIV from shared needles.

When users stop taking heroin, they experience agonizing symptoms including nausea, shaking, chills, vomiting, and pain. Stopping the psychological dependence on heroin is even more difficult, because addicts have poor self-belief and rely on the drug to escape from reality.

Treating Drug Abuse

Although weaning drug abusers from their physical dependence on drugs can be difficult, it is easier than overcoming their psychological dependence. Typical drug abusers have negative self-belief, low self-confidence, and a feeling of helplessness. Drugs are a way to escape this bleak outlook on life. *Unless the underlying attitudes of the abuser change, he or she is likely to return to the use of the drug.* Recovering from drug addiction is a long-term process with three stages (see Figure 6–1):

> **Stage 1: Wanting to stop.** Motivation is the key during stage 1. People wanting to stop drug use must learn to trust, love, and respect themselves.

FIGURE 6–1

Recovering from drug abuse is a three-stage process: (1) wanting to stop, (2) stopping, and (3) staying stopped. The third stage is often the most difficult.

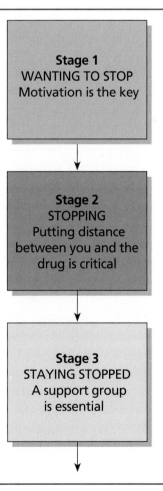

Stage 2: Stopping. During this stage it is critical for users to distance themselves from the drug. That may mean distancing themselves from the people and circumstances associated with drug use.

Stage 3: Staying stopped. During the recovery period, a support group is essential. Support groups meet all over the country to help recovered drug users stay off drugs.

If you or someone you know needs treatment for drug abuse, you can call the U.S. Center for Substance Abuse Treatment for referrals to local programs. Their hotline number is 1-800-662-HELP.

SEXUALLY TRANSMITTED DISEASES

Protecting yourself against sexually transmitted diseases (STDs) is a commonsense way to maintain your good health. These diseases are widespread; they are not limited to specific portions of the population. The most common STDs are gonorrhea, chlamydia, and genital herpes.

Gonorrhea is an infection of the genital mucous membranes. In men, symptoms are painful urination with a discharge of pus. In women, the symptoms are often mild or undetectable. Untreated gonorrhea can lead to sterility in both sexes. Fortunately, gonorrhea can be cured with antibiotics.

Chlamydia is an infection of the genital and urinary tracts. It is the most common of the STDs, and its symptoms are similar to those of gonorrhea, although milder. Three-quarters of infected women and half of infected men have no symptoms. Chlamydia can be treated with antibiotics. If it is left untreated, it can cause severe pelvic inflammatory disease in women and sterility in both women and men.

Genital herpes is caused by a virus similar to the one that causes cold sores and fever blisters. The first symptoms are a tingling in the genital area and small, sometimes itchy, blisters. Genital herpes flares up and dies down periodically, and stress seems to aggravate the condition. Although it cannot be cured, there are drugs that can control the symptoms and reduce the number of relapses.

Syphilis is a highly infectious STD caused by a bacterium. The first symptom is a small hard sore in the genital area, mouth, or anus. By the time this symptom has appeared, the syphilis infection has already spread to the blood. If left untreated, early-stage syphilis causes fever, sore throat, headache, and sores. The disease then seems to disappear, sometimes for years. In the final stage, blindness, paralysis, insanity, and death can result. Syphilis can be treated with antibiotics, but any damage that has already occurred cannot be reversed.

HIV-AIDS (acquired immune deficiency syndrome) is a group of diseases or conditions resulting from the gradual destruction of a person's immune system. A person infected with the human immunodeficiency virus (HIV) gradually loses T-cells and so becomes unable to fight off infection and disease. The time between infection with HIV and the onset of AIDS can vary considerably, from one or two years to over a decade. Drugs now enable people with HIV to keep their T-cell counts high for years. Although AIDS is usually transmitted sexually, it can also be transmitted through contact with blood (by sharing needles among drug abusers or by accident) or passed from an infected mother to her baby.

If you think you have a sexually transmitted disease, see a doctor or go to a clinic immediately. Pregnant women with a history of sexually transmitted disease should inform their doctor, since some diseases are passed from mother to child. The best strategy for dealing with sexually transmitted disease is prevention. The spread of these diseases can be prevented through celibacy or by practicing "safe sex" using latex condoms. Note that condoms do not provide complete protection from all STDs.

The Information Highway

GETTING UP TO SPEED

There are many Web sites and discussion groups about health issues:

- The President's Council on Physical Fitness and Sports provides information and advice about exercise, weight control, and fitness for disabled and older people (www.fitness.gov).
- The Substance Abuse and Mental Health Services Administration, a part of the U.S. Department of Health and Human Services, provides information on the treatment and prevention of various types of substance abuse <http://www.samhsa.gov>.
- Another government agency, the National Institute on Drug Abuse, provides information about drugs and statistics on drug abuse <http://www.nida.nih.gov>.
- The Centers for Disease Control and Prevention provide extensive government data on disease. Particularly useful is the feature "Health Topics A–Z," which gives information about diseases, including sexually transmitted diseases and HIV-AIDS <http://www.cdc.gov>.
- The HealthScout Network is a commercial consumer health site with personalized health management tools. These include health alerts, newsletters, mini-checkups, and family health pages <http://www.healthscout.com>.

In addition, you can use a search engine to find information about specific types of exercise and sports; sleep; alcohol, tobacco, and other specific drugs; sexually transmitted diseases, and other health issues.

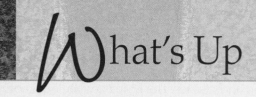

What's Up

Name _____ Date _____

1. List and briefly describe five aspect of physical fitness.

_____
_____
_____
_____
_____

2. What are the benefits of aerobic exercise?

_____
_____
_____

3. What are the benefits of weight training, calisthenics, and stretching?

_____
_____
_____

4. What are the results of irregular sleep habits?

_____
_____
_____

5. What is drug abuse?

_____
_____
_____

6. What is the difference between a stimulant and a depressant? Give an example of each.

_____
_____
_____
_____
_____

Name _____   Date_____

7. Describe some of the long-term effects of nicotine.

_____

_____

_____

_____

_____

8. What are the effects of drinking alcohol?

_____

_____

_____

_____

_____

9. Describe the three stages in the process of recovering from drug abuse.

_____

_____

_____

_____

_____

_____

10. How can sexually transmitted diseases be prevented?

_____

_____

_____

_____

_____

Case Studies

THE CASE OF THE BREATHLESS WEIGHT TRAINER

Gabe worked out with weights and was proud of the way he looked. He felt strong and able to take on anything. One weekend his friend Sue asked him to help her move. Sue's new apartment was in a building with no elevator, and Gabe had to carry Sue's furniture and other things up three flights of stairs. He was up and down the stairs all morning, and to his surprise, he was out of breath and needed frequent rests. Lifting the furniture was no problem, but the stairs were wearing him out.

1. How would you rate Gabe on the five aspects of physical fitness?

_____

_____

_____

_____

_____

2. Suggest an exercise program that would help Gabe develop all-around physical fitness.

_____

_____

_____

_____

THE CASE OF THE "SOCIAL" DRINKER

Each weekend, Tessa goes out with friends and has four or five drinks. Although she binge drinks, she never feels sick or hungover. After a while, Tessa starts to have a drink each evening before dinner, just enough to make her feel relaxed. One day when she ran out of wine and beer, she became anxious—so anxious she immediately went out to buy more. Tessa thinks of herself as a "social" drinker—someone who drinks a little with friends to relax.

1. Do you agree with Tessa that she is a social drinker? Why or why not?

_____

_____

_____

_____

2. Does Tessa have a problem with alcohol? Explain your answer.

_____

_____

_____

_____

_____

Journal

Answer the following journal questions.

1. What sport or type of exercise do you enjoy the most? What fitness benefits do you gain as a result of this activity?

_____
_____
_____
_____
_____

2. How can you improve your sleep habits to get more rest?

_____
_____
_____
_____

3. Describe someone you know who abuses drugs. What problems does this person—and the people around him or her—have as a result? What approach might help this person get off drugs?

_____
_____
_____
_____

4. Describe your ideal of perfect fitness and health.

_____
_____
_____
_____

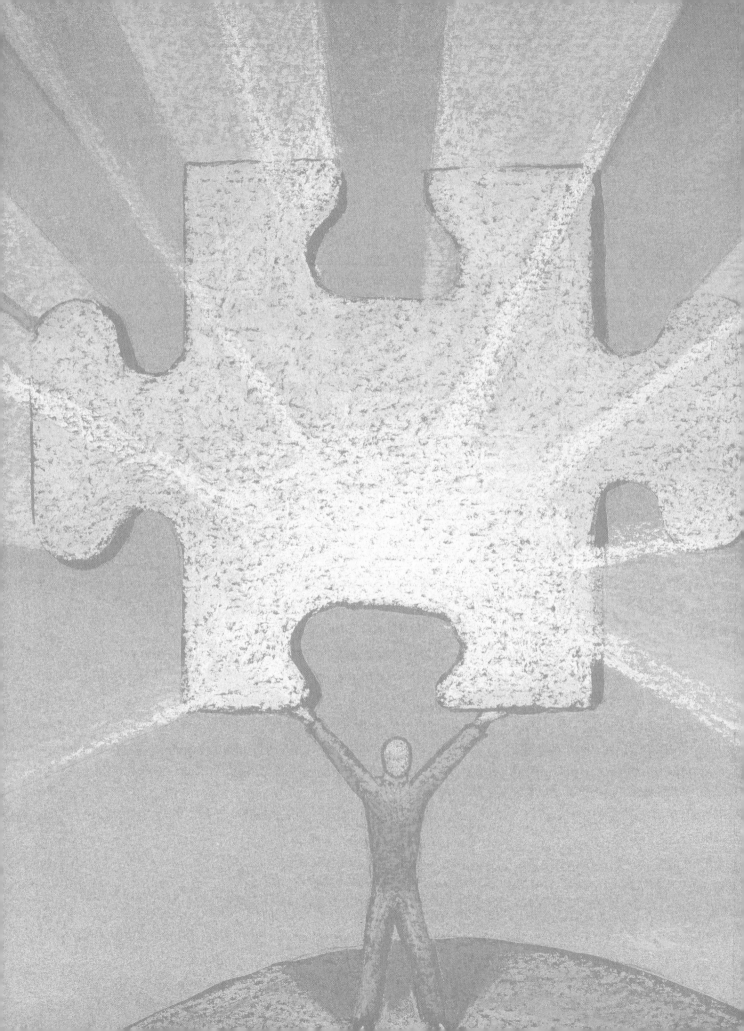

Developing Your Social Potential

So far you have explored your emotional, intellectual, and physical potential—all aspects of the inner you. In this unit you will turn your attention outward to improve your relationships with others. You will learn how to be a more effective communicator and how to get along with other people, both one on one and in groups.

Trained as an actor, President Ronald Reagan used clear, simple language and spoke in a relaxed and direct manner. He communicated so effectively with the American people that he earned the nickname "the Great Communicator." *(AP/Wide World Photos/Ron Edmonds.)*

Chapter 7

Communicating Effectively

At six months, a baby cries, laughs, smiles, makes faces, and waves its arms and legs to communicate. Although strangers may not know what the baby is trying to say, the parents probably do. By 18 months, babies speak a few words and can change their tone of voice to reflect their moods. Still, people who don't know the baby well can't understand much of what the baby's trying to communicate. Frustration often results because the baby can't get the people close by to respond properly. As babies grow into children, they acquire more communication skills. They speak, listen, write, and read, and the quality of their communication improves. As children mature and become adults, they become even more effective communicators, and their ability to get along with others, as well as their own sense of well-being, improves.

Although most of us take communication for granted, its importance cannot be overestimated. Good communication is the basis of our social potential. Without it, each of us would live dreary lives in isolation. It's no accident that solitary confinement is one of the harshest punishments. We need other people, and our connections to others are forged by communication.

> *The level of success that you experience in life, the happiness, joy, love, external rewards, and impact that you create is the direct result of how you communicate to yourself and to others. The quality of your life is the quality of your communication.*
>
> anthony robbins,
>
> motivational writer

In one-way communication, the speaker speaks and the receiver doesn't get a chance to respond. *(Courtesy of PhotoDisc.)*

Yet because we learned how to communicate gradually, as we grew up, most of us have never really thought about this valuable skill. For example, have you ever thought about the difference between communicating in your private life and communicating on the job? When you communicate at home, the communications belong to you. However, when you communicate on the job, your communications belong only partly to you. Your communications also belong to your employer. On the job, the written and oral messages you create represent not only you but also your employer. Thus you can see that although communication is an everyday matter, the quality of your communication is extremely important for your success in all areas of life. In fact, good communication skills are so important for reaching your potential that there are three chapters on communication in this book.

In this chapter you will learn the basics of communication, starting with what communication is—both verbal and nonverbal. You will learn about the problems we face when we communicate and the different communication styles that people have. Last, you will learn how to communicate effectively by improving your rapport with other people.

WHAT IS COMMUNICATION?

Communication is the exchange of messages. Messages can be verbal, using spoken or written words, or they can be nonverbal, using symbols, gestures, expressions, and body language. For communication to take place, there must be a sender, a person who transmits the message. There must also be a receiver, a person who receives the message. Effective communication occurs when the sender and the receiver have the same understanding of the message (see Figure 7–1).

One-Way and Two-Way Communication

There are two basic patterns for the communication process. The first is one-way communication, and the second is two-way communication.

In one-way communication, the sender transmits a message, the receiver gets it, and the process is complete. When a mail order house sends you a catalog, and you look at it and throw it away, one-way communication has taken place. Another example of one-way communication occurs when your instructor tells you the next assignment and you write it down and leave the classroom.

In two-way communication, the sender transmits a message, the receiver gets it, and the receiver responds with another message.

FIGURE 7–1

The communication process: The sender transmits a message, the receiver gets the message, and the receiver sends another message—the feedback—to the sender, and the process starts again.

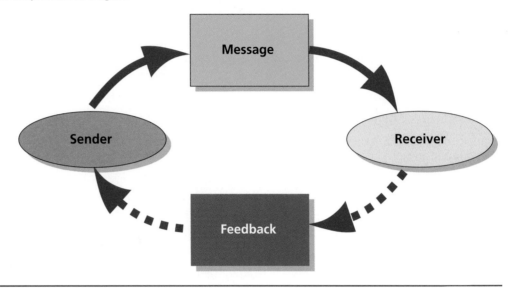

Sender and receiver alternate roles, giving one another feedback. Conversations and correspondence are examples of two-way communication.

One-way communication has the advantage of being fast. It also maintains the speaker's authority, since no feedback—either negative or positive—is expected of the listener. For example, in the armed forces, one-way communication is used to transmit orders and maintain the authority of rank. But one-way communication is far less effective than two-way communication. In one-way communication, the speaker has no way of determining whether the receiver has received the correct message, because there is no feedback. In contrast, two-way communication provides an opportunity for both parties to correct mistakes and misunderstandings.

Both one-way and two-way communication can take place in many types of situations and between different types of senders and receivers. Both patterns can take place between two people, between one person and a small group, between one person and a large group, and even between groups. Table 7–1 shows examples of one-way and two-way communication between different types of senders and receivers.

In two-way communication, both the sender and the receiver get and give feedback. *(Courtesy of PhotoDisc.)*

TABLE 7–1   Examples of One-Way and Two-Way Communications

Sender and Receiver	Example of One-Way Communication	Example of Two-Way Communication
Two individuals	An employer dictates a letter to her assistant.	Employer and assistant discuss a business problem.
An individual and a small group	A teacher sends a change-of-address e-mail message to all his e-mail correspondents.	A teacher leads a discussion in a small class.
An individual and a large group	The president of the United States delivers the State of the Union address to all U.S. citizens (and the world).	The president of the United States has a press conference with newspaper, magazine, and broadcast journalists.
A group and an individual	The Internal Revenue Service sends a tax refund check to a taxpayer.	The Internal Revenue Service notifies a taxpayer that she must respond to a question about unreported income.
Two groups	A student group puts posters advertising a rock concert all over campus.	A student group negotiates an agreement with a rock group to perform on campus.

> **The face [is] the index of a feeling mind.**
>
> *george crabbe,*
>
> *18th–19th century*
>
> *english poet*

Nonverbal Communication

Most people think of words as the chief means by which we communicate. Being clear, concise, and courteous in your choice of words is important. However, studies of face-to-face communication have shown that 80 to 90 percent of the impact of a message comes from nonverbal elements—facial expressions, eye contact, body language, and tone of voice. Nonverbal communication can be far more revealing of the content of a message than its words. The speaker usually has more control over choice of words than over facial expressions, eye contact, body language, and tone of voice. The expression, "It wasn't what he said, it was how he said it" reflects this truth. Words may say one thing while the body communicates another message.

Nonverbal communication varies from culture to culture, as the News & Views on page 159 describes. Because the United States is a multicultural society, it's important to be sensitive to cultural differences in communication. Sometimes it may be necessary to alter interactions with others based on the perception of cultural differences in nonverbal communication.

Facial Expressions   Smiling, frowning, and raising your eyebrows are just a few of the thousands of movements of which your face is capable. These movements communicate feelings. Researchers have found that many facial expressions are universal. A frown means the same thing in Detroit as it does in Bombay. The intensity and frequency of facial expressions vary from culture to culture.

Most people are good at judging a speaker's feelings from his or her expressions. Sadness, anger, hostility, excitement, and happiness are easily conveyed by expressions. But people are less accurate when it comes to judging character from facial expressions. For example,

News & Views

GESTURES: ONE CULTURE'S "GOOD LUCK" IS ANOTHER CULTURE'S INSULT

Some gestures do not need words to have meaning. Gestures such as a salute and a shake of the head have meaning without words. Each culture has its own gestures that people use to communicate. However, sometimes the same gesture has different meanings in different cultures. When that happens, people from different cultures can unintentionally confuse or offend one another.

In most parts of the world, for example, "victory" is conveyed by an upraised palm with the second and third fingers in a V-shape. If you make that gesture in Great Britain, however, you will be giving someone a sexual insult (similar in meaning to the middle-finger upward jerk of the United States).

The thumbs-up gesture means that all is well in much of Europe and North America. But in Greece and Turkey, the thumbs-up sign is a sexual insult. Another insult in Greece and Turkey is called the hand of Moutza. It is an open palm with the fingers extended, held facing the person being insulted. The origin of the palm of Moutza goes back 1,500 years. At that time ordinary citizens helped punish prisoners by pressing handfuls of dung into their faces. So be careful not to signal "five things" using your hand when in Greece or Turkey!

Another gesture that can cause misunderstanding is the sign of the University of Texas football team, the Longhorns. At a college football game, extending the second finger and the pinkie is a sign of encouragement and victory to the Longhorns. However, the same gesture in Italy and other parts of Europe means that a man's wife has been unfaithful—a terrible insult.

Similarly, crossing your fingers means luck in the United States. But in some Asian countries, crossing your fingers means you are making a sexual offer.

So be aware when you are communicating with people from another culture. The gestures whose meanings you take for granted may not mean what you think they mean to a person from another culture.

Sources: Peter Marsh, ed., *Eye to Eye: How People Interact,* Topsfield, Mass., Salem House, 1988, p. 54; Carole Wade and Carol Tavris, *Psychology,* 4th ed, New York, HarperCollins, 1996, p. 670.

many people think that a person who nods and smiles a lot is warm and agreeable, but studies have shown no such correlation.

Eye Contact   Smiles and frowns may have a common meaning throughout the world, but eye contact does not. In some cultures, looking downward while speaking to someone is a sign of respect. In mainstream U.S. culture, however, a person who doesn't meet your eyes during conversation is thought to be hiding something. Making eye contact with someone when speaking to them is considered desirable in the United States.

In mainstream American culture, eye contact is used to establish communication. For example, if you want salespeople to help you, you try to make eye contact with them. If you don't want your instructors to call on you in class, you avoid their eyes in the hope that they will not notice you.

Body Language   Try to speak for two minutes and hold your head, arms, and legs completely still. Impossible? Probably. Without being aware of it, people move their bodies constantly while they talk. They nod, shrug, gesture with their hands, and shift their weight. Body language can indicate a wide range of emotion from boredom (yawning) to impatience (tapping your fingers or feet) to enthusiasm (gesturing with your hands).

A smile communicates good feeling among people all over the world.
(Courtesy of PhotoDisc.)

In addition to communicating meaning by moving the body, people communicate by the distance they leave between themselves. In mainstream U.S. culture, people who are lovers, close family members, or intimate friends are comfortable standing about a foot apart. Acquaintances or colleagues, on the other hand, usually stand four to twelve feet apart when communicating. The tone of an interaction can be changed just by changing the distance between two people.

The meaning of body language and distance varies from one culture to another. In some cultures, gestures are expansive and expressive. In other cultures, body language is controlled to avoid showing too much emotion. Each culture has extensive unwritten rules about body language. For example, if a stranger walked up to you and stopped one foot away, you would feel threatened. That's because a person you don't know has entered space that's reserved for people you know intimately.

Voice Qualities A voice can be loud or soft, high or low pitched, fast or slow. Its tone can be pleasant, harsh, or monotonous. Voice qualities can convey whether you are interested, bored, tired, or happy.

It's sometimes risky to make generalizations about what voice qualities mean. For example, a New Yorker may speak faster than someone from Atlanta. When they speak to one another, the New Yorker may feel the Southerner is slow to understand and the Southerner may perceive the New Yorker as rude. Neither one of them would necessarily be right. On the other hand, people who know one another well are very good at picking up meaningful changes in voice quality. You probably have had the experience of knowing that something was bothering a friend because of the tone of voice you heard.

BARRIERS TO COMMUNICATION

Too much activity and noise can interfere with effective communication. *(Courtesy of Tom Stock.)*

Effective communication means that both sender and receiver have the same understanding of the message. The first prerequisite is that the message, both verbal and nonverbal, should be clear. But beyond the message itself are factors that influence both the sender and the receiver. Each person brings a distinct set of abilities, knowledge, experience, attitudes, and feelings to the communication process. Miscommunication may occur because of physical, mental, or emotional barriers on the part of the communicators.

When you communicate, you can take responsibility for your share of the process.

Your Turn 7–1

OBSERVING NONVERBAL COMMUNICATION

Here's an activity that will improve your awareness of nonverbal communication. Observe a conversation at a supermarket or mall. Pay particular attention to nonverbal communication. Write what you observed in the space provided.

1. What facial expressions did you notice?

_____

_____

2. Did the people maintain eye contact throughout the conversation? If not, when was eye contact broken?

_____

3. What body postures, head movements, and gestures did they use?

_____

_____

4. Describe the voices.

Volume _____

Pitch _____

Speed _____

Tone _____

You can try to overcome barriers to communication by making the message you send clear. If you receive a negative or unexpected response, examine yourself first to see if your message is the cause. You may have to overcome communication barriers by revising your message.

Physical Barriers

Any disturbing factor in the physical environment or your body can prevent full communication. If the room is noisy, you may not be able to hear or make yourself heard. If there is a lot of other activity, you may find yourself distracted. If you are sitting or standing in an awkward position, your discomfort may act as a barrier to communication. In some cases, hearing loss makes it difficult to understand what's being communicated.

Mental Barriers

Every person has a unique set of knowledge and experience that influences what he or she does. When you communicate, for example, you tend to interpret what's being said in light of your previous knowledge and experience. People make assumptions all the time, and frequently they are wrong. For example, when a father tells his young child to turn off a cartoon program, he assumes the child knows that's the end of that cartoon. The child, on the other hand, assumes that a TV program is the same as a videotape or DVD, which can be watched at any time. Later the child is upset when she realizes she will never see the remainder of the cartoon program.

Another type of mental barrier that prevents good communication is selective attention. People tend to focus on what interests them and pay little or no attention to the rest. Or we pay attention to positive matters and ignore unpleasant ones. During a performance evaluation, for example, an employee may remember each word of praise, while his boss's criticisms don't even register!

Another mental barrier to good communication is choice of words. In some cases, communication breaks down because one of the people simply doesn't understand the vocabulary of the other. When someone uses technical, specialized words to explain how a machine works, for example, a nontechnical person may not understand. Or communication may break down because one person "talks down" to another, and the second person becomes resentful. In other cases, the words being used are emotionally charged. Discussions about politics, for example, frequently go nowhere because people have long-standing emotional associations with words such as *conservative, liberal, left, right, Republican,* and *Democrat.*

Emotional Barriers

Feelings and emotions can also create barriers to communication. Stress, fear, happiness, anger, and love can all prevent effective communication. A person who is worried about something, for example, finds it hard to pay attention to a class lecture. Someone who just won the lottery may have trouble focusing on ordinary conversation.

People's long-held feelings and attitudes can also cause communication problems. Prejudice, which is a negative attitude toward people because of their membership in a group, is a communication barrier. It prevents people from communicating

> **Hating people because of their color is wrong, and it doesn't matter which color does the hating. It's just plain wrong.**
>
> *muhammad ali,*
>
> *boxing champion*

effectively as individuals because their attitudes can cloud the sending and receiving of messages.

Shyness is another emotional barrier to effective communication. Shy people are afraid to communicate with others because they think they will be judged negatively. They lack confidence in themselves, so they tend to withdraw and be quiet.

Lack of Rapport

The physical, mental, and emotional barriers to communication all have the same basic effect: They drive a wedge between the two communicators. In essence, the two communicators lack rapport, or harmony. This situation is so common that there are several expressions to describe it: "They're not on the same wavelength," "They're out of sync," "There's no chemistry between them," and "They're two ships that pass in the night."

Without rapport, people who try to communicate have a difficult time. Misunderstandings, hard feelings, and mistakes are the consequences. How can you establish rapport and communicate effectively? We'll try to answer that question in the rest of this chapter.

COMMUNICATION STYLES

The key to effective communication is awareness—of yourself but, more important, of the people with whom you communicate. You must be conscious of the feelings, needs, and personalities of the people around you. Once you become sensitive to others, you will find that their response to you is more positive. You will be on the way to establishing rapport, the foundation of effective communication.

Naturally, both people and the communication process are extremely complex. No two people or communication situations are alike. So how can you even begin to improve your awareness of others as communicators? The answer lies in using a model that simplifies a complex process and gives you insight into what's really going on.

There are many communication models, but the model we use in this chapter is based on the work of David Merrill and Roger Reid. They proposed that people show two major forms of behavior when they communicate: responsiveness and assertiveness.[1] Responsiveness is the degree to which a person is closed or open in his or her dealings with others. Someone with a low degree of responsiveness hides emotion and is very self-controlled. On the other hand, a person with a high degree of responsiveness shows emotion and seems friendly. Reid defines assertiveness as behavior ranging from asking questions (low assertiveness) to telling others what's expected (high assertiveness).

WHATEVER IT TAKES
Elizabeth Vargas

(AP/Wide World Photos/Jennifer Graylock.)

The one constant in Elizabeth Vargas's childhood was her family. Vargas's father, who was in the Army, moved his family to bases all over the world. Vargas was born in Paterson, New Jersey. By the time she graduated from high school in Stuttgart, Germany, she had lived in Heidelberg, Brussels, Okinawa, Kansas, and San Francisco.

A life of constant mobility prepared Vargas for the life of a journalist—ready to travel at a moment's notice to the latest story. Vargas studied journalism at the University of Missouri and got her first job there at KOMU-TV. She spent several years as a broadcast journalist at various local TV stations. Vargas recalls that early in her TV career she received mail suggesting that she go back to Mexico. She was very surprised by the letters, not only because of their rudeness but also because her family was originally from Puerto Rico.

In 1993 Vargas made the big move—from local to national broadcasting for NBC News. At the time, she was one of the few Hispanics on national TV news. Her current assignment is with ABC's *20/20* news magazine program. Says Vargas, "There were no Latina or Latino role models." Instead of focusing on being Hispanic, Vargas concentrated on being a good journalist. Her advice to aspiring journalists is to "read, read, read." Interestingly, given her career, Vargas grew up in a home with no TV.

Sources: Elinor J. Brecher, "Elizabeth Vargas: Tuning In at the Top," *Hispanic,* June 2002, pp. 24–25; Luis Fernando Llosa, "Elizabeth's Reign," *Latina Magazine,* February 1999 <http://www.latina.com/new/magazine/books/99/feb/triunfos.html>, accessed March 6, 2003; "Elizabeth Vargas" <http://www.abcnews.com>, accessed March 6, 2003.

News & Views

E-MAIL ETIQUETTE

In the past, you might have written a letter, made a phone call, or typed a memo. Today you are more likely to communicate with friends, family, and coworkers by e-mail. E-mail is so fast and convenient that people often dash off messages without much thought or care. The result can be ineffective communication or, worse, miscommunication.

WRITING AN E-MAIL MESSAGE

Here are some pointers for writing effective e-mail:

- Use an informative subject line. That way the recipient can easily see the topic of your message.
- Start your message with a salutation (*Dear Mr. Brenner* or *Hi Mom*), just as you would a written or typed letter.
- Keep your message short and to the point. People don't like to do lots of reading on a computer.
- Don't write anything you wouldn't want the whole world to see, because e-mail is not private. Your recipient may decide to forward your message to a large group of people. In addition, many companies routinely review and save employee e-mails, whether business or personal.
- DON'T USE ALL CAPITAL LETTERS BECAUSE THEY ARE HARD TO READ. THEY ARE ALSO CONSIDERED BAD MANNERS, LIKE SHOUTING.
- Don't write "flame" e-mails, messages that are insulting and meant to hurt. Wait until you cool down to send any e-mail message.
- As a courtesy, put your name at the end of your message. To make this easier, create signature blocks you can insert automatically.
- Check and proofread your message. Use a spell-checker, too.

SENDING E-MAIL

Once your message is written and checked, think about the transmission options before you hit any keys.

- Send CC copies of the message only to those who really need to see it. (The abbreviation CC means "carbon copy" and dates back to typewriter days.)
- Use BCC copies when you are sending a message to a group of people who don't know one another and who might not want their e-mail addresses seen by strangers. (BCC means "blind carbon copy.") With BCC copies, recipients see only their own e-mail address and yours.
- Don't spam—send impersonal e-mail messages to large groups.

continues

USING SMILIES

When you talk to someone face to face, you see the other person's facial expression and gestures. These supplement the message in the words. E-mail users have a group of keyboard symbols that add visual cues to e-mail messages. Called smilies, they usually appear at the end of a sentence and refer back to the sentence.

Here are some of the common smilies and their meanings. Tilt your head to the left to see the faces.

: -)	Smiley face; happiness	; -)	Wink; light sarcasm
: - l	Indifference	: - >	Wicked grin; heavy sarcasm
: - D	Shock or surprise	: - /	Perplexity; puzzlement
: - (	Frown; anger or displeasure	: - e	Disappointment

Note that smilies are used only in personal e-mails. They are not considered appropriate for business e-mail.

Sources: Suzy Girard, "Was It Something I Typed?" *Success,* February/March 2001, p. 42; "E-Mail Etiquette," <http://www.learnthenet.com/english/html/65mailet.htm>, accessed February 27, 2003; "E-Mail Etiquette," <http://www.iwillfollow.com/emailetiquette.html>, accessed February 27, 2003.

FIGURE 7–2

A person's communication style can be characterized by the assertiveness and responsiveness he or she shows. By plotting these characteristics on a grid, you can determine the person's communication style.

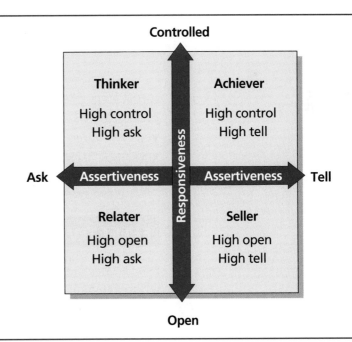

The two communication behaviors can be combined in a diagram, as shown in Figure 7–2. You can see that placing the two behaviors of responsiveness and assertiveness at right angles to each other results in a model with four boxes. When you plot a person's degree of responsiveness and assertiveness, the intersection of the two lines falls in one of the boxes. Each box represents a communication style: Thinker, Achiever, Seller, and Relater.

The Thinker

Thinkers are people who tend to be guarded in their interactions with others. Self-control is very important to them. Thinkers don't reveal much of themselves. Rather, they deflect attention from themselves by asking questions of the other person.

The Achiever

Like Thinkers, Achievers are self-controlled and guarded about revealing their inner selves. Achievers are very assertive, however. They express their expectations clearly.

The Seller

Sellers tend to be warm and outgoing in their dealings with others. Like Achievers, they are assertive and express themselves forcefully.

The Relater

Relaters are usually warm and friendly in their interactions. They are less concerned about themselves than about others. Relaters ask questions that are sometimes personal in nature.

Understanding the Communication Styles

At one time or another, each of us has used aspects of each communication style. For example, when you communicate with a close friend or spouse, you may be very open and personal (Relater). But when you communicate with your boss, you may be very self-controlled and unassertive (Thinker). In general, over time, each of us tends to favor one style in most of our interactions with others.

EFFECTIVE COMMUNICATION

Why is effective communication so important? Imagine visiting a place whose language you do not speak and whose people don't speak your language. Every message you send will probably be misunderstood or, at best, only partially understood. Everything you try to do will be difficult. Every relationship you try to establish will be based on very limited understanding. Now imagine that your communications with your friends, family, and peers suffer similar problems. The messages you send are partially misunderstood, and the feedback you receive is not what you need or understand. Not only is your communication with others affected, but your relationships with them suffer as well.

Your Turn 7–2

WHAT IS YOUR COMMUNICATION STYLE?

You can find out what your dominant communication style is by checking each of the communication characteristics that apply to you. The box with the most check marks represents your preferred communication style.

Thinker	**Achiever**
____ Quiet, level tone of voice	____ Factual speech
____ Leans back or away	____ Leans forward and faces others
____ Limited eye contact	____ Limited facial expressions
____ Stiff posture	____ Limited body movements
____ Uses big words	____ Fast-paced speech
Relater	**Seller**
____ Little emphasis on detail	____ Dramatic or loud tone of voice
____ Touches others	____ Animated facial expressions
____ Smiles, nods	____ Direct eye contact
____ Casual posture	____ Lots of body and hand movement
____ Talks about relationships	____ Uses voice to emphasize points

If you improve the quality of your communication with others, you will improve your relationships with them. And that, in turn, will improve the quality of your life.

You can use your knowledge of communication styles to improve the quality of your communication. By identifying your own style and the style of the person with whom you are communicating, you can identify potential communication problems. Once you understand the problems, you can take action to improve your rapport, and consequently your communication, with the other person.

Identifying Communication Problems

You've already identified your own preferred communication style in Your Turn 7–2. By listening and observing, you can identify the preferred communication styles of others. Do they look you in the eye or turn away? Do they ask personal questions or do they tell you just what's on their mind? Are they friendly or aloof? Are their voices loud or soft? By noticing such aspects of their behavior, you can use

FIGURE 7–3

A communication effectiveness map is a way to plot the communication styles of two people. Each person's style is represented by a circle. The closer the circles, the more similar their styles, and the fewer communication problems they are likely to have.

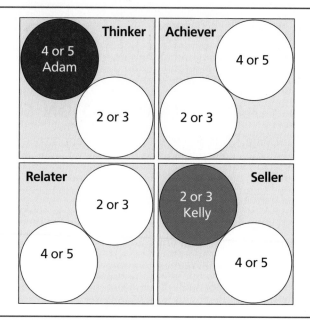

the chart in Your Turn 7–2 on page 169 to determine other people's preferred communication style.

If a person shows four to five characteristics of a style, he or she has a high preference for it. Two to three characteristics of a style reveal a moderate preference for that style. One characteristic is not significant.

Now let's use the information we have gathered. Let us suppose that Kelly has a moderate preference for the Seller style, that is, she has checked two or three characteristics in the Seller box. After observation, Kelly has decided that the person with whom she is communicating, Adam, shows a high preference for the Thinker style, with four or five characteristics of that style.

We can plot this style information by using a communication effectiveness map as shown in Figure 7–3.[2] You can see that a communication effectiveness map uses the same four boxes as the communication style model. In each box there are two circles. The outer circle represents the style of people who show four to five indicators of the style's behavior. The inner circle represents the style of people who show two to three indicators of the style's behavior.

In the example we've been discussing, Kelly's style is Seller with two or three indicators, and Adam's style is Thinker with four or five indicators. This is shown by the colored circles in the communication effectiveness map. You'll notice that Kelly's circle and Adam's circle do not touch. There is a gap between their communication styles. What does the gap mean? It means that Kelly and Adam are likely to have communication problems. The difference in their styles indicates they lack rapport.

Improving Rapport

How can Kelly, a Seller, and Adam, a Thinker, improve the quality of their communication? The answer is they must improve their rapport. In other words, they must become more alike in their communication styles. The way people do this is by imitating one another's behavior, or mirroring.

People do a certain amount of mirroring without being aware of it. If you have ever observed people deep in conversation, you may have noticed that their postures were similar or they both spoke softly. You can take this unconscious process further by paying attention to the other person's behavior and mirroring it. Mirroring does not mean imitation so obvious that the other person notices it. Rather, mirroring consists of subtle, small adjustments in your communication behavior to more closely match your companion. When you mirror successfully, the other person feels that you are in harmony. People are most comfortable with those they feel are like themselves.

Mirroring does not always improve rapport, so there are times it should not be used. For example, mirroring the behavior of someone who is angry or verbally aggressive will only make the interaction escalate. Instead, to calm the tone of the interaction, you can respond in a quiet, evenhanded way.

Mirroring the Body and Voice   You can make people with whom you are communicating more comfortable by gradually mirroring some of their body movements and voice qualities. For example, suppose you are talking to someone who is slouching in his or her chair. Without taking the same position, you can relax your posture to more closely match his or her position. Or perhaps the person you are talking with occasionally smiles or nods; you can respond in kind.

People often mirror one another's body language while communicating, even though they may not be aware of it. *(Courtesy of Tom Stock.)*

There are many aspects of nonverbal communication that can be mirrored: facial expressions, eye contact, posture, gestures, rate of speech, and pitch, volume, and tone of voice. The important thing is to match the other person's behavior in such a way that it is not noticeable. In addition, select just a couple of aspects of the person's style to mirror. Trying to mirror too much is distracting.

Mirroring Words   Another useful way to mirror others' communication style is to match their use of words. People tend to use words that reflect how they perceive the world. As you recall from Chapter 3, we perceive through our senses of sight, hearing, touch, taste, and smell.

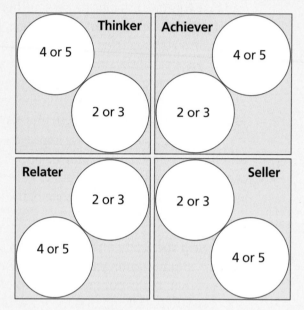

Your Turn 7–3

MAP YOUR COMMUNICATION

Choose a friend or classmate and observe him or her communicating. Use the indicators in Your Turn 7–2 to decide which communication style he or she favors and how many indicators he or she shows. Then plot your style and your friend's or classmate's style in the communication effectiveness map below.

1. What is your style?

_____

2. What is your friend or classmate's style?

_____

3. Do your styles overlap or touch?
If yes, describe the quality of your communication with this person.

_____

_____

4. Is there a gap between your styles?
If yes, describe any communication problems you may be having.

_____

_____

Your Turn 7–4

SAY IT AGAIN

How could you say the same thing to three different people who prefer different senses for perception? Rewrite the question, "What do you think it means?" using words that each person might choose.

1. Visual person:

_____

_____

2. Auditory (hearing) person:

_____

_____

3. Feeling (touching) person:

_____

_____

Each person has a preferred sense, and you can often tell which it is by listening to them talk. Most people prefer the senses of sight, hearing, or touch:

- Visual people say things like "I'll watch out for that," "It's clear to me," and "I can see that."
- People who rely on the sense of hearing use phrases such as "That rings a bell," "I hear what you're saying," and "That sounds good to me."
- People who favor the sense of touch say things like, "This feels right," "I can't get a hold on it," or "I grasp the meaning of that."

A few people rely on the sense of taste or smell:

- Those who rely on the sense of taste use phrases like "Let me chew on that a while," "That leaves a bad taste in my mouth," or "He's so delectable."
- People who favor the sense of smell say things like, "That idea stinks," "It seems fishy to me," or "She came out of it smelling like a rose."

When you've determined a person's preferred sense, you can increase your rapport by speaking the same language. For example, if the person is visual, you can ask, "Do you see what I mean?" If the person relies on hearing, you can phrase your question, "Does that sound right to you?"

Overcoming Shyness   Bernardo Carducci, a psychology professor at Indiana University Southwest, has some suggestions to help people overcome shyness with small talk.[3]

- Before a gathering, think about the people who will be there and what they may discuss.

- Arrive early. It's easier to start a new conversation than to break into a conversation that's in progress.

- Start a conversation by talking about something you and the other person share—the place, the weather, the host, and so on. Then introduce yourself.

- When the other person introduces a topic, support his or her remark. Make a comment on the topic, or throw out another topic.

These small talk pointers show that you need not be brilliant to be an effective communicator. You simply need to be responsive to other people.

The Information Highway

GETTING UP TO SPEED

Communication is a huge topic, and finding specific information on the Internet can be difficult unless you narrow your search. Here are Web sites that provide starting-off points:

- The Communication Institute for Online Scholarship offers resources to students and faculty in the field of communication. To use all its services, you must be a member or attend a school that is a member <http://cios.org>.

- If you are interested in nonverbal communication, visit the Web site of the Center for Nonverbal Studies. It has links to other interesting sites and maintains a dictionary of nonverbal communication <http:members.aol.com/nonverbal2>.

You can try searching on your own by using key words such as *nonverbal communication, facial expressions, e-mail etiquette, prejudice,* and *rapport.*

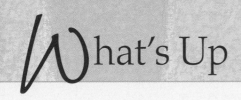
What's Up

Name _____ Date _____

1. What is communication?

_____

_____

_____

2. What is effective communication?

_____

_____

_____

3. Why is two-way communication generally more effective than one-way communication?

_____

_____

_____

4. What is nonverbal communication?

_____

_____

_____

5. Describe the three types of barriers to communication and give an example of each.

_____

_____

_____

_____

_____

_____

6. How can a knowledge of communication styles be helpful in improving communication?

_____

_____

_____

_____

continues

Name _____ Date_____

7. What is the purpose of mirroring?

_____

_____

_____

_____

_____

8. Give two examples of mirroring a person's body movements or voice during communication.

_____

_____

_____

_____

_____

9. Describe how you can mirror a person's preferred way of perceiving the world.

_____

_____

_____

_____

_____

_____

10. Why does mirroring aspects of a person's communication style lead to more effective communication?

_____

_____

_____

_____

_____

Case Studies

THE CASE OF THE IRRITABLE EX-SMOKER

It was Bob's third day without cigarettes, and he was beginning to feel the effects of quitting. He awoke with a headache, feeling grouchy, and during breakfast he snapped at each person in his family. He found it harder than he had expected to have his coffee without smoking. By the time he got to the office, he felt anxious and somewhat ill.

When Bob walked in, his assistant greeted him with a cheery "Good morning." "What's good about it?" Bob growled in reply.

1. What barriers to effective communication is Bob experiencing because he has quit smoking?

_____

_____

_____

_____

2. What can Bob and the people around him do to prevent the communication situation from getting worse?

_____

_____

_____

_____

_____

THE CASE OF THE ODD COUPLE

Rajiv and Barb were paired off by their instructor to work on a marketing problem together. As soon as they were seated in a corner of the room, Rajiv leaned forward, facing Barb, and started listing the facts of the case. Barb was a little taken aback by his desire to get right down to work. She smiled at him and nodded in appropriate places, but her attention was still partly on the rest of the class. "Rajiv," she said, tapping his arm lightly, "Why do you suppose Mrs. Valk picked us to be a team?" Rajiv looked at her in surprise, his train of thought completely thrown off.

1. What communication style does Rajiv prefer? Describe the behavior that supports your conclusion.

_____

_____

_____

_____

_____

continues

2. What communication style does Barb prefer? How can you tell?

_____
_____
_____
_____

3. What would Rajiv have to do to improve his rapport with Barb?

_____
_____
_____
_____

4. What would Barb have to do to improve her rapport with Rajiv?

_____
_____
_____
_____

Journal

Answer the following journal questions.

1. Describe your family's use of nonverbal communication. What facial expressions, eye contact, and body language are used to communicate in your home?

_____
_____
_____
_____
_____

2. Which of the barriers to communication—physical, mental, or emotional—poses the greatest problem for you? How can you overcome this barrier?

_____
_____
_____
_____
_____

3. Use the communication effectiveness grid and map in Your Turn 7–2 and 7–3 to plot your communication style and that of your spouse, significant other, or close friend. Are your communication styles similar or different? How does this affect your relationship?

_____
_____
_____
_____
_____

4. If you are shy, make a plan for being more communicative at your next social gathering. If you are not shy, offer advice to a shy friend on how to communicate effectively.

_____
_____
_____
_____
_____

**Musicians develop excellent
listening skills by playing in groups.**
(AP/Wide World Photos/
Delta Democrat Times, *Donald Adderton.)*

Improving Your Listening Skills

Tanisha was explaining to her friend Joanna why she had decided to quit her job. As Tanisha described the events that led to her decision, Joanna nodded and said, "Uh-huh." When Tanisha finished her story she paused expectantly, waiting for Joanna to say something. Startled by the silence, Joanna said, "Oh, I'm sorry, Tanisha, what were you saying?"

At one time or another, all of us have been in Tanisha's position—exasperated because someone with whom we thought we were communicating was not listening. And we all have been guilty of behaving as Joanna did—seeming to pay attention while our minds were elsewhere. Failing to listen to a friend can damage the friendship. Failing to listen to instructors, bosses, and coworkers has repercussions, too. It can lead to misunderstandings, mistakes, and hard feelings. "If each of America's more than 100 million workers prevented just one $10 mistake by better listening, their organizations would gain over $1 billion in profits," says Lyman K. Steil, president of Communication Development Inc., a consulting firm that teaches listening skills.[1] Since most communication—both personal and professional—involves listening, it's important to improve your listening skills. In this chapter, you will learn why listening is so hard. You will also learn about techniques you can use to become a more effective listener.

Listening means concentrating on what's being said. The student in the back is clearly not paying attention to what's happening in the classroom.
(Courtesy of PhotoDisc.)

WHY IS LISTENING SO HARD?

Listening seems like such an easy thing to do. After all, you just have to keep your ears open. But listening is more than hearing. You hear with your ears, but you listen with your brain. Imagine talking with an interesting person at a party. You can hear many conversations in the room, but you are listening to just one.

So why is listening so hard? Listening requires concentration. That means ignoring the hundreds of other things going on around you as well as in your head. Distractions, preconceptions, self-absorption, and daydreaming can all interfere with your ability to listen.

Distractions

It's easy to be distracted when you're listening to someone. Perhaps there's other activity in the room that draws your eyes or ears. Perhaps the person with whom you are speaking is wearing earrings that you can't stop looking at. Or another individual may pace or gesture or exhibit a mannerism that's hard to ignore. Whatever the distraction, it competes with the communication for your attention. And once your attention is divided, it's hard to listen well.

Preconceptions

Preconceptions about the speakers or what they have to say are barriers to effective listening. If you think that the speaker is a fool or has opinions that are the opposite of yours, you may close down your brain and pay no attention. What you lose is an opportunity to learn something—even if your preconceptions turn out to be true. You may even be surprised to hear something of interest if you decide to listen in spite of your presumptions about the speaker or the message.

Self-Absorption

Another cause of poor listening is that you focus on yourself rather than on the person who is talking. Instead of listening carefully to the other person, you are busy thinking about your own agenda. While the individual talks, you are planning and rehearsing your response. In effect, you are just waiting for the other person to be quiet so you can jump in with your contribution to the conversation.

Daydreaming

Have you ever fallen into a mental "black hole" during a conversation? Your body is there, but your eyes are glassy, and anyone looking closely at you can tell your mind is miles away. Unfortunately, it's easy to fall into the trap of daydreaming while you are supposed to be listening. That's because your brain can process words much faster than the speaker can say them. What does your brain do with this down time? It fills it with daydreams.

LISTENING EFFECTIVELY

Many people listen with just one ear. They understand just enough of what the speaker is saying to keep the conversation going with nods, smiles, and a well-placed "Uh-huh." With these responses, the listener is trying to convince the speaker that he or she is paying attention. In reality, the listener is listening passively. He or she is paying just enough attention to avoid seeming rude. This type of passive listening may be sufficient for some types of casual conversations, but it will not do for important personal and professional communications.

Instead, active listening is required when you communicate in most situations. Active listening means that your mind is engaged with the message and the speaker. You are concentrating on the speaker, and you are participating in the communication.

There are many techniques you can use to practice active listening. These techniques include being physically prepared, being open to the other person, being curious, asking questions, and listening for the meaning of the words and the unspoken message.

Be Physically Prepared

Listening is both a physical and a mental activity. If you cannot hear properly, you will have trouble listening. So the first prerequisite for effective listening is the ability to hear. If you always have trouble hearing, you should have your hearing checked to make sure it's normal. Don't assume that hearing problems are confined to older people; young people sometimes have damaged hearing because of overexposure to loud music or noisy machinery.

You can maximize your ability to hear by making sure the environment is free of noise and other distractions. In classrooms, lectures, and meetings, make sure you sit close to the speaker so you can hear well. You should also be able to see the speaker, because your sense of sight helps you listen. Watching the speaker's nonverbal cues helps you understand the message.

People who are frequently exposed to loud noise may damage their hearing. In noisy work areas, workers wear ear protectors.
(Courtesy of Tom Stock.)

Be Open

The Japanese symbol for the word *listen* shows the character for "ear" placed within the character for "gate." When we listen to someone, we are in effect passing through the other person's gate and entering his or her world. When we listen effectively, we are receiving the speaker's message in an open, nonjudging way.[2]

This is not always easy. Being open to another person means you risk having to change your feelings, ideas, or attitudes. Yet listening in an open, nonjudging way does not necessarily mean you must agree with everything the speaker says. You must just be willing to accept their right to say it and to listen.

Being willing to accept the speaker's message means that you stop focusing on finding contradictions and errors. Instead, you let the message get through. Then you can evaluate the message—after you've actually listened to it.

If you can listen openly, you will communicate to the speaker that you think he or she is important and has ideas worth hearing. You communicate an attitude of respect for the other person. The bonus of open listening is that the speaker will feel less defensive and more open to you.

Be Curious

Part of being an open listener is being curious about other people. If you can really listen to what another person has to say, you will find that you can learn a lot. Try to be observant and objective about listening, and you will be able to gather a great deal of information.

To do this, you must let your curiosity overcome your need to judge the other person and justify your own position.

Ask Questions

You can express your curiosity about the speaker as well as clarify your understanding of the message by asking questions. Effective listeners ask questions in a way that will elicit informative answers.

Your Turn 8–1

HOW GOOD A LISTENER ARE YOU?

Take a moment to think about your own qualities as a listener. Then answer the following questions to see what your strengths and weaknesses are.

		Yes	No
1.	Is your hearing normal?	☐	☐
2.	Do you look at the person who is speaking?	☐	☐
3.	Do you try to ignore other sights and sounds when you listen to someone speak?	☐	☐
4.	While listening, do you avoid doing something else at the same time (like reading or watching TV)?	☐	☐
5.	When someone is talking to you, do you concentrate on him or her rather than on your own thoughts?	☐	☐
6.	Do you think that other people can teach you something?	☐	☐
7.	If you don't understand something, do you ask the speaker to repeat it?	☐	☐
8.	Do you listen even when you disagree with what the speaker is saying?	☐	☐
9.	If you think the subject is dull or too hard, do you tune out?	☐	☐
10.	Do you frequently have to ask people to repeat themselves because you've forgotten what they have said?	☐	☐
11.	If the speaker's appearance or manner is poor, do you pay less attention?	☐	☐
12.	Do you pretend to pay attention even when you are not listening?	☐	☐

If you answered *yes* to the first eight questions and *no* to the last four questions, your listening skills are good. Even if you got a perfect score, the tips and techniques that follow will help you improve your listening skills.

Your Turn 8–2

ASKING GOOD QUESTIONS

For each of the following items, write a question that will elicit the response indicated. Then say whether the question is open-ended or closed-ended.

1. **Question:**

_____

_____

Response: The coat is black leather with a belt.
Type of question: _____

2. **Question:**

_____

_____

Response: I feel uncomfortable because he gives me orders rather than asking me to do something.
Type of question: _____

3. **Question:**

_____

_____

Response: I like the red one better. _____

Type of question: _____

4. **Question:**

_____

_____

Response: First we decided what type of playground we wanted, then we made a plan, and finally we enlisted other people to help us build it.
Type of question: _____

5. **Question:**

_____

_____

Response: No, I don't like it.
Type of question: _____

Effective listeners ask questions in a way that will elicit information.
(Courtesy of PhotoDisc.)

In general, the most effective questions are open-ended questions. **Open-ended questions** cannot be answered with just a *yes* or a *no;* they require an explanation as a response. Questions that begin with *what, how,* and *why* are generally open-ended questions. For example, "What happened at the meeting?" "How do you feel about that?" and "Why did he leave?" are questions that require an informative response. Open-ended questions are used to get more detail and to clarify messages.

On the other hand, **closed-ended questions** can be answered with a simple *yes* or *no.* "Did you agree with her?" and "Do you like it?" are examples of closed-ended questions. Closed-ended questions tend to limit the exchange of information, especially when the speaker is shy or reserved. Effective listeners can use closed-ended questions, however, when information needs to be checked. "Do you mean you'll be a day late?" is a closed-ended question that verifies the listener's understanding of the message.

Remember, good questions, both open- and closed-ended, arise out of the conversation. That means that you, the listener, must be paying attention. The next time you watch someone doing an interview on television, notice whether they stick to a script of questions, no matter what the response, or whether they allow their questions to arise from the content of the interview. Good interviewers are good listeners, and their questions are relevant to the conversation.

Listen for Meaning and Verbal Cues

We mentioned earlier that listeners can understand verbal messages far faster than speakers can say them. Rather than using the brain's down time for daydreaming, effective listeners use it to think about the meaning of what they hear.

As you listen to the speaker's words, use your critical thinking skills (see Chapter 3). Try to identify the ideas and facts and the relationships between them. Ask yourself, What is the most important thing being said? What facts or ideas support the main idea? Does one thing cause another? Is sequence or time involved? Does this represent a fact or an opinion? Thinking critically about the message will help you understand it and keep your attention focused on the communication.

In addition, thinking about the meaning of the speaker's message can give you cues about your own responses. For example, if you are being interviewed for a job, you should listen carefully to what the interviewer is saying. If the interviewer talks a lot about the company's

> **If you wish to know the mind of a man, listen to his words.**
>
> *chinese proverb*

> **We have two ears and one mouth that we may listen the more and talk the less.**
>
> *zeno,*
>
> *ancient greek philosopher*

LISTENING: A CORNERSTONE OF PSYCHOTHERAPY

A woman in her late thirties was having marital and family problems, and she went to a psychotherapist for help. Here is a brief excerpt from one of their sessions:

Woman: You know this is kind of goofy, but I've never told anyone this and it'll probably do me good. . . . For years . . . I have had . . . "flashes of sanity" . . . wherein I really feel sane . . . and pretty much aware of life. . . .

Therapist: It's been fleeting and it's been infrequent, but there have been times when it seems the whole you is functioning and feeling in the world, a very chaotic world to be sure. . . .

Woman: That's right. . . .

Notice how the therapist took the woman's first statement and rephrased it, trying to clarify her meaning. He must have been listening carefully. All psychotherapy involves close listening, but in client-centered psychotherapy listening is a crucial tool.

In client-centered psychotherapy, the therapist tries to help the client release his ability to understand and manage his or her life—what we have been calling *reaching your potential*. According to psychologist Carl Rogers, this personal growth will occur if three conditions exist in the relationship between therapist and client:

- The therapist must be thoroughly herself or himself by expressing feelings and attitudes toward the client, not opinions or judgments. By being open with the client, the therapist builds the client's trust.

- The therapist must accept the client as he or she is—a condition known as unconditional positive regard. By doing so, the therapist shows care for the client, no matter what the client is feeling or thinking.

- The therapist must aim for a thorough, empathic understanding of the client through active listening. By clarifying the meaning of what the client is saying, the therapist can promote the client's even deeper understanding of self.

This last component of client-centered therapy is based on listening. "Therapists can learn, quite quickly, to be better, more sensitive listeners, more empathic. It is in part a skill as well as an attitude," says Rogers.

How can client-centered therapy help people? According to Rogers, when clients find a therapist listening to and accepting their thoughts and feelings, they are better able to accept their own thoughts and feelings—even the negative ones. This increased acceptance leads to a feeling of having greater self-control. As clients become more self-aware and self-accepting, they find some of the freedom to grow and change as a human being.

Source: Carl Rogers, *On Personal Power: Inner Strength and Its Revolutionary Impact,* New York, Delacorte Press, 1977, pp. 9–12; *On Becoming a Person,* Boston, Houghton Mifflin, 1961, pp. 61–62, 89.

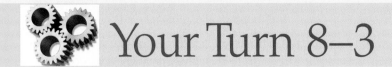

Your Turn 8–3

FACT OR OPINION?

Distinguishing between fact and opinion is important for effective listening. Indicate whether each of the following statements is a fact or an opinion.

1. You don't need reservations to eat dinner at that restaurant. _____

2. The food there is pretty good. _____

3. The last time we had dinner there, the waiter spilled coffee on the table. _____

4. I thought the chocolate sundae was too sweet. _____

5. The bill came to $29 without the tip. _____

There are no visual cues when you listen on the telephone, and when you encounter a voice mail system, you can't even ask questions. Instead, you must rely on your ears to pick up the message.
(© *Walter Hodges/Corbis.*)

reputation for high-quality service, you can describe your own commitment to high quality in some aspect of your life. If the interviewer asks an open-ended question, give a full response.

Listen Between the Lines

Effective listening requires more than just paying attention to the words. An active listener also focuses on nonverbal cues. As we learned in Chapter 7, voice qualities, eye contact, facial expressions, and body language all contribute to the meaning of a message. By paying attention to the nonverbal aspects of communication, you can improve your ability to listen.

Most nonverbal communication cues are visual, so it's important for the listener to be able to see the speaker. You can get a sense of how sight contributes to effective listening by comparing the experiences of talking face to face and over the telephone. When you talk face to face, you can perceive the person's feelings and unstated messages by looking at the other person's face, eyes, and gestures. In contrast, when you listen on the telephone, you rely on your ears to pick up both the words and the voice cues. Your ability to detect the unstated message is reduced because you cannot see the speaker. When you communicate by e-mail or instant messaging, you lose both sight and voice cues and depend entirely on words for meaning.

> *Everything becomes possible by the mere presence of someone who knows how to listen, to love, and to give of himself.*
>
> elie wiesel,
>
> holocaust survivor and writer

Take Notes

Another way to ensure that you listen actively is to take notes. Taking notes forces you to pay attention to the message and decide what's important enough to write down. As we discussed in Chapter 4, taking and reviewing notes also helps you remember what you hear.

Although you may be used to taking notes in class, there are other situations in which note taking is a good way to ensure effective listening. When you are listening to directions, for example, it's helpful to write them down. When you are doing business on the phone, take notes about the details. That way you'll be sure to get the message accurately and completely.

The Information Highway

GETTING UP TO SPEED

There is a wealth of information about listening skills on the Internet, ranging from sales pitches for listening seminars to sites posting suggestions for improving listening skills.

- ■ A good place to start is the International Listening Association's site, which has links to listening resources <http://listen.org>.
- ■ For resources on hearing protection and hearing aids, check the Web site of HEAR (Hearing Education and Awareness for Rockers), a nonprofit organization started by a rock musician who suffered hearing loss <http://www.hearnet.com>.
- ■ Dave's ESL Café on the Web is a comprehensive site of interest to speakers of English as a second language. Their search engine provides links to ESL listening resources on the Internet <http://www.eslcafe.com>.

In addition, to learn more about topics in this chapter, you can do searches using the key words *listening skills, hearing education, client-centered psychotherapy, Carl Rogers,* and *noise.*

WHATEVER IT TAKES
Chan Ho Yun

(Courtesy of Tannery Hill Studios.)

When Kika Keith looked for music lessons for her daughter, she found that Colburn, a famous performing arts school in downtown Los Angeles, was too far away from her neighborhood. Private violin lessons there were too expensive as well. But she also found Chan Ho Yun at Colburn. A violinist and teacher, Yun offered Keith a deal. If Keith would find space in her neighborhood and more kids to take lessons, he would teach them free of charge.

So began Sweet Strings, a classical music program for the kids of South Central Los Angeles. For Keith, the way Sweet Strings took off was a complete surprise. South Central, better known for its rap fans, turned out to have a lot of classical music lovers, too. When word of free violin lessons got around the neighborhood, people flocked to join the program. The first class, in 1999, had 25 children and no instruments. By 2000, there were 60 students and 50 donated violins. Soon the program was giving free violin, viola, cello, and bass lessons to over 100 African American, Latino, and Korean kids, with a waiting list of more than 300.

Today Sweet Strings relies on donations from Hollywood celebrities, large corporations, and foundations. It has some paid as well as volunteer music teachers. Because their resources are limited, Sweet Strings can't admit everyone. They accept the students with the greatest need—those whose schools do not have a music program. Students from Sweet Strings have played at the opening night of the Hollywood Bowl and at an event where President Clinton was the featured speaker.

As the children learn music, the community has also benefited in other ways. Yun required that parents accompany their children to lessons. So parents learned to read music, too. In addition, they got to know their neighbors. People of different backgrounds found that stereotypes were breaking down and friendships were forming because of the shared interest in children and music. Says Yun, "No matter where we come from or what color we are, the only color I recognize is the color of the sound of the music we make."

Sources: Amy Reeves, "Sweet Strings in South Central L.A.," *Strings,* January 2001, No. 91 <http://www.stringsmagazine.com/issues/strings91/Newsprof.shtml>, accessed February 28, 2003; Christina Cheakalos and Caren Grigsby Bates, "Strings of His Heart," *People,* March 19, 2001, pp. 69–70; "Chan Ho Yun, Violin Teacher and Performer, Co-founder, Sweet Strings" <http://www.digitalheroes.org/dhc/bios/bio_yun.html>, accessed February 28, 2003.

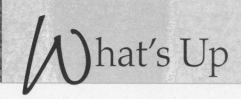

What's Up

Name _____   Date _____

1. What is the difference between hearing and listening?
_____
_____
_____

2. Why is effective listening so hard?
_____
_____
_____

3. Why is it easy to daydream while listening?
_____
_____
_____

4. What is the difference between passive and active listening?
_____
_____
_____

5. Describe two things you can do to make sure you are physically prepared to listen.
_____
_____
_____

6. Why it is important to listen in an open, nonjudging way?
_____
_____
_____

continues

Name _____   Date _____

7. What is an open-ended question? Give an example.

_____

_____

_____

8. What is a closed-ended question? Give an example.

_____

_____

_____

_____

_____

9. When you are listening, your brain has down time. What should you use this down time for?

_____

_____

_____

_____

_____

10. How do nonverbal cues help the listener understand the message?

_____

_____

_____

_____

_____

Case Studies

THE CASE OF THE ABSENT-MINDED EMPLOYEE

Julio was the night manager at a fast food restaurant. Each night, he gave instructions to the staff about what needed to be done. One of the employees, Rick, was always interrupting, chatting about other topics, and daydreaming. He made a lot of mistakes, and he had to be told what to do again and again.

1. Why does Rick make so many mistakes at work?

_____

_____

_____

_____

2. What might Julio do to get Rick to listen attentively?

_____

_____

_____

_____

THE CASE OF THE MISTAKEN MESSAGES

Jill had just started a part-time job as a receptionist for a travel agency. Part of her job was to answer the phone and take messages for the agents when they were busy. The phone was constantly ringing, people told her messages to pass on, and she had to greet visitors, too. Jill had a good memory, and she usually remembered to tell the agents about their calls. But at the end of the first week, a couple of agents complained that they weren't getting all their messages. Some of the messages they did get were wrong.

1. What is wrong with Jill's approach to taking messages on the phone?

_____

_____

_____

_____

2. What can Jill do to improve her listening skill and make sure she is passing messages on correctly?

_____

_____

_____

_____

Journal

Answer the following journal questions.

1. What barriers to listening interfere with your ability to listen effectively? How can you overcome these barriers?

_____
_____
_____
_____
_____

2. In what situations do you find yourself not paying attention to a speaker? How can you be more open to hearing the messages of others?

_____
_____
_____
_____
_____

3. What role does listening play in your life at home? At school? At work? In which situation is your listening most effective? Why?

_____
_____
_____
_____
_____

4. If you improved your listening skill at school, how would this benefit you?

_____
_____
_____
_____

People with speech problems understand the value of speaking skills. Joseph Kalinowski, a speech pathology professor, has been stuttering since childhood. He helped develop a small device, worn in the ear, that suppresses stuttering. *(Courtesy of Cliff Hollis, East Carolina University.)*

Improving Your Speaking Skills

From the time you get up in the morning until you go to sleep at night, you use your voice to communicate. At home you converse with your family about the events of the day. With your friends you talk about whatever concerns you. You use the telephone to speak about business and personal matters. At school you ask and answer questions in class and talk with other students. At work you give directions, explain things, ask and answer questions, participate in meetings, and talk with customers and coworkers. You may occasionally give oral presentations at school or work.

Since talking is the basic form of communication among people, you are judged to a great extent by your ability to speak. People recognize you by your speech. The words you choose, your gestures, the expressions on your face, the sound of your voice, and the way you pronounce words add up to an instantly recognizable person. The way you speak is an expression of your personality. In this chapter, you will learn that speaking involves more than words. You will discover that your appearance, your voice qualities, and how you say things all have a great impact on the people around you. You will learn techniques for effective face-to-face and telephone conversations. Last, you will learn some ways to improve your ability to speak to groups, both informally and formally.

FIGURE 9–1

Your appearance and voice have far more impact on your listeners than what you actually say.

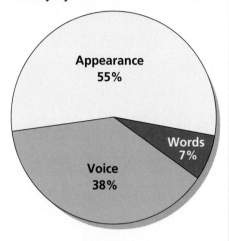

FIRST IMPRESSIONS

Speaking is not limited to the words you say. In addition to the words of your message, listeners perceive the way you look and the way you sound. In studies of face-to-face communication, Dr. Albert Mehrabian has found that the impact on the listener of appearance and voice is far greater than that of words (see Figure 9–1). In fact, since listeners see you before they hear you, your appearance has a great effect on your ability to get your message across. You have 7 to 10 seconds to make a good first impression!

If people's visual impression of you is poor, they are less likely to listen to what you have to say. Most people are put off by bad posture, lack of cleanliness, and sloppiness. Good posture, hygiene, and grooming are essential to forming a favorable first impression.

Also important in creating a good first impression is the way you dress. In recent years, dress standards have changed considerably. It's no longer possible to prescribe appropriate dress for every situation. Rather, you should think of your listeners. If their opinions are important to you, then you should dress in a way that is acceptable to them. So ask yourself, On what basis will my listeners judge the way I dress? Do I want to wear a navy blue suit or casual clothes? Should I look conservative or fashionable? Whatever type of clothing you decide on, it should be clean and neat. Your clothes should not distract your listeners from your message.

SPEECH QUALITIES

Once your listeners have gotten a first impression of you from your appearance, they get their second impression from your speech. Forgetting for a moment the specific words of your message, what do you want to communicate with your speech? Most people want to be perceived as intelligent, competent, and attractive. To be perceived this way, you must speak well. You must control the qualities of your voice—volume, pitch, rate, and tone. You must pronounce words accurately; enunciate, or speak clearly; and use correct grammar and appropriate vocabulary.

In the United States, there are four basic varieties of spoken American English: standard English, dialects, accented English, and substandard English.

- **Standard English** is the English spoken by national news broadcasters, actors, and others who have rid themselves of regional or social dialects.

- **Dialects** are variations of American English that are spoken in particular areas or by particular social groups. The most familiar regional dialects are those of the South, New York City, Boston,

National news broadcasters are trained to speak standard English. Many people learn standard English by listening to them on TV. *(AP/World Wide Photos/ Gino Domenico.)*

and the Midwest. Black English, a dialect spoken by many African Americans, is found in all regions of the United States. It is sometimes called Ebonics.

- **Accented English** is spoken by the many Americans for whom English is a second language.
- **Substandard English** is English spoken with poor pronunciation, enunciation, grammar, and vocabulary.

Largely through the influence of television, standard English is understood easily throughout the United States. It has therefore become the norm against which people's speech is judged. Since the purpose of speaking is to communicate, it makes sense to communicate in language that people from all social groups and regions of the country understand. So if you are trying to improve your speech, you should be imitating the standard English you hear on national news broadcasts. As you practice improving various aspects of your speech, you should try to record your voice so you can hear what you sound like.

Volume

The **volume** of your voice refers to its intensity or loudness. In most situations, a moderate volume is appropriate for standard English and will enable listeners to hear you. Of course, if you are addressing a large group, you will have to raise the volume of your voice or use a microphone. In addition, a good speaker uses changes in volume to emphasize parts of the message.

If you are having trouble speaking loudly enough, you should practice breathing properly. If you take quick, shallow breaths, your lungs do not have enough air to produce sounds loud enough to be heard easily. Instead, you should breathe deeply and control your breath as singers and actors do.

Pitch

Pitch refers to the level of sound on a musical scale. People who speak with a high-pitched voice sound shrill and unpleasant. On the other hand, people whose voices are pitched too low can be hard to hear. And people whose pitch never varies speak in a monotone, which is boring for listeners. A moderate pitch with variations is best for standard English.

Pitch carries different meanings in standard English and regional dialects. For example, when you ask a question in standard English, the pitch of your voice rises toward the end of the sentence. The rising pitch at the end of the sentence conveys a question, doubt, or hesitation. Since a rising pitch at the end of a sentence means uncertainty in standard English, many Northerners are confused when they listen to people speaking a Southern dialect. Southerners have a slight rise in pitch at the ends of most sentences. This rise doesn't mean uncertainty; rather it's meant to convey courtesy, a meaning that's lost on the Northerners. You can see from this small example that using standard English can prevent the miscommunication that results when dialect differences are not understood.

Rate

Standard English is spoken at a moderate rate. Indeed, because of the long vowel sounds in English, it's hard to speak the language very fast. As with pitch, there are regional differences in the rate of speech. Northerners tend to speak faster than Southerners, and people from the Northeast speak faster than those from the Midwest.

To avoid sounding boring, you can vary the rate of your speech. You can slow down to emphasize important facts or ideas or to accommodate a listener who can't keep up with you. You can also pause to emphasize major points. A moment of silence has the power to refocus your listener's attention. Avoid filling your pauses with sounds like "um" and "uh." These fillers are distracting to your listeners.

Tone

As you know, tone of voice reveals the speaker's feelings and attitudes. A voice can be depressed, cheerful, angry, or neutral. Because tone of voice is so revealing, you should be aware of what you sound like. Sometimes it's appropriate to convey your emotions through the tone of your voice. For example, you may want to communicate your happiness that your friend is getting married. At other times you may want to change your tone to avoid communicating a feeling you would rather hide. You may wish to sound neutral rather than angry, for instance, when you are disagreeing with your boss.

Enunciation

Enunciation refers to the clarity with which you say words. Saying "didja" for "did you" or "talkin'" for "talking" are examples of poor enunciation. Poor enunciation is the result of leaving out sounds, adding sounds, and running sounds together. Poor enunciation in standard English may be the result of speaking a regional dialect.

Commonly left out sounds are the final *t, g,* and *d* when they follow another consonant. For example, many people say "stric" rather than "strict," "goin'" rather than "going," and "pon" rather than "pond." Some vowels are frequently swallowed as well. When two vowel sounds occur together, one is often lost. For example, many people say "pome" rather than "poem" and "crule" rather than "cruel." Sometimes entire syllables are lost, as in "praps" for "perhaps" and "lil" for "little."

Another type of poor enunciation is the addition of unnecessary sounds. "Umberella" for "umbrella," "disasterous" for "disastrous," and "exshtra" for "extra" are some examples.

Finally, slurring words—saying them indistinctly and running them together—makes you difficult to understand. "C'mere, I wancha t'gimmee a hand" is an example of slurred speech. Unless you enunciate clearly, your listeners may pay more attention to decoding your speech than to interpreting its meaning.

Pronunciation

Pronunciation is closely related to enunciation. Whereas enunciation refers to the clarity with which you say words, **pronunciation** refers to the correctness with which you say words. A person who says "Febyuary" instead of "February" or stresses the wrong syllable in "harassment" is mispronouncing words. Many pronunciation errors in English arise from the quirks of spelling. The *t* in "often," for example, is not pronounced. The letters *ea* sound different in "break" and "beak." In addition, some words have more than one acceptable pronunciation. When in doubt about the pronunciation of a word, look it up in the dictionary. Generally, the preferred pronunciation is listed first. Table 9–1, page 202, shows some commonly mispronounced words.

Grammar and Vocabulary

You may enunciate clearly and pronounce words correctly, but if you've chosen the wrong words or put them together incorrectly, you will not be considered a good communicator. A good vocabulary allows you to present your thoughts with precision. You don't need to use fancy words, just have a wide enough vocabulary to express yourself clearly.

Good grammar is also essential. However, the rules of grammar are not necessarily the same in a dialect as in standard English.

Most speech pathologists work with people who have speech problems. However, some of them help people get rid of accents, learn new dialects, and change their speech patterns. (© Bob Rowan; Progressive Image/Corbis.)

For example, "He runnin" is a grammatical Black English sentence, but the same sentence in grammatical standard English would be "He is running." If you are used to speaking a dialect informally, pay closer attention to the rules of grammar when speaking standard English. Justly or not, people who constantly make grammatical errors when speaking standard English are considered poorly educated and unprofessional. If you think your grammar could use improvement, try reading more. By reading you will absorb many of the rules of standard English grammar. If you think you need more help than that, you can enroll in a course at your school or an adult education center.

TABLE 9–1   Commonly Mispronounced Words

Incorrect	Correct	Incorrect	Correct
Omost	Almost	Liberry	Library
Irrevelant	Irrelevant	Fas*t*en	Fas(t)en
Probly	Probably	Nucular	Nuclear
Akst	Asked	Idear	Idea
Oways	Always	Sophmore	Sophomore
Famly	Family	Drownded	Drowned
Mischievious	Mischievous	Burgular	Burglar
Cor*ps*	Cor(ps)	Of*t*en	of(t)en
'Po-lice	Po-'lice	'Di-rect	Di-'rect
Jest	Just	Preventative	Preventive

EFFECTIVE CONVERSATIONS

An attractive appearance and good speech contribute to your effectiveness as a communicator, but they are not enough to ensure good communication. In face-to-face communication, it's important to think as much of the person with whom you are conversing as you do about yourself and your message. So in addition to knowing what you want to communicate, you must make others feel comfortable by establishing a positive atmosphere, using appropriate body language, listening, letting others speak, and mirroring their speech.

Know What You Want to Say

If a conversation has a purpose other than social chitchat, you should be mentally prepared for it. That means you know beforehand what message you want to communicate. You have decided what points you need to cover and what your approach will be. When you are mentally prepared, instead of floundering, you will be able to direct the conversation where you want it to go.

There's another side to knowing what you want to say, and that's knowing what you *don't* want to say. It's important to respect confidences and to be discreet and tactful. Communicating private matters to people who are not directly concerned will eventually result in your being perceived as untrustworthy and rude. To avoid this, make sure you keep confidences and speak to others with tact and discretion.

A rumor goes in one ear and out many mouths.

chinese proverb

Your Turn 9–1

RATE YOUR SPEECH QUALITIES

Answer the following questions to evaluate your speech qualities. You may have to ask a friend to help you if you're not sure how you sound.

		Yes	No
1.	I usually speak standard English.	☐	☐
2.	I speak at a moderate volume, neither too loud nor too soft.	☐	☐
3.	I speak at a moderate pitch and vary the pitch to convey different meanings.	☐	☐
4.	I speak at a moderate rate, neither too fast nor too slow.	☐	☐
5.	I use pauses to emphasize major points.	☐	☐
6.	I control the tone of my voice in order to better communicate my messages.	☐	☐
7.	I usually enunciate clearly and distinctly.	☐	☐
8.	When I'm not sure of the pronunciation of a word, I look it up in a dictionary.	☐	☐
9.	I use a wide range of words when speaking.	☐	☐
10.	When I speak, I use correct grammar.	☐	☐

A *no* answer to any of these questions indicates that you can improve your speech.

> ***One of the greatest pleasures of life is conversation.***
>
> *sydney smith, 19th-century*
>
> *english clergyman and writer*

Establish a Positive Atmosphere

The environment of a conversation has a great effect on the quality of the communication that takes place. No one would expect to have a mutually satisfying conversation, for example, in a police interrogation room with bright lights trained on the suspect. Sitting behind a large desk or in an imposing chair or standing over the person with whom you're conversing sends a similar message: You are in control. Any setup that makes the speaker appear dominant has the effect of stifling the free flow of communication.

So if you want to converse openly and honestly with someone, be sure that the environment contributes to a relaxed atmosphere. Make sure there are no physical barriers between you and your listener. Move out from behind a table or desk, sit if the listener is sitting, and move the furniture to get comfortable seating if necessary.

Use Body Language

You are already aware of how much facial expressions, eye contact, posture, and gestures can communicate. When you speak, try to use the vocabulary of body language to add to the meaning of your verbal message. Smiling, looking people in the eye, holding yourself tall but relaxed, and gesturing for emphasis will help hold the attention of your listeners. On the other hand, do not exaggerate your use of body language, because that is distracting. It's also important to control any mannerisms you may have, such as biting the end of a pen or playing with objects in your hands.

Listen

Nothing conveys your interest in the other person as much as listening carefully to what he or she has to say. Your success as a speaker is dependent on your effectiveness as a listener. Only if you listen carefully will you get feedback to your message. And good feedback is necessary to keep a conversation effective. Listening is so important that we devoted a whole chapter to it. If you need to brush up on your listening techniques, review Chapter 8.

Let Others Talk

A conversation is a dialogue, not a monologue. If you monopolize the conversation, you will find that effective communication is not taking place. Part of being a good speaker is knowing when to let the other person talk. Be attentive to your listener so you will know when he or she wants to say something. Then be silent and listen.

Mirror the Speech of Others

As you recall, people are most comfortable communicating with those who are like themselves. Part of establishing rapport with another person is to mirror aspects of their communication style (see Chapter 7). When you have a conversation, you can mirror the speech of the other person. You can match the pace, pitch, tone, or volume of others' speech, the words they use, and their body language. Mirroring aspects of the other person's communication style will help the person relax and be more open with you.

In addition to reacting to the other person's communication style, you can affect that style by your actions. For example, suppose

Silent? Ah, he is silent! He can keep silence well. That man's silence is wonderful to listen to.

thomas hardy,

19th-century english novelist

People can achieve greater rapport when they are talking if no one person is dominating the others. *(Courtesy of PhotoDisc.)*

you are talking to someone who speaks very slowly. You can try to speed him up by mirroring his pace, then gradually speaking faster. Without even being aware of it, he will speed up a bit to match *you*. If you want someone to relax, make sure your own posture is relaxed, your voice is calm, and your facial expression interested and pleasant. Changing aspects of other people's communication style by getting them to mirror you is called leading.

SPEAKING ON THE TELEPHONE

The visual dimension of communication is lost when you talk on the telephone. The power of facial expressions, eye contact, and gestures to communicate is gone. Instead, you must rely on your words and voice to convey your message. You must concentrate on identifying yourself and being courteous and attentive in order to communicate effectively on the telephone. You should also learn the best way to handle the telephone itself.

Using the Telephone Properly

Telephones, answering machines, and voice mail are everywhere, and you have been using them for years. But do you use this technology properly? Here are some tips to help you master the telephone.

> **It takes two to speak the truth,— one to speak, and another to hear.**
>
> henry david thoreau,
> 19th-century author
> and naturalist

- Talk directly into the mouthpiece of the telephone, with your lips about an inch from the phone. Don't let the telephone slip below your chin. The listener will have trouble hearing you, or your voice may not be properly recorded on an answering machine or voice mail system.

- If you are using a speaker phone, face the unit so your voice will be picked up properly.

- Speak at a normal volume. It's usually not necessary to shout. If the connection is bad, place the call again.

- Enunciate clearly so you will be understood.

- If you get a wrong number, don't just hang up. Apologize for the mistake. Not only is this good manners but also it protects your reputation for professionalism. Remember that many phones have caller ID and you can be identified.

- If you have to leave the line, tell the other person what you are doing. Inform her if you are putting her on hold or responding to a call-waiting signal. If you are gone more than a minute, check back and ask if she would like to continue to hold. That tells her that she hasn't been forgotten.

WANTED: BILINGUAL WORKERS

"What is an extra language worth?" That question is being asked all over the country by bilingual workers. As American companies and governments do more business with non-English speakers, the demand for bilingual employees is rising. Bilingual workers are needed in health care, technology, social work, teaching, public safety, and administrative jobs in both the private and public sector.

Being bilingual in today's job market is a plus. Many employers want to hire employees who are bilingual and bicultural as well, meaning that they understand the language, customs, and traditions of foreign-born customers. A survey conducted by Hispanic Times Enterprises revealed that, when two people with equal qualifications apply for a job and one of them is bilingual, most companies will hire the bilingual applicant.

In some places, the need for extra languages is so great that local governments are beginning to mandate the hiring of bilingual workers. For example, in 2001, the city of Oakland, California, passed an ordinance requiring that bilingual workers be hired. Oakland was looking for people who were bilingual in Spanish or Chinese for positions, including police officer, firefighter, sanitation worker, and recreation worker, that involve contact with the public.

But will the bilingual employee be paid more for his or her language skills? Some bilingual employees are paid more, especially those with higher-level jobs. Bilingual financial analysts, merchant bankers, stockbrokers, and middle- and upper-level managers are often paid extra for their relevant language skills. For lower-level jobs, the situation varies considerably, although the trend is toward extra pay. For example, MCI pays its bilingual telephone operators a 10 percent bonus if they speak another language more than half the time on the job. Clark County, Nevada, is planning to pay its bilingual workers an extra $100 a month if at least 20 percent of their work involves dealing with Spanish-speaking clients.

Whether bilingual workers are paid more sometimes depends on whether a second language is considered a job requirement or just an added talent. For example, at MCI knowledge of a second language is a job requirement for certain operator positions, and so these positions pay more.

Whether bilingual employees are paid more also depends on the regional job market. In Miami, Florida, so many people speak both English and Spanish that companies don't need to pay extra to attract bilingual employees. On the other hand, in San Francisco, a Charles Schwab & Co. broker who speaks Chinese is paid a higher base salary than other brokers, because this language skill is relatively rare among brokers.

If you are bilingual and want to use your language skills, the Internet will make your job search easier. In addition to checking general-purpose jobs sites, you can check a national database of bilingual job opportunities <http://www.bilingual-jobs.com>. You can search there for jobs by language, by location (including international jobs), by company, and by key word.

Sources: Rich Heinz, "Employers Eager to Buy Lingual Skills," *California Job Journal,* September 2, 2001 <http://www.jobjournal.com/article_printer.asp?artid=333>, accessed March 4, 2003; Timothy Pratt, "Plan to Increase Pay for Bilingual Workers Closer to Fruition," *Las Vegas Sun,* July 26, 2002 <http://www.lasvegassun.com/sunbin/stories/text/2002/jul/26/513768608.html>, accessed March 4, 2003. Peter Fritsch, "Bilingual Employees Are Seeking More Pay, and Many Now Get It," *The Wall Street Journal,* Nov. 13, 1996, pp. A1, A15; Elaine McShulskis, "Bilingual Employees More Valuable," *Human Resources Magazine,* Apr. 1996, p. 16; Jane M. Rifkin, "The Competitive Edge," *Hispanic Times Magazine,* Dec./Jan. 1996, p. 10.

Your Turn 9–2

CAN YOU IMPROVE THIS CONVERSATION?

For each of the following scenarios, make a suggestion that will improve the quality of the conversation.

1. Carl went to his instructor's office to discuss his term project. They sat together and Carl outlined his ideas. As he got more involved in the details of the project, the instructor stood up and began to pace.

_____

_____

_____

2. Kiyoko and Tamara ran into one another in the cafeteria and sat down to eat together. They had just met in their English class the previous week. Tamara chatted on about this and that, never running out of things to say. By the end of the meal, Kiyoko was bored and restless. She had barely gotten a word in.

_____

_____

_____

3. Jessica was a bit upset about work when she ran into a coworker, Carlita. She told Carlita about the problem. Carlita offered some suggestions, but Jessica didn't seem to hear them. She went right on with her own thoughts.

_____

_____

_____

- Don't drop the receiver or put it down hard on a table or desk. The noise it makes is amplified and will disturb the person at the other end of the line.

- When you hang up, gently put the receiver in its cradle.

Using Automated Telephone Systems

When you make a call these days, you are as likely to get a machine as a person on the other end of the line. So it pays to be prepared. If you are making a personal call and an answering machine or voice mail system picks up, you can just leave your name, number, and a brief message. However, if you are making a business or information call,

> **To speak, and to speak well, are two things.**
>
> ben jonson,
>
> 17th-century english dramatist
>
> and poet

be ready to deal with an automated telephone system. Here are some suggestions to help you get the most from these computerized systems:

■ **Have a pencil and paper handy.** You may be given some menu choices depending on the purpose of your call; for example, "For account balances, press 2." Jot down the choices so you can pick the best one.

■ **Have all the information you will need right by the telephone.** If you have to enter information such as an account or personal identification number, have it handy. It's hard to ask a computer to hold on while you go look for something!

If you wind up going around and around an automated system without accomplishing anything, don't give up. Just hold on or try pressing 0. Eventually a human being may answer!

Using a Cell Phone

As more people use cell phones, a whole new set of etiquette issues has arisen. Nearly everyone has had the experience of being interrupted by a cell phone ringing at a movie or religious service or on a bus or train. Beyond the distraction of the phone ringing is the distraction of having to listen to someone's cell phone conversation. Bad cell phone manners are not limited to social events and public places, however. They are also widespread in schools and businesses, where cell phones interrupt classes and business meetings.

Because cell phones are relatively new, people are still working out the social rules that apply to their use. The level of public irritation at cell phone use is so great that policies and legislation are being considered to ban their use in classrooms, theaters, restaurants, and public transportation. Some places have already made it illegal to talk on a cell phone and drive, which is a matter of safety rather than etiquette.

Regardless of the law, it makes sense to use a cell phone without disturbing others. Here are some suggestions.[1]

■ Never take or make a personal call in class or during a business meeting, including interviews. If you are expecting an *emergency* call, set the ringer to vibrate and excuse yourself to answer the phone.

■ Don't use a cell phone in classrooms, lecture halls, elevators, libraries, museums, restaurants, theaters, waiting rooms, places of worship, buses, trains, or other indoor public spaces.

■ Don't talk on the phone while conducting personal business, such as banking.

" The telephone gives us the happiness of being together yet safely apart. "

mason cooley,

american aphorist

- Keep conversations brief.
- Use an earpiece in noisy places so you can hear how loud you sound and modulate your voice.
- Tell callers you are on a cell phone so they are not surprised by being disconnected.
- Don't set your ringer to a loud or annoying tune.

Talking to a Person on the Telephone

Identify Yourself   Because you cannot be seen, the first step of any telephone conversation is to greet the other person and identify yourself. Even if the person you are calling has caller ID, he or she may not recognize your phone number when it is displayed. So, identification is still needed. If you do not do this immediately, the conversation may be confusing to your listener, who is trying to figure out who you are. If you are at home, you can identify yourself by name. If you are at work, you should identify your organization as well as yourself. For example, you might say, "Good morning, this is Sonia McClellan from Bay State Insurance." If you're answering the phone, you might say, "Bay State Insurance, Sonia McClellan speaking." Whatever greeting you use, be sure the other person understands who you are.

Be Courteous and Attentive   Courtesy and attention are the basics of effective telephone conversations. Courtesy conveys your interest in, and respect for, the person with whom you are speaking. And attentiveness is needed to listen effectively and communicate well.

Courtesy can be communicated by the words you speak as well as by your tone of voice. If you are calling to conduct business, be sure you make any requests in a polite way. Keep your voice pleasant and friendly so the listener knows you want to be helpful.

Attentiveness is especially important when you speak on the telephone. It's easy to be distracted by what's going on around you or to work on other tasks, since the other person can't see that your attention has wandered. To communicate your attentiveness, you can't rely on body language as you would in face-to-face communication. Rather, you must use your voice to indicate you are paying attention. Instead of nodding, for example, you can say, "I see" or "yes." If the content of the call is important, take notes. Your notes will help you be sure you have a complete and accurate understanding of what's been communicated.

He has occasional flashes of silence that make his conversation perfectly delightful.

sydney smith, 19th-century english clergyman and writer

WHATEVER IT TAKES
Gary Locke

(AP/Wide World Photos/Louie Balukoff.)

Growing up in the housing projects of Seattle, Washington, Gary Locke didn't learn to speak English until he started kindergarten. At home with his parents, brothers, and sisters, he spoke Chinese. Today, Gary Locke is the first Chinese American governor of a U.S. state. "The family is very proud," he said. "It really is the American dream."

Over a hundred years ago, Locke's grandfather came to the United States and worked as a house boy in Olympia, Washington, before returning to China. Locke's father emigrated to the United States, fought in the U.S. Army during World War II, and settled in Seattle. Gary was the second of five children the Lockes raised in a housing project for veterans. Locke's parents ran a small grocery store that was open 365 days a year. To keep busy, Locke joined the Boy Scouts and became an Eagle Scout at the age of 14.

Locke attributes his rise to governor of Washington to education. "Education is the great equalizer," he said on the night he was elected. Locke paid for college through financial aid, scholarships, and part-time jobs. After college, Locke went to law school and then returned to Washington.

His family hoped he would pursue a career in law or medicine, but Locke entered politics. His family was disappointed but became his biggest supporters when he ran for office as a Washington state legislator. He served 11 years in the state legislature and 3 years as county executive of King County before being elected governor in 1996 and again in 2000. Locke lived in the governor's mansion in Olympia, the capital of Washington, less than a mile from the house where his grandfather worked as a house boy.

Sources: "Our Governor," on the State of Washington Web site <http://www.governor.wa.gov/>, accessed March 6, 2003; Bill Donahue, Don Campbell, and Tina Kelley, "American Tale: Washington Governor Gary Locke Explores His Roots in Jilong, China," *People*, Nov. 24, 1997, pp. 169–170; Timothy Egan, "The 1996 Elections: The States—The Governors; Chinese Roots of Winner Delight the Pacific Rim," *New York Times*, Nov. 7, 1996, p. B8; Rachel Zimmerman, "Chinese Village Swells with Pride as Washington Governor Seeks His Roots on a Pilgrimage," *New York Times*, Oct. 12, 1997, p. A14.

Your Turn 9–3

WHO IS IT?

Lauren Smith has temporarily forgotten her telephone manners. Rewrite the following sentences so they are courteous and informative.

1. (Answering the phone at home) Yeah? . . . Never mind who *this* is, who's calling?

_____

_____

_____

2. (Making a doctor's appointment) I need to see Dr. Dubler for a checkup.

_____

_____

_____

3. (Answering on behalf of her employer, Southwest Distribution) Hello.

_____

_____

_____

SPEAKING TO GROUPS

Many people are perfectly comfortable speaking over the phone or to one person but find speaking to groups very difficult. Yet since so many of our activities are accomplished in groups—social, educational, and business—it's important to learn to speak well in group situations. Most of the time you will find yourself speaking informally as you participate in a group activity. Occasionally, you may be asked to make a formal presentation to a group.

Speaking Informally in a Group

Whether it's a class, club, committee, or meeting of coworkers, the chances are that at least once a day you will find yourself

People who work in teams spend a lot of time speaking informally in a group. *(Courtesy of PhotoDisc.)*

communicating in a group. People who are good at speaking in groups have a great deal of influence over the actions of the group. Good speakers are generally well prepared, assertive, and courteous.

Be Prepared　Preparation is the first prerequisite of effective participation in groups. You cannot speak well unless you know something about the topic under discussion. To prepare for classroom discussions, you should keep up with the assigned readings. To prepare for other types of group discussions, you must keep abreast of the subjects that are likely to come up by paying attention to the news and reading trade or professional publications.

Before some meetings, the person leading the meeting distributes an agenda, a list of topics to be discussed. If you have an agenda, study it before the meeting and learn more about things with which you are unfamiliar. If you don't have an agenda, try to find out before the meeting what subjects are to be covered.

Be Assertive　You may be thoroughly prepared, but unless you speak up you will not contribute to a group's efforts. Speaking up in a group requires assertiveness, the self-belief and determination to make your opinions heard. To be assertive, you must believe that you have something worth saying. You must have confidence in your own ability to contribute to the group.

Being assertive also means you must achieve a balance between your own right to be heard and the rights of others to express themselves. A good communicator speaks up but also yields the floor to someone else who wants to speak. Being assertive does *not* mean that you monopolize the discussion.

Be Courteous　There are often as many opinions as there are people in a group. So it is important, when you express an opinion, to speak tactfully. Even when you think someone else is wrong, you should acknowledge others' right to their opinions before you express your own ideas.

When you speak in a group, respect the rights of others. That means that you must not interrupt, fidget, daydream, or carry on side conversations. You should listen carefully to what others say and express yourself firmly but politely.

Making a Presentation

When you make a presentation, you are the featured speaker and your listeners are your audience. People who are normally relaxed and open when communicating may experience great anxiety when making a presentation. Fearful of making mistakes, they appear rigid and wooden. A person who makes effective presentations, however, has learned to project the same personality on stage as in one-to-one conversations.

It's normal to feel anxious about making presentations. However, you can minimize your anxiety by following several basic suggestions for making a good presentation. You can prepare your presentation in advance, relate to your audience, and be yourself.

Prepare Your Presentation   The most effective speakers are prepared. No matter what the subject or the audience, effective presenters have planned their presentations in advance. They know what information they want to communicate and how they will deliver it. Effective presenters follow these basic steps when preparing presentations.[2]

A good presenter is well prepared, makes the message meaningful for the audience, and communicates some of his or her own personality. *(Courtesy of Comstock Images.)*

- **Think about the audience and the setting.** Is the audience young or old, experienced or inexperienced, male or female? Is the setting formal or informal? The answers to these questions will help you tailor your presentation.

- **Outline your message.** Think about your objective and include only information that supports your objective. Remember, people can't absorb too much information at once, so keep the presentation simple. Three or fewer main points are usually enough.

- **Prepare supporting materials.** You can reinforce the impact of your message by preparing audio or visual material that supports your message. Presentation software packages like Powerpoint make it easy to produce professional-quality supporting materials on a computer.

- **Rehearse.** Run through your presentation a few times. Then find an audience, even if it's only one person. Give your presentation and ask for feedback.

Relate to Your Audience   Presenters who rely primarily on the weight of facts and figures to engage their audiences usually fail. That's because people relate to speakers who relate to them. A good speaker gives a presentation that is relevant and meaningful to the audience, in terms of both its message and how the message is delivered.

Your Turn 9–4

DO YOU SPEAK UP?

Spend a day keeping track of the number of groups you interact with and the number of times, if any, you speak in each group situation. You can record this information in the chart below.

Description of Group	Number of Times You Spoke

Once you've recorded a day's participation in groups, answer the following questions:

1. Did you speak in each group of which you were a part?

_____

_____

If not, why not?

_____

_____

_____

_____

2. Did you find it easier to speak up in some groups than in others?

_____

If yes, why?

_____

_____

_____

_____

If you have considered your audience and setting before you prepare your presentation, the chances are your message will be meaningful to your listeners. For example, suppose you are giving a talk on the latest browser software. Is your audience made up of experienced computer programmers or people who use computers as appliances? Your presentation will be very different to each of these audiences.

Your presentation will also be more effective if you can relate to your audience in the way you deliver your message. Address yourself to the audience. Talk *to* them rather than *at* them. Get them to participate by asking questions, recalling well-known events or people, and having them use their imaginations. If the group is small, the audience can actively participate. If the group is large, you can persuade them as they participate silently.

Be Yourself   Truly effective presenters take these suggestions one step further by communicating something of themselves as individuals. They take off the formal mask and let people see the real person beneath. To be an effective presenter, you must be willing to be open and disclose parts of yourself to the audience.

The Information Highway

GETTING UP TO SPEED

There are many Internet Web sites related to speaking skills. Here are a few to get you started:

- *The Columbia Guide to Standard American English* is a reference work available on Bartleby.com <http://bartleby.com>.
- If you are interested in learning more about American dialects, including Black English, visit the Web site of the American Dialect Society <http://www.americandialect.org>.
- Dave's ESL Café on the Web is a comprehensive site of interest to speakers of English as a second language. Their search engine provides links to ESL resources on the Internet, including speaking skills resources <http://www.eslcafe.com>.
- Toastmasters, a worldwide organization dedicated to improving oral presentation skills, has a Web site with information on speaking to groups <http://www.toastmasters.org>.

In addition, you can search using key words such as *speaking skills, standard English, Ebonics, American English dialects, English as a second language, voice training, bilingualism* (or a specific language), and *oral presentation.*

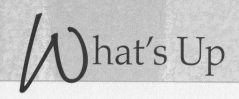
What's Up

Name _____   Date _____

1. On what basis are people's first impressions of you formed?

_____

_____

_____

_____

_____

2. Define the following terms:

Standard English: _____

_____

Dialect: _____

_____

Accented English: _____

_____

Substandard English: _____

_____

3. What does your tone of voice communicate?

_____

_____

_____

_____

4. What is enunciation?

_____

_____

_____

_____

5. What is pronunciation?

_____

_____

_____

_____

continues

Name _____ Date_____

6. What are the essentials of effective conversation?

_____

_____

_____

_____

7. Why it is important to identify yourself at the beginning of a telephone conversation?

_____

_____

_____

_____

_____

8. How can you communicate that you are paying attention when talking on the telephone?

_____

_____

_____

_____

_____

9. Why is it important to be assertive when speaking in groups?

_____

_____

_____

_____

_____

10. List the four basic steps of preparing a presentation.

_____

_____

_____

_____

Case Studies

THE CASE OF THE CLASHING SPEAKERS

Brenda, who lived in Boston, had a part-time job as a telemarketer, selling over the phone to people in New England. She was good at her job, and some evenings she made as much as $15 an hour in commissions. When her firm got a major new client in Georgia, she started calling potential customers in the Southeast. Within a week, her average hourly rate had dropped to $8.

1. What speech qualities may have contributed to Brenda's success in selling to customers in the Northeast?

2. Why might Brenda have trouble selling to Southern customers?

3. How can Brenda improve her ability to sell to Southerners?

THE CASE OF THE INTERRUPTED JOB INTERVIEW

Tyson dressed in his only suit for a job interview with a recruiter from a large consumer goods corporation. A college senior, Tyson was anxious to have a job lined up by the time he graduated. During the interview, the recruiter asked him what he would like to be doing in five years. In the middle of his response, Tyson's cell phone rang. He said, "Excuse me" to the recruiter and took the call.

1. What did Tyson do wrong during his interview?

2. After the interview, Tyson never heard from the company again. What should he do in the future to improve the impression he makes at job interviews?

Journal

Answer the following journal questions.

1. If you could hire a dialect coach, what aspect of your speech would you change or improve? How would this change in speech benefit you?

_____

_____

_____

_____

_____

2. Describe someone you know who is a good conversationalist. What makes this person so skillful?

_____

_____

_____

_____

_____

3. What role does the telephone play in your life? If you use a cell phone, how has it changed your behavior?

_____

_____

_____

_____

_____

4. In polls, fear of making a speech ranks high, along with fear of snakes. If you get very anxious before you have to speak in public, what can you do to reduce the stress you feel? Given what you have learned in the chapter, what strategies might you try in the future?

_____

_____

_____

_____

_____

On the International Space Station, diverse groups of people work together in close quarters for long periods. There's nowhere to go when conflict arises, so astronauts have to learn to resolve their problems and get along. *(©Corbis.)*

Chapter 10

Getting Along with Others

Have you ever watched actors, directors, and other movie people accept an Oscar for their work? Nine times out of 10, Oscar winners thank the people—parents, spouses, friends, or colleagues—who made it possible for them to succeed. People who lead full, successful lives have a tremendous respect for and appreciation of others. They understand that good relationships with the people around them are important to their well-being. People who reach their potential are able to form and maintain good relationships with family, friends, coworkers, customers, and neighbors.

When people start working, they find that it's no longer possible to associate only with people they like. Instead, they are expected to get along with all sorts of people, whether they like them or not. You may be surprised to learn that most people who are dismissed from their jobs are not fired because they can't handle the work. Rather, they are dismissed because they can't get along with colleagues and customers.

In this chapter, you will learn that having positive, effective relationships with the people around you means striking a balance between your needs and their needs. It means committing yourself to ethical values. You will learn what's important to you, what's important to other people, and how you relate to others. You will discover how to give and get feedback from the people around you. And you will learn to handle conflict and anger in a productive way.

BEGIN WITH YOURSELF

What kind of person are you? How do other people see you? Your values, attitudes, beliefs, and emotions are the foundation of your uniqueness. How you act upon these states of mind determines how other people react to you. We have already discussed, in Chapter 1, how certain values and beliefs can contribute to your success in life. Now let's reexamine some beliefs and values—those that are essential for good human relations.

Self-Belief

As you recall, people with good self-belief are convinced of their own worth. They believe in their ability to influence events, and they approach new people and new challenges with self-confidence. When you believe in yourself, it's easy to believe in others. You recognize that other people are as important and unique as you are. The inner confidence of self-belief means that you don't feel threatened by everyone around you.

Trust, Respect, and Empathy

Whether you get along well with people depends on you. A good relationship with another person is built on the values of trust, respect, and empathy.

- **Trust** means that you can rely on someone else, and he or she can rely on you.
- **Respect** means that you value the other person, and he or she values you.
- **Empathy** means you can experience another person's feelings or ideas as if they were your own.

When there is trust, respect, and empathy between two people, there is rapport. Rapport is the essence of good human relations. As you learned in Chapter 7, rapport is achieved through effective communication. Good communication can establish and improve the rapport between two people, and poor communication can just as easily break down rapport. People who value trust, respect, and empathy are careful communicators. They avoid SAD comments—*s*arcastic, *a*ccusing, and *d*emeaning messages that destroy rapport.

Assertiveness

Trust, respect, and empathy show a concern for the feelings and rights of others. Assertiveness shows that you understand the importance of your own feelings and rights as well. Let's suppose, for example, that someone asks you to chair a fund-raising committee for a

Some people are naturally assertive, but others can learn. Assertiveness training workshops teach people how to speak up for themselves and how to achieve a good balance between their own rights and those of others. *(Courtesy of PhotoDisc.)*

neighborhood group. You really don't feel comfortable asking for money, and you have no time to spare. If you are passive, you will agree to chair the committee even though it will be an uncomfortable and inconvenient chore. If you are aggressive, you'll shout that you have too much to do to deal with such nonsense. You'll be standing up for your rights but trampling on the feelings of others. If you are assertive, you will refuse the assignment politely.

Framing an Assertive Communication   How can you be assertive and tell people *no* or disagree with them—and still be polite? You can try framing your response as a three-part communication using these key phrases: (1) I feel . . . , (2) I want . . . , and (3) I will. . . . Here is an example: "*I feel* uncomfortable asking people for money, but *I want* to support your efforts even though I don't have time to spare. *I will* be glad to help on a different committee later in the year." Notice that this response focuses on the speaker's thoughts and feelings but also shows trust, empathy, and respect for the receiver. It gives as much due to the speaker's feelings as to the receiver's needs.

Achieving a Balance between Passivity and Aggression
Achieving a good balance between your own needs and those of others is hard for many people to do. For some people, the problem is not being assertive enough. They feel they are not important enough, or they don't have rights, or their feelings don't matter. The truth is that being passive often leads to resentment and unhappiness. Failing to acknowledge that you have important rights and feelings means you're shortchanging yourself. In these situations, others win, but you lose.

Other people have trouble distinguishing assertive behavior from aggressive behavior. They assert themselves in such a hostile, angry way that they create problems for themselves. Aggressive people tend to alienate those around them. In these situations, everyone loses.

Assertiveness is somewhere between passivity and aggression. It takes thought and practice to be assertive. When you are assertive, you share your feelings in a clear, positive, and courteous way. You are not so polite that people misunderstand your message, and you're not so rude that people feel attacked. In these situations, you win, but others win, too.

Assertiveness is a skill that can be learned. Many companies think it is such an important interpersonal skill that they give employees training in assertiveness techniques.

" Precision of communication is important . . . in our era of hair-trigger balances when a false or misunderstood word may create as much disorder as a sudden thoughtless act. "

james thurber,

american humorist

Your Turn 10–1

THE FINE LINE BETWEEN ASSERTIVENESS AND AGGRESSION

Think for a moment about a situation in which you reacted passively and found yourself doing something you really didn't want to do, or in which you reacted aggressively and found yourself involved in an argument.

1. What was the situation?

_____

_____

2. How did you react?

_____

_____

3. What do you think you could have done to protect your rights and feelings without harming the other person?

_____

_____

_____

4. Reframe your response using the "I feel . . . , I want . . . , I will . . ." model.

_____

_____

_____

CONSIDER YOUR ETHICAL VALUES

Many of the values you hold are shared by society in general, and much behavior that our society views as wrong is also against the law. If people break the law, they are punished. Stealing, for example, is both unethical and illegal.

But people also have beliefs about what is right and what is wrong that are not dealt with by the law. For example, lying is unethical, but it is not usually illegal. If you value honesty, you don't lie, your conscience is clear, and you feel comfortable with yourself.

> *Watch your thoughts;*
>   *they become words.*
> *Watch your words;*
>   *they become actions.*
> *Watch your actions;*
>   *they become habits.*
> *Watch your habits;*
>   *they become character.*
> *Watch your character;*
>   *it becomes your*
>   *destiny.*

frank outlaw

actor

Each of us has a set of ethical values by which we try to live. You may value honesty, trustworthiness, and loyalty, for example. You do your best to behave in a way that reflects these values, and your ethical conduct becomes part of your character.

Schools and employers have expectations about the ethical conduct of students and employees. For example, students are expected to do their own work and not to cheat on exams or to plagiarize reports. In a work situation, employers expect workers to put in an honest day's work in return for their pay. Beyond that basic contract, employers expect employees to behave honestly in the dozens of day-to-day situations that arise in the workplace. Taking merchandise home, stealing supplies, using the telephone for personal or long-distance calls, and using a company computer to surf the Internet are examples of unethical behavior.

The argument that "everyone does it" is no excuse for unethical conduct. Unethical behavior has the effect of diminishing self-belief, because the person behaving this way is compromising his or her values. Beyond its negative effect on self-belief and character, unethical behavior in the workplace usually means that employees are stealing from their employers. If they are caught, they may be fired or even prosecuted under the law.

When it comes to ethical issues, you can behave according to your values fairly easily when the situation involves only yourself. For example, you can easily refrain from taking office supplies home with you. But your sense of what's right may not be the same as your friend's or your boss's. In fact, most people don't give much thought to questions of right and wrong until there is a conflict between their values and other people's values. When an ethical conflict involving others arises, you must decide what to do.

In some situations, you may be able to ignore what you consider wrong behavior on the part of others. For example, if a coworker is making lots of personal phone calls, you may feel it's better to tolerate the situation than to upset it. In other circumstances, you may feel it's necessary for you to act to prevent the unethical behavior or to stop yourself from becoming part of it. An example of this type of situation might be when the behavior has the potential to harm others, such as when an ambulance driver turns off the communication device in order to run an errand and thus doesn't respond in time to an emergency call.

When you have an ethical problem that involves others, think about the situation. Before doing anything, ask yourself what effect your action will have on others and on yourself. It sometimes takes courage to stand up for what you believe is right.

Your Turn 10–2

DO THE RIGHT THING

What would you do in each of the following situations? Explain your response.

1. You've been put in charge of ordering supplies. Your coworker tells you to order some extra supplies for yourself, because everybody helps themselves to what they need for home use.

   _____
   _____
   _____
   _____
   _____
   _____
   _____

2. You're about to take the written part of a licensing exam that you need to pass to be employed in your field. Although you've studied quite a bit, you're so anxious to pass that you're considering cheating if the opportunity arises.

   _____
   _____
   _____
   _____
   _____
   _____
   _____

3. You process invoices from suppliers of services to your employer. You've noticed that invoices billed to a particular production supervisor are consistently higher than those billed to other supervisors. One day you overhear the production supervisor telling a supplier to overcharge the company by $1,000 so that each of them can pocket $500.

   _____
   _____
   _____
   _____
   _____
   _____
   _____
   _____

REACH OUT TO OTHERS

Do you like to be treated with courtesy and respect? Of course you do. And so does everyone else. The key to getting along with other people is to treat them with the same courtesy and respect with which you would like to be treated. Of course, doing this is not always easy. For example, people often have difficulty communicating with people of other races or ethnic backgrounds. The meanings people attach to the use of language, facial expressions, and gestures differ from culture to culture, and misunderstandings may be frequent (see Chapter 7). To overcome cultural barriers, it's important to be open to different ways of life and to communicate carefully. Don't assume you have been understood completely, and don't assume you have understood the other person completely, either.

While acknowledging that each person is different, keep in mind that people have many things in common. There are basic hopes, fears, and emotions that we all experience. Understanding these human feelings and empathizing with others form the basis for good relationships with people.

What Do People Need?

The quality of empathy is the basis for good human relations skills. Being able to imagine what another person feels, thinks, and needs means that you are able to interact with him or her in an intelligent and caring way. And when people sense that you are attuned to their needs, they react positively to you.

In the course of a day, you may encounter many people, all of them unique, with whom you must interact in a positive way. How can you make sense of the bewildering variety of emotions, thoughts, feelings, and needs of each person you meet? You may find it helpful to think of people's needs in terms of a hierarchy, as shown in Figure 10–1. Abraham Maslow, a psychologist, proposed that people are motivated by different levels of needs depending on their circumstances. Homeless people, for example, have basic survival needs: They must find food or starve. Once hunger is satisfied, they can attend to their personal safety. If security needs are satisfied, people can think about meeting the need for love and relationships with others. Once feeling secure in their ties to others, people can focus on meeting their needs for achievement, competence, and self-respect.

For most people, their family provides the shelter, food, security, and love they need. *(Courtesy of Getty Images, Inc.)*

FIGURE 10–1

Maslow's hierarchy of needs provides a way to think about human needs. In general, people try to satisfy lower-level needs before higher-level needs.

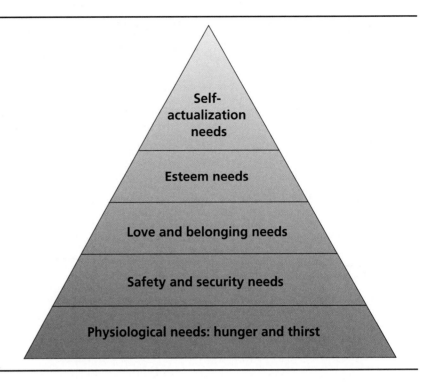

When people feel healthy, safe, loved, and competent, they can pursue the highest level of needs—what Maslow called self-actualization (and what we have been calling "reaching your potential"). Self-actualization is reached when people are fulfilled in every aspect of their being. Not many of us experience complete and lasting self-actualization. Occasionally, we may have peak experiences in which we feel moments of perfect happiness or fulfillment. These feelings might come from creating a work of art, falling in love, running a race, or having a baby. Unfortunately, the peak experiences do not last long.

Maslow did not view his hierarchy of needs as rigid. In other words, people do not always focus on their needs in sequential order. They sometimes focus on higher-level needs even when lower-level needs remain only partly fulfilled. Parents, for example, may neglect their own needs to give loved children something extra, or good Samaritans may neglect their need for personal safety to come to the aid of someone in trouble. Even though people may not always attend to their needs in hierarchial order, Maslow's model is helpful when you're trying to figure out a person's motivations. It's also helpful to use the model when you are setting goals (see Chapter 2).

How Do You Relate to Others?

Another way of thinking about human relations is to focus on the dynamics of the relationship itself, rather than on your needs or the needs of the other person. When you first meet someone, you tend to be cautious and guarded about revealing yourself. As you reveal more

Your Turn 10–3

UNDERSTANDING THE NEEDS OF OTHERS

1. According to Maslow's hierarchy of needs, which need would be your focus in the following situations?

a. You want to get an A on your term project.

_____

b. You've moved to a new town or neighborhood and have no friends in the area.

_____

c. You're hiking in the mountains and get lost for three days.

_____

d. You're walking home alone one night, and someone tries to mug you.

_____

e. You have just thought of a wonderful idea for starting your own business.

_____

2. Where would you place yourself on Maslow's hierarchy? Which level of needs are you trying to satisfy most? List three ways you try to satisfy this need.

_____

_____

_____

_____

about yourself to the other person, trust and empathy develop. The other person also lets her or his guard down and reveals more to you. Gradually, the relationship deepens and becomes more intimate. The quality of a relationship depends on the degree of mutual trust and openness.

The Johari Window   One way of diagramming the effect of mutual understanding and knowledge on a relationship is to use the Johari window (see Figure 10–2, page 230).[1] The Johari window is named after its inventors, Joseph Luft and Harry Ingham. It is a square with four sections, each section representing information known or unknown to yourself and to others.

FIGURE 10–2

The Johari window is a way of diagramming the amount of shared and unshared knowledge in a relationship. The more shared knowledge there is between people (Box 1), the more openness and trust in the relationship.

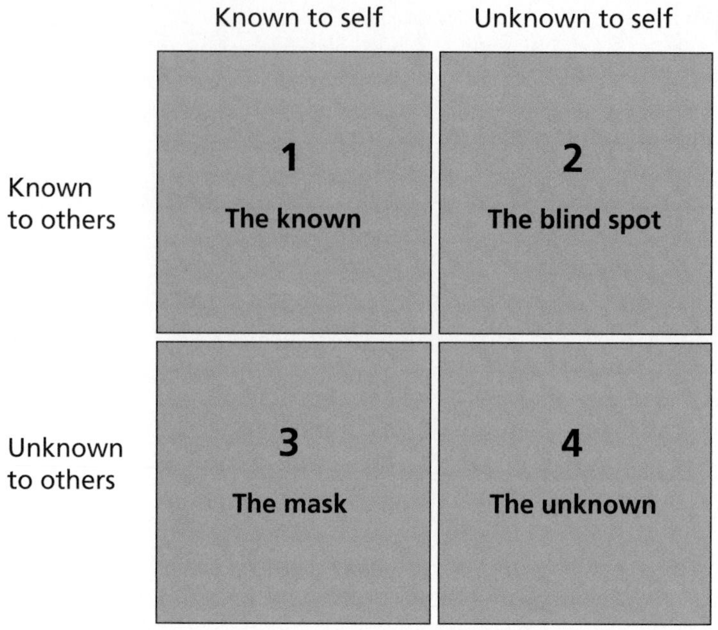

	Known to self	Unknown to self
Known to others	1 The known	2 The blind spot
Unknown to others	3 The mask	4 The unknown

The Known.   The first section of the Johari window represents the part of the relationship characterized by openness, shared information, and mutual understanding. In this section are matters known to yourself and to the other person as well. The more intimate and productive the relationship, the larger this section grows. If you sketched a Johari window representing your relationship with a close friend, this section would be large. It might be small, however, if you sketched your relationship with an instructor or manager. If you are shy, this section might be small in most of your relationships.

The Blind Spot.   The second section of the Johari window consists of feelings, behaviors, and information that is known to the other person but not to you. This section is sometimes called the blind spot. The unknown matters may include your annoying mannerisms (of which you are unaware) or the other person's hidden motivations. Whatever is unknown to you in the relationship is a handicap. Therefore, the larger this section, the less effective you are in the relationship.

The Mask.   The third section of the Johari window also limits your effectiveness in a relationship, but in a different way. It is everything that you know but the other person doesn't. This information, unknown to the other person, provides you with a protective mask. At first glance, it might seem that the more you know that the other person doesn't, the better off you are. If power is your object, this may be true. But if the mask becomes so large that it crowds out openness (the first section of the Johari window), the relationship suffers from a lack of trust and rapport. So, for example, if you are asked to show a coworker how to do something, and you withhold critical information, the coworker may fail and you may look competent. But in the long run, you have set the tone for a relationship in which there is little trust or cooperation.

The Unknown. The fourth section of the Johari window consists of matters that are unknown to both people. These matters include information about the context of the relationship, each person's psychological makeup, personality traits, creative potential, and so on. As a relationship develops, the size of this section of the Johari window may decrease.

Using the Johari Window to Improve Relationships As you may have realized, the four sections of the Johari window are not fixed in size. As a relationship develops and changes, the internal vertical and horizontal lines, which separate the known from the unknown, can move. In other words, you can take actions that will increase the size of the first section, the known, to make a more effective relationship. By being open, trusting, and sharing information, you can decrease the size of your mask (section 3). Doing this is not always easy, especially for shy people. It involves expressing your feelings and knowledge in a way that exposes you to possible harm. As anyone who has ever asked another person for a first date can attest, disclosing your feelings and needs may be hard. Yet if you want to get to know another person, self-disclosure is necessary, and its rewards may be great.

You can also increase the size of the first section, the known, by decreasing your blind spot. One way to do this is through honest introspection. That is, you must examine your feelings and behavior to understand your needs and motivations. Another way to decrease your blind spot is to ask another person for feedback. What information does the other person have that will help you in the relationship? Using feedback to decrease your blind spot requires the cooperation of the other person. And the amount of cooperation you get will depend in part on your own willingness to be open and to share. You can see that you can exercise a lot of control over the quality of your relationships.

FEEDBACK IN RELATIONSHIPS

Giving and getting feedback makes relationships grow and develop. Whether the growth is healthy or stunted depends in large part on our ability to give feedback in a nonthreatening way and to receive feedback without being crushed by it. Of course, some feedback is positive. Praise and affirmation are good to give and to receive, and most of us thrive on it. Dealing with negative feedback is much more difficult.

DIAGRAM TWO RELATIONSHIPS

Use the Johari windows below to diagram two relationships. Use the first window to model a relationship with a spouse, lover, or friend. Use the second window to model a relationship with a fellow student, coworker, or acquaintance.

	Known to self	Unknown to self
Known to others	**1** **The known**	**2** **The blind spot**
Unknown to others	**3** **The mask**	**4** **The unknown**

	Known to self	Unknown to self
Known to others	**1** **The known**	**2** **The blind spot**
Unknown to others	**3** **The mask**	**4** **The unknown**

Giving Feedback

Why is giving feedback a necessary part of every relationship? Feedback is part of a communication loop that helps create the knowledge, openness, and mutual trust necessary for effective relationships. As we saw from the Johari window, the larger the area of mutual knowledge, the more effective the relationship. Giving feedback is one way to increase what is known about a relationship.

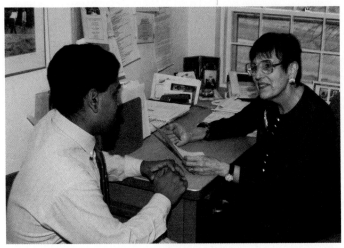

Most companies have regular performance appraisals to ensure that their managers give employees feedback about their work. *(Courtesy of Tom Stock.)*

However, it takes skill to give negative feedback in a way that helps the other person. The person who is being helped must feel respected and valued, not demeaned. If those being helped are made to feel defensive, they will not be receptive to feedback. So it's important when giving feedback to be calm, concerned, and encouraging. You must accept the other person without judging him or her, and direct the criticism at behaviors, not at personality. For example, if a parent criticizes children's behavior by telling them they are bad, the children feel demeaned and worthless. If, on the other hand, the parent gives specific feedback about behavior—such as it's rude to interrupt—the children's self-esteem is intact and they have some idea how to behave in the future.

When you give feedback in a relationship, keep these things in mind:

- Understand your own feelings and motivations.
- Be accepting and nonjudgmental about the other person.
- Be sensitive to the other person's resistance. Pressure doesn't work in the long run.
- Criticize specific behavior, not personality.
- Give feedback only on matters that the other person can change. If something can't be changed, there's little value in discussing it.
- Don't tell others what to do.

Receiving Feedback

Even harder than giving productive criticism is being on the receiving end of negative feedback. Even though on one level we know we are not perfect, still, no one likes to be told he or she is in some way inadequate. In fact, our first reaction to criticism is often defensive. Rather than being open to the criticism, we react by protecting our self-belief.

WHO DO YOU THINK YOU ARE? IT DEPENDS . . .

Your cultural background influences every aspect of your life. Some of these influences are very apparent—for example, the holidays you celebrate. But other influences are harder to see because they involve the way you think about yourself and relate to others. One example of culture influencing the way people think and behave is the idea of the self.

Some cultures define the self primarily as an individual. In these cultures, the individual is thought of as being an independent entity. The individual is emotionally separate from groups, including family groups. Individual-centered cultures place a high value on self-reliance and competitiveness. Does this sound familiar? It should, because mainstream culture in the United States is individual-centered.

Other cultures define the self in relation to a group. In these cultures, the individual's core identity is closely embedded in that of the group. These cultures place a high value on solidarity, concern for others, and cooperation. Group-centered cultures include those of Japan and other East Asian nations, as well as Mexico and other Latin American countries.

You can see that the way you think of yourself influences how you relate to others. Keep these ideas of the self in mind when you are thinking about your relationship with others, especially those whose view of the self may differ from yours.

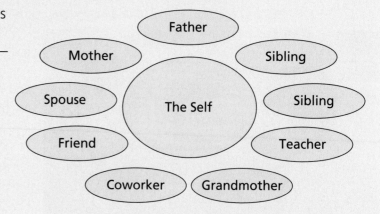

The Self in an Individual-Centered Culture

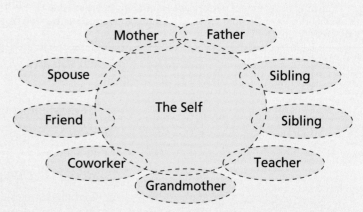

People from an individual-centered culture like that of the United States see themselves as independent, with clear boundaries between themselves and others. People from a group-centered culture like those of Japan or China see themselves as interdependent with others.

(Adapted from Hazel R. Markus and Shinobu Kitayama, "Culture and the Self," *Psychological Review,* Vol. 98, No. 2, 1991, p. 226.)

Sources: Bruce Bower, "Western Notions of the Mind May Not Translate to Other Cultures," *Science News,* Vol. 152, Issue 16, Oct. 18, 1997, p. 248ff.; Gina M. Shkodriani and Judith L. Gibbons, "Individualism and Collectivism among University Students in Mexico and the United States," *Journal of Social Psychology,* Vol. 135, Issue 6, Dec. 1995, p. 765ff.

Protecting Your Self-Belief   Our self-belief is so important to our well-being that people have evolved many ways to defend it. These processes, which reduce anxiety and protect our self-belief, are called **defense mechanisms**. Some common defense mechanisms are withdrawal, rationalization, substitution, fantasy, and projection. The defense mechanisms are not unhealthy unless they come to dominate our interactions with others.

1. **Withdrawal.** People who feel threatened sometimes deal with their anxiety by trying to avoid the situation that caused the stress. Trying to escape from negative feedback is called **withdrawal**. People who have difficulty with the give and take of close relationships often withdraw. Separation, divorce, quitting a job—all may be examples of withdrawal.

2. **Rationalization.** Another way to defend your self-belief is to **rationalize**, that is, to explain or excuse an unacceptable situation in terms that make it acceptable to yourself. Rationalizing involves distorting the truth to make it more acceptable. For example, if you are criticized for forgetting an important customer at work, you may rationalize that it was your boss's responsibility to remind you, whereas in truth it was your responsibility.

3. **Displacement.** **Displacement** is a defense mechanism in which you react to a negative situation by substituting another person for the person who aroused your anxiety or anger. For example, if your instructor criticizes you in front of the class, you may go home and yell at your sister. In general, the person you choose as the substitute is less likely to harm your self-belief.

4. **Fantasy.** **Fantasy** is a form of withdrawal in which daydreams provide a boost to self-belief when reality threatens. For example, if you've been told that you'll be off the team unless your grades improve, you may fantasize about being indispensable to your team and leading it to victory. Everyone fantasizes to a degree; fantasy becomes a problem only when it is a substitute for reality.

5. **Projection.** **Projection** is a defense mechanism in which you attribute your own unacceptable behaviors and feelings to another person. If you are criticized for treating a coworker discourteously, for example, you may project that the coworker was being rude to *you*.

Handling Feedback Positively   All the defense mechanisms can help us maintain our self-belief. But at what cost? People who are always on the defensive find it hard to change and grow. Their relationships with others are characterized by a lack of openness and trust. On the other hand, people who can handle negative feedback constructively have an opportunity to develop and grow. Their relationships with others become more, not less, effective.

Your Turn 10–5

DEFENDING YOURSELF

1. Identify which defense mechanism is being used in each situation.

   a. A person having difficulty in school drops out.

   _____

   b. A person criticized for poor judgment goes home and picks a fight with her husband.

   _____

   c. A person who is told he needs training decides that his manager doesn't know what he's doing.

   _____

2. Most people consistently use one or two defense mechanisms when they feel threatened. Which defense mechanism(s) do you use? Give an example of a situation in which you reacted defensively.

   _____

   _____

   _____

   _____

How can you handle negative feedback in a positive way? Learning to accept feedback means paying less attention to how criticism makes you feel and more attention to what's actually being said. If you remember that criticism is information that can help you, you will be able to deal with it more effectively. Try these tips for handling negative feedback:

- Consider who is criticizing you. Is the person in a position to know what he or she is talking about? If not, the criticism may not be valid. If so, it's worth listening to.

- Is the person criticizing you upset about something else? If so, he or she may just be blowing off steam. If he or she is calm, though, you should pay more attention.

- Ask for specific information. Many people who offer criticism do so in the most general terms, which is not helpful.

- Think about what you've heard. Give yourself time to react.

- Decide whether the criticism is appropriate. If it is, think about what you will do to change your behavior.

> *Anybody can become angry—that is easy; but to be angry with the right person, and to the right degree, and at the right time, and for the right purpose, and in the right way—that is not within everybody's power and is not easy.*
>
> *aristotle, ancient greek philosopher*

Conflict is part of everyday life. People who can control their anger have a better chance to resolve their conflicts than people who lose control. *(Courtesy of PhotoDisc.)*

CONFLICT

Throw any two people together for any length of time and they are sure to disagree about something. The conflict may be over what time they go to the movies or whether war can be morally justified. If they cannot settle the disagreement, they may become frustrated and angry. This scenario is so common that you may think conflict is always a negative experience. Yet if handled properly, conflict can have healthy and productive results.

What Causes Conflict?

Differences over facts, ideas, goals, needs, attitudes, beliefs, and personalities all cause conflict. Some conflicts are simple and easy to resolve. A difference of opinion about a fact, for example, usually does not escalate into an emotional battle. If you and a friend disagree about who holds the world's record for the 100-meter dash, you can easily resolve the conflict by checking a sports almanac.

But conflicts about personalities, values, needs, beliefs, and ideas can be more serious. Such conflicts often cause frustration and anger. The issues are more fundamental, and they can have an emotional component that makes disagreement threatening. Unless the anger is dealt with properly, the conflict is not resolved.

In addition, when people feel that the outcome of a conflict is a reflection of their self-belief, conflict can be damaging. For example, Brian and Ann disagreed in a meeting about how to market a new product, and Ann's plan was adopted. Instead of thinking that his plan had been rejected, Brian felt that his self-belief had been attacked. Such a conflict is not easily resolved.

Anger

Anger, the result of unresolved conflict, is a powerful emotion. Think about the last time you got angry. What did you do? Did you tell the other person why you were angry? Did you snap at them about something else? Or did you keep your feelings to yourself? People express anger in different ways.

Expressing Anger Directly   People often express their anger directly. If someone annoys you, you tell them so, or you glare at them, or you shove them, or you tailgate them on the road. Obviously, the direct expression of anger can run the gamut from assertiveness to aggression to violence. How people express anger directly depends on their personalities and the extent to which they are provoked. People with negative self-belief often have an underlying attitude of hostility that is easily triggered by even minor events. Others, more secure in their self-belief, can express anger more calmly without being aggressive. (See the discussion of assertiveness on page 222.)

Expressing Anger Indirectly   Another way to express anger is indirect. Instead of confronting the person with whom you are angry, you direct your anger at a third party, who is less threatening. Since this process is similar to the defense mechanism of displacement, it is often called displacement.

In many situations it is inappropriate to express anger at the person with whom you are angry. Suppose you've just started your own business and one of your clients keeps changing his mind about what he wants you to do. You are angry, because he's wasting your time. Yet expressing anger directly will cause you to lose a customer. In this case your anger may find an outlet when you snap at your child or a friend. This is certainly unfair to the person at the receiving end of your wrath!

Internalizing Anger   The third way to deal with anger is to keep it bottled up inside you. Many people consider the expression of anger to be threatening, bad, or rude, and so they internalize it. Unfortunately, the result of internalizing anger is that you feel a growing resentment. Since your anger is not expressed, there is no way for the conflict to be resolved, and it festers. Internalized anger can cause stress and harm your emotional and physical health.

Controlling Anger   You can minimize the destructiveness of anger by trying to control it. There are several approaches that you can take.

- Don't say or do anything immediately. It's usually best to cool off and give yourself a chance to think. Counting to 10 may help.
- Figure out why you are angry. Sometimes the cause of the anger is something you can easily change or avoid.
- Channel your anger into physical exercise. Even a walk can relieve the tensions of anger.
- Use relaxation techniques such as deep breathing to calm yourself.
- Find a friend who will listen and offer constructive suggestions.

Resolving Conflicts

Once your anger is under control, you can try to resolve the conflict that caused it. The energy created by your anger can be channeled into solving the problem. Here are a few suggestions.

- Commit yourself to resolving the problem that caused the conflict. Don't just decide to keep the peace.
- Ask yourself what you hope to achieve by resolving the conflict. Is it critical to get your way, or is your relationship with the other person more important? Your priorities will influence how you settle the conflict.

Your Turn 10–6

TAKE AN ANGER INVENTORY

Some people get angry easily, and others remain calm. Where are you in this spectrum? Raymond W. Novaco of the University of California devised an anger inventory upon which the following questionnaire is based.

For each item, indicate whether you would be very angry, somewhat angry, or not angry by circling the numbers 1, 2, or 3.

	Very Angry	Somewhat Angry	Not Angry
1. Your coworker makes a mistake and blames it on you.	1	2	3
2. You are talking to a friend, and she doesn't answer.	1	2	3
3. You lose a game.	1	2	3
4. An acquaintance always brags about himself.	1	2	3
5. Your boss tells you your work is poor.	1	2	3
6. You are driving on a highway and someone cuts in front of you.	1	2	3
7. At a store, a salesperson keeps following you and offering help.	1	2	3
8. A car drives through a puddle and splashes you.	1	2	3
9. Someone turns off the TV while you are watching a program.	1	2	3
10. You are studying and someone is tapping his fingers.	1	2	3

Add the numbers you circled in each column. Then add the subtotals to get your grant total.

_____ + _____ + _____

Grand Total _____

If your score was:

10–15 You get angry quickly.

16–20 You get angry fairly easily.

21–25 You have a moderate level of anger.

26–30 You are slow to get angry.

WHATEVER IT TAKES
Colin Powell

(AP/Wide World Photos/J. Scott Applewhite.)

Colin Powell's story is an American classic. The son of immigrants from Jamaica, Powell grew up in the South Bronx. He attended New York City public schools. Even though Powell was not an enthusiastic student, his parents made him do his homework every day and do his best. As a result, says Powell, "I got a pretty good education."

Colin Powell was an average student in college, too. Indeed, what interested him most was the ROTC military program he joined at the City College of New York. "The discipline, the structure, the camaraderie, the sense of belonging were what I craved," said Powell. After graduation with a degree in geology, Powell joined the army.

Powell's career as a soldier spanned 35 years. He began as a junior lieutenant and retired as a four-star general. During his years with the army, he had many jobs ranging from battalion commander in Korea to chairman of the Joint Chiefs of Staff, the highest-ranking position in the armed services. Powell was the first African American and the youngest man ever to be appointed to that position, which he held during the Persian Gulf War in the early 1990s.

After his retirement from the military, Powell twice had the opportunity to run for president. Both times he declined, indicating that he didn't have the necessary passion to be a politician. In 2001, President George W. Bush appointed Powell secretary of state, the first African American to hold this position. As secretary of state, Powell's job is to accomplish U.S. foreign policy goals through diplomacy.

With so much experience of war, Powell understands how terrible violence is. "Soldiers know what it's like to be scared in battle—that's why soldiers hate war and try to avoid violence," Powell said in an interview with students. "Always try to avoid violence, to avoid fighting. Try to solve problems by respecting each other and by talking to each other."

Sources: "Biography: Colin L. Powell, Secretary of State," U.S. Department of State, <http://www.state.gov/r/pa/ei/biog/1349.htm>; "Colin L. Powell," Thomson-Gale, <http://www.galegroup.com/free_resources/bhm/bio/powell_c.htm>; "General Colin Powell: Symbol of Integrity Walks Moderate Path," ABC news, <http://abcnews.go.com/sections/politics/DailyNews/profile_powell.html>; "Meet General Colin L. Powell: Interview Transcript," Scholastic, <http://teacher/scholastic.com/barrier/powellchat/transcript.htm>; all accessed March 13, 2003.

- Make sure you and the other person have the same understanding of the reason for conflict. Ask questions and really listen. You may be surprised: Some conflicts are the result of misunderstanding.

- Be assertive, not aggressive. Remember that the other person has rights and feelings, too.

- Try to keep to the facts. When discussing the issue, make sure you understand the difference between facts and feelings. The more you can keep feelings out of it, the better your chance for resolving the conflict.

At first, you may find it difficult to control your anger and to approach conflicts in a more thoughtful, rational way. With practice, you will become more comfortable in dealing with conflict. You may find that effectively resolving conflict is a way to learn more about yourself and to grow, as well as to improve the quality of your relationships with the people around you.

The Information Highway

GETTING UP TO SPEED

Some Web sites related to the topics covered in this chapter include the following.

- You can take an inventory to see how assertive you are at a site that focuses on women's health issues (men can take the inventory, too <http://www.queendom.com>).

- Ethics Web maintains a site that provides links to ethics resources on the Internet, including links to business ethics <http://www.ethicsweb.ca>.

- You can find tips on how to deal with aggression on the road, known as road rage, from "Dr. Driving" <http://www.drdriving.org>.

- If you are interested in different approaches to conflict resolution, check the Web site of the Association for Conflict Resolution <http://www.acresolution.org>.

In addition, you will find thousands of possible sites by using a search engine and entering the key words *assertiveness, aggression, road rage, ethics, interpersonal relationships,* and *conflict resolution.*

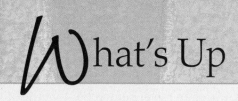
What's Up

Name _____ Date _____

1. Why are most people fired from their jobs?
_____
_____
_____
_____
_____

2. How do trust, respect, and empathy affect good human relations?
_____
_____
_____
_____
_____

3. What is the difference between aggressiveness and assertiveness?
_____
_____
_____
_____

4. Describe the different levels of needs in Maslow's hierarchy.
_____
_____
_____
_____
_____
_____

5. What is self-actualization?
_____
_____
_____
_____
_____

continues

Name _____   Date_____

6. What does the Johari window show? How can it be used?

_____

_____

_____

_____

_____

7. Why is it important to give specific, behavior-related feedback?

_____

_____

_____

_____

_____

8. What is the purpose of a defense mechanism?

_____

_____

_____

_____

_____

9. What causes conflict between two people?

_____

_____

_____

_____

_____

10. Why should you try to control your anger before resolving a conflict with someone else?

_____

_____

_____

_____

_____

Case Studies

THE CASE OF THE WORRIED MAN

Paul works as a technician for an electronics firm that has just been acquired by a large multinational corporation. Before the takeover, Paul had been working hard to show he was ready to be promoted to supervisor. Since the takeover, however, there have been rumors that the plant will be downsized or closed. Paul has lost interest in the promotion. He just worries about whether he'll have a job tomorrow.

1. Before the takeover, what needs were uppermost in Paul's mind?

_____

_____

2. After the takeover, Paul's needs changed. What was his new need?

_____

_____

3. According to Maslow, why did Paul's needs change?

_____

_____

THE CASE OF THE "SICK" EMPLOYEE

Julie was hired to help Mary run her small housewares shop by doing record keeping and accounting. On the last day of each month, Julie had to balance the accounts, pay vendors, and send statements to customers with account balances. She wasn't very good at this task, and she made quite a few mistakes the first two months. Mary criticized her sharply about the errors. On the last day of the third month, Julie called in sick.

Mary was annoyed, because in addition to helping customers she had to do the end-of-month accounting. Mary became really angry when Julie called in sick on the last day of the fourth month as well. But she said nothing, and the next day it was business as usual.

1. Why is Julie calling in sick on the last day of each month?

_____

_____

2. Describe the conflict between Julie and Mary.

_____

_____

3. How did Mary deal with her anger?

_____

_____

4. How might Mary and Julie resolve this problem?

_____

_____

Journal

Answer the following journal questions.

1. How good are you at getting along with others? What aspects of your relationships with others would you like to improve?

_____

_____

_____

_____

_____

2. Explain your code of ethics. What ethical values are most important to you? Least important? Why?

_____

_____

_____

_____

_____

3. Describe the most successful relationship in your life. What makes this relationship work? How can you improve it?

_____

_____

_____

_____

_____

4. Describe a conflict you've recently experienced. How was the conflict resolved? In your view, was the resolution successful? Explain.

_____

_____

_____

_____

_____

One of the purposes of basic training is to forge
group bonds. As soldiers gain more experience,
some will demonstrate leadership skills
and be promoted up the ranks.
(©Kevin Fleming/Corbis.)

Chapter 11

Functioning in Groups

From the time you were born into a family until this moment, when you are reading these words for a class, you have belonged to hundreds of groups. Psychologists define a group as the conscious interaction of two or more people. This means that the members of a group must be aware of one another. So, for example, people shopping at JC Penney are not a group unless an incident takes place that makes them pay attention to one another. If a security guard starts chasing a shoplifter and people stop to watch, they become members of a group.

The group at JC Penney lasts just a few minutes and breaks up. Other groups, such as the U.S. Senate or the Dave Matthews Band, last for years. And some groups, like the one in the department store, are informal. Informal groups are loose associations of people without stated rules. Passengers on a bus, a group of friends, or people at a party are all part of informal groups. Other groups are formal; that is, they have clear goals and established rules. Political parties, businesses, schools, labor unions, orchestras, baseball teams, and other such associations are all formal groups.

In this chapter, you will learn that all groups, whether formal or informal, have goals, roles for members to play, and standards of behavior. You will discover that different groups have different patterns of communication. You will learn how people behave as members of groups and as leaders of groups. Understanding how groups work will help you be an effective group member or leader—vital skills in all areas of life.

GROUP DYNAMICS

Group dynamics is the study of how people interact in groups. All groups have goals they try to achieve; roles for members to play; norms, or standards of behavior; communication patterns; and a degree of cohesiveness.

Goals

All groups have goals, whether they are explicitly stated or taken for granted, short-term or long-term. People at a party, for example, are there to have a good time. A business's goal may be to make a profit by serving a particular market. A hockey team's goal is to win as many games as possible.

In groups, the goals can be cooperative or competitive. When the goals are cooperative, people in the group work together to achieve an objective. A group putting on a play, for example, has a cooperative goal. When group goals are competitive, people in the group work against one another to achieve their objectives. Four people playing Monopoly have competitive goals; only one can win the game.

The swimmers on this team have a cooperative goal: to beat the opposing swim team. But they also have a competitive goal: Each swimmer wants to have the best time in the freestyle event, beating her teammates as well. *(Courtesy of PhotoDisc.)*

Of course, in real life things are seldom so clear-cut. In most groups, there are both cooperative and competitive goals at the same time. Take the example of a theater group: Clearly, the cooperative goal is to have the play ready to perform on opening night. Yet the actors in the group may have competitive goals. Each may be trying to win the most applause or the best reviews.

Most of the groups you will encounter, both at school and at work, will have both cooperative and competitive goals. Today, for example, many businesses organize their workers into project teams. Members of the team cooperate with one another to achieve the goals of the team. At the same time they compete with other teams in the organization. They may even compete with each other. Consider a corporation that creates teams of workers to develop new products. People on the widget team cooperate with one another to design, produce, and market the best and most profitable widget. At the same time, they compete with people on the gadget team, who are trying to design, produce, and market the best and most profitable gadget. The widget people are also competing among themselves for recognition, promotion, raises, and power.

Studies have shown that groups with cooperative goals have better communication and are more productive. In groups with competitive goals, members tend to spend too much energy on rivalry. However, competitive goals can be positive forces. They can create a feeling of challenge and excitement that motivates people to do their best.

Roles and Norms

If you pitch for your baseball team, you are expected to stand on the pitcher's mound, try to strike out the opposing batter, catch any fly balls that come your way, and so on. On the team, your role is pitcher, and your norms are the rules of baseball. In a group, a **role** is a set of expected behaviors for a particular position. **Norms** are the rules by which people in particular roles are expected to behave.

Norms cover almost all aspects of our interactions with other people, although they vary from one culture to another. For example, when in public, women in many Muslim countries are expected to wear a chador, a cloth that covers the head and veils the face. In the United States, in contrast, most women cover their heads only when it is cold. Norms change gradually over time and through the influence of one culture on another. For example, 50 years ago blue jeans were considered appropriate wear for people who did manual labor or farm work. Today blue jeans are acceptable on a wide range of people in all but the most formal or conservative settings.

There are many roles that have a substantial number of norms associated with them. Mother, father, wife, husband, child, friend, boss, employee, teacher, and student are common roles with dozens of norms. Employees, for example, are expected to be punctual, conscientious, hardworking, and loyal. Friends are expected to be supportive and loyal. The norms for these roles are deeply ingrained in our society, and they help make it function smoothly.

In many formal groups, explicit roles are assigned to members. In a committee a chairperson leads and a secretary records the minutes. In a band, there may be a singer, guitarist, keyboard player, and drummer. In a large business, there are salespeople, marketing staff, research and development staff, engineers, manufacturing workers, and administrative support workers (see Figure 11–1).

In many companies, an employee plays a role in different work teams, not just in his or her department. For example, an engineer

Your Turn 11–1

YOUR CLASS AS A GROUP

Think about the class for which you are reading this book. Then answer the following questions.

1. What are the cooperative goals of the class, if any?

_____

_____

2. What are the competitive goals of the class, if any?

_____

_____

3. What class roles can you identify? What role do you play?

_____

_____

4. What norms do you associate with each role you identify?

_____

_____

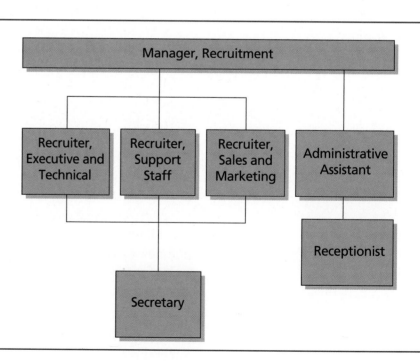

FIGURE 11–1

An organization chart shows the roles people play in an organization. Here a small part of a corporation's human resources department is shown.

Manager, Recruitment

Recruiter, Executive and Technical

Recruiter, Support Staff

Recruiter, Sales and Marketing

Administrative Assistant

Receptionist

Secretary

One person can have many roles in life. This man is a husband, father, athlete, and worker. *(Courtesy of Tom Stock.)*

may be on the staff of the engineering department. But she may also be on several work teams with people from other departments of the company. The engineer may represent her department on several project work teams with different designers, manufacturing supervisors, and marketing managers. Not only does she need technical engineering skills but also she needs people skills to work well with others on her teams.

Communication

As you participate in groups, observe the communication patterns. Does one person dominate, telling everyone else what to do? Do two

FIGURE 11–2

There are three basic communication patterns in groups: In the *chain pattern*, a message is passed from one person to the next. In the *wheel pattern*, the person at the hub communicates with each person on the spokes, but the people on the spokes don't communicate with each other. In the *all-channel pattern*, all members communicate with each other.

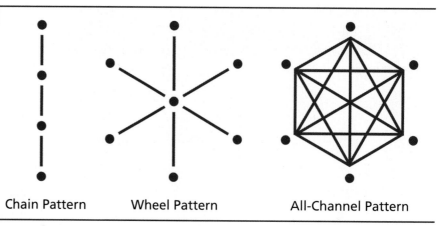

Chain Pattern   Wheel Pattern   All-Channel Pattern

or three people talk among themselves while the rest observe? Is communication like a chain, with messages passed from one person to another? Or do all members communicate with all other members?

Communication patterns can tell you a great deal about groups. In formal groups, communication patterns may be rigid. For example, in the armed services, the communication pattern looks like a chain (see Figure 11–2). Messages are passed down the chain from the higher ranks to the lower ranks and occasionally in the other direction. Skipping a link of the chain is a serious breach of group norms in the armed services.

Another example of a formal communication pattern is called the wheel. One person at the hub communicates with each group member on the spokes, but the members do not communicate with each other. An example of this is a dispatcher directing the activity of a group of electronics service technicians, or an office manager supervising a group of clerks.

In smaller, less formal groups, such as a project team, social group, or small business, members communicate more freely with one another in the all-channel pattern. In theory, each group member communicates with every other group member, although in practice the pattern may be more random.

Cohesiveness

All groups have a certain amount of cohesiveness, that is, the degree to which members stick together. Very cohesive groups have a strong identity and clear goals and norms, and their members are very loyal to one another. Families usually have a high degree of cohesiveness, as do some religious congregations and social groups.

A certain amount of cohesiveness is good; it keeps the group from falling apart and it keeps members cooperating to achieve group goals. One of the jobs of a coach or manager, for example, is to encourage the cohesiveness of the team or department. But too much cohesiveness can cause problems, as we shall see.

Your Turn 11–2

DRAW A COMMUNICATION PATTERN

In the space below, draw the typical communication pattern of your class and your family.

Your Class   **Your Family**

HOW PEOPLE BEHAVE IN GROUPS

Have you ever found yourself doing something you wouldn't ordinarily do because "everyone else is doing it"? You might have cheated on an exam, gotten your navel pierced, or spent too much money on something fashionable. The cohesiveness of your group caused you to behave in a way that was contrary to your beliefs or values. You found yourself conforming or complying with the group's norms. In some groups this condition goes so far that it has been given a special name, "groupthink."

Conformity

Changing your opinion or behavior in response to pressure from a group is called conformity. The urge to conform can be extremely powerful, as was shown in a famous experiment conducted by psychologist Solomon Asch.[1] Groups of seven students were told

PREJUDICE, STEREOTYPES, AND DISCRIMINATION

In 1902, Takuji Yamashita, a Japanese immigrant, graduated from the University of Washington law school. He passed the bar exam with honors, but the State of Washington said that Yamashita could not be a lawyer. At the time, Japanese immigrants could not apply for American citizenship, and a person had to be a citizen in order to be a lawyer. Yamashita argued his own case in court, saying that laws excluding people based on race were unworthy of "the most enlightened and liberty-loving nation of them all." The court agreed that Yamashita was "intellectually and morally" qualified to be a lawyer. However, he lost his case because the prejudices of the time were built into the legal system.

As a young man, Takuji Yamashita was denied the right to practice law based on his ethnicity. *(Courtesy of the descendants of Takuji Yamashita.)*

Ninety-nine years later, the laws excluding nonwhites from citizenship were no longer on the books. So in 2001, 42 years after Yamashita's death, the State of Washington finally admitted him to the bar. In a special ceremony attended by his descendants, Yamashita was awarded the honor for which he had studied and fought.

Like all victims of prejudice, Yamashita was prejudged because of his background. Prejudice is a negative attitude about people based on their belonging to a particular group, without any regard for their individuality. Stereotypes are the simplified beliefs that people have about the characteristics of members of a particular group. And discrimination is action taken against someone we are prejudiced against.

Where does prejudice come from? Psychologists have different ideas about the origins of prejudice. Some think that prejudice is the result of competition between groups. When blacks and whites, or Americans and Mexicans, for example, compete for jobs, members of both groups become prejudiced against the other group.

Other psychologists believe that prejudice is learned behavior. In this view, children acquire the prejudices of the adults around them, much as they learn any other type of behavior.

Another theory holds that people with certain personality traits are more likely to be prejudiced. People who are rigid and conventional, and who have poor self-belief, are prone toward prejudice. They feel better about themselves when they can feel better than others.

Still another point of view is that prejudice is a result of lazy thinking. Because the world is so complex and hard to understand, people resort to stereotypes to simplify their thinking and to categorize people.

Most people have prejudices, and most people are either unaware of them or won't admit to them. Prejudice that results in unfair discrimination harms the people discriminated against, like Yamashita. Today legislation makes discrimination based on sex, age, race, ethnicity, or religion illegal. Yet discrimination still persists in the attitudes and behavior of individuals.

FIGURE 11–3

Which of the lines on the right-hand card matches the line on the left-hand card?

they were participating in an experiment about perception. They were shown these cards and asked to select the line on the right-hand card that matches the line on the left-hand card (see Figure 11–3).

No doubt you picked the correct line without any trouble. But how would you do in the following situation? In Asch's study, six of the seven students were "in" on the true nature of the experiment. The group was given the same task: to match the sticks. The six were instructed to answer unanimously, out loud in front of the group. The seventh, the true subject, answered last, also out loud. At first, the six answered correctly, and so did the true subject. But then the six started to unanimously select the incorrect line, contradicting what the seventh subject could see perfectly well. In one out of three groups, the true subjects conformed—that is, they gave the wrong answer to go along with the group.

In follow-up interviews, it became apparent that both the conformers and the ones who stuck to the evidence of their senses were disturbed by what happened. The conformers reported that their feelings of self-confidence had been eroded by the unanimous judgments of the other group members. Those who remained independent of the group reported feeling embarrassed and uneasy at being the odd one out.

Why do some people conform and others do not? Psychologists think that people who conform to group behavior that is contrary to their beliefs and values suffer from poor self-belief. They lack the confidence necessary to act independently. Those who act independently when group values contradict their own values tend to have good self-belief. In addition, the size of the unanimous majority influences the degree of conformity in a group. When confronted with one or two people who hold a different opinion, a person is not so likely to conform. But when three or more people hold a differing belief, others are more likely to go along with the majority.

Of course, it's important to realize that conformity is not always bad. In common social situations such as waiting in line, entering an elevator, or taking a class, conformity is simply convenient behavior. It means that these situations will take place in a way that everyone expects. It relieves people of the necessity of making a decision about what to do all day long.

The important thing about conformity is to know when it is appropriate. In most circumstances, it probably is appropriate. But when the beliefs, values, and behavior of a group run counter to your own beliefs, values, and codes of behavior, then whether to conform becomes an important decision. Do you go along to get along, or do you act independently? This can be a hard question to answer.

Groupthink

When a group is very cohesive and its members very loyal to one another, a special type of conformity sometimes arises. Called groupthink, it is an uncritical acceptance of a group's beliefs and behaviors in order to preserve its unanimity. When loyalty to the group becomes more important than anything else, the members are suffering from groupthink.

When a group is suffering from groupthink, its members lose their ability to think critically and independently. They lose sight of their own values and of moral consequences. Some political groups suffer from groupthink. Loyalty to a leader, party, or ideology creates an atmosphere in which the group makes poor decisions.

PARTICIPATING IN GROUPS

You can use your knowledge about how groups work to improve the way you interact with others. By analyzing the goals, roles, and norms of the groups you belong to, you will be able to understand the nature of each group. You can also get the most out of groups by learning to be an active participant.

Analyzing Group Goals, Roles, and Norms

When you first join a group, are you quiet at first? Do you keep to yourself, observing how people interact? Most people behave this way when they join a new group. Unconsciously, they are trying to understand the group's goals, roles, and norms. A good example of this is your first few days in a new school or on a new job, when you are figuring out who's who and how things work.

You can sharpen your powers of analysis by asking yourself some questions when you first encounter a group. As you observe, try to answer the following questions:

- What are the objectives of the group?
- Are the group's goals cooperative or competitive?
- Does the group function as a team, or are there rivalries among members?

Your Turn 11–3

CONFORMITY IN YOUR CLASS

Think about your class again, and answer the following questions.

1. Give two examples of conformity in the classroom.

_____

_____

2. Describe a situation in which a member of the class did not conform to group norms.

_____

_____

3. Does the class suffer from groupthink? Give evidence to support your answer.

_____

_____

■ Are some members pursuing individual goals rather than group goals?

■ Does the group have a leader? Who is the leader?

■ What other roles are apparent in the group?

■ What are the norms of the group? Is it formal or informal?

■ What communication patterns are being used?

By answering these questions, you will better understand the nature of the group and your role in it. As you begin to feel comfortable with the norms of the group, you can start to participate more actively.

Participating Actively

Groups tend to accept those who adopt their norms, and reject those who ignore them. So once you figure out the norms of a group, you will have better success if you behave accordingly. If the group is formal, with rules of order, then you too will have to be formal. If the group is informal, you can behave in a more casual manner.

WHATEVER IT TAKES

Mike Krzyzewski

(AP/Wide World Photos/Hans Deryk.)

When Mike Krzyzewski arrived at Duke University in 1981 to coach its basketball team, the school newspaper wrote "that is not a typo" next to his name. Krzyzewski, pronounced "sha-shef-ski," thought that was pretty funny. Known as Coach K at Duke, Krzyzewski has built an impressive men's basketball program. Duke's team, the Blue Devils, has won three national championships and has had six national players of the year. In addition, all but two of Coach K's players who played all four years have graduated. Many have gone on to play in the NBA.

What makes Coach K's teams so successful? Krzyzewski has created a special Blue Devils culture that is not focused on winning. Instead, Krzyzewski emphasizes the kids on the team and the coaches who assist him. He values them even when they fail. As a result, the team "tries to play hard for him and tries to play great for him" in the words of a former player.

In 2001, in honor of his coaching achievements, Krzyzewski was inducted into the Basketball Hall of Fame. In his acceptance speech, Krzyzewski said, "I hope that all of those youngsters who have played for me and the people who have worked with me will share in this honor. My mom always told me to associate myself with great people and great institutions, and I have tried to do that."

According to Krzyzewski, the son of Polish immigrants, his mother taught him not to fear losing. "She loved me no matter what happened. I didn't realize how powerful that was until I got older," says Krzyzewski. His parents pressured him to join the armed forces and so he found himself at the U.S. Military Academy at West Point, playing basketball. However, Krzyzewski didn't want to be an Army officer. He wanted to be a basketball coach. After he graduated, he coached service teams for a couple of years. When he resigned from the Army, he went to Indiana University as an assistant coach to Bobby Knight. From there he went to Duke, where he has been for more than 20 years.

After Duke won the 2001 national championship, Krzyzewski said, "I thoroughly loved coaching these kids. . . . They've given me their hearts, their minds, and not only that, they've given to each other. That's the most rewarding thing about what I do."

Sources: "Mike Krzyzewski," *GoDuke.com* <http://www.goduke.ocsn.com/sports/m-baskbl/mtt/krzyzewski_mike00.html>; accessed January 14, 2003; "Mike Krzyzewski," Hall of Famers, Basketball Hall of Fame, <http://www.hoophall.com/halloffamers/Krzysewski.htm>, accessed March 14, 2003; "Duke's Winning Coach Isn't Afraid of Losing," America's Best Society and Culture, CNN.com <http://www.cnn.com/specials/2001/americasbest/time/society.culture/pro.mkrzyzewski.html>, accessed March 14, 2003.

FIGURE 11–4

An agenda can be used to prepare for a meeting and to make sure the group covers all the necessary business in a logical order.

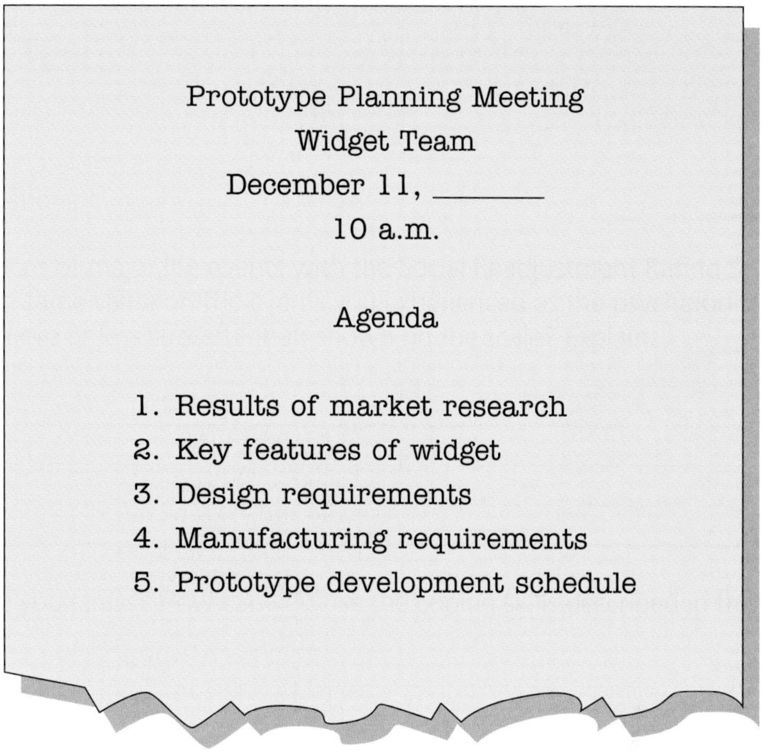

Prototype Planning Meeting
Widget Team
December 11, _____
10 a.m.

Agenda

1. Results of market research
2. Key features of widget
3. Design requirements
4. Manufacturing requirements
5. Prototype development schedule

If the group is formal—perhaps at work or school—you may be given an agenda before the group meets. An agenda is a list of matters to be discussed or decided at the group's meeting (see Figure 11–4). Read the agenda and make sure you are prepared to discuss the subjects that will come up at the meeting. Preparation may involve thinking, reading, or researching. You should bring the agenda and any relevant information to the meeting.

Whether the group is informal or formal, you will get more out of it if you participate actively. In addition to being prepared, active participation requires that you:

- Pay attention. Use your listening skills to follow what's going on. In some situations, it may be appropriate to take notes.
- Acknowledge what other people think and feel. Even if you disagree with them, you should not tear down others' ideas.
- Be assertive. Speak up when you have something to say.
- Contribute your own ideas. Realize that what you think may have value for the group.
- Be courteous. Remember that groups are more productive when members cooperate with one another.

Norms for Classroom Behavior

If you had a class in which the instructor often came late, was poorly prepared, and took phone calls during lectures, you would probably drop it as soon as possible. Instructors, however, can't drop a class when students come late, are poorly prepared, and pay no attention. For a class to function smoothly, everyone should have the same expectations about the class's norms—how students and teachers will behave. In some classes, the instructor is very explicit about the behavior expected. But most often, instructors simply assume that students will adapt to acceptable group norms. Here are some norms of good classroom etiquette.

Attend Class   Just as you expect the instructor to be present at every class, you should plan to attend every course session. Students who attend class usually get better grades than students who skip class. An occasional absence due to illness or emergency may be necessary, but beyond that, absences show a lack of commitment to your education.

Arrive on Time   Make sure you arrive on time and are seated and ready to begin before the class starts. It's disruptive to everyone when a student walks in late. If your schedule means you can't make it to a particular class on time, then drop the class.

Stay until the End   Plan to stay in class until it's over. Don't schedule appointments, jobs, or other personal business to interfere with class sessions. If you must leave early on occasion, inform the instructor *before* class that you have to leave early.

Respect the Instructor's or School's Policies about Eating and Drinking   Some teachers tolerate an early-morning cup of coffee, but others don't want any food or drink in their classrooms. The smells are distracting, food winds up on the desk and floor, and trash accumulates. If you do bring something to eat or drink to class, be sure to clean up after yourself.

Turn off Cell Phones during Class   We've already discussed cell phone etiquette in Chapter 9, but in case a reminder is necessary, cell phones and pagers should be turned off during class. If you are expecting an extremely important emergency call, inform the teacher beforehand. Then set the ringer on vibrate, and take the call outside in the hall.

Listen to Others during Discussions and Presentations   Be courteous and pay attention to your fellow students. You might even learn something. At the very least, you will be helping to ensure that people pay attention to you when you speak up during discussions or give an oral report.

Your Turn 11–4

RATE YOURSELF AS A MEMBER OF YOUR CLASS

How well do you function as a member of your class? Think about the last few class sessions you've attended, and then answer these questions:

1. What do you do, if anything, to prepare for class meetings?

_____

_____

2. Do you take notes in class? _____

3. What do you do if you disagree with something that's said?

_____

_____

4. How frequently do you participate in class discussions?

_____

5. Are you courteous to other group members?

_____

_____

6. Compare your class's norms to the classroom norms listed on page 260. How are they similar? How are they different?

_____

_____

_____

_____

Treat Others with Respect When You Speak   A classroom contains many people who may have attitudes very different from yours. Whatever your private opinions are about people, respond to them with respect, even when you are disagreeing with them. Don't interrupt, don't dominate a discussion, and don't make personal comments about anyone, including the instructor.

Use a Computer Appropriately   If you bring a laptop or handheld electronic device to class, use it only for class business. Do not surf the Web, do your on-line shopping, catch up on your e-mail, play games, or keyboard an assignment for the next class. Use the device for taking notes or accessing course-related materials on line.

Resolving Issues with the Instructor   If you have a disagreement with the instructor or are upset by something you think is unfair, don't bring up the issue in class. Instead, discuss the problem after class or during a scheduled appointment.

These are just some common norms to help people get along in class groups and thus get more out of their courses.

> *Either lead, follow, or get out of the way.*
>
> *sign on broadcast executive*
>
> *ted turner's desk*

LEADING GROUPS

In every group there is usually someone who takes charge. The leader may be the person who has formal authority, like the highest-ranking manager at a business meeting, or the leader may be a group member who simply directs everyone, like a student who takes charge of a project group. Leadership, then, is more than a title. **Leadership** is a set of behaviors, beliefs, and values that enables the leader to persuade others to act.

People become the leaders of their groups in several ways. A leader may be elected, such as the president of a parent-teacher association or labor union. A leader may be appointed, as are the members of the president's cabinet, who head various departments of the federal government. Or a leader can simply emerge from the group, as happens in groups of workers, students, or friends.

Qualities of a Good Leader

Some people seem born to leadership. They have a quality known as **charisma**, a special magic to their personalities that inspires great popular loyalty. Martin Luther King Jr., Billy Graham, Magic Johnson, and Princess Diana are examples of people with this natural leadership quality.

A good leader need not be charismatic, however. He or she must simply possess a variety of qualities that many ordinary people have. First and foremost, leaders have good human relations skill. The ability to get along well with others is the foundation of true leadership. Second, leaders are very goal oriented and very motivated. They know what they want to accomplish, and they are able to focus on doing what's necessary to achieve their goals. Third, leaders have good self-belief. Their outlook on themselves and on life is positive. They can communicate the confidence they have in themselves and in life to help motivate others.

Basic Leadership Styles

Just as people have different personalities, they approach the task of leading a group in different ways. People differ in the emphasis they put on[2]

- the task itself—getting a job done
- relationships with others—being interested primarily in people

Democrats   Leaders who stress both task and relationships can be called Democrats. They tend to derive their authority from the cooperative ideals and goals of the group. They are good at getting individuals to participate, because they are not overly concerned with maintaining their own authority or power. They are interested in motivating group members to share the responsibility for achieving the group's goals.

Taskmasters   Leaders who stress the task over the group's relationships are Taskmasters. They are more concerned about getting the job done than fostering fellowship. They tend to be confident, independent, and ambitious. To get group members to do what's necessary, they try to control behavior with rewards and punishments. This type of leader assigns tasks and responsibilities to group members.

Nurturers   Leaders who put relationships over the task at hand are Nurturers. They believe that people come first. They emphasize the personal development of group members. Because of this, they tend to be sympathetic, approving, and friendly. They create a secure atmosphere in which the group can operate.

After the September 11, 2001, attack on the World Trade Center in New York City, Mayor Rudolf Giuliani showed exceptional situational leadership skills. Normally a taskmaster in style, Giuliani became strong yet flexible, demonstrating elements of all the leadership styles as the situation demanded. *(AP/Wide World Photos/Kathy Willens.)*

Bureaucrats   Leaders who are oriented neither to the task nor to relationships are Bureaucrats. They behave in a cautious, orderly, and conservative way. They prefer facts and established procedures to risk-taking behavior. Such leaders pay attention to detail and accuracy.

Situational Leadership   Which of these four basic leadership styles is best? The answer to this question is: the style that is most effective in a particular set of circumstances. Although each of us may possess traits and values that make us tend naturally to one of the four basic styles, good leaders can adapt their styles to the situation. The ability to adapt your leadership style to different circumstances is called **situational leadership**.

A team of researchers working together on a long-term project would probably do best with

Your Turn 11–5

WHICH LEADERSHIP STYLE WORKS BEST?

1. Indicate which of the following leadership styles is best suited to the groups listed below.

Democrat style: emphasizes cooperation and shared responsibility

Taskmaster style: focuses on the tasks that need to be done, not on people

Nurturer style: focuses on group members, not on tasks

Bureaucrat style: focuses on procedures rather than people or tasks

a. a platoon of soldiers in battle _____

b. employees of a state motor vehicles bureau _____

c. the head of a family _____

d. a professional association _____

e. a church choir _____

f. a youth group _____

g. a group of volunteers for a neighborhood block party _____

h. employees in a research "think tank" _____

i. a department in a college _____

j. the staff of a college yearbook _____

2. Which style would you favor for leading a group? Why?

_____

_____

_____

a leader who thinks both task and relationships are important—a Democrat. In this situation the contributions of motivated, creative individuals are important in achieving the best results. In contrast, a factory gearing up for a seasonal crunch would benefit from a leader who stresses task over relationships, assigning jobs and responsibilities as necessary—the Taskmaster.

A self-help group such as dieters needs a leader who stresses relationships over tasks—the Nurturer. Since the achievement of goals is closely related to the psychological well-being of the individuals, the leader must emphasize the interpersonal relations of the group members. In a situation in which neither the task nor the relationships are particularly important, the leader can focus on process and procedure. The Bureaucrat does well in situations in which the means are as important as the ends—government agencies, for example.

The Information Highway

GETTING UP TO SPEED

There are many sources of information about groups on the Internet. Here are a few places to start your search:

- A professor at Virginia Commonwealth University maintains a page with links to resources on group dynamics. See "Forstyh's Research in Groups" page at <http://www.has.vcu.edu/>.

- Many colleges post guidelines for classroom etiquette on their Web sites. Check your own school's Web site for such a list of norms or search for "classroom etiquette" at the Web sites of the Kellogg School of Management at Northwestern University <http://www.kellogg.northwestern.edu/>, or Palm Beach Community College <http://www.pbcc.edu/>.

- A site puts together informal groups based on shared interests and sets up meetings, although there's no guarantee anyone will show up <http://www.meetup.com>.

- You can find an Internet discussion group that interests you and join in the conversation by selecting "groups" <http://www.google.com/>.

You can search for more resources by using the key words *group dynamics, roles and norms, conformity, classroom etiquette, work teams, leadership styles, prejudice,* and *discrimination*.

What's Up

Name _____ Date_____

1. What is the difference between a formal group and an informal group?

_____
_____
_____
_____

2. Briefly state what the cooperative and competitive goals of a basketball team might be.

_____
_____
_____
_____

3. What are norms?

_____
_____
_____
_____

4. Describe these group communication patterns:

Chain _____
_____
_____

Wheel _____
_____
_____

All-channel _____
_____
_____

5. What is conformity?

_____
_____
_____
_____

continues

Name _____   Date_____

6. What is groupthink?

_____
_____
_____
_____
_____

7. Why do people generally observe quietly when they first join a new group?

_____
_____
_____
_____
_____

8. What is the purpose of an agenda?

_____
_____
_____
_____
_____

9. What is leadership?

_____
_____
_____
_____
_____

10. Why is situational leadership effective?

_____
_____
_____
_____
_____

Case Studies

THE CASE OF THE GARBLED MESSAGES

Alex, Gayle, Jennifer, and Keith all worked for the same large department of an insurance company. Alex was the department manager, and Gayle was his administrative assistant. Jennifer was their secretary. Keith, who did word processing, reported to Jennifer. Frequently all four of them worked to produce a large, complex report for Alex's boss.

When such a report needed to be done, Alex told Gayle what he needed. Gayle, in turn, explained to Jennifer what she had to do. Jennifer then coached Keith about his share of the work. Usually, there were several drafts because each of them made mistakes or forgot to tell the next person something critical. The process was frustrating, and they dreaded doing these reports.

1. Describe the communication pattern this group uses when they have to prepare a report.

_____

_____

2. How would you change the way the group operates in order to make the preparation of these reports less frustrating and more efficient?

_____

_____

_____

THE CASE OF THE INEXPERIENCED TEACHER'S AIDE

Lisa got a part-time job as a teacher's aide in a day care center. She loved helping the teacher lead the four-year-olds in the various activities of their morning. One morning the teacher called in sick and Lisa was on her own. Many of the children seemed cranky that day, and Lisa tried to soothe each one affectionately. She spent a lot of time with a little girl who wouldn't take her coat off. By the middle of the morning, some children were fighting over a toy, the little girl still had her coat on, and another group refused her suggestion that they clean up the toys they had played with. Lisa was getting upset. It was clear to her that she had lost control of the class.

1. What leadership style is Lisa using?

_____

_____

2. To get the group back on track, what leadership style might Lisa try? Why?

_____

_____

_____

_____

Journal

Answer the following journal questions.

1. Describe the role you play in your family and the norms for your behavior. To what extent is having a role and norms useful? To what extent does it limit you?

_____

_____

_____

_____

_____

2. Have you ever felt prejudice toward someone else and been mistaken about what they were really like? Describe what happened and what changed your attitude.

_____

_____

_____

_____

_____

3. What was the least successful group you've been in? What made the group function poorly? How might its group dynamics been improved?

_____

_____

_____

_____

_____

4. Describe a person who has played a great leadership role in your life. What qualities made this person an outstanding leader?

_____

_____

_____

_____

_____

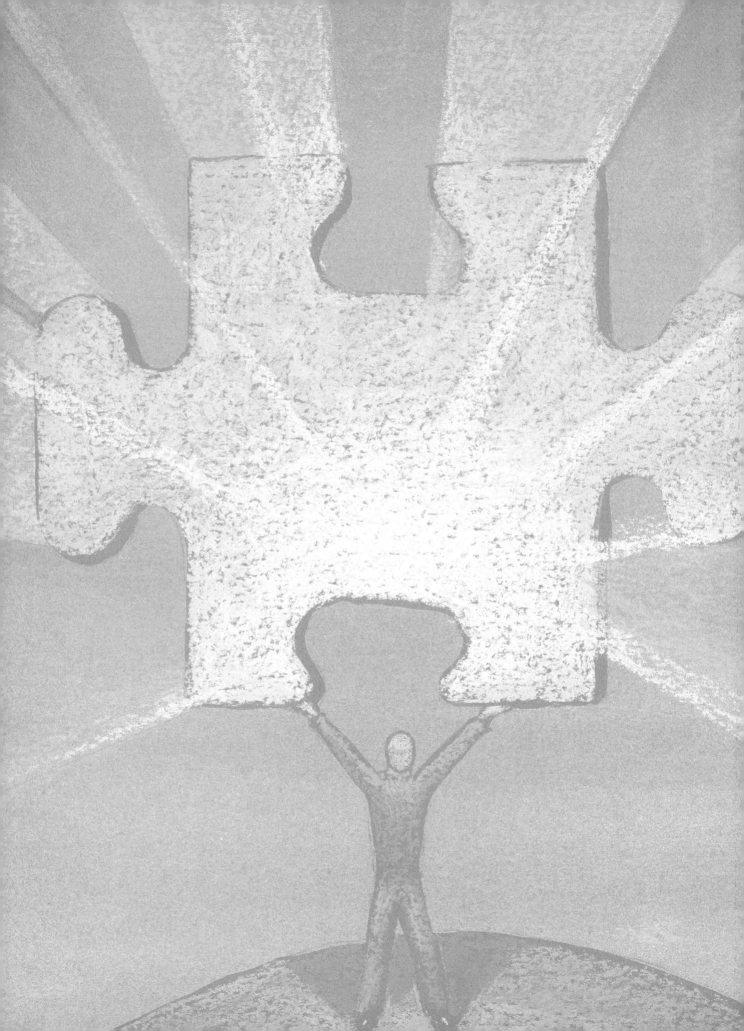

Developing Your Action Plan

In previous units, you learned how to make the most of your emotional, intellectual, physical, and social potential. Now you are going to put these aspects of yourself to use. In this unit, you will learn some practical tips for managing stress, time, and money, and you will use all you have learned to start planning your career.

One person's stress is another person's sport. At the age of 70, former President George H. W. Bush jumped out of an airplane for old times' sake. When he was younger, he had been a Navy pilot during World War II. *(Courtesy of Joe Jennings.)*

Chapter 12

Handling Change and Stress

Two factory workers learned that in six months their plant would shut down. Both felt extremely stressed about losing their jobs. The first, after a brief period of feeling angry and anxious, decided he would go back to school and acquire skills that would enable him to get off the factory floor and into a more promising career. The second worker tried to get factory work elsewhere, but no one was hiring. After months of job hunting, he lost the willpower to look for a job. Two years after the plant shut down, one man is on his way to a new career and another is counted among the "permanently unemployed."

Why did one person become energized by the prospect of a layoff and another become demoralized? Many psychologists think that, like beauty, stress is in the mind of the beholder. An event in and of itself is not enough to cause stress. Rather, **stress** is the emotional and physical reaction that results when a person has trouble *coping* with a situation, event, or change. In most situations, people feel stress when they interpret a situation as likely to overtax their ability to deal with it. Whether they think and feel that a situation is stressful depends on previous experience with similar situations and their ability to cope. Thus, one person's stressful situation is another person's enjoyable challenge. To give an extreme example, most of us would feel tremendous stress if we were pushed out of an airplane with a parachute on our back. Skydivers, on the other hand, would take the jump much more calmly.

People respond to stressful situations both physically and psychologically. Physical reactions to stress include increased levels of adrenaline, which helps the body produce more energy, higher blood pressure, and faster heart rate. These responses can help us deal with stress in the short run by improving our ability to "fight or flee." But when stress continues over a long period, it can result in illness. Prolonged stress can contribute to heart disease and cancer, and it can weaken the body's ability to fight infection.

The psychological reactions to a stressful event are varied. In a stressful situation, most people feel that they have lost control over their lives and that life is unpredictable. Consequently, they feel helpless, anxious, and upset. These feelings can develop into anger or depression, sometimes severe enough to require treatment.

Despite the potentially serious effects of stress, it's a mistake to think that stress is a completely negative experience. Stress has positive aspects as well. Many people experience growth when they seek new experiences they are not sure they can handle. When you start a new job, choose a difficult course of study, or decide to get married, you are seeking stress, whether you are aware of it or not. But if you constantly played it safe and never tried something new or challenging, you would never reach your potential. You would stop growing. To live a successful life, you must handle the stress you seek and the stress that comes unpredictably.

You can learn to live with stress. By studying this chapter, you will learn about the causes of stress, the relationship of personality and stress, and the signs of stress. In addition, you will discover and use some strategies for coping with stress.

Major life changes can cause stress. Even positive changes, like getting married, can throw people off balance for a while. *(Courtesy of PhotoDisc.)*

CAUSES OF STRESS

As we've already seen, what causes stress for you may be a routine event or even stimulating for someone else. Nevertheless, we can make some generalizations about what causes stress for most people.[1]

- Negative events cause more stress than positive events; for example, getting a divorce is more stressful than getting married.

- Unpredictable events are more stressful than predictable events; getting sick unexpectedly causes more stress than an annual case of hay fever.

- Uncontrollable events cause more stress than controllable events; being expelled from school is more stressful than quitting.

- Uncertain events are more stressful than definite events; not knowing whether you've gotten a job causes more stress than knowing whether you've gotten it or not.

Events that cause stress can be roughly divided into two types: major life events, like marriage, pregnancy, moving, going back to school, losing a job, and death, and daily events, like traffic jams, being late, noisy neighbors, and misplacing your keys.

Major Life Changes

Thomas H. Holmes, a psychiatrist, and his colleagues did research on the relationship of major life changes, the amount of adjustment they require, and illness.[2] They found that the more major changes individuals have experienced in a short time, the more likely they are to become ill. In addition, they surveyed a group of 394 adults to find out how much adjustment each major change required.

As a result of these studies, Holmes and his colleagues came up with the Social Readjustment Rating Scale (see Table 12–1, page 276). Basically, this is a list of major life changes, each of which is assigned a rating depending on the amount of readjustment it requires. According to this scale, the death of a spouse is the most stressful event, with a rating of 100, and minor violations of the law the least stressful, with a rating of 11. Holmes found that when people experience a number of major life changes within a year, they are more likely to become ill. About half of the people with scores of 150 to 300 and 70 percent of those with scores over 300 developed an illness within a year or two.

What's interesting about the results of these studies is that events normally thought of as happy can be quite stressful. Having a baby, moving to a new house, getting married, and even starting school, for example, require readjustment and cause stress. So when people experience many major life changes, even positive ones, within a short period of time, they are more likely to become sick.

Daily Irritations

Major life events are not the only causes of stress. Dealing with a bureaucracy, traveling in rush hour, breaking a glass, fighting with your sister, misplacing your driver's license—all these minor, everyday irritations can add up to varying degrees of stress. Minor events are most stressful when we can't predict them or control them.

Some researchers think that minor irritations are actually more stressful than major life events. In their view, the effects of many major life events are actually caused by the daily hassles they create.

The minor irritations of daily life can cause stress. For example, getting stuck in a traffic jam, especially when you don't expect it, can be upsetting. *(Courtesy of PhotoDisc.)*

TABLE 12–1   Social Readjustment Rating Scale

Life Event	Value	Life Event	Value
Death of spouse	100	Son or daughter leaving home	29
Divorce	73	Trouble with in-laws	29
Separation from spouse	65	Outstanding personal achievement	28
Jail term	63	Spouse begins or stops work	26
Death of close family member	63	Starting or finishing school	26
Personal injury or illness	63	Change in living conditions	25
Marriage	50	Change in personal habits	24
Fired from work	47	Trouble with boss	23
Reconciliation with spouse	45	Change in work hours or conditions	20
Retirement	45	Moving	20
Change in health of family member	44	Change in schools	20
Pregnancy	40	Change in recreational habits	19
Sex difficulties	39	Change in social activities	18
Addition to family	39	Change in sleeping habits	16
Change of financial status	38	Change in number of family gatherings	15
Death of close friend	37	Change in eating habits	15
Change of career	36	Vacation	13
Change in number of marital arguments	33	Christmas or major holiday	12
Foreclosure of mortgage or loan	30	Minor violation of the law	11
Change in work responsibilities	29		

Source: Reprinted with permission from *Journal of Psychosomatic Research,* vol. 11, p. 213, Thomas H. Holmes and Richard H. Rahe, "The Social Readjustment Rating Scale," copyright 1967, Pergamon Press plc.

For example, having a baby, a major event, is stressful for new parents. But it may be stressful not only because they experience intense love and joy but also because they are constantly feeding, soothing, rocking, doing laundry, and going without sleep.

PERSONALITY AND STRESS

As we saw in the case of the two factory workers who lost their jobs, individuals have different reactions to the same events. One saw the layoff as an opportunity to grow; the other became paralyzed and unable to act. The same event held a very different meaning for each of their lives. One man was able to take risks, think positively, and adapt well to his new situation. The other man avoided risk, became demoralized, and adapted poorly.

Your Turn 12–1

ASSESS YOUR MAJOR LIFE CHANGES

Review the major life events in Table 12–1. How many have happened to you in the last 12 months? Write the event and its point value in the space below. Then add the point values to get a total.

Event	Value

Total Value _____

Now find your chance of becoming ill within two years:

150 or less	30 percent chance of becoming ill
151 to 299	50 percent chance of becoming ill
300 or above	80 percent chance of becoming ill

Your Own Experience

Remember that each person reacts differently to stress. You may have a high chance of becoming ill, according to the Social Readjustment Rating Scale, but you may remain healthy. Describe your own health after the events you listed above.

_____

_____

_____

> **A pessimist is one who makes difficulties of his opportunities and an optimist is one who makes opportunities of his difficulties.**
>
> *harry truman, american president*

Risk Takers and Risk Avoiders

Some people believe that change is the fundamental condition of life. They feel that new things are challenges rather than threats. Such people tend to be open and flexible, and they take risks when necessary. Risk takers accept that they will feel a certain amount of stress. They have positive self-belief, and they are confident in their ability to cope.

On the other hand, many people find change to be threatening. They are much more comfortable when life settles into a predictable

Your Turn 12–2

ASSESS THE STRESS OF DAILY LIFE

As you know, there are good days and there are bad days. One day this week, keep a log of what causes you the most stress. You may discover interesting connections between daily events and your level of stress.

Date _____

	Situation	People Involved	Your Reaction
Most stressful			
Somewhat stressful			
Relaxing			

routine. The thought of doing something new and different makes them very anxious. Risk avoiders feel that new situations threaten their fragile self-belief. So they use up more energy trying to maintain the status quo. Ironically, the effort to avoid risk also creates stress.

Stress-Producing Thought Patterns

As you recall from Chapter 1, your beliefs influence your behavior. People with self-confidence believe they can influence events and take control of their lives. On the other hand, people who are in the

WHATEVER IT TAKES

Roy P. Benavidez

(Courtesy of the Roy P. Benavidez Estate.)

One morning in 1968, Roy Benavidez, a staff sergeant with the Army's Green Berets in Vietnam, got a radio call for help from other Special Forces soldiers. Benavidez jumped into a helicopter and flew to the scene. "When I got into that helicopter, little did I know we were going to spend six hours in hell," Benavidez told the *San Antonio Express* years later.

When the helicopter landed, Benavidez jumped out and was immediately wounded by enemy fire. He found the soldiers and dragged the wounded back to the helicopter. The pilot was killed as they tried to take off, and the helicopter crashed and burned. Benavidez got the wounded men off the aircraft and set up a defensive perimeter. Over the next few hours, he organized return fire, called in air strikes on the enemy, tended the wounded, and retrieved classified documents. He was bayoneted, clubbed, and shot, but he survived and continued to help the others. Finally, a second helicopter arrived to take them out. Benavidez was so spent that he couldn't walk or talk. The doctors thought he was dead until he spit at one of them to show he was still alive!

Benavidez became a soldier to improve his life. Born in South Texas, Benavidez was the son of a sharecropper and his wife, both of whom died young. He and his brother were raised by an uncle. Working as migrant laborers, the family moved around so much that Benavidez got little schooling. To get an education, improve his English, and live a better life, Benavidez joined the Army when he was 20. He decided to make a career of the Army after attending airborne school. He was injured by a land mine in Vietnam, and doctors thought he would never walk again. However, Benavidez recovered and became a Green Beret. It was during his second tour of duty in Vietnam that he carried out the rescue mission that brought him such great recognition.

For his actions in saving the lives of eight men, Benavidez was awarded the Distinguished Service Cross and the Medal of Honor, the military's highest award for valor. His fellow Texans have honored him by naming schools, a National Guard armory, and an Army Reserve center after him. In 2000, the Navy announced it would name a ship after him—a rare honor for an enlisted Army man.

Sources: "Roy Benavidez," *San Antonio Express-News,* November 29, 1998; Richard Goldstein, "Roy P. Benavidez," *New York Times,* December 4, 1998; "Ship's Name to Honor Army Hero Benavidez," *San Antonio Express-News,* September 17, 2000; "Navy Names New Roll-On/Roll-Off Ship for U.S. Army Hero" and Medal of Honor citation at <http://www.mishalov.com/Benavidez.html>, accessed February 18, 2003.

> *God, give us the
> serenity to accept
> what cannot
> be changed;
> give us the courage
> to change what
> should be changed;
> give us the wisdom
> to distinguish one
> from the other.*
>
> *reinhold niebuhr,*
>
> *religious and social thinker*

habit of thinking in negative ways believe they are unable to cope with change. Because of their negative thought patterns, they find many events stressful. Some typical thoughts of a stress-prone person are:

"I can tell she doesn't like me."

"I must get this right the first time."

"I can't do anything right."

"I'll never get another job."

"It's the worst thing that could happen."

"I'm a loser."

With thoughts like these, it's no wonder that these people feel stressed about their lives. All these thoughts are sending the message: I am helpless. Believing you are helpless means you lose the will to exert control over your life and your surroundings. The feeling of helplessness leads to stress. In extreme cases, it can lead to depression or even death.

Adaptability

People who feel they are helpless are vulnerable to stress, because they believe they cannot take control and influence their environment. At the other extreme are people who feel they must be in control at all times. Since this is impossible, of course, they react with stress even to the slightest changes they haven't initiated.

People who fall between these two extremes—the helpless and the controlling—are best able to deal with change and stress. They have the ability to change what they can change, adapt to what they can't change, and understand the difference between the two. Such people are hardy and resilient. When they experience stress, they respond with a positive attitude. Their ability to cope with stress enables them to bounce back to a more relaxed state fairly quickly.

SIGNS OF STRESS

The symptoms of stress are varied, and different people experience different combinations of symptoms. Learning to recognize the many signs of stress, which include physical symptoms, mental changes, emotional changes, and behavioral changes, will help you cope with stress.

- ■ **Physical signs.** The most common physical manifestations of stress are shortness of breath, increased or irregular heart rate, chest pains, fatigue, headache, insomnia, muscle tension (especially in the neck and shoulders), abdominal cramps, and nausea. People who experience stress over a long period often get colds.

Your Turn 12–3

ARE YOU PRONE TO STRESS?

How well are you described in the items below? In the space provided, write the numbers 1 through 4 as follows: **1 Never   2 Sometimes   3 Frequently   4 Always**

1. I try to do as much as possible in the least amount of time.　_____

2. When I play a game, I have to win in order to feel good.　_____

3. I find it hard to ask for help with a problem.　_____

4. I'm very critical of others.　_____

5. I'm very ambitious.　_____

6. I try to do more than one thing at a time.　_____

7. I spend little time on myself.　_____

8. I am very competitive.　_____

9. I get involved in many projects at the same time.　_____

10. I have a lot of deadlines at work or school.　_____

11. I have too many responsibilities.　_____

12. I become impatient with delays or lateness.　_____

13. I speed up to get through yellow lights.　_____

14. I need the respect and admiration of other people.　_____

15. I keep track of what time it is.　_____

16. I have too much to do and too little time to do it.　_____

17. My friends think I'm very competitive.　_____

18. I feel guilty if I relax and do nothing.　_____

19. I talk very quickly.　_____

20. I get angry easily.　_____

Total　_____

Now total your answers and rate yourself:

Over 70　　You are very prone to stress.

60–69　　You are moderately prone to stress.

40–59　　You are somewhat prone to stress.

30–39　　You occasionally feel stress.

20–29　　You rarely feel stress.

- **Mental signs.** Stress changes the way people think and perceive. Common changes in mental functioning include decreased concentration, increased forgetfulness, indecisiveness, confusion, and the mind racing or going blank.
- **Emotional signs.** People under stress can experience anxiety, nervousness, depression, anger, frustration, and fear. They may become irritable and impatient, and their tempers may grow short.
- **Behavioral signs.** All these changes in the body and brain often manifest themselves in behavioral changes. Typical behaviors of those under stress include pacing, fidgeting, and nail biting; increased eating, smoking, and drinking; crying, yelling, swearing, and blaming; and throwing things or hitting.

When people have serious symptoms of stress that impair their ability to carry out the normal tasks of daily life, they may be suffering from a psychological disorder. They may have posttraumatic stress syndrome (common among war veterans and victims of disasters or violent crimes) or clinical levels of anxiety or depression. Stress that interferes with daily life calls for seeking professional help.

COPING WITH STRESS

It's important to deal with stress before you suffer from stress overload. There are three basic ways you can cope with stress: You can deal with the sources of stress, change the way you think about what's causing your stress, or simply relieve the physical and emotional symptoms of stress. You can use a combination of approaches to manage stress. In addition, you can draw on the support of your family and friends to help you deal with stress.

Dealing with the Cause

The most direct way of coping with stress is to eliminate its cause. For example, suppose you have a job that's causing you stress, like driving a cab in Manhattan or working as a short-order cook in a diner. The most effective way to eliminate stress in this situation is to get another job.

As you recall, too many major life events within a short period can cause great stress. Sometimes it's possible to control the number of such events. For example, suppose your mother is ill, you are getting married, and you are moving to a new apartment around the same time. To prevent stress overload, it might be wise to postpone other changes, such as starting school, getting a new job, or having a baby.

Lack of time and lack of money are common problems that contribute to stress. By improving your time and money management skills, you will be able to decrease the stress that shortages of time

Your Turn 12–4

STRESS SIGNALS CHECKLIST

Are you suffering from stress? More than two or three of the following signs may be an indication that you should examine your life for sources of stress. Place a check mark next to any symptoms that apply to you.

Physical Signs
- ☐ Shortness of breath
- ☐ Fast or irregular heartbeat
- ☐ Muscle tension
- ☐ Nausea
- ☐ Insomnia

Mental Signs
- ☐ Difficulty in concentrating
- ☐ Increased forgetfulness
- ☐ Confusion
- ☐ Mind racing or going blank
- ☐ Indecisiveness

Emotional Signs
- ☐ Anxiety
- ☐ Depression
- ☐ Anger
- ☐ Frustration
- ☐ Fear

Behavioral Signs
- ☐ Pacing, fidgeting
- ☐ Nail biting
- ☐ Changes in eating, drinking, or smoking
- ☐ Crying, yelling, or swearing
- ☐ Throwing things or hitting

and money can cause. We'll discuss time and money management in detail in Chapters 13 and 14.

You can also bring your problem-solving skills to bear on situations that can't be eliminated. Perhaps you need to be more assertive, improve your communication skills, or resolve a conflict in order to reduce the stress you are feeling.

Reframing Your Thoughts

You can also cope with stress by changing how you think about a stressful situation (see Figure 12–1). The meaning that an event has for us depends on the frame through which we see it. By reframing your perceptions, you can change the meaning of an event. Often

---

FIGURE 12–1

Stress involves an event and the way you perceive the event. By changing the way you think about a stressful event, you can reduce the stress you feel.

Negative Thought Pattern

Positive Thought Pattern

DRUGS TO RELIEVE STRESS: A TREATMENT, NOT A CURE

People who are suffering from anxiety and stress are sometimes prescribed antianxiety drugs by their physicians. Although these drugs can be effective in reducing anxiety, they do not reduce the *causes* of anxiety. They are relieving the symptoms of stress but not curing it, much as a cold tablet can relieve congestion but not cure a cold. And unlike exercise, relaxation, and rest, which can also relieve the symptoms of stress, antianxiety drugs have side effects and other risks.

The most frequently prescribed antianxiety drugs are Valium and Xanax. Both are benzodiazepines, a type of drug that relieves anxiety symptoms without causing extreme drowsiness. Benzodiazepines act by slowing down the activity of the central nervous system. This has the effect of calming people. If used properly, benzodiazepines are effective for treating a general, chronic state of anxiety. They are less effective for treating the stress associated with a specific event, like a death in the family or giving a speech.

Benzodiazepines have undesirable side effects. First, they can cause drowsiness and lack of coordination. People taking benzodiazepines should not drive or operate machinery. Second, they can interfere with thinking and cause memory loss, so taking benzodiazepines when you are studying is not a good idea. Third, benzodiazepines can multiply the effects of other drugs such as alcohol. When taken in combination with those drugs, they can cause coma or even death. Benzodiazepines can also be addictive. Patients who stop taking it can experience tremors, nausea, and hallucinations, and their anxiety returns.

So benzodiazepines, although helpful for some people, must be used with caution under the supervision of a physician. It's important not to abuse these or any other drugs, because the results of abuse can be deadly.

people reframe an event or situation by using one of the defense mechanisms we discussed in Chapter 10. Withdrawing, rationalizing, displacing, fantasizing, and projecting are ways in which we try to deal with anxiety-provoking situations. These may be effective in the very short term, but they do not relieve stress in the long run. They just drive it deeper.

Instead of trying to escape or focusing on the fear, worry, or anxiety you are feeling about something, try to focus on something you can positively influence or control. For example, if you are feeling stressful about giving a speech, instead of worrying about your performance, reframe your thoughts and focus your energy on preparing and rehearsing. In this way, you can acknowledge your nervousness without letting it take control.

Positive self-talk can be helpful in changing your approach to stressful situations. As you recall from Chapter 1, telling yourself about a situation in positive terms encourages constructive behavior.

For some people, the physical and emotional symptoms of stress can be relieved through relaxation techniques such as meditation. *(Courtesy of PhotoDisc.)*

You can increase your resiliency—your ability to cope with change and stress—by focusing on positive rather than negative thoughts.

You can also help change your thinking by taking a time-out from a stressful situation. Even something as simple as a short walk can provide a break and allow time for stress levels to diminish. After the break you will feel refreshed and have a new perspective on the problem.

Relieving Stress through Lifestyle Changes

The third basic way to cope with stress is to make lifestyle changes that can relieve the symptoms of stress. There are changes you can make to your diet, exercise regimen, and sleep patterns that will improve your ability to cope with stress.[3]

- **Decrease or cut out caffeine.** As you recall, caffeine is a stimulant; it has some of the same effects on the body that stress does. Avoiding coffee, tea, colas, and chocolate will reduce the physical symptoms of stress.

- **Eat a well-balanced diet.** A healthy diet will improve the body's ability to cope with stress. Avoid junk food, which is high in sugar and fat. In addition, you can eat certain foods such as grains, fruits, and vegetables; these are thought to have a calming effect.

- **Eat slowly.** Try to relax and enjoy your meals rather than racing through them.

- **Get enough sleep.** You know how many hours of sleep you need to feel good the next day. Try to get that amount every night. Lack of sleep makes people more susceptible to stress.

- **Get regular physical exercise.** Aerobic exercise such as walking, jogging, or swimming has been shown to decrease stress levels (see Chapter 6). Regular physical activity or sports can decrease tension and improve your strength and ability to cope.

- **Do relaxation exercises.** Activities such as resting, meditation, yoga, and deep breathing help relax the body and calm the mind.

- **Take a break each day.** Put a few minutes aside for yourself each day as a respite from the pressures of life. Pursue interests and hobbies that are a source of pleasure and distraction. Even a short rest can leave you relaxed and better able to cope.

Seeking Social Support

If you have family or friends, you will be able to cope with stress better than people who are on their own. Your family or friends may help you with the cause of your stress. For example, if you are overwhelmed by the conflicting demands of studying and housework, someone may take over a few of your chores. They may give you information that you need to solve a problem. In some cases, they can offer emotional support, reassuring you that someone cares about you.

It's interesting to note that women feel more comfortable about asking for help than men do. In times of stress, they are more likely to turn for help to their family or friends. Men tend to try to deal with stress on their own.

The Information Highway

GETTING UP TO SPEED

There are many stress-related resources on the Internet. Here are a few sites to get you started.

- A physician and his wife provide a good overview of the causes, symptoms, and control of stress <http://www.teachhealth.com>. The site is available in both English and Spanish.
- Tips for coping with stress can be found at <http://www.stressfree.com>.

To find more information about topics covered in this chapter, you can do a search using the key words *stress, stress management, Social Readjustment Rating Scale, posttraumatic stress disorder, anxiety, depression,* and *diazepam.*

Your Turn 12–5

YOUR SUPPORT GROUP

To whom would you turn if you were feeling stress? Use the circles below to represent members of your support group.[4] Write the names of the people to whom you feel closest in the circles that touch the central "me" circle. In the outer circles, write the names of those to whom you feel connected. The people you choose may live near or far or be from the past or present; they may even no longer be alive except within your memory.

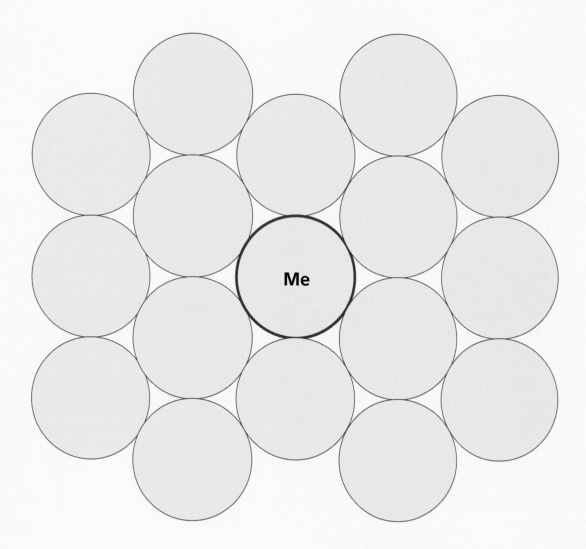

Me

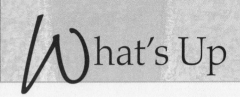
What's Up

Name _____ Date _____

1. What is stress?

_____
_____
_____
_____
_____

2. Why can certain stress-related circumstances be a positive experience?

_____
_____
_____
_____
_____

3. What are four characteristics of events that generally cause stress?

_____
_____
_____
_____
_____

4. What often happens to people who experience a large number of major life changes within a short time?

_____
_____
_____
_____
_____

5. Describe the difference between risk takers and risk avoiders.

_____
_____
_____
_____
_____

continues

Name _____ Date_____

6. Why do people with negative thought patterns experience a lot of stress?

_____

_____

_____

_____

_____

7. List physical, mental, emotional, and behavioral signs of stress.

_____

_____

_____

_____

_____

8. How does reframing your thoughts help you cope with stress?

_____

_____

_____

_____

_____

9. What are three lifestyle habits that help you cope with stress?

_____

_____

_____

10. How can people in your support group help you cope with stress?

_____

_____

_____

_____

_____

_____

Case Studies

THE CASE OF THE WOMAN WHO WAS TOO LUCKY

Right after she completed a course of study at a secretarial school, Heather got a job in a firm downtown. Two months later, she got married and moved from her parents' house into a new apartment with Jim. Her husband also started a new job.

Heather thought she should be happy about how well her life was going, but in reality she felt jumpy and anxious much of the time. When Heather's husband began to press her about starting a family, she was surprised to find she didn't want a baby. She had a new home, new job, and new husband to worry about. Why did Jim want to add to her problems? Yet Heather had always wanted children. What had happened to her? she wondered.

1. Why was Heather feeling jumpy and anxious about all the positive events in her life?

_____

_____

2. Why did Heather react negatively to her husband's desire to have a baby?

_____

_____

3. Do you think Heather's attitude toward having children will change in the future? Explain your answer.

_____

_____

THE CASE OF THE STRESSFUL JOB

Ramon had been working at a high-pressure job filled with daily deadlines for about three years. At the beginning of the fourth year, his workload increased when a colleague took a leave of absence. Ramon began experiencing shortness of breath and irregular heartbeat. When these symptoms persisted, he became convinced he was going to have a heart attack. He went to the doctor for a checkup and was told he was healthy. But the symptoms didn't go away.

That summer Ramon's boss talked him into taking three weeks off for vacation. By the end of the three weeks, Ramon's symptoms had disappeared.

1. What was the cause of Ramon's shortness of breath and irregular heartbeat?

_____

_____

2. Why did Ramon's symptoms disappear when he went on vacation?

_____

_____

3. What might Ramon do to cope with his stress?

_____

_____

Journal

Answer the following journal questions.

1. Compare your own experiences of major life events with the Social Readjustment Rating Scale on page 276. Do you put the same value on the events you experienced as the psychologists did? Do you feel they were more or less stressful than shown on the scale? Explain.

_____
_____
_____
_____
_____

2. What everyday hassles cause you stress? How can you use the coping skills described in this chapter to deal with them?

_____
_____
_____
_____
_____

3. Describe someone you know who has a resilient personality that enables him or her to recover quickly from stress. What does this person do to cope?

_____
_____
_____
_____
_____

4. What situation at home, at school, or on the job is causing you stress? How might you cope with the situation? What problem-solving, thinking, lifestyle, and social skills can you use to reduce the stress you are experiencing?

_____
_____
_____
_____
_____

Travelers hate losing time because of delayed flights. One reason Southwest Airlines is doing so well is that it has one of the best long-term on-time arrival rates of any airline. *(Courtesy of Benelux Press/Index Stock.)*

Chapter 13

Managing Time

Nothing symbolizes our culture's sense of time more than the digital clock and watch. Now, instead of the circular analog dial, which has hands sweeping around in a never-ending circle, we use digital displays, which show that each second and minute slip away forever.

Try this simple test with a friend who has a watch that measures seconds. Sit back, relax, and close your eyes. When your friend says, "Go," try to feel how long it takes for a minute to pass. If you are like most people, you'll stop the watch after about 30 seconds. Most of us have a speeded-up perception of time.

With such a view of time, we feel pressure to use time before it disappears. Time is a limited resource: If we don't use it, it's gone forever. The need to use time can lead to a great deal of stress, because in many cases, people feel that they are helpless to control it. And while it's true that we can't control the passage of time, we can do something about controlling our use of time. Using time management techniques, we can overcome some natural human tendencies like procrastinating and wasting time. We can try to make the most of the limited time we have.

In this chapter, you will learn some reasons why you may put off doing things and techniques you can use to overcome this problem. You will learn the importance of planning and setting priorities. You will also discover what you actually do with your time by keeping a time log. Finally, you will practice using a planner and "to do" list to improve your use of time.

THE TYRANNY OF TIME

Many of us are victims of our attitudes about time. We put things off, we complain about the lack of time, and we misuse the time we have. The purpose of time management is to help us overcome these problems.

Procrastination

Procrastination is putting off until tomorrow what you really ought to do today. Some people have developed procrastination into such a fine art that figuring out ways to postpone doing things takes up much of their time!

What Causes Procrastination? There are many causes of procrastination. Some people procrastinate because they are afraid to fail. When they are faced with a difficult task, the uncertainty they feel about its outcome causes great stress. Instead of going ahead, they find reasons for delaying.

Other people, who feel they don't control their lives, look for cues outside themselves that indicate they should start a task. You're familiar with the excuses of this type of procrastinator: "I'll start dieting (or whatever) on Monday," or "It's too cold (or hot or rainy) to do that." Some of these procrastinators even rely on astrology, numerology, or biorhythms to indicate the "right" time to perform a task.

Still other procrastinators fool themselves into thinking that the decision to perform a task is as good as actually finishing it. Such people might reason that since they decided to do their reading assignments sometime today, they'll go to the movies first. In this case, the reward comes before the accomplishment.

Overcoming Procrastination Why try to overcome procrastination? The most obvious reason, of course, is that if you can start a task on time, you are more likely to finish it on time. If you procrastinate, you'll find yourself pushing and missing deadlines or cramming for exams, situations that create stress. Another reason for overcoming procrastination is that timely performance of a task gives you more control over the task. When you start promptly, you are allowing yourself more time, more control, and therefore less stress.

> **If you wait, all that happens is you get older.**
>
> larry mcmurtry,
>
> american novelist

Procrastination can be a serious problem on the job. People who work at home, where there are many distractions, have to be on guard against procrastinating.
(Courtesy of Andersen Ross/Getty Images, Inc.)

DO YOU PROCRASTINATE?

Many people procrastinate, but not in all areas of their lives. Some keep up with personal matters and social relationships and let school or work responsibilities slide. Others do the opposite. Use the following checklist to see which areas you tend to procrastinate in.

SCHOOL

_____ Going to class

_____ Doing homework

_____ Keeping up with reading

_____ Preparing papers or projects

_____ Completing degree requirements

_____ Studying for exams

WORK

_____ Arriving on time

_____ Planning a career

_____ Meeting deadlines

_____ Looking for a job

_____ Making phone calls or appointments

_____ Solving a problem

PERSONAL

_____ Eating a proper diet

_____ Stopping smoking or drug use

_____ Pursuing hobbies

_____ Getting medical and dental checkups

_____ Exercising

_____ Setting goals

_____ Doing community service

SOCIAL

_____ Visiting relatives

_____ Visiting friends

_____ Ending a relationship

_____ Giving gifts or cards

_____ Asking for a date

_____ Returning phone calls

HOUSEHOLD AND FINANCES

_____ Daily chores

_____ Minor repairs

_____ Paying bills

_____ Balancing a checkbook

_____ Car maintenance

_____ Major repairs

_____ Budgeting

_____ Paying back loans

A third reason for overcoming procrastination is that you may actually get things done. The satisfaction you'll experience from doing something difficult is far greater than the satisfaction you'll get from postponing it indefinitely.

If procrastination is your problem, how can you overcome it? There are several basic approaches, one or more of which may work for you.[1]

- **Set a deadline for starting.** Some tasks take effort over time, so having a deadline for finishing is not enough. Set a time to start, and then stick to it.

- **Get yourself going with something easy.** If the task you face is tough and you can't plunge right in, start by doing something routine or easy. For example, if you have to write a difficult letter, prepare the envelope first. Then shift into the harder aspects of the task.

- **Reward yourself for progress.** If the task is large, reward yourself for accomplishing part of it. Save the biggest reward for completing it.

"Lack" of Time

Many people complain that they don't procrastinate, they just don't have enough time. They are beset by family, school, work, civic, and household responsibilities. Their spouses, children, parents, lovers, bosses, teachers, friends, and neighbors are making constant demands on their time. How can they ever get anything done?

The truth is that we all have the same number of hours each week: 168. How we use those hours is the critical factor. When they are pinned down, most people cannot account for how their time was spent.

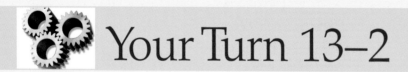# Your Turn 13–2

HOW DO YOU SPEND YOUR TIME?

You may be surprised to find out how you actually spend your time. Use the time log on pages 297–298 to record what you do for a week. For convenience, you can remove it from the book and carry it with you. Include all activities, even commuting, errands, watching TV, and "doing nothing."

Time	Monday	Tuesday	Wednesday
7 A.M.			
8			
9			
10			
11			
12 NOON			
1 P.M.			
2			
3			
4			
5			
6			
7			
8			
9			
10			
11			
12 MIDNIGHT			
1 A.M.			
2			
3			
4			
5			
6			

continues

Time	Thursday	Friday	Saturday	Sunday
7 A.M.				
8				
9				
10				
11				
12 NOON				
1 P.M.				
2				
3				
4				
5				
6				
7				
8				
9				
10				
11				
12 MIDNIGHT				
1 A.M.				
2				
3				
4				
5				
6				

Your Turn 13–3

HOW WELL DO YOU USE TIME?

Study the time log you did for "Your Turn" 13–2. Then answer the following questions:

1. Total the number of hours you spent on each of the following activities.

Sleeping _____ Eating _____ Working _____ Classes _____ Commuting _____

Studying _____ Chores _____ Exercising/sports _____ Socializing with friends/family _____

Watching TV _____ Doing nothing _____ Other (specify) _____

2. How much time did you spend on worthwhile activities?

_____

3. How much time did you waste on meaningless or trivial activities?

_____

4. Which activities do you wish you had spent more time on?

_____

5. Which activities do you wish you had spent less time on?

_____

6. List any activities you meant to do but never got around to during the week you kept the time log.

_____

7. After analyzing your use of time for the week, describe how you would "redo" the week if you had the opportunity to do so.

_____

_____

> *Employ thy time well, if thou meanest to gain leisure.*
>
> benjamin franklin,
> 18th-century statesman,
> scientist, and writer

Wasted Time and Misused Time

People who believe they don't have enough time to accomplish everything they want to accomplish may be facing two problems. First, they may be wasting time. They may be dawdling over meals, taking more time than necessary to finish a task, or doing nothing. (Of course, a certain amount of doing nothing is good for your mental health. But too much amounts to laziness.)

The second problem they may be facing is that they are misusing time. They are spending too much time on unimportant matters and too little time on what's important. Their days are eaten away by the trivial, and they never have time for the significant tasks and for leisure.

Another way to misuse time is to drift mentally and lose focus. It's important to stay in the moment and make sure your attention doesn't wander. As the saying goes, "Pay attention to your attention."

Why Manage Your Time?

You can see that without some effort on your part, time can easily slip away. Procrastinating, not having enough time, wasting time, and misusing time can add up to a life spent without reaching your potential. If you want to be in control of your life and achieve your goals, you will have to take charge of your time. Time management will help you do the things you must do, so that you'll have time to do the things you want to do.

GETTING ORGANIZED

The key to time management is being organized. This means you must keep your goals and tasks in mind and learn to plan ahead.

Remembering Your Goals

Do you remember the goals you set for yourself in Chapter 2? You set long-, intermediate-, and short-term personal, educational, professional, and community service goals for yourself. How many of these goals have you already lost sight of?

Setting goals is important, as we have learned. However, you will not reach your goals unless you learn to keep them in mind. Write them down and put them someplace where you'll see them, perhaps on your refrigerator or in your wallet.

Planning

A goal or project without a plan is a dream. **Planning** is a thinking process in which you devise an orderly and systematic approach to achieving an objective. Planning comes before doing. When you plan, you consider:

- what you have to do
- what resources—time, money, people, things, or information—you will need to do it
- how best to break the task down into manageable steps

You have already had some experience in creating action plans for your most important goals. No doubt you considered each goal separately and created plans for each. What happens, though, when your plan for one goal interferes with your plan for another goal?

Setting Priorities   Time management would be simple if you just had one goal to reach or one task to perform. But most of us have many goals and tasks on top of the dozens of routine activities we face each day. So every day, whether we're conscious of it or not, we make choices about how we will spend our time.

Part of planning is setting priorities—that is, deciding what tasks are the most important and must be done first. When you set priorities, you review everything you need to do and ask yourself:

1. What tasks must be done immediately (for example, buying your mother a birthday present when today is her birthday)?
2. What tasks are important to do soon?
3. What tasks can safely be delayed for a short period?
4. What tasks can be delayed for a week, a month, or longer?

Assign each matter you must take care of to one of these four categories. That will establish your priorities. Tasks in the first two categories have the highest priority and deserve your immediate attention.

Setting priorities helps you decide which tasks are most pressing. You will find that you may have to postpone one or more tasks to achieve the others.

There are time management tools, discussed in the next section, that can help you set up a schedule. But before you get into the specifics of your schedule, remember these tips:

- Be realistic about how long activities take. Some people routinely underestimate the time needed for a particular task. For example, if you commute to school or work during rush hour, don't allow 20 minutes when it's really a 30-minute trip with traffic.
- Some tasks have to be finished so that others may start. For example, if you have to write a paper, you will need to schedule research time before writing time.
- Remember that you have peak energy levels at certain times of day. Try to schedule difficult or important tasks at those times.
- Use what you learned about the way you actually spend your time from keeping the time log. What activities can you limit, eliminate, or combine with others? Are there any periods of time you're not using wisely?

Scheduling   Once your priorities are set, you can effectively schedule your time. First, of course, you must account for the time you spend on fixed daily activities such as sleeping, eating, personal hygiene, work, and

Planners and personal digital assistants (PDAs) are excellent tools for time management. They come in different formats, sizes, and prices to suit different needs. *(Courtesy of Tom Stock.)*

Your Turn 13–4

SET YOUR PRIORITIES

To give you practice in setting priorities, think about the most important things you want to do this week. Write each activity below, and assign it a priority number from 1 to 4.

1. highest priority, cannot be delayed

2. important, should be done as soon as possible

3. less important, can be done next week

4. least important, can be postponed more than a week if necessary

_____

_____

_____

_____

_____

_____

_____

attending class. Then you can allocate the time left over to the tasks with the highest priority.

USING TIME MANAGEMENT TOOLS

To help you schedule your time, you can use a planner for intermediate- and long-term scheduling and "to do" lists for daily activities.

Planners for Intermediate- and Long-Term Activities

Planners are basically calendars designed to be used for planning. They take the form of pocket calendars, weekly planners, diaries, personal digital assistants (PDAs), and computer-based calendars, and they are available in pharmacies, discount department stores,

VIEWS OF TIME

How long would you wait for someone if you had arranged to meet at noon and he or she didn't show up at noon? Fifteen minutes? Half an hour? If you are like most people in industrialized cultures, you might wait half an hour at most. After that, you would go on to your next appointment or task. That's because people in industrialized nations have a linear view of time. We see time as an arrow moving forward in a straight line. On this time line, yesterday is gone forever, today is a brief moment, and tomorrow is coming up fast. We divide our days into appointments, schedules, and routines, and we do one thing at a time. We see time as a resource in short supply, so we don't want to waste it.

Not everyone shares this view of time. In rural cultures, time is seen as an endless circle. Days follow days, seasons follow seasons, and time is nature's time, not man's time. If one day is "wasted," another day will come. People in rural cultures do not understand the rigid and compulsive attitude toward time that those of us in industrialized societies have. Without the need to coordinate work in large factories or organizations, where work can be done day or night, rural people still tell time by the rhythms of nature.

An interesting contrast in two cultures' views of time can be seen from their calendars. In many countries of the West, including the United States, the years are counted from the year of Jesus' birth. The year 2003 means 2,003 years after the birth of Jesus. In this type of linear calendar, the years add up one by one. China has used this Western calendar since 1911, but the traditional way of naming the years in China is cyclical. Every year is given an animal sign according to a cycle that repeats: Rat, Ox, Tiger, Rabbit, Dragon, Snake, Horse, Sheep, Monkey, Rooster, Dog, and Boar. In this calendar, each animal sign repeats every 12 years. The animal signs are associated with horoscopes, just as the signs of the zodiac are in Western astrology. The Chinese consider the animal horoscopes fun, but they do not take them seriously. Rather, they use the animal signs to find out a person's age without asking directly. If you know that someone was born in the year of the Rat, for example, you can guess which cycle the person was born in and so deduce his or her exact age.

office supply stores, and electronics stores. They come in a variety of formats and prices, and they are all designed to help you schedule weeks and months ahead.

When you open them, some planners display a month at a time, some a week at a time, and some two days at a time. For most people, the month-at-a-time display doesn't provide enough room to enter all their appointments and commitments. The week-at-a-time or two-day format is better, because it allows more room to write.

FIGURE 13–1

A daily "to do" list helps you plan and keep track of tasks. Crossing off items as you do them can give you a sense of accomplishment.

To Do
~~Read Ch. 12 of Stephenson~~
Do Ch. 12 of Stephenson study guide
Study for English quiz
~~Work 1:30~~
~~Return videos~~
Call Kaylee

Whichever format you select, make sure the planner is a convenient size for you to carry with you all the time.

Your planner should be your single source of information about your time schedule. In other words, don't put goal schedules in one place, social appointments in another calendar, and school activities in a third. Use the planner to plan and record all commitments on your time. Keep it up to date.

"To Do" Lists for Daily Activities

In addition to keeping a planner, making a daily "to do" list can help you get things done. A "to do" list, prepared each morning or the night before, lists all the tasks you want to accomplish that day (see Figure 13–1). The act of creating the list helps you plan your day. Consulting the list during the day helps you remember what you need to do. And crossing an item off when you finish it will give you a sense of accomplishment.

> **You may delay, but time will not.**
>
> *benjamin franklin,*
> *18th-century statesman,*
> *scientist, and writer*

It's hard to get things done when family members need you. Parents of young children may find it is less stressful to attend to their children's needs first and try to get their own work done later. *(Courtesy of PhotoDisc.)*

TIME MANAGEMENT STRATEGIES

Part of effective time management is recognizing that life rarely proceeds exactly as planned. You may be great at organizing yourself, making plans, schedules, and lists. But what happens to you when the unexpected interferes, as it always does? Do your plans and schedules go to pieces, or are you able to recover and accomplish something?

The ability to be organized *and* flexible about the use of time characterizes a truly effective time manager. Effective time managers can handle interruptions and the demands of others. They have learned to say no when their time is already committed. They can shift priorities if necessary. And they are good at using unexpected gifts of time.

Dealing with the Demands of Others

When people start prioritizing and scheduling their time, sometimes they forget that they are certain to be interrupted by friends, family, and colleagues. Some of this can be avoided, of course. If you know that your brother will want your attention when you're studying at home, you can try studying in a library. Or you can ask the person interrupting you if you can get back to him or her later.

But, in reality, the people you live with, work with, and socialize with have a right to some of your time and attention. Ignoring this fact will cause you a lot of stress, because your plans will constantly be falling apart and your relationships with others will suffer.

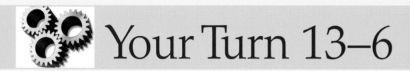

Your Turn 13–5

USE A PLANNER

Practice using a planner by filling in your time commitments for the next week using the weekly planner on pages 306–307. Start by entering your routine commitments and any special appointments, whether business, school, or social. Then plan study time, goal time, and leisure time. You can remove the weekly planner from the book and carry it with you for convenient use.

Your Turn 13–6

MAKE A "TO DO" LIST

In the space below, make a "to do" list of all the tasks you wish to accomplish tomorrow. Assign each one a priority number from 1 to 4 as follows:

1. highest priority, cannot be delayed
2. important, should be done as soon as possible
3. less important, can be done within a few days
4. least important, can be postponed a week or more if necessary

_____
_____
_____
_____
_____
_____
_____
_____
_____
_____

Tomorrow, as you finish each item, cross it off.

Time	Monday	Tuesday	Wednesday
7 A.M.			
8			
9			
10			
11			
12 NOON			
1 P.M.			
2			
3			
4			
5			
6			
7			
8			
9			
10			
11			
12 MIDNIGHT			
1 A.M.			
2			
3			
4			
5			
6			

continues

Time	Thursday	Friday	Saturday	Sunday
7 A.M.				
8				
9				
10				
11				
12 NOON				
1 P.M.				
2				
3				
4				
5				
6				
7				
8				
9				
10				
11				
12 MIDNIGHT				
1 A.M.				
2				
3				
4				
5				
6				

Therefore, you should plan to be interrupted. Leave what's called "response time" in your schedule: a cushion of time you can use to respond to the people around you. If you plan more time than you think you'll actually need to finish a task, you will still be able to finish it by your deadline even if you are interrupted. And you will remove a source of stress—the conflict between your plan and someone else's needs.

Learning to Say No

There are just so many hours in a day, and an effective time manager knows this. Therefore, he or she has developed the ability to say no to additional projects, responsibilities, or demands when accepting them would mean being overcommitted. You need to set priorities on the demands for your time. Developing assertiveness and the willingness to say no will help you accomplish your tasks and goals.

Using Unexpected Gifts of Time

Every once in a while, something unexpected happens and you have 10 minutes or an hour with "nothing" to do. How do you respond to these gifts of time? If you are an effective time manager, you use these small bits of time to get something done.

The key to using time that you might otherwise just spend waiting is to be prepared with small tasks you can do. For example, you might carry some reading material or schoolwork with you. You can use the time to take a walk or get some other exercise, or you can run the errand you've been putting off. You can make a start on the big project you've postponed. In other words, don't just wait for the time to pass. Use it.

An unexpected gift of time can be used to get things done, or it can be used to relax and gather your energy for the rest of the day. *(Courtesy of Steve Cole/Getty Images, Inc.)*

WHATEVER IT TAKES

Donna Fujimoto Cole

(Courtesy of Kaye Marvins/Houston.)

Growing up in the small town of McAllen, Colorado, Donna Fujimoto Cole was the daughter of a farmer and a high school cafeteria worker. There was one other Asian family in town besides the Fujimotos, and Cole remembers being teased by kids in elementary school.

When she was 18, Cole left McAllen to attend a junior college in Texas. Within a year, she quit school and moved to Houston, Texas, where she married John Cole and had a daughter four years later. By that time, Cole needed a job badly to help pay off her husband's debts. During an interview for a secretarial job at a one-man chemical trading company, she answered the telephone when it rang. Her initiative landed her the job on the spot.

Over the years, Cole learned a lot about the business of buying and selling chemicals. In 1978 her employer spun off Del Ray Chemical International to take advantage of a minority set-aside program. Cole and two Hispanic partners were the minorities, owning a small stake in the business. But Cole didn't care for the financial arrangement. So in 1979, newly divorced, Cole used $5,000 of her own savings to start Cole Chemical & Distributing Company.

At first Cole ran her business out of a friend's office. Money was so tight that she didn't pay herself a salary. Her mother gave her groceries or sent her cash to keep going. Cole depended heavily on the help of her parents, friends, and day-care centers to help take care of her daughter while she built up the business. Today, Cole's company has sales of about $60 million a year.

Cole attributes her success in part to hard work and in part to luck. "There were a lot of people who did business with the government who felt they had to buy from small minority business owners," she says. "They also saw somebody who was going to care about their business."

In recent years, Cole has broadened her activities beyond her business. She volunteered her time with 22 organizations until she decided she was spreading herself too thin. At that point Cole decided to focus on business-related organizations. For her work, Cole has received dozens of awards over the years; her company is one of the top 100 minority-owned businesses in the United States

"There's a need for Asian women to be able to grow and to learn to lead," says Cole. "They have so much to give back."

Sources: Asian Women in Business, "The AWIB 2002 Entrepreneurial Leadership Award Winner, Donna Fujimoto Cole" <http://www.awib.org/content_frames/DonnaFujimotoCole.html>, accessed March 31, 2003; Janean Chun, "Take the Lead," *Entrepreneur*, June 1996, p. 46; Tuck School of Business Web site, Jan. 26, 1998 <http://www.dartmouth.edu/tuck>; Houston Chemical Association, "Honorary Members, Donna Fujimoto Cole" <http://www. houstonchemical.org/honorary.html>, accessed March 31, 2003; "100 Leading Asian American Entrepreneurs: Donna Fujimoto Cole; Chemical Distribution," *Transpacific,* No. 67 (1996), pp. 72–73.

The Information Highway

GETTING UP TO SPEED

You can start your search for time management resources on the Internet on the following sites.

- Mind Tools provides general suggestions for time management on its Web site <http://www.mindtools.com>.
- The George Mason University Web site has a "time management tips" section for college students <http://www.gmu.edu/>.
- If you are interested in different viewpoints on time and calendars, check "calendar wonders" at the Mie Net Web site <http://www.mienet.net/>.

Use a search engine and the following key words to find information related to topics in this chapter: *procrastination, time management strategies, getting organized, calendars,* and *planners.*

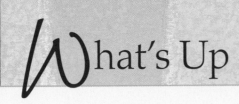

What's Up

Name _____ Date _____

1. Why do people procrastinate?

_____
_____
_____
_____
_____
_____
_____

2. List three techniques for overcoming procrastination.

_____
_____
_____

3. What are the benefits of time management?

_____
_____
_____
_____
_____

4. What is planning?

_____
_____
_____
_____

5. Why is it important to set priorities?

_____
_____
_____
_____
_____
_____

continues

Name _____   Date_____

6. When you set up a schedule, what items do you schedule first?

_____

_____

_____

_____

_____

7. What is the purpose of a planner or PDA?

_____

_____

_____

_____

_____

8. How can a daily "to do" list be used?

_____

_____

_____

_____

_____

9. Why it is important to plan on being interrupted?

_____

_____

_____

_____

10. How can you be prepared to use unexpected gifts of time?

_____

_____

_____

_____

Case Studies

THE CASE OF THE HARRIED STUDENT

Barbara always complained to her friend Alyssa that she had no time. Alyssa found this hard to believe, since Barbara had a light course load at school and didn't work. One day the two friends spent the day together, and Alyssa got to see what Barbara's school was like.

Barbara was late in meeting Alyssa, because she had gotten up late and spent too much time over breakfast. After Barbara's first class, which they barely got to in time, they had an hour's break. Barbara said she needed to get some information from the school library in order to complete an assignment that night. But instead of going to the library, they ran into some friends and had some coffee. After the second class, they had an hour for lunch. Barbara was scheduled for an hour in the computer lab, which turned out to be only 45 minutes, since the friends got there late. Then Barbara had a doctor's appointment, and it was clear she would be late for that, too. When Alyssa left her friend, she realized they had never gotten to the library.

1. Describe three problems that Barbara has with time.

_____

_____

_____

2. Do you think Barbara has enough time to do what she needs to do in the course of the day? Explain.

_____

_____

_____

_____

_____

THE CASE OF A MAN AND A PLAN

Leon went to school, worked part-time, and had a wife and son, so it was important to him to manage his commitments efficiently. He bought a handsome planner and carefully scheduled his routine school and work commitments, study time, school projects, household chores, and exercise time.

The first couple of days that Leon used the planner everything went as scheduled. But on the third day, Leon's son got sick, and Leon stayed home to take care of him. He missed classes and the opportunity to do some research for a special project.

On the fourth day, Leon's son was better and could go to day care, but his wife wanted him to come to an office party during the time he had planned on working out. In the evening his son

continues

wanted him to play with him, not study. On the fifth day he unexpectedly had to work overtime, and that bumped several things right off his schedule. Leon was starting to feel frustrated and annoyed. He was beginning to think the planner had been a waste of time and money.

1. Was it a good idea for Leon to use a planner?

_____

_____

2. What was wrong with the way Leon was scheduling his time?

_____

_____

3. How could Leon become a more effective time manager?

_____

_____

_____

Journal

Answer the following journal questions.

1. Assess your current approach to time management. Are you a procrastinator? Are you organized? Do you meet all your deadlines? Do you use any time management tools?

2. What activity do you consider your biggest time waster? What benefit do you get from this activity? Is it worth the amount of time you spend?

3. How do you meet the demands of your family and friends, as well as the demands of school and work? What might make juggling these easier for you?

4. How do you keep track of everything you have to do now? How can you improve your ability to plan and schedule activities?

5. What would you do if you had a day with no demands on your time?

Some people use their success to benefit good causes. Actress Marlo Thomas continues the work of her father, comedian Danny Thomas, who founded St. Jude Children's Research Hospital. *(AP/Wide World Photos/Mario Suriani.)*

Chapter 14

Managing Money

What are your dreams and goals? Do you want to start your own business, take a winter vacation in Hawaii, or go to school full-time? The chances are that no matter what your goals and dreams are, you will need money to achieve them. And that's money over and above the amount you need for the basics of life—food, shelter, clothing, and so on.

For almost all of us, money, like time, is a limited resource. We earn or receive a limited amount, and with that we try to get by—often from paycheck to paycheck. But just as you must manage your time to get the most out of it, you must learn to manage money for the same reason.

This chapter covers the basics of money management. Before we begin, you will assess your attitudes toward money. Then you will see how the financial pyramid, with your values and goals at its base, provides a model of lifelong personal money management. With this as background, you will go on to track your income and expenses and prepare a monthly budget. You will review the basics of banking, savings, credit, and insurance. Finally, you will weigh the pros and cons of home ownership and learn about the importance of investing now for future expenses such as retirement.

ATTITUDES TOWARD MONEY

Money is a resource that carries a high emotional charge for many people. Time, or lack of it, can cause anxiety and stress, but attitudes toward money are often tangled up with a person's self-belief. American culture places great importance on achieving material success. In this view, the possession of money is often equated with a person's inner worth. The more money you have, the better you are as a person. When money defines self-belief, people depend on possessions to boost their feelings of worth. And possessions, although nice, are not a solid foundation for a positive self-belief.

How do you feel about money? Do you see money as making you a better person? Or do you view money as a tool, something you can use to achieve your goals, whether educational, professional, or personal? The following activity will help you define your attitudes about money.

> **Misplaced emphasis occurs . . . when you think that everything is going well because your car drives so smoothly, and your new suit fits you so well, and those high-priced shoes you bought make your feet feel so good; and you begin to believe that these things, these many luxuries all around, are the really important matters of your life.**
>
> *martin luther king jr.,*
> *civil rights leader*

THE FINANCIAL PYRAMID

Now that you have thought about your attitudes toward money, try putting these aside for a while. You'll be a better money manager if you can separate your decisions about money from your feelings. In the remainder of this chapter, we will focus on various aspects of money management. First we will look at the big picture of money management, and then we will consider some of the details that will help you make financial decisions.

The big picture of personal money management is shown by the financial pyramid (see Figure 14–1 on page 320). The financial pyramid provides a visual model of the main aspects of personal finance. At the base of the financial pyramid are your values and goals. These should be the foundation of all your money decisions. The next step up is your basic living expense—shelter, food, clothing, and so on. Before you can go on to spend money on other things, you must take care of your basic living costs. Once you've budgeted for the basics, you can move up a step to consider savings, credit, and insurance. When these are incorporated in your financial plan, most people are ready to move up a step to home ownership, the main investment of many families. Finally, people devote resources to long-term investing. Common goals for long-term investment are saving for their children's education and saving for retirement.

The financial pyramid helps people set priorities on using their money resources and provides a reminder of important long-term financial goals that people need to act on even when they are young. However, the financial pyramid model may not apply equally to everyone. For example, some families never own a home; others do

Your Turn 14–1

HOW DO YOU FEEL ABOUT MONEY?

This exercise will give you an idea about your attitudes toward money. Circle the answer that corresponds most closely with your feelings.

■ When you think of having money, you imagine it
  1 coming from your parents.
  2 belonging to your spouse or significant other.
  3 belonging to you.

■ As a child, you spent your allowance or pocket money on
  1 anything you wanted.
  2 necessities.
  3 birthday and holiday presents for your relatives.

■ When you were younger, you hated math and did poorly in it. Now that you need to make money decisions, you
  1 figure you can't balance a checkbook, much less use your money wisely.
  2 put off making money decisions because you dislike math.
  3 tell yourself that math has nothing to do with your ability to handle money.

■ You have just $35 to spend on food and other necessities until payday, four days from now. Passing a pizza place, you
  1 splurge on a pizza with all the toppings.
  2 keep going, since you can't even afford to look in the window.
  3 promise yourself to stop in after payday to buy a pizza.

■ You get an unexpectedly large gift of $500. You
  1 blow it on an expensive watch and new clothes.

  2 invest in bank certificates that will tie up the money for 30 months.
  3 put the money in a savings account to which you have access.

■ You want to go back to school. You have enough money for only a quarter of the total tuition for the degree or program. You
  1 enroll anyway. Something will come up to pay for the other three quarters.
  2 enroll for a couple of courses, even though they're likely to be your last.
  3 make a plan for financing the whole program through work, grants, and loans.

■ You won $30,000. You desperately need a new refrigerator and TV. You
  1 hold off until the refrigerator breaks down and TVs go on sale.
  2 put all the money in the bank and do without a new refrigerator and TV.
  3 buy both.

■ Word of your luck has spread at school. The first time your fellow students don't ask you to join them at lunch, you
  1 feel sorry you won the money.
  2 spend lunch time buying them presents.
  3 ignore them and visit a financial planner during your lunch.

To get your score, add up the numbers you circled. Check the results below.

Your score   What it means

8–10 points   You tend to be very emotional about money. You should beware of making sudden money decisions.
11–17 points   You are shaky about making money decisions. Although you probably won't make major mistakes, you also won't get the most out of your money.
18–24 points   You have an objective attitude toward money and its uses. Be sure you consider all the consequences before making a money decision.

FIGURE 14–1

The financial pyramid provides a model for financial planning. The foundation of the pyramid is your values and goals. All decisions about money should arise from that foundation.

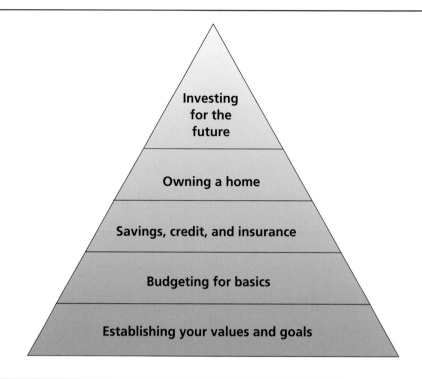

- Investing for the future
- Owning a home
- Savings, credit, and insurance
- Budgeting for basics
- Establishing your values and goals

not use credit. In addition, the model is not always sequential. Although most people consider these aspects of financial planning in the order shown, from bottom to top, this sequence does not always apply. For example, if you are living with your parents, you may not need to contribute to basic household expenses, but you may already have dealt with credit when you applied for student loans. Once families are well established, however, they are probably making personal finance decisions on each level of the pyramid—at the same time.

BUDGETING FOR THE BASICS

Planning how you will use your money is called budgeting. A **budget** is a plan based on your short-, intermediate-, and long-term financial goals. The purpose of a budget is to keep your spending within the limits of your income and to distribute your spending appropriately.

Budgeting has important benefits. The first, of course, is that you will have a better idea of exactly where your money comes from and where it goes. But just as important, budgeting helps you focus on your goals and set priorities for achieving them. Right now you probably don't have enough money for all the things you want to do. Does it surprise you to learn that you will probably never have enough money for all the things you want to do? Even though your income may increase in the future, so will your financial responsibilities and your wants. This means you must think about your goals and decide what's most important to you. Budgeting forces you to make choices,

Your Turn 14–2

REVIEW YOUR VALUES AND GOALS

Now is a good time to turn back to Chapters 1 and 2 and review your values and goals. Summarize your most important values and goals below. Underline the goals that involve money.

1. Most important values

_____

_____

_____

2. Short-term goals

_____

_____

_____

_____

3. Intermediate-term goals

_____

_____

_____

_____

4. Long-term goals

_____

_____

_____

_____

plan ahead, and control your spending.[1] But before you can budget, you must have a thorough knowledge of your income and expenses.

Income and Expenses

If you are like most people, you have a pretty good idea of where your money comes from. Your **income** is the total amount of money coming in. You may have just one or several sources of income:

- a salary you earn by working
- an allowance from your parents or spouse
- alimony or child support payments

- welfare payments or food stamps
- social security payments
- disability payments
- student financial aid
- tax refunds
- gifts
- interest earned on savings
- dividends earned on investments

The total amount of your income, from all sources, is called your gross income. If you are working, your employer withholds amounts from your paycheck to pay federal and local taxes, if any, social security (FICA), group insurance premiums, union dues, pension contributions, and other deductions. Thus the amount of money you actually receive, called your net income, is less than your gross income.

Far harder to account for—at least for most people—is where the money goes. The amounts you spend are called expenses. Most people have fixed expenses, which are the same from month to month or are due quarterly or yearly. Examples of fixed expenses are rent or mortgage payments, car payments, telephone and utility bills, cable TV bills, installment loan payments, savings plans, and insurance payments. Variable expenses differ from one period to another. Food, clothing, entertainment, gas, repairs, gifts, furniture, books, and education are just a few examples of variable expenses.

Needless to say, if your expenses are greater than your income, or if you are unable to put away money to achieve long-term objectives, you have a problem. You can improve your money situation by budgeting.

The Four A's of Budgeting

Budgeting has four basic steps, called the four A's of budgeting.[2]

1. accounting for income and expenses
2. analyzing your situation
3. allocating your income
4. adjusting your budget

Accounting for Income and Expenses   The first step of budgeting is accounting for your income and expenses. What this means, in practice, is that you have to keep track of income and expenses for a couple of months. You keep track not only of big expenses like car payments but small expenses like renting a DVD or buying a snack. If you have a checking account or make most purchases with a credit or debit card, you will have good records of many of your expenses.

To track income and expenses, you can keep a notebook set up as shown on pages 324–325. Divide the notebook into two sections—

> **The use of money is all the advantage there is in having money.**
>
> *benjamin franklin,*
>
> *18th-century statesman,*
>
> *scientist, and writer*

Your Turn 14–3

TRACK YOUR INCOME AND EXPENSES

Use the income and expense record on pages 324–325 to keep track of all your income and expenses for two months. You can remove the chart from your book and carry it with you for convenience.

a small section for income and a large section for expenses. When you get paid or receive money, enter the date, source, and amount in the income section. When you spend money—even 50 cents for a newspaper—jot down the date, what you bought, and how much you paid in the expenses section. Remember to enter items you purchase with a credit card. For example, if you charge a pair of shoes, enter the amount you charge in the Clothing column. To make record keeping easier, you can divide your expenses into categories such as rent, telephone, utilities, food, clothing, transportation, medical/dental, entertainment, personal items, gifts, and so on. At the end of each month, total your income and expenses by categories. These figures will be the basis for your budget.

Allocating Your Income   Now comes decision-making time. You've kept track of income and expenses for a couple of months and you've reviewed your spending patterns. You probably think that at this rate you'll never have money to reach your goals! But there are things you can do.

Analyzing Your Situation   After you've kept track of income and expenses for a couple of months, you should analyze your situation. Ask yourself some questions:

- Did your expenses exceed your income?
- Were you able to pay all your fixed expenses?
- Did a large periodic expense such as an annual insurance premium or tuition bill throw you off?
- Are you spending too much money on some types of things?
- Did you pay off all your credit card balances, or did you get by with the minimum payment?
- Were you able to save money for one of your goals (vacation, tuition, a new stereo, a car, down payment on a house, retirement, etc.)?

Your answers to these questions will point up any weaknesses in your current money situation.

Income and Expense Record, Month of _____

Income

Date	Source	Net Amount
	Total	

Expenses

Date	Rent/Mortgage	Telephone	Utilities	Insurance	Loan	Transportation	Food
Totals							

Date	Clothing	Household	Medical	Education	Savings/Emerg.	Personal	Other
Totals							

Total expenses for month _____

Income and Expense Record, Month of _____

Income

Date	Source	Net Amount
	Total	

Expenses

Date	Rent/Mortgage	Telephone	Utilities	Insurance	Loan	Transportation	Food
Totals							

Date	Clothing	Household	Medical	Education	Savings/Emerg.	Personal	Other
Totals							

Total expenses for month _____

First, figure out how much you must allocate to each of your monthly fixed expenses. You must allocate money for bills you pay monthly (such as rent, electricity, and credit card payments), as well as bills you pay quarterly, semiannually, or annually (insurance premiums, tuition, excise taxes, real estate taxes, and so on). Perhaps you noticed that you were unprepared to pay that semiannual auto insurance premium or some other periodic large bill. If you set aside a certain amount of money each month, you would be ready to pay those large, occasional, but regular expenses. For example, if the cost of your auto insurance premium is $600 a year, you should be allocating $50 each month toward that expense.

After you've budgeted your fixed expenses, review your variable expenses to see where you are overspending. Here you must make judgments between what you really need and what you want. For example, are you spending a lot more than you thought on personal items and restaurant meals? If you could cut down on these expenditures, you could use the money you save to pay down your credit card balance or start saving. Try to allocate money for things that are really important to you in the long run.

Next, consider what you would do if your car broke down and needed a $300 repair. These things happen all the time, but if you haven't set aside money in an **emergency fund**, you'll be caught short when something unexpected happens. A minimum of two months' income is recommended for your emergency fund. That will help cover unplanned expenses such as repairs and loss of income through disability or unemployment. Remember to replenish the fund as soon as you can if you take money out of it.

Finally, consider your goals. If you want to take a vacation in Europe or buy a house, start saving now—even if you can only afford a few dollars a month. (If your goal is more important to you than anything else, you might want to start the allocation process with money toward the goal. Then you'll have to reduce your other expenditures until your goal is met. Some people live frugally for years in order to meet an important financial goal, such as paying for an education, buying a house, or starting a business.)

Adjusting Your Budget   A budget is not carved in stone. As you try out your budget you may find that you haven't planned realistically or you've forgotten some items altogether. Your income will change, your expenses will change, and your goals will change. For these reasons, you should plan to review your budget periodically and revise it as necessary.

Your Turn 14–4

MAKE UP A MONTHLY BUDGET

Use the information you gathered and analyzed to allocate your income on a monthly basis. In the space below, enter the dollar amounts you plan to spend on each of the following expenses for a period of one month.

Item	Budgeted Amount
Rent or mortgage	_____
Telephone, cell phone	_____
Utilities (gas, oil, electricity, water, sewer)	_____
Cable TV/Internet access	_____
Insurance (auto, health, life, homeowners', disability, etc.)	_____
Installment loans, car payments	_____
Transportation (gas, maintenance, repairs, parking, carfare)	_____
Food (groceries and restaurant meals)	_____
Clothing	_____
Household items and repairs	_____
Gifts	_____
Medical/dental	_____
Education (tuition, books, fees)	_____
Personal (include entertainment)	_____
Emergency fund	_____
Taxes not withheld (self-employment, excise, real estate)	_____
Savings toward goals	_____
Other_____	_____
_____	_____
_____	_____
_____	_____
_____	_____

SAVINGS AND DEBIT CARDS

Savings and Banking

Most people find it's not safe or convenient to have all their money in cash. They put the money they don't need for day-to-day expenses in a bank or financial institution. The institution may be a commercial bank, savings and loan, or credit union. When selecting a financial institution to deposit your money, you should consider:

- Up to what amount your deposits are insured and by whom. Federal insurance, such as the FDIC, is a better risk than state insurance funds, some of which have gone broke in the past.
- Interest rates.
- The accessibility of your money.
- Convenience of location and service.
- The types of accounts that are offered.
- Fees charged for various services.

You may need more than one account to manage your money. Most people need a **checking account** to pay routine bills (see Figure 14–2). They deposit part of their earnings and write checks to pay bills, keeping a record of each transaction in a check register. Checking accounts vary a great deal. Some pay interest if you keep a minimum balance. Some charge you for each check and ATM transaction; others charge a monthly fee with unlimited service. Some allow you to pay bills on-line. You should shop around to find the best services for your needs.

Large sums of money shouldn't be kept in a checking account, especially an account that pays no interest. Instead, you can put extra money into a savings account that pays compound interest. With compound interest, you get interest both on the money you deposited and the interest it has already earned. Over time, that can add up. A quick way to figure out how long it will take for your savings to double is called the "rule of 72." Just divide 72 by the interest rate

FIGURE 14–2

People keep money in checking accounts for cash and for paying bills. Each month the bank sends a statement listing all deposits, withdrawals, and checks. Some banks provide on-line access to account information as well.

```
FIRST TRUST BANK                                              - - -           PAGE    1 OF 1
Central Avenue Branch                        JOHN J. BROWN                          992 613 CY
Anytown, USA 00000                          Central 123 Elm Court
                                            Anytown, USA 00000                        13435711
                                                                                    6134357116
          STATEMENT OF YOUR ACCOUNT(S) FOR PERIOD 4-15-05 THROUGH 5-13-05
**************************************************************************************
                    SUMMARY OF REGULAR ACCOUNT # 18 485711

BALANCE ON 04/15                502.10
DEPOSITS AND INTEREST         1,551.08
WITHDRAWALS                   1,494.28
BALANCE ON 05/13                558.90       TAXPAYER ID NUMBER    123 45 6789
```

DATE	CHECK #	TRANSACTION DESCRIPTION	AMOUNT	BALANCE
4/15		BEGINNING BALANCE		$ 502.10
4/18	4951	THE BOOK STORE	−25.00	477.10
4/22		POS PURCHASE/GAS STATION, ANYTOWN, USA 00000	−15.00	462.10
4/23		DEPOSIT	650.15	1,112.25
4/23	4949	THE CABLE COMPANY	−48.25	1,064.00
4/25		POS PURCHASE—4/24 THE STORE, ANYTOWN, USA 00000	−67.20	996.80
4/28		ATM WITHDRAWAL-4/27, ROBIN ST., ANYTOWN, USA 00000	−80.00	916.80
5/01		BILL PAY—NATURAL GAS COMPANY ON-LINE 1234 ON 5/1	−123.76	793.04
5/03	4950	THE PET STORE	−33.34	759.70
5/03		BILL PAY—INSURANCE COMPANY ON-LINE 1234 ON 5/3	−155.00	604.70
5/05	4952	CREDIT CARD COMPANY	−96.73	507.97
5/07		DEPOSIT	650.15	1,158.12
5/08	4953	MORTGAGE COMPANY	−750.00	408.12
5/10		ATM WITHDRAWAL—5/09, CENTRAL AVE., ANYTOWN, USA 00000	−100.00	308.12
5/12		DEPOSIT	250.00	558.12
5/13		INTEREST PAYMENT	.78	558.90

```
CHECKS POSTED   (# INDICATED SEQUENCE BREAK)
  CHECK . . . . AMOUNT . . . . DATE    CHECK . . . . AMOUNT . . . . DATE    CHECK . . . . AMOUNT . . . . DATE
    4949          48.25        4/23      4951          25.00        4/18      4953         750.00        5/08
    4950          33.34        5/03      4952          96.73        5/05
```

you expect to earn. So, for example, if you are earning 6 percent interest, it will take 12 years for your money to double.

There are a variety of savings options to choose from:

- **Passbook accounts** can be opened with very little money; they pay the least interest.
- **Money market accounts** have interest rates that fluctuate with market rates, but some may require a minimum balance or limit your access to the money.
- **Certificates of deposit** (CDs) offer the highest interest rates, but they tie up your money for a stated period. If you need to withdraw your funds before the certificate comes due, you will pay a penalty.
- **Individual retirement accounts** (IRAs) are used to put aside money for retirement. If you withdraw the funds at an earlier age, there may be a stiff penalty.

As your financial responsibilities increase, you may need more than one savings account. If you are unsure which type of account is right for you, ask your financial institution's customer service representative for advice.

Debit Cards

About two thirds of American households now use a **debit card** as a form of payment beyond cash and checks. A debit card allows you to pay for something with money from your checking or savings account without using cash or a check. When you use a debit card, the amount of the payment is subtracted from the balance in your checking or savings account.

There are two basic types of debit cards. The first is an "on-line" debit card. This is usually an ATM card that includes the debit feature. To access your bank account at a store, you use the card as you would at an ATM machine, identifying yourself with your personal identification number (PIN). The second type of debit card is an "off-line" debit card. This card looks like a credit card, and the transaction is more like a credit card transaction. Instead of using a PIN number, you sign a receipt.

Many people like debit cards because of their convenience and the "pay now" feature. With a debit card, they cannot spend more money than they have.

CREDIT

Buy now, pay later. Sounds wonderful, doesn't it? **Credit** is a financial arrangement that gives you the right to defer payment on merchandise or services. In essence, you are using someone else's money to

> **Money is like a sixth sense, and you can't enjoy the other five without it.**
>
> somerset maugham, novelist

pay for something. But—you must pay back what you borrowed, plus a charge for using the money, called **interest**. So anything you buy on credit will cost you more than if you pay cash.

There are times when using credit is worth the price you pay. A genuine emergency like a large medical bill, a genuine necessity like a car repair, or paying tuition for a degree program are all examples of situations in which it is appropriate to borrow money. On the other hand, buying a luxury item because the credit terms look easy and borrowing when you have no prospect of being able to pay the money back are two situations in which you should not use credit.

So be careful when you are considering using credit. It's tempting—and easy—to borrow money and use credit cards. But unless you keep tight control on the amounts you borrow, the debt mounts up until you can't manage the monthly payments. In that situation your creditors can repossess the merchandise, garnish your salary (get a portion of what you make until the loan is paid), and give negative information about your creditworthiness to a credit bureau. Credit may be attractive, but misusing it can lead to stress and financial crisis.

The Cost of Credit

Because buying something on credit costs more than paying cash, you should shop around when you're taking out a loan or applying for a credit card. Different retailers and financial institutions lend money on different terms. The total cost of credit may vary widely.

When you use credit, make sure you know the **annual percentage rate** (APR), which is the interest rate you will be charged per year on the amount you finance. Also make sure you know the **finance charge**, the total of all costs associated with the loan or credit card—interest, fees, service charges, insurance, and so on—before you sign anything. APRs and fees vary widely, so you should shop around for the best deal. Never sign a credit card application or loan contract unless you fully understand its terms.

Credit Cards

Credit cards allow you to buy merchandise and services and borrow cash up to a certain dollar amount, called your **credit limit**. All you do is sign your name. In return for this convenience, you agree to pay for your purchases in full once a month or in part over an extended period. If you pay your credit card account balance in full each month, you are not charged interest on your purchases. If you pay for only part of your purchases, the unpaid balance is treated as a loan. You pay interest on it, often at a very high APR.

Credit cards have many advantages. They relieve you of the need to carry large amounts of cash when shopping. They allow you to charge travel, entertainment, and merchandise all over the world.

Most retail stores, supermarkets, and restaurants accept payment by credit card or debit card. The ease with which purchases can be made without cash has contributed to both the rise in consumer debt and the popularity of debit cards for those who prefer to "pay now." *(Courtesy of Getty Images, Inc.)*

Your Turn 14–5

BANKING A TAX REFUND

You just received a tax refund of $1,625 from the IRS. What are you going to do with that money? Here's the plan:

- Keep a certain amount of cash—your choice—to spend immediately.
- Open an IRA (minimum amount, $500).
- Save the rest in one or more types of accounts.

Use the space below to list what you are going to do with the money.

_____

_____

_____

_____

_____

_____

They make ordering merchandise by mail, phone, or on the Internet easy. And they allow you to take advantage of buying items on sale even when you don't have the cash. Of course, the flip side is that credit cards can lull you into a false sense that you have lots of money—until you get the bill. So while they have many advantages, credit cards should be used cautiously.

There are several types of credit cards:

- Credit cards, such as Visa and MasterCard, are issued by banks or private companies such as AT&T. They are the most common type of credit card. They can be used for just about anything, from buying a coat to paying for a health club membership. They charge an APR, often as high as 13 to 21 percent, and most have an annual fee as well.
- Travel and entertainment cards, such as American Express and Diner's Club, are used mostly for airline tickets, hotels, and restaurants, although some retailers accept them, too. The balance on a travel card usually must be paid in full each month or the card is canceled.
- Gasoline cards are issued by oil companies, and they are used to pay for gas and oil at that company's gas stations.
- Retail cards are issued by specific stores, such as JC Penney or Sears. They can be used to make purchases only in the store that issues them.

Loans

People borrow money for many purposes. Among them are financing an education, buying a house, and buying a high-ticket item such as a car or major appliance.

Student Loans If you need money for your education, you should consider a **student loan** whose interest rate is subsidized by the federal government. Financial institutions make loans to students on the condition that the students will repay the loans after they graduate. The lender assumes that the education will make the student employable, so he or she will be able to pay the loan back. The government insures the loans, so banks are paid back even when a student defaults.

Although you may be reluctant to borrow money to pay for most things, borrowing to finance a college education usually pays off in the long run. A college education is an investment in your future. As you can see in Figure 14–3, the lifetime earnings of people with college degrees and beyond is far greater than those of high school graduates.

If you are interested in applying for federal student grants and loans, check with your school's financial aid office or visit the U.S. Department of Education's financial aid Web site at <http://www.fafsa.ed.gov>.

Installment Loans **Installment loans** are paid back in monthly installments for a fixed period of time. The most common installment loan for most Americans is the auto loan. When you take out an

---

FIGURE 14–3

According to the U.S. Census Bureau, on average college graduates make almost twice as much as high school graduates over the course of a lifetime. People with professional degrees (such as doctors and lawyers) make almost four times as much. (*Source: U.S. Bureau of the Census.*)

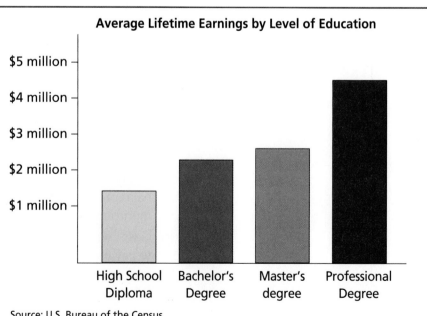

Average Lifetime Earnings by Level of Education

Source: U.S. Bureau of the Census

---

installment loan, you sign a contract agreeing to pay the loan back on the terms outlined in the agreement. If possible, you should not have more than one installment loan at a time, so your monthly payments for credit are not too high.

Sources of Loans   When you need to borrow money, you must look around for someone who thinks you are a good credit risk and for the lowest APR you can find. Some sources of loans are:

- Your relatives, although this can be an uncomfortable situation. If you do borrow from relatives, you should draw up a contract and plan a payment schedule.
- Credit unions, if you are a member.
- Banks and savings institutions.
- Licensed small loan companies, which often charge higher interest because they take on riskier customers.

Whatever you do, avoid borrowing on your credit card and pawnbrokers and loan sharks. Credit card cash advances have extremely high interest rates. Pawnbrokers lend small amounts, keep your assets, and charge extremely high interest rates. Loan sharks often operate outside the law.

Credit Records and Your Rights

The first time you apply for a credit card or loan, you may be refused because you have no credit record. You have no credit record, of course, because you have never been given credit. How can you get out of this loop? You can try one of several approaches to establish a credit record:

- Take out a small installment loan and ask someone with a credit record to cosign with you. The cosigner will be responsible for paying if you do not.
- If you have a savings account with a bank, use it as collateral to borrow money from the same institution. Collateral is property—in this case, money—that you give the lender access to as a guarantee that you will pay back the loan.
- Some banks offer credit cards with low credit limits if you have a student identification card or if you have been employed for one year.
- Sign up for utilities in your own name, even if you have to pay a large deposit.
- Pay your bills on time.

Credit records are maintained by companies called **credit bureaus**. In recent years these companies have been criticized for making errors in credit records and being slow to correct them. You

DEALING WITH DEBT

Owing more money than you can pay back is sometimes the result of poor money management: People simply borrow too much money and charge too much to their credit cards. Sometimes debt becomes unmanageable when income drops because of events such as divorce, unemployment, or illness. No matter what the cause, however, debt can easily grow until it is too large to pay off. In fact, more than 1.5 million Americans filed for bankruptcy in 2002 because they couldn't resolve their debt problems in any other way.

Well before people get to the bankruptcy stage, they should be aware of the warning signs that financial trouble may be getting serious. Take this test to see if any of the warning signs apply to you. Do you:

- pay only monthly minimums on your credit cards?
- skip some bills to pay others?
- panic when faced with an unexpected major expense, such as a car repair?
- depend on overtime or moonlighting to pay your monthly bills?
- borrow from friends and relatives to cover your basic expenses?

If you answered *yes* to any of these questions, you may be headed for financial trouble.

How can you regain control of your finances? The first step is to know how much you earn, how much you spend, and how much you owe. If you can't get a handle on these three things on your own, you need help. There are organizations whose purpose is to help people having financial difficulties. For example, American Consumer Credit Counseling <http://consumercredit.com> and the National Foundation for Consumer Credit <http://nfcc.org> are two organizations that provide credit counseling services (either free or for a small fee; the organizations are financed by lenders). Credit counselors help people work out long-term debt payment plans while learning how to budget and change their spending habits.

Sources: American Bankruptcy Institute, "U.S. Bankruptcy Filings, 1980–2002," <http://www.abiworld.org/stats/1980annual.html>, accessed April 3, 2003; *The Consumer Reports Money Book,* Yonkers, N.Y., Consumer Union, 1992, p. 153; "Danger Signs of Financial Trouble," American Consumer Credit Counseling Web site <http://accc.pair.com/danger.htm>, Feb. 6, 1998; "Take a Step in the Right Direction: A Guide to Managing Your Money," National Foundation of Consumer Credit, Silver Spring, Md., 1997.

have the right to see your credit record and to know who else has seen it in the previous six months. A small fee is charged for this service unless you were recently denied credit. If the information is inaccurate, you can have it investigated and corrected, and copies of the corrected report will be sent to anyone who received an incorrect report. You may also add a notation to your file about any information you consider unfair. You can help prevent some errors if you always use the same form of your name on all contracts, accounts, credit cards, and other documents.

Your Turn 14–6

FILL IN A CREDIT APPLICATION

A creditor wants a lot of information in order to make a decision about extending you credit. Give yourself some practice in gathering this information by filling in the credit application form on page 336.

Your Credit Obligations

When you use credit, you are obliged, legally and morally, to pay back what you have borrowed. There may be times when for some reason you miss a payment or series of payments. If this happens, you should notify your creditor immediately and explain your situation. Most creditors will help you work out another payment schedule to give you time to recover. You may also draw on the services of a credit counseling organization, which can help you work 336out credit problems.

INSURANCE

Why do you need insurance? You need insurance to protect yourself and your dependents against financial ruin in the event of illness, accident, theft, fire, or death. Insurance works on the principle that not everyone who buys it will actually need it. People pay premiums to an insurance company in case an unforeseen hazard occurs—an illness, hospitalization, accident, fire, and so on. If a misfortune does occur, the insurance company pays the insured person under the terms of the insurance contract.

There are many types of insurance available, including health insurance, medical coverage, auto insurance, life insurance, disability insurance, renter's insurance, and homeowner's insurance.

Medical Coverage

An accident or serious illness can mean paying medical bills for years if you are not insured. Yet because of the high cost of medical coverage, millions of Americans are uninsured. Most people who have medical coverage have it through their employers. In some cases the company pays the full premium, but in most cases the employee pays part or all of the cost. There are several types of medical coverage:

- **Traditional health insurance.** When the insured person sees a doctor or is hospitalized, the insurance company pays

ACME
Car Sales

CREDIT
APPLICATION
FORM

APPLICANT:

1. Name (Last)	(First)	(Initial)	2. Birthdate	3. Social Security No.

4. Address (Street)	(City)	(State)	(Zip)

5. Area Code/Tel. Number	6. Lived At Present Address Years Months	7. ____Own ____Rent ____Other	8. Monthly Payment

9. Previous Street Address (if less than 2 years at present address)	10. Lived At Previous Address Years Months

11. Previous Employer	12. How Long Employed	13. Job Title	14. Mo. Net Income

15. Employer's Address (Street)	(City)	(State)	(Zip)	16. Area Code/Tel. Number

17. Previous Employer	18. How Long Employed	19. Job Title	20. Mo. Net Income

21. Employer's Address (Street)	(City)	(State)	(Zip)	22. Area Code/Tel. Number

23. Other Sources of Income	24. Net Income per Month

CO-APPLICANT: Complete this section only if a joint account is requested. (Spouse can be a co-applicant.)

25. Name (Last)	(First)	(Initial)	26. Birthdate	27. Social Security No.

28. Address (Street)	(City)	(State)	(Zip)

CREDIT REFERENCES:

48. Savings Account (Institution Name)	(Account No.)	(Balance)

49. Checking Account (Institution Name)	(Account No.)	(Balance)

LOANS AND OUTSTANDING DEBTS: List all debts owing. Attach additional sheet if necessary.

50. Auto, Make, Model, & Year	51. Financed by	52. Account No.	53. Balance	54. Mo. Payment

55. Name of Creditor/Lender		56. Account No.	57. Balance	58. Mo. Payment

The above information is given to obtain credit privileges. I (we) hereby authorize the obtaining of information about any statements made herein, and I (we) agree to be bound by the terms of the National Credit Card agreement. Signers shall be jointly and severally liable.

Applicant's Signature	Date	Authorized User(s)	

Co-Applicant's Signature	Date	Relationship to Applicant	No. of Cards Requested

a portion of the cost, usually 80 percent. The remaining 20 percent of the cost is paid by the insured person. Traditional health insurance is usually the most expensive type of medical coverage because insured people can go to the doctor and hospital of their choice.

- **Managed care plans.** Managed care plans are similar to traditional health insurance, except that the insured person is limited in his or her choice of physicians and hospitals to those in the managed care network. Managed care coverage usually costs less than traditional health insurance.

- **HMOs.** Health maintenance organizations are associations of thousands of patients and hundreds of medical professionals. When you are sick, you visit one of the HMO's physicians. If you need a specialist, you are referred to a doctor on staff. The advantages of HMOs are their relatively low cost (although their costs are rising fast), the convenience of having a wide array of medical care in one organization, and their emphasis on preventive care. The main disadvantages are that your choice of doctors is limited and access to specialists is often tightly controlled.

- **Medicaid and Medicare.** Low-income people are often eligible for Medicaid, and elderly and disabled people are usually eligible for Medicare, which are federally financed health insurance plans. In addition, some states provide free or low-cost health insurance for poor children.

Auto Insurance

Each year, thousands of people die, millions of people are injured and disabled, and billions of dollars are spent as the direct result of automobile accidents. Most states require that car owners buy liability coverage, which protects you against the claims of others in case you cause property or other damage while operating a motor vehicle. In addition to liability coverage, auto insurance policies can include:

- Collision coverage to repair damage to your car if a collision occurs. You agree to pay a deductible—$500, on average—and the insurance company pays the balance. If your car is old, it's not worth buying collision coverage. The insurance company will not pay any claim higher than the total book value of the car.

- Comprehensive coverage in case your car is stolen, catches fire, or is the victim of other perils such as flood.

- Medical coverage for your medical bills if you are injured while riding in your car.

- Uninsured motorist coverage in case you are killed or injured, or your car is damaged in an accident caused by a driver who has no insurance.

Some states have "no fault" auto insurance. Under this type of insurance, your own insurance company pays you benefits, regardless of whose fault the accident was.

The cost of auto insurance varies widely, with young male drivers in urban areas paying the highest premiums. When you buy auto

Liability coverage protects you from having to pay a person whose property or health you have damaged. The insurance company pays on your behalf. *(Courtesy of PhotoDisc.)*

insurance, it pays to shop around and compare coverage. You can economize on the cost of a policy in several ways:

- Buy a less expensive or used car.
- Buy a car with airbags, an alarm system, or another antitheft device.
- Choose the highest deductibles on collision and comprehensive coverage that you can afford. (The **deductible** is the amount you pay before the insurance company starts paying. The higher the deductible, the cheaper the coverage.) A week's salary is a good rule of thumb.
- Don't buy collision or comprehensive coverage if your car is old.
- Participate in approved driver education courses to get a "good driver" discount.

What happens if you are turned down for insurance or your policy is canceled because of a poor driving record? In that case, you go into your state's assigned risk pool and get insurance from a company servicing high-risk drivers. The cost of this insurance is greater than regular auto insurance. If your driving record is good for a few years, you should be able to buy standard insurance.

Other Types of Insurance

Other types of insurance that you may need now or as your financial responsibilities increase are:

- life insurance, which provides financial protection to your dependents in case of your death
- disability insurance, which pays you a certain amount per month in the event you are injured or too sick to work
- renter's insurance, which protects against damage or loss of personal property and liability claims
- homeowner's insurance, which protects against property damage and liability claims
- long-term care insurance, which provides coverage for lengthy nursing home stays.

OWNING A HOME

Buying a home—whether it is a house, condominium, or cooperative apartment—is the biggest investment most people make during their lifetimes. Despite the high cost of finding, buying, and maintaining a home, most Americans still regard home ownership as part of the American dream. Thus the decision to buy a home is complicated and involves both financial and emotional factors. Before you take the plunge, it's important to consider the advantages and disadvantages of buying a home.

Home ownership is a major financial commitment. Most people need to plan and save for several years before they are ready for this step. *(Courtesy of PhotoDisc.)*

Advantages of Home Ownership

Home ownership has many advantages, not the least of which are the emotional advantages. For many people, owning a home is the realization of a dream. It provides them with a sense of security and control over their lives. In general, homeowners have a greater commitment to their communities than do renters. They tend to be more involved in civic issues such as education and community improvement.

Home ownership also has financial advantages. The biggest advantage is that paying off a mortgage (the loan you take out when you buy a home) is a way to build a nest egg for retirement. Mortgage payments are a form of forced savings because you build equity (ownership) in your home. In addition, the interest on your mortgage and the property taxes on your home are tax deductible, meaning that your income tax bill will be less. A home can be a source of cash in the future because you can borrow against it with a home equity loan. Finally, if you own the home over a long period of time and then sell it, you have a good chance of making some money on the sale.

Disadvantages of Home Ownership

Home ownership does have a down side. First, you may be in a stage of life that is full of uncertainty, such as at the beginning of a marriage or career or after a divorce, or your work may require frequent moves. In these situations, your housing needs may change rapidly, and home ownership would restrict your mobility. Not only does selling a home cost time and money but also,353 if buyers are scarce, you may be stuck covering the costs of the home long after you've moved out. Second, home ownership is expensive. In most cases you need to make a substantial down payment—10 percent or more of the price—to qualify for a mortgage. Then the mortgage payment is just part of the monthly cost. Owning a home means paying for property taxes, insurance, routine maintenance, and repairs. Last, owning a home is not a sure way to make money. Home prices rise and fall in the short term. In some places, prices are flat for years. On the other hand, in some major cities home prices go up fairly steadily.

If you have the discipline to invest the money you'd save by renting, you may do better financially in the long run than someone who depends on rising home values.

Making the Decision to Buy or Rent

If you need help in making the decision to buy or rent, you can consult one of the many books or Web sites devoted to home ownership or

Your Turn 14–7

YOUR PERSONAL INSURANCE PLAN

Think about your current circumstances. What kind of insurance do you need? For each of the following, indicate why you do need this form of insurance or why you don't need it.

1. Medical coverage

_____

_____

_____

2. Auto insurance

_____

_____

_____

3. Life insurance

_____

_____

_____

4. Disability insurance

_____

_____

_____

5. Renter's insurance

_____

_____

_____

6. Homeowner's insurance

_____

_____

_____

Your Turn 14–8

SHOULD YOU OWN YOUR HOME?

1. What are your feelings and attitudes toward owning your own home?

_____

_____

2. At this stage of your life, does it make sense to own your own home? Explain.

_____

_____

3. Do you have the financial resources to own a home? Explain.

_____

_____

personal finance. Many of these have worksheets or calculators that help you estimate costs and benefits. In addition, there are software packages on the market that help you with financial analysis and lead you through the decision-making process.

INVESTING FOR THE FUTURE

In the long term, you will encounter situations in which you need a lot of money. For example, you may want to start a business or pay for your children's college educations. These are large expenses that most people cannot cover with current income. Later, during your retirement years, you will need money to supplement social security benefits and pension plans, if any.

Long-term financial planning is critical, but it is something that people find very difficult to do. A woman in her twenties usually does not have retirement on her mind. A father holding his newborn baby may worry more about the cost of diapers than college. Still, the sooner you start to plan and invest for the future, the better off you will be. If you start young, the amounts you need to invest will be smaller because they have more time to grow. If you start late, you will have to invest large amounts each year, which may seriously

WHATEVER IT TAKES
Rosario Marín

(AP/Wide World Photos/Mike Fuentes.)

You probably are carrying her signature in your wallet. Rosario Marín became the highest ranking Latina in the Bush administration when she was sworn in as U.S. Secretary of the Treasury in 2001. Until she resigned in June 2003, her signature was printed on all the paper money issued by the United States. Marín is the first immigrant to serve as secretary of the treasury.

Born in Mexico, Marín moved to California with her family at the age of 14. She was sad about the move, because she thought she would miss her *quinceanera,* her coming of age party. Even though she spoke no English when she arrived, she graduated from high school with honors.

After high school, Marín started working at a bank to help her family's finances. She attended community college at night, earning her associate's degree in four years. Then she transferred to California State University, where she earned a bachelor's degree, also at night. By that time, she had been promoted up the ranks at the bank, and she had married.

The birth of her first son, who had Down syndrome, changed the course of her life. Before Eric was born, Marín's ambition had been to be the president of her own bank. After his birth, she became an advocate for the disabled. She took on the state of California to protect her son's interests and was appointed to Governor Pete Wilson's administration. In this capacity, she fought for laws and programs to serve the disabled. After numerous positions in the state of California, she was elected mayor of Huntington Park, a city that's 99 percent Hispanic. From there she and her husband and three children moved to Washington, D.C., so Marín could fulfill her duties as secretary of the treasury.

One of Marín's goals during her stay in Washington was to educate Americans about personal financial health. With personal bankruptcies at an all-time high, Marín wanted money management to be part of every student's education.

Sources: Julia Bencomo Lobaco and Cathy Areu Jones, "Hispanas Making a Difference" <http://www.hispaniconline.com/vista/febhisp.htm>, accessed January 21, 2003; Ana Radelat, "Rosario Marín: A Latina Who's Right on the Money," *Hispanic,* June 2002, p. 26; "Rosario Marín '04" <http://rosarioforsenate.com>, accessed August 24, 2003; U.S. Department of the Treasury, "Treasurer Rosario Marín" <http://www.ustreas.gov/education/history/treasurers/marin.html>, accessed January 21, 2003.

Because people are living longer, they can look forward to many years of retirement. To help finance your retirement, you need to start saving when you are young. *(Courtesy of Getty Images, Inc.)*

interfere with your lifestyle. It is crucial to get in the habit of investing regularly, even if the amounts are small.

Home ownership is one form of long-term savings, as we have seen. However, there are other ways to invest money for long-term goals such as financing your children's education or building a retirement fund. Some of the most common long-term investments are:

- **Stocks.** When you buy stock, you become a part-owner of a corporation. Your profit may come from dividends paid when the company does well, or from selling the stock at a price higher than you paid. Needless to say, you may not profit but may lose instead. Still, over the long run, stocks have been the best choice for long-term increases in value.

- **Bonds.** When you buy a bond, you are lending money and will be repaid on a specific date, usually with interest payments in the meantime. Bonds usually involve less risk than stocks, but they do not have as much profit potential.

- **Mutual funds.** Mutual funds pool the money of a group of people and make investments on their behalf. There are stock mutual funds and bond mutual funds as well as funds that combine various types of investments.

- **IRAs, Keoghs, and 401(k) plans.** These are all plans for retirement savings. The money in these plans is usually invested through mutual funds or banks.

- **Education Savings Accounts.** Coverdell and other education savings accounts are designed to encourage people to save for tuition and other school expenses. The money in these accounts grows tax-free and is not taxed when withdrawn for educational expenses.

Keep in mind that all these forms of investment pose some risk. Unlike money in a savings account in a bank, the money you invest in stocks, bonds, and mutual funds is not insured by the federal government. Therefore, when you invest you must be prepared to lose money as well as to make money. Choosing the right types of investments for you means balancing risk and reward. One way to decrease risk is to diversify. That means you spread your investments in different types of stocks, bonds, and mutual funds. If one of your investments does poorly, it is likely to be balanced by another doing well.

WHAT ARE YOUR LONG-TERM FINANCIAL GOALS?

Think about large expenses you are likely to have in the future. Then answer the following questions.

1. List some future events or situations for which you will need large amounts of money.

_____

_____

_____

_____

2. What have you done, if anything, to prepare for these events?

_____

_____

_____

_____

3. How can you improve your long-term financial planning?

_____

_____

_____

_____

The Information Highway

GETTING UP TO SPEED

The Internet is a gold mine of sites devoted to personal money management. Many of them are interactive, allowing you to input your personal data and come up with financial projections. For example, on some sites you can calculate how much you can afford to borrow when buying a home.

■ A few of the personal finance sites are:

<http://www.kiplinger.com>

<http://moneycentral.msn.com>

"Money & Business" at <http://channels.netscape.com>

■ You can find a glossary of financial terms at <http://www.quicken.com/glossary>.

■ An excellent source of student financial aid information is the on-line database of scholarships maintained by fastWEB (which stands for *financial aid search through the web*). You input your personal profile, and a search for appropriate sources of financial aid is performed for you <http://www.fastweb.com>.

In addition, you can use a search engine and the following key words to find more on topics covered in this chapter: *personal finance, personal financial planning, money management, household budgeting, savings institutions, consumer credit, credit counseling, insurance* (and specific types of insurance), *home ownership, education savings accounts,* and *retirement planning.*

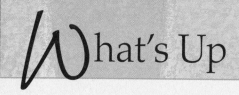

What's Up

Name _____ Date _____

1. Sketch the financial pyramid in the space below.

2. List five possible sources of income.

_____
_____
_____
_____
_____

3. What is the difference between fixed and variable expenses?

_____
_____
_____

4. What is budgeting? Why is budgeting important?

_____
_____
_____

5. What are the four basic steps of budgeting?

_____
_____
_____
_____

continues

Name _____ Date_____

6. What is a checking account used for?

_____

_____

_____

7. When you borrow money or use credit, there is an annual percentage rate and a finance charge. What is the difference between them?

_____

_____

_____

8. How can you first establish a good credit history?

_____

_____

_____

9. What is the purpose of insurance?

_____

_____

_____

10. Describe two ways to cut the cost of auto insurance.

_____

_____

11. Describe two advantages and two disadvantages of home ownership.

_____

_____

_____

_____

12. Why is it important to invest now for large future expenses such as a child's college education?

_____

_____

_____

Case Studies

THE CASE OF THE BIG SPENDER

When Felipe got his first full-time job, he was thrilled with having his own money. His mother asked him to pay room and board, and he willingly agreed. In the first month he was working, he bought a stereo on the installment plan and clothes for work on his new bank credit card. He borrowed money to buy a new car. He was stunned at how much he would have to pay for auto insurance. His extra cash was spent on restaurants and entertainment.

Within a few months, Felipe discovered he was constantly broke. The great feeling he had had about earning his own money was replaced by a sinking feeling of being broke—and worse, in debt. Room, board, credit card payments, auto loan payments, insurance, dates—there simply was not enough money for it all.

1. Felipe has two basic problems with his handling of money. What are they?

_____

_____

2. When Felipe first started working, what should he have done about money for the first few months?

_____

3. What can Felipe do to improve his present situation?

_____

_____

THE CASE OF THE LAID-OFF ASSISTANT

Noreen moved into a new, much larger apartment and bought a kitchen table, chairs, and two sofas on the installment plan. Although her rent was higher and she also had car payments to make, she had enough room in her budget to take on the additional monthly payments on the furniture.

Several months later, Noreen lost her job as an administrative assistant. For the first time in her life, she missed a loan payment—on the furniture. Noreen was frantic. She didn't know what to do until she found a new job. Her unemployment checks were not large enough to cover her expenses.

1. What is Noreen's problem?

_____

2. What should Noreen do about her auto loan and furniture loan?

_____

3. How will Noreen solve her problem in the long run?

_____

_____

Journal

Answer the following journal questions.

1. Describe your family's attitudes toward money. Is money discussed openly, or is it considered a private topic? Who controls the family finances? How are decisions made? What role do you play?

_____
_____
_____
_____

2. What are your three most important financial goals? What are you doing to reach these goals?

_____
_____
_____
_____

3. Do you have a budget? Do you follow it? What improvements can you make in your budgeting?

_____
_____
_____
_____

4. Describe your use of banks, if any. What types of accounts do you have? What do you use them for? What savings goals do you have?

_____
_____
_____
_____

5. What is your attitude toward credit? How can you use credit more wisely?

_____
_____
_____
_____

6. If you won a huge sum in the lottery, what would you do with it? How would it change your life?

_____
_____
_____
_____

In San Jose, California,
Pallas Hansen founded Career Closet,
a nonprofit organization that provides
poor women with professional-looking
clothing for job interviews and new jobs.
There are similar organizations
in many cities across the country.
(Courtesy of Pallas Hansen.)

Chapter 15

Preparing for Your Career

For many people, work is drudgery, a place to which they drag themselves each day. Others enjoy themselves so much on the job that they hardly consider what they do work. Indeed, one of the seven beliefs of highly successful people is that "work is play" (see Chapter 1). As you prepare yourself for a career, keep in mind that you'll be spending a large part of your waking hours working. Wouldn't it be better to be paid to do something you are good at and enjoy?

A large part of reaching your potential can take place in the context of work. If your work is satisfying, the contentment you feel at work will spill over into your personal life. If your career makes good use of your abilities and interests, you will feel you are contributing to the world. If your work is challenging, you will grow and develop as a person. In short, a satisfying career can help you reach your potential as a human being.

You may be thinking that this is a very idealistic view of work. Real jobs aren't like that, you say. Perhaps you are remembering a boring job you had—or still have. A job that required a tenth of your brainpower and had no future, perhaps. True, there are jobs like that out there. But why should you settle for a job like that?

Now turn your mind away from that boring job. Think instead about something you once did that you really enjoyed. When you were working on this activity, you were absorbed. Time flew by. You got a great feeling of satisfaction when you were done. Work should be like that. It can be, too, if you take the time to make some discoveries about yourself and about the world out there before you start job hunting.

You can use the time you have now to prepare yourself for a career. In this chapter, you will get ready for your job search by figuring out what you have to offer as well as what you want out of a career. You will learn where to find economic and job news that may affect you. You will pull together a resume and explore employment resources. You will practice filling in application forms and preparing for interviews. And most important, you will start planning your short- and long-term career goals.

WHAT CAN YOU OFFER?

A lot of people, including students, homemakers returning to work, and people changing careers, think they have little or nothing to offer employers. "But I can't do anything. I have no skills or experience" is the common refrain. If you think of yourself this way, now is the time to stop. The fact is, everyone has skills, interests, education, and experience that would be of value to some employer. Many employers will train new employees if they feel they have basic skills, the ability to learn, and the commitment to do well.

Personal Qualities, Skills, and Interests

When you are thinking about jobs and careers, the place to start is with yourself. Look at the personal qualities and foundation skills listed in Table 15–1. According to the U.S. Department of Labor, these qualities and skills are necessary for solid job performance in the modern workplace. Which of these qualities are you confident you possess? Which of the foundation skills have you developed during the course of your life? A well-prepared person should have most of these qualities and skills. They are necessary for any type of employment, from sales clerk to mechanic to computer programmer, although particular occupations will require more of some qualities and skills than others. Many of them are qualities and skills you have developed through your upbringing and your education. In addition, you have been improving these qualities and skills in the course of working through this book.

The next set of general skills considered necessary for success on the job by the Department of Labor are the workplace skills (see Table 15–2). These are skills involving the use of resources, interpersonal

The skills you use in a favorite activity or hobby can sometimes be the basis for a career. For example, a person who enjoys metalworking might be suited to a career in auto body repair and refinishing.
(Courtesy of PhotoDisc.)

TABLE 15–1 Personal Qualities and Foundation Skills Needed for Solid Job Performance

Personal Qualities	Individual responsibility	
	Self-belief	
	Self-management	
	Sociability	
	Integrity	
Foundation Skills (Transferrable Skills)	*Basic Skills:*	*Thinking Skills:*
	Reading	Ability to learn
	Writing	Reasoning
	Arithmetic	Creative thinking
	Mathematics	Decision making
	Speaking	Problem solving
	Listening	

Source: U.S. Department of Labor, Secretary's Commission on Achieving Necessary Skills (SCANS), *Learning a Living: A Blueprint for High Performance,* Washington, D.C., 1992, p. 3.

TABLE 15–2 Workplace Skills Needed for Solid Job Performance

Resource Skills	Allocate time, money, materials, space, and staff
Interpersonal Skills	Work on teams
	Teach others
	Serve customers
	Lead
	Negotiate
	Work with people of diverse backgrounds
Information Skills	Acquire and evaluate data
	Organize and maintain files
	Interpret and communicate
	Use computers to process information
Systems Skills	Understand social, organizational, and technological systems
	Monitor and correct performance
	Design or improve systems
Technology Skills	Select equipment and tools
	Apply technology to specific tasks
	Maintain and troubleshoot equipment

Source: U.S. Department of Labor, Secretary's Commission on Achieving Necessary Skills (SCANS), *Learning a Living: A Blueprint for High Performance,* Washington, D.C., 1992, p. 3.

relationships, information, systems, and technology. Like the foundation skills, the workplace skills are very general and are needed in varying degrees for different occupations. For example, an airplane mechanic should have lots of technology skill, but some of the interpersonal skills, such as negotiating, are less important in that occupation.

In every job, workers must deal to a degree with all five skill categories—resources, interpersonal, information, systems, and technology. Yet most jobs are weighted toward one or two skill categories. That is, the skills that are critical for success in the job fall into one or two of the five categories. For example, it is critical that a teacher have a high level of interpersonal skills, because teaching involves working with people. But he or she should also possess information skills, because a teacher must interpret and communicate information (the content of a course or subject). In addition, a teacher must have systems skills in order to deal with a social system (the class and the school) and to monitor and correct performance (of students).

When you read over the workplace skills in Table 15–2, you may be alarmed by how grand and abstract they sound. Don't be. What you have to consider when thinking about careers is how your own specific skills fit into these general categories. For example, you may be skilled at running a forklift and other heavy machinery. How does that very specific skill fit into the workplace skills in Table 15–2? In fact, what you are using when operating a forklift is a technology skill. You are applying technology to a specific task. Let's consider another example, that of a woman with little paid work experience who has served as president of a parent-teacher association. In that role, she has developed resource skills by fund-raising, interpersonal skills by leading and working with people of diverse backgrounds, and systems skills by managing the PTA, a social system.

Having a skill is not quite enough, however. You must also enjoy using it. Let's consider a computer technician as an example. He has a high level of technology skill, acquired through education and on the job. He is very good in repairing computer systems, but he is bored by his work. What he really enjoys are the occasions when he helps a customer and explains things. Perhaps this technician would be happier in a job that requires more interpersonal skill, such as computer sales or training.

When taking inventory of your skills and interests, don't overlook volunteer work or internships. For example, women returning to work after a period of child raising often have acquired skills that are useful in the workplace. *(Courtesy of PhotoDisc.)*

Your Turn 15–1

WHAT ARE YOUR SKILLS AND INTERESTS?

What skills do you use when you are enjoying yourself the most? First think of three activities you really enjoy: they can be work, school, sports, recreation, home, or community activities. List them here:

1. _____

2. _____

3. _____

    For each activity you listed, write down the skills you enjoyed using as you performed that activity. Use the skills described in Tables 15–1 and 15–2.

Skills You Enjoyed Using in Activity 1:

_____

_____

_____

_____

_____

_____

Skills You Enjoyed Using in Activity 2:

_____

_____

_____

_____

_____

_____

Skills You Enjoyed Using in Activity 3:

_____

_____

_____

_____

_____

_____

Which skill or skills do you use the most during activities you enjoy? How might these skills be used in a work environment?

_____

_____

_____

So when you think about skills, don't think just about what you are good at. Think about what you enjoy as well.

Education and Experience

In addition to your skills and interests, you can offer employers the benefit of your education and experience. Your education is an indication not only of what you know but also of what foundation skills you have—reading, writing, and computation skills. In addition, your education shows that you have the ability to learn and to manage yourself, important qualities that employers look for.

Your work experience is also something you have that's of value. If you have never worked for money, worked only part-time, or worked a long time ago, you may think you have nothing to offer in this area. Yet you should think of work experience as something broader than full-time paying jobs. Work experience can also include:

- part-time or summer jobs
- baby-sitting, newspaper delivery, yard work
- community or church work
- other volunteer work
- apprenticeships or internships

Many people develop significant skills through occasional or unpaid work experiences. You shouldn't overlook these activities when you are taking stock of your background.

WHAT DO YOU WANT?

The skills, interests, education, and experience you bring to your job hunt are critical from the employer's point of view. But there are other factors you must also consider—factors that are critically important to you.

There are millions of jobs in this country in thousands of occupations. By taking a careful inventory of your skills, interests, education, and experience, you can narrow your focus. And by carefully thinking about what you want in a career, you can eliminate many more occupations from consideration. In essence, you must evaluate what factors are important to you in a career.

- your preference for working with resources, people, information, systems, or technology
- within the category or categories you choose, what type of resources, people, information, systems, or technology do you prefer? For example, money or natural resources, children or immigrants, numbers or words or images, social or technological systems, hand tools or electrical engineering?

Your Turn 15–2

TAKE A SELF-INVENTORY

Take some time to consider what you really want from a job or career. Answer the following questions.

1. Do you prefer to work primarily with resources, people, information, systems, or technology?

_____

2. With which type of resources (environment, money, employees, etc.) would you enjoy working?

_____

3. With which type of people (children, peers, travelers, old people, the poor, etc.) would you enjoy working?

_____

4. With which type of information (books, Internet, pictures, video games, numbers, words, etc.) would you enjoy working?

_____

5. With which type of systems (social groups, work processes, information systems, etc.) would you enjoy working?

_____

6. With which type of technology (computers, hand tools, cooking equipment, manufacturing, etc.) would you enjoy working?

_____

7. In which area of the country would you like to work?

_____

8. Would you like to work in an urban, suburban, or rural environment? Would you like to work indoors or outdoors?

_____

9. Are you interested in a casual or formal work environment?

_____

continues

10. What values are important for you in your work (truth, beauty, competence, risk, ambition, helping others, etc.)?

_____

11. How much job security is necessary for you?

_____

12. How much money do you need or want in salary?

_____

> **It is work, work that one delights in, that is the surest guarantor of happiness.**
>
> ashley montagu,
>
> anthropologist

- the region of the country where you want to live
- urban, suburban, or rural lifestyle
- large corporation, small company, or self-employment (note that many people become self-employed after gaining experience by working for companies)
- casual or formal environment for work
- the values associated with the work or company (for example, competitiveness, excellence, helping others, creativity, and so on)
- job security
- money

By making choices in each of these areas, you will be able to focus more clearly on occupations that could be right for you.

MATCHING YOURSELF TO AN OCCUPATION

Now that you've spent some time thinking about your skills and your wants, you are ready to match yourself to occupations that would be suitable for you. Many career information resources are available to help you do this. In addition to using these resources, you should keep up with economic and job news. If you do your "homework," you will be able to come up with a career that's right for you.

Using Career Information Resources

Personal contacts, libraries and career centers, counselors, professional organizations, government agencies, and the Internet are all sources of information about careers.

People You Know   Your friends, relatives, coworkers, instructors, and fellow students are good resources for job and career information. (In fact a U.S. Department of Labor survey showed that 48 percent of job hunters learned of their jobs through personal contacts.) People you know can answer questions about what they do. More important, they can put you in touch with other people who work in fields you think you might be interested in. Networking can give you insights into occupations that may be hard to get from written descriptions.

Libraries and Career Centers   Your public and school libraries and your school's career center all have information about jobs and careers. One of the first books you should look at is the *Occupational Outlook Handbook,* published every two years by the U.S. Department of Labor's Bureau of Labor Statistics. This book covers employment trends, sources of career and job information, tips on finding a job and evaluating a job offer, and descriptions of hundreds of occupations. Some libraries and schools may subscribe to the *Occupational Outlook Quarterly,* also published by the U.S. Department of Labor. This periodical describes trends in the job market and predicts areas of job growth and decline. You can also access these books on-line at the Department of Labor Web site <http://www.dol.gov>.

Both the *Occupational Outlook Handbook* and the *Occupational Outlook Quarterly* are general in their coverage. Ask the librarian or office staff to help you find books, pamphlets, or other materials about particular occupations of interest to you.

Counselors   If you are having trouble figuring out your career interests, you may need the help of a career counselor. You can find counselors in several places:

- high school guidance offices
- career planning and placement offices in colleges and vocational/technical schools
- community organizations
- private counseling firms
- government employment service offices

Counselors are trained to help you discover your strengths and weaknesses. Counselors can administer aptitude and interest tests and interpret the results. They can help you match your aptitudes and interests with suitable occupations. Although counselors won't tell you what to do, they can help you better understand yourself and your work experience. They may also be able to offer advice about the local job market and educational and training opportunities.

Professional and Other Organizations   Professional organizations, trade associations, labor unions, and large businesses all provide career information. In addition, there are organizations that provide career information for specific groups, such as veterans, women, the handicapped, minority groups, and older workers. To find these organizations, you can check the *Encyclopedia of Associations* in the reference section of your library. If you need further help, ask the reference librarian.

Government Agencies   Federal and local government employment agencies are another source of career and job information. State employment services coordinate their efforts with the U.S. Employment Service. There are more than 2,000 local offices whose primary function is to help job hunters find jobs. However, they also provide counseling and testing for those who are exploring their futures.

Internet Resources   Much of the information you can find in libraries, career centers, guidance offices, professional and trade organizations, and government agencies is also available on the Internet. Companies, professional groups, and government agencies maintain Web sites with career-related information. In addition, you can find interactive sites that produce a career profile when you input your personal data. The amount of career-related information on the Internet is huge, so be prepared to spend quite a bit of time searching for information that is relevant to you. (See Getting Up to Speed on the Information Highway on page 385 for specific Web sites to get you started.)

Keeping Up with Economic and Job News

When thinking about occupations, you should keep up with current events and job projections. It won't do you much good to select an occupation that's disappearing across the country or declining in your area.

One source, already mentioned, is the *Occupational Outlook Quarterly,* which can be found in the library or on-line. This describes national trends in the job market. You can also check the U.S. and your state's Department of Labor Web sites on the Internet for recent national and state job trend information. You should also keep up with local economic news as well. Local newspapers and television stations cover economic and business news that affects employment in your area.

WHERE THE JOBS WILL BE IN THE YEAR 2010

When you choose an occupation, you should consider the long-term job outlook for that field. The U.S. Bureau of Labor Statistics publishes employment trend information, some of which is highlighted here.

The three industries with the fastest job growth between 2000 and 2010 are computer and data processing services, residential care, and health services. This reflects the continuing importance of computers in business and personal life, as well as the aging of the baby boomers, who will require more health care in the next decades. Following the top three are cable and pay television services and personnel supply services. Notice that all the fastest growing industries are in the service sector—manufacturing jobs will continue to decline in the United States.

The bar graph shows the number of new jobs expected this decade in the 10 occupations with the largest job growth. Jobs in the service industries dominate, with the largest growth in some of the lowest paying sectors, such as fast food preparation and retail sales. These figures underscore the need for higher education to compete effectively for better paying jobs that may be less numerous.

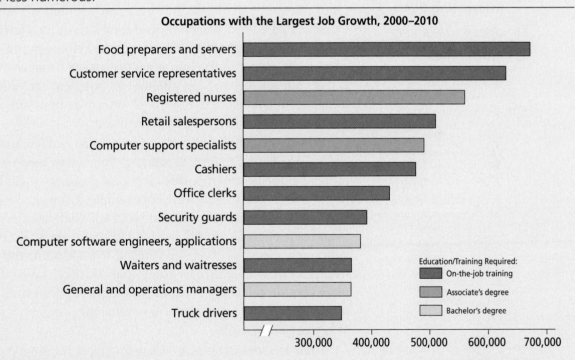

Occupations with the Largest Job Growth, 2000–2010

(Source: Bureau of Labor Statistics, "Table 4. Occupations with the Largest Job Growth, 2000–2010," *Monthly Labor Review*, November 2001, www.bls.gov/emp/emptab4.htm, accessed April 8, 2003.)

Among the occupations with the largest projected decline during this decade are farmers and ranchers, order clerks, tellers, insurance clerks, and word processors and typists. Most of these occupations are declining because technology and workflow changes are making them less necessary.

Job Shadowing

Once you have narrowed your career interests, you may want to spend a few hours or a day "shadowing" someone in your chosen occupation. By observing firsthand what a job involves, you will get a better idea of whether the occupation would be a good match for you. To find someone to shadow, ask people you know or your school placement office to help you.

Setting an Occupational Objective

The result of all this thinking and research is that you should be able to narrow your career objective to one or two occupations. Knowing what you are looking for will help you when you begin your job search. For a person with a job objective, job hunting is a self-directed activity. You will be much more likely to find a job that you will like if you look for a specific type of work.

I want the kind of job that is interesting but doesn't take very much time.

anonymous 14-year-old girl

TAKING ACTION ON YOUR JOB SEARCH

Once you've got an objective, you are ready to start job hunting. Occasionally, a lucky person finds a good job within a few days. But most people job hunt for weeks or months before finding something suitable. Be prepared: job hunting is itself a job. It can also be a severe test of your self-belief. Most job hunters experience rejection and disappointment before they get a job offer. It's important not to feel too discouraged when this happens to you.

When you've been job hunting for a while and feel that you're getting nowhere, you have to motivate yourself to keep going. First, remember the power of positive self-talk: Praise yourself for the job-hunting tasks you handle well. For example, if you get an appointment for an interview, congratulate yourself. That's an accomplishment in and of itself! And second, use the technique of visualization to keep your motivation high. Imagine yourself at work, doing the job you want. Picture what you're wearing, your coworkers, the office or other place you can call yours. Keep these images in mind when your job hunt plateaus and you feel you're not making progress. If you keep at it, you *will* get a job.

There are several tasks associated with job hunting: preparing a resume, preparing a career portfolio, looking for job leads, filling out employment applications, going on interviews, and handling a job offer.

Your Turn 15–3

IDENTIFY YOUR OCCUPATIONAL OBJECTIVE

If you've done your thinking and research, you should be ready to name some occupations that would suit you. Use the space below to list a few occupations that interest you.

_____

_____

_____

_____

_____

_____

_____

Preparing a Resume

A **resume** is a short summary of your experience and qualifications. Employers often use resumes to screen job applicants or as an agenda for the employment interview. From the job hunter's point of view, preparing a resume is a good way of presenting past experiences and skills.

How Resume Databases Affect Resume Formats   Many medium-sized and large companies maintain their own searchable databases of resumes. When you send them a paper or e-mail resume, it will be entered into the database and searched by a computer—it won't necessarily be read by a human being. The scanning and searching technologies of these systems affect how job hunters prepare resumes. There are three important things to keep in mind:

1. Resume databases search by key words such as particular skills, job titles, job functions, and educational degrees. Therefore, your resume must include such key words in order to be a "hit" in a search.

2. Scanners and other input technology can't deal with fancy formatting or colored paper. Therefore, you must have a **plain text resume**, a paper and electronic version saved in "text only" or ASCII format (see Figure 15–1). This is your default resume, to be used in most circumstances.

FIGURE 15–1

A plain text, or ASCII, resume is used when the resume will be scanned or otherwise entered into a resume database system. It can be sent to an employer in paper form, as a text file, or pasted into an e-mail message.

```
Marianne Guilmette
134 Dobson Street
Pittsburgh, Pennsylvania 15219
(412) 555-5489
mguilmette@cybermail.com

Objective

A sales and marketing position

Summary of Qualifications

Retail sales experience including advertising, special promotions, product
display, and selling to customers. Telemarketing experience selling magazines.
Associate's degree in marketing.

Work Experience

June 2003 to Present
Campus Store, Pittsburgh Community College, Pittsburgh, Pennsylvania

Senior Sales Associate (part-time)
Responsibilities include product display, customer sales, special marketing
promotions, and using computer to produce marketing communications and campus
newspaper advertisements.

Special Accomplishments
Named Sales Associate of the Month for December 2002 and March 2003.

July 2002 to May 2003
MDS Marketing Group, Pittsburgh, Pennsylvania

Telemarketer (part-time)
Sold magazine subscriptions, books, videos, and DVDs by telephone.

Education

Associate's Degree, Marketing, Pittsburgh Community College, Pittsburgh,
Pennsylvania, 2004

Associations

Future Marketers Club

References and Career Portfolio

Available upon request.
```

3. You also should also have a formatted resume that is visually appealing, with different fonts, indents, bold and italicized type, and so on (see Figure 15–2). This can be used as part of your career portfolio or sent to a recruiter who asks you for it.

How to Organize the Information in a Resume   Resumes usually contain the following information:

- your name, address, telephone number, fax number, and e-mail address
- your employment objective
- summary of your qualifications that includes key words
- education, including school names and locations, dates you attended, type of program, highest grade completed, or degree earned

FIGURE 15–2

A formatted resume uses bold, italic, and display type and other design elements to make a visually appealing document. The information in this resume is organized chronologically.

Marianne Guilmette
134 Dobson Street
Pittsburgh, Pennsylvania 15219
(412) 555-5489
mguilmette@cybermail.com

Objective	A sales and marketing position
Summary of Qualifications	Retail sales experience including advertising, special promotions, product display, and selling to customers. Telemarketing experience selling magazines. Associate's degree in marketing.
Work Experience	***June 2003 to Present*** Campus Store, Pittsburgh Community College, Pittsburgh, Pennsylvania ***Senior Sales Associate (part-time)*** Responsibilities include product display, customer sales, special marketing promotions, and using computer to produce marketing communications and campus newspaper advertisements. ***Special Accomplishments*** Named Sales Associate of the Month for December 2002 and March 2003. ***July 2002 to May 2003*** MDS Marketing Group, Pittsburgh, Pennsylvania ***Telemarketer (part-time)*** Sold magazine subscriptions, books, videos, and DVDs by telephone.
Education	***Associate's Degree, Marketing*** Pittsburgh Community College, Pittsburgh, Pennsylvania, 2004
Associations	Future Marketers Club
References/Career Portfolio	Available upon request.

- work experience, paid or volunteer, and for each job, usually the job title, name and location of employer, and dates of employment
- any professional licenses
- military experience, including branch and length of service, major responsibilities, and special training
- membership in organizations
- special skills, foreign languages, honors, awards, or achievements
- an indication that references and career portfolio are available on request

The information on a resume can be organized in two basic ways. The first, and most common, format is the **chronological resume** (see Figures 15–1 and 15–2). It lists your most recent job first, followed by other jobs in reverse chronological order. If you've had a lot of work experience, it is presented before education on a chronological resume. Students with little or no work history generally list education before work experience on a chronological resume.

The second basic organization is the **functional resume** (Figure 15–3). It presents work experience in terms of the functions and skills used on the job. Functional resumes are often used by people changing careers, because they highlight general skills and functions that can be used in another occupation. They can also be used by people with little formal work experience, because they can highlight skills acquired in nontraditional settings. For example, a homemaker wanting to return to work can list skills acquired in running a home and doing volunteer work for the community, church, or school. Or students with skimpy work histories can show what skills they have acquired from school activities and part-time jobs.

Whichever format you use, your resume should be no longer than one or one and a half pages. Use key words to describe your skills and

---

FIGURE 15–3

A functional resume highlights the functions and skills you have acquired on the job and in school. It is a good way to organize a resume if you have little work experience or want to change industries or occupations.

WILLIS L. LeMOYNE
67 West Green Street
Pittsburgh, PA 15220
Telephone: (412) 555-3497
Fax: (412) 555-2803
E-mail: WillisLLeMoyne@aol.com

OBJECTIVE
A position in sales and marketing

OVERVIEW
An excellent job candidate with a degree in marketing, experience in marketing and promotion, and special training in oral presentation skills and computer-aided design for marketing communications. Strong background in outdoor activities such as camping.

SKILLS AND ACHIEVEMENTS
➤ As marketing coordinator of the Student Activities Association, implemented a marketing plan that increased student membership by 27 percent
➤ Promoted Student Activities Association through newspaper ads, posters, direct e-mail, and pop-ups on school web site
➤ Used computer-aided design skills to create promotional materials
➤ Improved communication skills by earning a certificate for special oral presentation course
➤ As Assistant Scout Master, organized and led Boy Scout troop on camping trips including winter survival camping, ice climbing, and mountain climbing expeditions
➤ As Eagle Scout, mentored younger scouts working up the ranks

EDUCATION
Associate's Degree, Marketing, Pittsburgh Community College, 2004

Marketing courses included:
➤ Consumer Behavior
➤ Marketing Management
➤ Computer-Aided Design for Marketing Professionals

ASSOCIATIONS
➤ Future Marketers Club

REFERENCES AND CAREER PORTFOLIO
Available upon request.

GATHER INFORMATION FOR YOUR RESUME

Use the data sheet on pages 368–369 to gather information in preparation for writing your resume. Make sure you double-check the spellings of all names and the accuracy of dates and addresses. You may not use all the information on your resume, but you will have it handy in case you need it.

responsibilities, and write in phrases, not full sentences, to save space. Remember, your resume should be perfect: neat, well organized, and without grammatical and spelling errors. Don't depend on your word processor's grammar and spelling check to catch all your errors. Ask someone with experience to help you edit and proofread the resume. In addition, resist the temptation to be funny as a way of getting attention. Attempts at humor rarely impress employers. And finally, do not lie on your resume. It's wrong, and if you are found out, you could lose a job offer or your job itself.

Preparing a Career Portfolio

A good resume lists your skills and achievements. A career portfolio, on the other hand, showcases them. A **career portfolio** is a collection of documents that illustrate what you have done on the job, in school, or in community service. A resume, letters of recommendation or commendation, certificates, awards, news articles, and examples of your work are items that typically appear in a career portfolio.

The items in the portfolio should target your job objective. For example, the marketing graduate whose resume is shown in Figure 15–3 might include copies of these items:

- a nicely formatted paper resume
- a letter of commendation from the faculty adviser of the Student Activities Association, praising his work to increase membership
- one or two computer-designed promotional items for the Student Activities Association
- the certificate he earned from the special oral presentation course
- a list of marketing courses with a brief description of each and his grade

Typically, you take a career portfolio with you to a job interview. When something comes up for which you have a relevant document,

DATA SHEET FOR YOUR RESUME

Name _____

Address _____

Phone No. _____ Fax No. _____ E-mail _____

Employment Objective _____

Your Qualifications (list key words)_____

Education

College or Other Postsecondary School _____

Address _____

Date Started _____ Date Ended _____

Years Completed or Degree Received _____ Course of Study _____

Courses Relevant to Employment Objective _____

_____

Honors _____

Extracurricular Activities _____

High School _____

Address _____

Date Started _____ Date Ended _____

Years Completed or Degree Received _____ Course of Study _____

Courses Relevant to Employment Objective _____

_____

Honors _____

Extracurricular Activities _____

Work Experience

Job Title _____

Employer's Name and Address _____

Supervisor's Name _____

Date Started _____ Date Ended _____

Description of Responsibilities and Skills Used _____

_____

Job Title _____

Employer's Name and Address _____

Supervisor's Name _____

Date Started _____ Date Ended _____

Description of Responsibilities and Skills Used _____

continues

DATA SHEET (continued)

Job Title _____

Employer's Name and Address _____

Supervisor's Name _____

Date Started _____ Date Ended _____

Description of Responsibilities and Skills Used _____

Professional Licenses

Name/Number of License _____

Licensing Agency _____ Date Issued _____

Military Experience

Rank _____ Branch of Service _____

Date Started _____ Date Ended _____

Description of Responsibilities and Skills Used _____

_____

Special Training _____

Personal Data

Awards, Honors, and Special Achievements _____

_____

Hobbies and Special Interests _____

Foreign Languages _____

Organizations and Offices Held _____

_____

Volunteer Work _____

References   List educational, employment, and character references. No relatives, please.

Educational Reference:

Name and title _____

Address _____ Phone _____

Employment Reference:

Name and title _____

Address _____ Phone _____

Character Reference:

Name and title _____

Address _____ Phone _____

Your Turn 15–5

PLAN A CAREER PORTFOLIO

List at least six items you could include in your career portfolio.

_____

_____

_____

_____

_____

_____

you can pull it out of the portfolio binder or case and explain it to the interviewer. He or she may ask you to leave the whole portfolio at the end of the interview, so be sure all the documents are photocopies and not originals. If you are Web-savvy, you can also post your career portfolio on a Web site, and the interviewer can look at it there.

Finding Job Openings

Most jobs are not advertised. If you limit your search to the jobs listed in the classified section of your local newspaper, you will be short-changing yourself. Furthermore, although many jobs are now posted on-line on job boards, the majority of jobs are not. So when you job hunt, you need to use as many approaches as you can. The more active you are in searching for a job, the more likely you are to find something. Among the sources of information are networking, employers, school placement offices, classified ads, private employment agencies, government employment agencies, registers and clearinghouses, and the Internet.

Networking When you are job hunting, you should ask your parents, other relatives, friends, fellow students, instructors, and coworkers for leads to jobs that might interest you. If you can list 50 people you know who might be helpful, each of them may be able to give you two or three names. Before you know it, your network may have a thousand potentially helpful people in it. To extend your network even further, join business or trade organizations, local community service groups, and organizations like Toastmasters. Remember, almost half of all successful job hunters find their jobs through networking, not through ads or the Internet. Being referred to a company by a person who is known there often will open the door to an opportunity.

Your Turn 15–6

START BUILDING A NETWORK

Most people can easily build a network of a thousand people. On a separate piece of paper, list 25 (or more) people you know and the jobs they hold. Then build the network by asking each of the people on your core list for two referrals. Working outward, add to your network. Keep a list of every person and their contact information for use when you begin job hunting.

Employers You can apply directly to an employer even if you're not sure there is a job available. To find employers that may have positions that meet your job objective, you can:

- check the employers' Web sites on the Internet (see Figure 15–4)
- consult directories of trade associations at the library
- check the directories of your local Chamber of Commerce
- look in the Yellow Pages
- Visit flipdog <http://www.flipdog.com>, a Web site that scans the Internet for job openings posted on employer Web sites.

FIGURE 15–4

Many corporations post job openings on their Web sites.

School Placement Offices   Many school placement offices provide job referral services to students and alumni. This is an excellent source of job leads for students, because employers list positions whose qualifications are likely to be matched by students or alumni. In addition, placement offices can put you in touch with alumni who work in the field that interests you. These alumni are happy to share information and job leads with students.

Classified Ads   Classified ads list hundreds of jobs, but many do not identify responsibilities, the employer's name, or the salary. Still, some people do find their jobs by responding to classified ads (see Figure 15–5).

You can find employment ads in local newspapers and professional and trade publications, both in print and on-line. Check these every day, early in the day. If you do decide to answer an ad, respond promptly. Some jobs are filled before the ad stops running. Keep a record of all ads you respond to.

Private Employment Agencies   Private employment agencies can sometimes be helpful. There are temporary agencies, general agencies, agencies that specialize in a particular field, and executive search agencies. The most important thing to remember about agencies is that they are in business to make money. Either you or the employer will have to pay a fee, usually a percentage of a year's salary, if you get a job through the agency. Before you decide to use a private employment agency, make sure you understand the financial arrangements.

Government Employment Agencies   Your state's employment service, sometimes called the Job Service, provides free statewide and local job referrals. Because the service is free, offices are often crowded, and you may have to wait a long time before you are helped. To find a state employment office, look in the phone book under your state's Department of Labor or Employment, or visit their Web site.

Registers and Clearinghouses   Registers and clearinghouses collect and distribute employment information. There are federal and private clearinghouses, and some specialize in certain fields. Some list employers' vacancies, some list applicants' qualifications, and some list both. The cost to the job hunter varies.

Internet Resources   Many of the job-hunting resources just mentioned can also be accessed over the Internet. Corporate Web sites often post job openings, school placement offices can be reached on-line, classified ads appear on a newspaper's Web site, and private and government employment agencies maintain job databases. Thousands of Web sites post job openings.

FIGURE 15–5

Even though most jobs are not advertised, it still pays to check the classified ads in your local newspaper.

Leading COSTUME JEWELRY DISTRIBUTOR

is seeking a

MARKETING ASSISTANT

to help regional marketing manager with sales and promotion.

College preferred. Marketing experience a plus.
Competitive salary and benefits.

E-mail resume to Mia Wall, MWall@fortaine.com.

Delores Kesler

(Courtesy of Delores Kesler, Adium, LLC.)

Although Delores Kesler grew up in a home without extra money, she was taught by her mother's example to give to others. When Kesler was about nine years old, her mother took her to visit a senior center for people with mental illness. Kesler found the experience sad and depressing, but the next week she went back, this time with some penny candy to give to the patients. "The fact that it wasn't pleasant didn't bother me," says Kesler. "In fact, I kept going when my mother stopped."

Today Kesler still gives to others, but now she's giving money she earned by founding a Jacksonville, Florida, temporary staffing agency in 1977. Starting with a $10,000 loan, Kesler built up Accustaff Inc. into a business earning $50 million a year. She was one of the first women to take a company public on the New York Stock Exchange. For her business achievements, she was awarded the Ernst and Young Entrepreneur of the Year Award and the Horatio Alger Award for Distinguished Americans.

In her business, Kesler instituted a policy that all employees had to devote some time to community service. She also made sure the company gave to charitable causes. After she retired in 1997, Kesler devoted herself to philanthropy, supporting causes that benefit children, education, and the environment through her foundation. Kesler believes that women who have made their own money should give back to the community. She hasn't forgotten the less popular causes, either. She is particularly devoted to her work with the Hospice Foundation for Caring.

Sources: "About Us," ATS Professional Services <http://www.consultats.com/aboutus.cfm>, accessed April 11, 2003; Laura Link Maggio, "Kesler Teaches the Art of Giving," *The Business Journal,* November 9, 2001 <http://jacksonville.bizjournals.com/jacksonville/stories/2001/11/12/focus1.html>, accessed April 11, 2003; Rather, Dan, "They Live the Dream," *Parade,* May 6, 2001, p. 6.

FIGURE 15–6

This is the home page of one of the many commercial job boards on the Internet.
(Courtesy of CareerBuilder LLC.)

In addition to these resources, there are approximately 20 huge Internet job boards that list openings around the world. For example, the U.S. Department of Labor and state employment agencies maintain America's Job Bank, a nationwide database of job listings. Some of the most comprehensive private job boards are CareerBuilder, Career Mosaic, CareerPath.com, Headhunter.net, HotJobs, JobOptions.com, Jobs.com, Monster.com, and NationJob Network (see Figure 15–6). Job sites usually update their listings every day, and you can search for openings by location and type of job. When a new job matching your profile comes in, the job board will e-mail you a notice.

Another way to use the Internet for job hunting is to post your resume in a resume database or a personal home page. Employers can find qualified job candidates by doing key word searches. For the job hunter, posting a resume is usually less effective than searching a job site because you are relying on an employer to find you instead of the other way around. Regularly repost your resume because some sites pull up newer resumes before older ones.

A certain amount of caution is needed when you are job hunting on-line. For example, identity thieves have been known to post false job openings on the larger job boards in an effort to get people's social security numbers and credit card data. So never give out such personal information over the Internet. Furthermore, if you are currently employed and want to keep your job search private, be careful where you post your resume on-line. Make sure you understand the degree of privacy the site will afford you. This can range from no privacy (anyone can access your resume) to sites that allow you to see which companies are interested in your resume before the resume is released. To be safe in general, you can create a resume that does not give your name and lists only an anonymous e-mail address, such as those available on Yahoo or Hotmail. You can then screen any responses you get before offering further information.

Finally, keep in mind that not all employers use the Internet, so do not stop using other job-hunting techniques when you start searching on-line.

Writing Cover Letters

Most employers don't want to be bothered with handling the phone calls of dozens of job applicants. When you respond to a classified ad or other job listing, or contact an employer cold, you usually mail, fax, or e-mail your resume and cover letter.

The cover letter demonstrates your interest in a particular job or company. Its purpose is to get the employer to look at your resume and call you in for an interview. So one all-purpose cover letter will not do. You must write a cover letter that is targeted to each job you're responding to. Here are some tips for composing cover letters:

- Whenever possible, address the letter to a specific person. Do some research, if necessary, to find the exact name of the person you are writing to.

- If you are e-mailing your cover letter and resume, they should go into one e-mail message. (Many employers will not open e-mail attachments for fear of viruses.) Keep the "cover letter" portion of the message short: just the salutation ("Dear Mia Wall"), an opening paragraph in which you indicate which job interests you, where you saw it advertised, and that you think you would be a good fit for the job. In the second paragraph, indicate your availability for an interview. Finish with a closing like "Sincerely," and add your name, phone number, and e-mail address. Then paste your plain text resume right into the e-mail. Figure 15–7 shows Marianne Guilmette's e-mail response to the ad for a marketing assistant.

- If you are sending your cover letter and resume by fax or regular mail, then use a business letter format. A paper cover letter can have an additional paragraph in which you explain why your skills, education, and experience would be valuable to the employer. Still, keep it short—three paragraphs maximum and no more than one page.

FIGURE 15–7

The "cover letter" portion of an e-mailed resume should be very short and to the point. A plain text (ASCII) version of the resume is pasted right below the closing of the "cover letter" portion of the message.

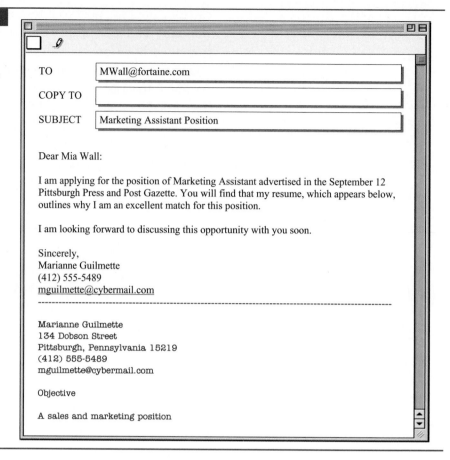

TO   MWall@fortaine.com

COPY TO

SUBJECT   Marketing Assistant Position

Dear Mia Wall:

I am applying for the position of Marketing Assistant advertised in the September 12 Pittsburgh Press and Post Gazette. You will find that my resume, which appears below, outlines why I am an excellent match for this position.

I am looking forward to discussing this opportunity with you soon.

Sincerely,
Marianne Guilmette
(412) 555-5489
mguilmette@cybermail.com

Marianne Guilmette
134 Dobson Street
Pittsburgh, Pennsylvania 15219
(412) 555-5489
mguilmette@cybermail.com

Objective

A sales and marketing position

Remember, the cover letter, like the resume, is an advertisement for you. Make it positive and upbeat in tone. And make it perfect: neat, well organized, and without errors. Have someone proofread it for you.

Filling Out Employment Applications

When you call on an employer directly, or before you are interviewed, you may be asked to fill out an employment application form. This form includes much of the information that is on your resume but arranged for the employer's convenience. So bring a copy of your resume when you call on employers. You can also use the resume data sheet from "Your Turn" 15–4, page 367, as a handy source of information when filling out an application form.

When you fill out an employment application, follow directions. Write neatly. Remember that spelling and grammar are as important on the application as they are on your resume and cover letter. If there is a section that doesn't apply to you, write a dash (—) or N/A (not applicable) in the space. You need not provide information that may be discriminatory—your age, race, religion, marital status, and arrest record, for example. The employment application form shown in Figure 15–8, page 377, is nondiscriminatory.

FIGURE 15–8

The information on an employment application form is similar to the information on a resume.

Fortaine, Inc.

APPLICATION FOR EMPLOYMENT
An Equal Opportunity Employer

PERSONAL INFORMATION

Name _Marianne Guilmette_   Date _Sept. 20, 20—_

Address _134 Dobson St._   Soc. sec. no. _555-2D-0020_

Pittsburgh, PA 15219   Telephone _(412) 555-5489_

E-mail address _mguilmette@cybermail.com_   Fax _—_

Are you 18 years of age or older? Yes ☑ No ☐

Are you either a U.S. citizen or an alien authorized to work in the United States?   Yes ☑ No ☐

EMPLOYMENT DESIRED

Position applied for _Marketing Assistant_ Full-time only ☑ Part-time only ☐ Full-time or part-time ☐

EDUCATION

Type of School	Name of School	Address	No. Years Completed	Major and Degree
High School	West Central H.S.	Fromer Rd., Pitts.	4	College prep
College	Pitts. Com. Coll.	East Main, Pitts.	2	Marketing, A.S.
Bus. or Trade School				
Prof. or Grad. School				

WORK EXPERIENCE

Dates (Month and Year)	Name and Address of Employer	Position(s) Held	Highest Salary	Reason for Leaving
June 2003 – present	Campus Store, Pittsburgh CC, East Main St., Pittsburgh	Senior sales associate	$7/hr	—
July 2002 – May 2003	MDS Marketing Group, Pittsburgh, Pa.	telemarketer	$6/hr +	Company relocated.

List work-related skills you have or special accomplishments. _retail sales, special promotions, product display, telemarketing. Was Sales Associate of the Month twice._

REFERENCES Give the names of three people, not relatives, who have known you for at least one year.

Name	Address	Phone	Relationship
Beth Martingale	Campus Store, PCC	(412)555-2051	Employer
John Hoisington	Dept. of Mktng, PCC	(412)555-3124	Professor
Rev. Wm. Starzyk	Trinity Church, Pitts.	(412)555-9024	Minister

I hereby certify that all information is true and complete and authorize Fortaine Inc. to contact former employers and references regarding this application.

Applicant Signature _Marianne Guilmette_   Date _Sept. 20, 20—_

Interviewing

If your resume and application have made a good impression, you will be invited for an employment interview.

There are three basic types of employment interviews:

- A gatekeeping interview screens a large group of applicants. Typically this is done by an employment agency, recruitment firm, or human resources department. You must do well in this interview to go on to the next stage.

- A job interview, with one or more people in the company, explores your qualifications, personal characteristics, and suitability. This interview is usually conducted by the person supervising the position. If you do well in this level of interview, you are passed to the next stage.

- In a final interview, a higher level executive assesses how well you would fit with the company and discusses any problems that may have come up during previous interviews.

If you are applying for a job at a large company, you are likely to go through all three types of interviews. In a small company, you may be interviewed by just one or two people.

Most interviews are done in person, but some are done over the phone to save the employer time and money. During an interview, the interviewer will evaluate your skills, experience, and character in order to decide whether you are a match for the job. Although an interview may last only 15 minutes, those minutes are very important. You should take time to prepare carefully for each interview. During the interview, you should try to make a good impression as well as learn as much as you can about the job. And after an interview, it's important to follow up to show your professionalism and interest.

Before the Interview   The interview is your big chance to impress someone who has the authority to approve you or give you a job. Because people know that interviews are so important, they get nervous. To minimize your nervousness and increase your self-confidence, prepare yourself for the interview beforehand. Here are some suggestions that will help you arrive at an interview well prepared.

- **Do some research about the company.** Get information from the company's Web site, public relations department, or from the library. Find out what it produces or sells, how big it is, what its reputation is, and what its problems are. Be ready to ask questions about the company.

- **Do some research about the job.** Make sure you understand the duties and responsibilities of the position. You can check the *Occupational Outlook Handbook* for a general description of

> **Work is life, you know, and without it, there's nothing but fear and insecurity.**
>
> *john lennon,*
>
> *british rock musician*

the position. Be aware, however, that different employers use different job titles and job descriptions.

- **Be ready to explain why your experience and skills qualify you for the job.** Which of your skills and experiences can be useful to the employer?

- **Be prepared to answer the questions that almost always come up.** These are variations on Tell me about yourself, What are your strengths? What are your weaknesses? Why should we hire you? What have you accomplished? What do you want to do in five years? How much salary do you want? Be specific, and be ready with examples.

- **Be prepared to handle discriminatory questions.** Although employers cannot legally ask questions designed to reveal your race, nationality, age, religion, or marital status, sometimes they do. You can either answer the question directly or try to return the interview to its proper focus, the requirements of the job. For example, you can respond with something like, "I know your company is committed to diversity by the statement posted in the lobby. I want to show you how hiring me will help you meet your company's business goals."

- **Make sure you are neat and well groomed and that your clothing is appropriate.** For most job interviews, stick to the basics. That usually means a clean, well-pressed suit for both men and women. Avoid extremes—trendy or skimpy clothes, gaudy colors, large jewelry or lots of jewelry, body piercings (except small earrings for women), lots of makeup, sunglasses, and sneakers. Do not wear perfumes or aftershave. In general, it's better to dress conservatively because that projects a professional image.

- **Bring several copies of your resume, your career portfolio, a pen, and a small notebook.** You may want to take some notes.

- **Be prepared to take one or more tests.** You may be asked to take an aptitude test, a skills test, a medical exam, or a drug test.

- **Know exactly where the interview is and how to get there.**

- **Plan to get to the interview 10 minutes early.**

Getting ready for an interview is a lot like getting ready for an exam. The more you prepare, the less nervous you will feel, and the better you will do.

During the Interview   The moment has come. You look great, you've done your homework, and you even got there with a few minutes to spare. Remember the importance of first impressions

> *"The sense of being perfectly well dressed gives a feeling of inward tranquillity."*
>
> ralph waldo emerson,
>
> 19th-century American writer

The employment interview is your chance to convince an employer that you are the right person for the job. It also gives you the opportunity to ask questions about the job and the company. *(Courtesy of PhotoDisc.)*

and act accordingly. You should be professional with everyone you encounter, including security guards and receptionists.

When you're called in for the interview, it's time to follow the interviewer's lead. After you've introduced yourself and shaken hands, if offered, wait to be seated until the interviewer shows you a chair. Put your things on a nearby chair—never on the interviewer's desk. While you are getting settled, the interviewer is usually reviewing your resume or application. Let the interviewer begin the conversation when he or she is ready.

Interviewers are individuals, too, so the interview process may be quite different each time you undergo it. Some interviewers ask very specific, directed questions and expect short, to-the-point answers. Others talk so much you hardly have any time to speak yourself, although you may learn a lot about the company. Still others just say, "Tell me about yourself," and expect you to start talking. So you have to be flexible enough to adapt to the interviewer's style.

The Basic Types of Interview Questions.   In an interview, you may be asked three types of questions:

- **Informational questions.** These questions are about your credentials—your experience, education, and skills. They are the easiest to answer. An example of an informational question is "What are your qualifications for this job?" Many job interviews consist only of informational questions.

- **Problem-solving questions.** These questions are more difficult because they are hypothetical. Interviewers may give you a problem scenario and ask what you would do. For example, they tell you that Employee X arrives late three times a week and ask how you would handle this situation. They may ask you to role play. For example, if you are applying for a sales job, interviewers might indicate an item on the desk and ask you to sell it to them.

- **Behavioral questions.** These questions are designed to assess your character, traits, habits, and attitudes by discovering how you handled challenging situations in the past. A typical behavioral question is "Tell me about a time when you made a big mistake" or "Tell me about a time when you made a great sale." You answer such a question by telling a story about a past experience. Even if the experience was negative—such as making a big mistake—you should frame it positively. "Although the client was upset that the installation was late, I learned the importance of good communication and follow-up."

Handling Personal and Discriminatory Questions.   What happens if interviewers ask you a sensitive or personal question? Saying that it's none of their business (even though it may be true) won't work. Instead, you must try to respond in a way that will put the interview back on track without embarrassing the interviewer. For example, if the interviewer asks how old you are, you can simply reply, if answering doesn't bother you. Or you can say something like "Your ad didn't indicate that you were concerned about age but rather focused on keyboarding speed. I'd like to show you that I am accurate at seventy-five words per minute."

Remember, questions having to do with your race, sex, age, religion, and marital status are discriminatory. However, some interviewers do ask such questions. If you find yourself in an interview that seems to dwell on these subjects, this might be an indication that you don't want to work for that company.

Asking Questions about the Company.   During the interview, keep in mind that you are there for two purposes. The primary purpose, of course, is to sell yourself to the employer. You want to convince the interviewer that you are the right person for the job. The second purpose is for you to assess the company and the job. The interview affords you a brief opportunity to get a feel for the company and to learn more about the job. Be sure you ask questions that show you've done your homework about the company. You may find, after an interview, that you really are enthusiastic about the possibility of working at that company. On the other hand, what you learn about the job and the company may convince you that you would be better off elsewhere.

Interview Tips.   Here are some suggestions to make the most of the opportunity provided by the interview:

- Don't eat, chew gum or candy, or smoke.
- Don't criticize former employers or complain about them.
- Don't discuss any of your financial or personal problems.
- Avoid controversial topics like politics.
- Don't make up answers that you think the interviewer wants to hear. This may backfire on you.
- Listen carefully, and be sure you understand each question. Remember that open-ended questions require more than a *yes* or *no* answer. It's okay to ask for clarification or to take time to think about your response. (Review your listening skills in Chapter 8.)

- Be courteous. Make sure you have the interviewer's name right. Listen carefully, and don't interrupt.

- Ask open-ended questions about the company and the job. In addition to gaining information, you will demonstrate your interest and enthusiasm.

- Let the interviewer bring up the subject of money. If you are asked what salary you expect, you can turn the question around by indicating you know what the average starting salary is in the industry and by asking what the company's salary range is. Try not to mention a specific salary first, because you may be too high or too low.

At the End of the Interview. Interviewers can bring the interview to a close in several ways. You may be thanked for your time and told you will hear from them. When this happens, it sometimes means that the interviewers do not think you are suitable for the job. They may let you know at a later date that someone else was hired. Try not to take it personally. Remember that the employer is looking for someone who fits into the organization.

Another way the interview can end is with your being invited back for a placement or other test or to talk to someone else in the company. If you're asked to take a drug test, find out which types of tests they are using and which foods or medications could trigger a false positive. (Three quarters of large and medium-sized companies test for drugs.) When you are invited back, make sure you write down the details of your next appointment. Don't rely on your memory, because you may be too excited to remember things correctly.

FIGURE 15–9

Writing a thank you note or letter to each interviewer demonstrates your interest in the company and the job.

TO MWall@fortaine.com

COPY TO

SUBJECT Interview for Marketing Assistant Position

Dear Mrs. Wall:

Thank you for taking the time to speak with me yesterday about the Marketing Assistant position in the Middle Atlantic region. I was very impressed with your company, and the job sounds wonderful. I'm more than ever convinced that my marketing experience can benefit your company.

Sincerely,
Marianne Guilmette
(412) 555-5489
mguilmette@cybermail.com

Your Turn 15–7

ROLE PLAY AN INTERVIEW

Choose a partner from your class and role play an interview. One of you will be Marianne Guilmette, whose resume appears on page 365. Marianne is looking for a marketing job. The other will play the part of the interviewer, who is looking for someone to fill the vacancy shown in the classified ad on page 372. Take a few minutes to prepare, and then role play the interview.

And last, the interview may actually end with a job offer. If this happens, *and you are absolutely sure you want the job,* then say yes. But in most circumstances, you should ask for a day to think it over. That extra time will give you a chance to think about the job and the company. You will have to decide whether the company, job, salary, and potential for the future are what you want.

After the Interview   Even if the interview does not result in a job offer, you should send interviewers a letter or e-mail message to thank them for their time (see Figure 15–9). A brief thank you note serves to demonstrate courtesy and interest on your part. Although you may not get the particular job you interviewed for, at some time in the future you may wish to apply to that company again.

After each interview, you should review your performance. What seemed to impress the interviewer? What could you have done better? Use each interview as a rehearsal for the next. That way you will improve your interview skills. Remember, you may have a dozen or more interviews before you get a job offer. Ideally, you will have more than one offer and can choose the job you prefer.

YOUR CAREER: A LIFELONG ENTERPRISE

Your working life will be long—40 or 50 years for many people. Your working life will also be varied: Gone are the days when a person worked at the same job for the same company for life. So when you consider a job offer, you must think of long-range as well as short-range consequences. Sometimes an offer of immediate employment is tempting simply because you've been job hunting for a while or need the money. While these are certainly factors influencing whether you take a job, you should try to evaluate how a job fits into your long-term professional goals. Essentially, if the job you are considering will help you achieve your career goals, then you should take it.

Do you remember the long-term professional goals you set in Chapter 2? Now that you have spent some time thinking about

Your Turn 15–8

YOUR LONG-TERM PROFESSIONAL GOALS

Take this opportunity to review and change your long-term professional goals, if necessary. Whether your goals have changed or not, answer the following questions. Renew your commitment to achieving your goals.

1. What is your long-term professional goal?

_____

_____

2. By when do you expect to reach this goal?

_____

3. What actions must you take to reach your goal?

_____

_____

_____

_____

_____

yourself and setting an employment objective, you should reevaluate your long-term goals. Perhaps you need an entirely new professional goal, or a slightly modified goal. Perhaps your action plan for achieving your long-term professional goal needs an overhaul.

Goal-setting in the context of a career is an ongoing process. As you gain experience, you may find that the goals you set at the start of your career no longer interest you or were unrealistic. You may find that your jobs are taking you in unexpected but interesting new directions. You will also find the world around you changing so fast that you must adapt to keep up. Changes in technology and the world economy can change the way businesses operate. If you don't keep up with such changes, your skills and experience may become obsolete. Continuing education and retraining are becoming a lifelong process.

The process of self-evaluation and learning that you have undertaken in this course is an ongoing process. It doesn't end when the course is over or when you get your first job. Rather, to reach your potential, you will use your inner resources and abilities to meet the challenges of your personal and professional life.

The Information Highway

GETTING UP TO SPEED

There are so many career- and job-related Web sites that you could spend days looking through them. Here are a few to get you started.

- To match yourself by ability, skills, and temperament to specific careers, you can answer a questionnaire at these sites and be given a list of suitable occupations. The College Board posts one career questionnaire <http://www.collegeboard.org> and the Princeton Review posts another in its Career section <http://www.review.com/>. In addition, the Princeton Review site has many job-hunting tips.

- Once you have a few occupations in mind, you can access descriptions of them from the U.S. Department of Labor Bureau of Labor Statistics, which posts the *Occupational Outlook Handbook* on-line <http://stats.bls.gov>. This site also offers the latest employment trend information.

- You can find suggestions and tips for preparing a resume at <http://www.free-resume-tips.com> and <http://resume.monster.com>.

- Search for career portfolio articles at <http://www.quintcareers.com/>.

- Ready to job hunt? Then try America's Job Bank, a nationwide database of job listings posted by the public Employment Service. In addition to specific job listings you will find links to your state's employment office <http://www.ajb.org>. Or you can try one of the commercial job boards, such as Career Builder <http://www.careerbuilder.com>, the Monster Board <http://www.monsterboard.com>, or Flipdog, where you can also post your resume <http://www.flipdog.com>.

In addition, there are sites devoted to careers and jobs in particular areas, such as education or health care. To find these sites, do a key word search using the name of the occupation.

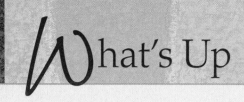
What's Up

Name _____ Date _____

1. List and describe the five categories of workplace skills.

_____

_____

_____

_____

_____

2. What career information can be found in a library?

_____

_____

_____

_____

_____

3. How can you use the Internet to find career information?

_____

_____

_____

_____

_____

4. Why should you keep up with job trends and economic news?

_____

_____

_____

_____

_____

5. What is a resume? What is its purpose?

_____

_____

_____

_____

_____

continues

Name _____   Date_____

6. What is a career portfolio? How does it differ from a resume?

_____
_____
_____
_____
_____
_____

7. Describe three ways of finding a job.

_____
_____
_____
_____
_____
_____

8. What is the purpose of a cover letter? a thank you letter?

_____
_____
_____
_____
_____
_____

9. List three things you can do to prepare for a job interview.

_____
_____
_____

continues

Name _____   Date _____

10. What are the two main purposes of a job interview?

_____

_____

_____

_____

_____

11. List and give an example of the three basic types of interview questions.

_____

_____

_____

_____

12. Why should you keep reviewing and changing your professional goals?

_____

_____

_____

_____

_____

Case Studies

THE CASE OF THE SELF-IMPORTANT APPLICANT

Jeff's uncle knew someone at the telecommunications company where Jeff wanted to start his career. As a favor to Jeff, who was about to graduate, Jeff's uncle set up an interview for him.

Jeff prepared his resume, took his only suit to the cleaners, and went to the interview full of confidence. He was surprised to hear the interviewer describe the entry-level position. Although he had never had a telecommunications job, he was sure he was too qualified to start at such a job. When he heard what the starting salary was, he informed the interviewer that he was not interested. Later that evening Jeff told his uncle about the interview. He couldn't understand why his uncle became so annoyed when he heard what had happened.

1. Was Jeff's uncle justified in being annoyed at Jeff?

_____

_____

_____

2. Why are Jeff's expectations about his first job so unrealistic?

_____

_____

_____

3. How would doing some research into the company and the industry have helped Jeff on his first interview?

_____

_____

_____

THE CASE OF THE DISCOURAGED JOB SEEKER

When Abby finished school, she started looking for her first full-time job. Every Sunday she looked through the classified employment ads and circled any that looked interesting. She sent out several resumes and cover letters each Monday, but with no results. After three weeks, she was discouraged and decided it was no use to check the ads.

1. What should Abby have had before she even started her job hunt?

_____

_____

_____

2. What's wrong with Abby's job search technique?

_____

_____

_____

3. What should Abby do to get her job search on track?

_____

_____

_____

Journal

Answer the following journal questions.

1. Describe the worst job you ever had. What did you learn from it? How did this job affect your career goals?

_____
_____
_____
_____
_____

2. What is your ideal job? What aspects of this job appeal to you? What "real world" work might this ideal job be similar to?

_____
_____
_____
_____
_____

3. Describe someone you know who loves his or her job. Why does this person enjoy work? How does this enjoyment affect the rest of her or his life?

_____
_____
_____
_____
_____

4. What is your career goal? What are you doing now to prepare yourself to reach this goal?

_____
_____
_____
_____
_____

After You're Done:
Self-Assessment

Now that you have worked through *Reaching Your Potential,* it's time to assess your progress. Read each of the following statements. Then circle *yes, maybe,* or *no* to indicate whether the statement is true of you at this time.

To the Lifelong Learner

1. I can name and describe the four areas of potential that each of us has.	Yes	Maybe	No
2. I have good self-belief, the foundation of success.	Yes	Maybe	No
3. I can learn new things and change my beliefs to change my behavior.	Yes	Maybe	No
4. I can set, pursue, and achieve realistic goals.	Yes	Maybe	No
5. I can envision a compelling future for myself.	Yes	Maybe	No
6. I have achieved personal mastery over at least some aspects of my life.	Yes	Maybe	No

UNIT 1   Developing Your Emotional Potential

Chapter 1   The Power of Self-Belief

7. I can explain my most important values and beliefs to another person.	Yes	Maybe	No
8. I usually think about things in a positive way.	Yes	Maybe	No
9. I recognize my good qualities and always make the most of them.	Yes	Maybe	No

Chapter 2   Setting Realistic Goals

10. I have a dream for my future.	Yes	Maybe	No
11. I have written personal, educational, professional, and community service goals.	Yes	Maybe	No

12. I have action plans for achieving my goals.	Yes	Maybe	No
13. I have the motivation needed to achieve my goals.	Yes	Maybe	No

UNIT 2 Developing Your Intellectual Potential

Chapter 3 Improving Your Thinking Skills

14. I use techniques to improve my memory.	Yes	Maybe	No
15. I am able to think critically.	Yes	Maybe	No
16. I try to solve problems in a systematic way.	Yes	Maybe	No
17. I use techniques to improve my creative thinking.	Yes	Maybe	No

Chapter 4 Improving Your Study Skills

18. I know my learning style and try to use it whenever possible.	Yes	Maybe	No
19. I have good study skills.	Yes	Maybe	No
20. I use special reading techniques when I read to learn.	Yes	Maybe	No
21. I take good notes on my readings and in class.	Yes	Maybe	No
22. I have good test-taking skills.	Yes	Maybe	No
23. I know how to use the resources of a library.	Yes	Maybe	No

UNIT 3 Developing Your Physical Potential

Chapter 5 Eating Well

24. I can list the basic nutrients and their food sources.	Yes	Maybe	No
25. I eat a balanced diet.	Yes	Maybe	No

Chapter 6 Staying Healthy

26. I am physically fit because I exercise regularly.	Yes	Maybe	No
27. I do not abuse drugs, including alcohol and tobacco.	Yes	Maybe	No
28. I understand how to prevent the spread of sexually transmitted diseases.	Yes	Maybe	No

UNIT 4 Developing Your Social Potential

Chapter 7 Communicating Effectively

29. I can explain the basic elements of communication.	Yes	Maybe	No
30. I know what my own communication style is.	Yes	Maybe	No
31. I use techniques to improve my communication with others.	Yes	Maybe	No

Chapter 8 Improving Your Listening Skills

32. I am an active listener, with respect for the speaker and comprehension of the message.	Yes	Maybe	No

Chapter 9 Improving Your Speaking Skills

33. I am a good speaker, with good voice qualities and a good command of standard English.	Yes	Maybe	No
34. I am good at conversing with another person.	Yes	Maybe	No
35. I have good telephone skills.	Yes	Maybe	No
36. I can prepare and deliver an oral presentation.	Yes	Maybe	No

Chapter 10 Getting Along with Others

37. I am assertive without being aggressive.	Yes	Maybe	No
38. I have ethical values that I try to live by.	Yes	Maybe	No
39. I am good at understanding the needs of other people.	Yes	Maybe	No
40. I give feedback tactfully and receive feedback openly.	Yes	Maybe	No
41. I use conflict resolution techniques to defuse angry situations.	Yes	Maybe	No

Chapter 11 Functioning in Groups

42. I can describe the basics of group dynamics.	Yes	Maybe	No
43. I function well as a member of a team or group.	Yes	Maybe	No
44. I can use different leadership styles in different situations.	Yes	Maybe	No

Chapter 12   Handling Change and Stress

45. I understand the relationship between change and stress.	Yes	Maybe	No
46. I know the signs of stress and watch out for them.	Yes	Maybe	No
47. I can reduce my feelings of stress by using coping techniques.	Yes	Maybe	No

Chapter 13   Managing Time

48. I perform tasks in a timely manner and I am punctual.	Yes	Maybe	No
49. I set priorities on the things I need to do.	Yes	Maybe	No
50. I use a planner and "to do" list to organize my time.	Yes	Maybe	No

Chapter 14   Managing Money

51. I know my values and goals and base short- and long-term financial decisions upon them.	Yes	Maybe	No
52. I have a written budget.	Yes	Maybe	No
53. I understand and use savings institutions, debit, credit, and insurance wisely.	Yes	Maybe	No
54. I know the factors that influence whether I should rent or buy a home.	Yes	Maybe	No
55. I invest now for large future expenses such as retirement.	Yes	Maybe	No

Chapter 15   Preparing for Your Career

56. I can match my skills and interests to one or more suitable occupations by using career resources.	Yes	Maybe	No
57. I have a good resume and can write a good cover letter.	Yes	Maybe	No
58. I know how to use various job-hunting resources.	Yes	Maybe	No
59. I am good at preparing for and undergoing employment interviews.	Yes	Maybe	No
60. I can evaluate whether a job fits into my long-term professional goals.	Yes	Maybe	No

Look over your self-assessment. Underline the statements to which you replied *maybe* or *no*. These statements reflect areas in which you may not yet have reached your potential. Pay particular attention to the chapters that cover these areas as you work through the book.

Look over your self-assessment. Underline the statements to which you replied *maybe* or *no*. These statements reflect areas in which you still may not have reached your potential.

Compare this self-assessment with the one you did before you began working through this book (see pages xxvi–xxix). In which areas have you succeeded in reaching your potential? Which areas still need work? You should review the chapters in which these areas are covered to improve your knowledge and skills.

Glossary

A

accented English English spoken by many Americans for whom English is a second language

aerobic exercise activities that improve cardio-respiratory endurance; for example, walking and swimming

agenda a list of topics to be discussed at a meeting

alcohol an addictive drug that decreases brain activity and lowers blood pressure

all-channel pattern a communication network in which each group member communicates with every other group member

amphetamine a drug that stimulates the brain

anabolic steroid an artificial form of a male hormone that stimulates the growth of muscle

annual percentage rate (APR) the interest rate charged per year on the amount borrowed

anorexia nervosa an eating disorder in which the person starves himself or herself because of a fear of being fat

assertiveness the self-belief and determination to make your needs or opinions known

associative thinking a method of problem solving in which you let your mind wander in order to get fresh insight

B

backburner thinking putting a problem aside and allowing your unconscious mind to take over solving it

barbiturate a type of depressant drug, also called *barbs, reds,* and *yellows*

beliefs specific opinions about yourself, other people, situations, things, or ideas

benzodiazepine a type of depressant drug, such as tranquilizers and sleeping pills

bodily-kinesthetic intelligence the ability to solve problems or make things by using your body or parts of your body

body composition the proportion of the body made of muscle compared with fat

body mass index a measure of weight in relation to height

brainstorming a process by which a group of people comes up with many ideas about a problem or issue

budget a plan for using your money in order to spend less than income and meet financial goals

bulimia an eating disorder in which the person consumes large amounts of food and then induces vomiting to avoid gaining weight

C

call number a unique identification number that indicates where a book or other item is shelved in the library system

calorie the amount of heat needed to raise the temperature of one kilogram of water one degree centigrade

carbohydrate a chemical substance that provides energy for the body; for example, sugar

cardiorespiratory endurance the ability to do moderately strenuous activity over a period of time without overtaxing the heart and lungs

career portfolio a collection of documents that illustrate what you have done on the job, in school, or in community service; used in employment situations

certificate of deposit (CD) a type of bank account in which your money is tied up for a period of time ranging from 30 days to 5 or 10 years

chain a communication pattern in which messages are passed from one person to another without skipping over anyone

charisma a special quality of personal leadership that inspires great loyalty

checking account a bank account used to write checks and pay bills

chlamydia a sexually transmitted infection of the genital and urinary tracts

cholesterol a fatty acid found in animal products such as meat, cheese, shellfish, and eggs

chronological resume a resume format that lists the most recent job experience first, followed by other jobs in reverse chronological order

circadian rhythm an inner daily clock that governs the operating of our bodies

citation a reference to a published work, including author, title, publisher or periodical, date, and page numbers

closed-ended question a question that can be answered with a simple *yes* or *no*

club drug any of a wide variety of drugs used at parties, dance clubs, raves, and bars, especially by young adults

cocaine an addictive drug that increases brain activity and makes the user feel happy and excited

cognition mental processes such as thinking and remembering

cohesiveness in a group, the degree to which members stick together

communication the exchange of messages, either verbal or nonverbal

community service goals objectives that relate to improving conditions in your neighborhood, town, or city

compelling future the driving force from your current reality to a future reality

complex carbohydrates complex sugars such as starch and whole grains, which usually contain fiber

conformity changing opinions or behavior in response to pressure from a group

cover letter in job hunting, the letter that accompanies your resume, demonstrates your interest in a company or job, and asks for an interview

crack a powerful form of cocaine whose name derives from the sound that rock cocaine makes as it melts

creativity the ability to see things in a new way and to come up with unusual and creative solutions to problems

credit a financial arrangement in which you can defer payment on merchandise or services

credit bureau a company that maintains credit records

credit card plastic identification card that allows the holder to buy merchandise and services up to a certain dollar amount and pay for them later

credit limit the highest amount of money you can charge against a particular credit card

D

debit card a card that allows you to pay for something by deducting money from your checking or savings account

deductible the amount an insured person pays to settle a claim before the insurance company starts paying

deductive reasoning a type of logical thinking in which the conclusion that is reached is true if the information it is based on is true

defense mechanism a mental process used to reduce anxiety and protect self-belief

depressant any drug that decreases brain activity and lowers blood pressure

depression a disorder characterized by sadness and difficulties in eating, sleeping, and concentrating

dialect a variation of standard English that is spoken in a particular geographic area or by a particular social group

dietary fiber undigestible matter in whole grains, fruits, and vegetables that aids digestion

discussion list a special interest discussion group on the Internet

displacement reacting to a negative situation by substituting another person for the person who aroused your anxiety or anger

drawing a visual image of something

drug a chemical substance that creates a physical, mental, emotional, or behavioral change in the user

drug abuse the nonmedicinal use of a drug, which results in physical, emotional, or mental harm to the user

E

eating disorder a condition in which eating habits are out of control; for example, bulimia

educational goals objectives that relate to learning or training

e-mail a method of exchanging messages over the Internet

emergency fund an amount of money, usually at least two months' salary, set aside for unplanned expenses or loss of income

empathy experiencing another person's feelings or ideas as if they were your own

enunciation the clarity with which words are spoken

expenses amounts you spend

extrinsic motivation needs and incentives that come from outside ourselves and make us act in particular ways; an outside reward for behavior

F

fact something that can be shown to be true

fantasy a form of withdrawal from a negative situation in which daydreams provide a boost to self-belief

feedback a response to a message; fundamental to two-way communication

finance charge the total of all costs associated with a loan or credit card

fixed expenses amounts you spend that are the same all the time and/or occur regularly; for example, rent

flexibility the ability to move a joint through its full range of motion

flowchart a diagram used to show the steps in a process or procedure

Food Guide Pyramid a model of a well-balanced diet, with foods that can be eaten in quantity at the base of the pyramid, and food that should be eaten sparingly at the top

formal group a group with clear goals and established rules

formatted resume a visually appealing resume saved as a formatted document with bold, italic, and other type; used when a paper resume is needed

functional resume a resume format in which work experience is presented in terms of the functions and skills used on the job

G

genital herpes a sexually transmitted disease caused by a virus

gonorrhea a sexually transmitted infection of the genital mucous membranes

gross income the total amount of money, from all sources, coming in

group the conscious interaction of two or more people

group dynamics the study of the patterns of response or adaptation that occur when people interact in groups

groupthink an uncritical acceptance of a group's beliefs and behaviors in order to preserve its unanimity

H

hallucinogen a drug that distorts perceptions and creates images of things that are not really there

heroin an addictive drug that affects the brain and lowers blood pressure

HIV-AIDS (human immunodeficiency virus–acquired immune deficiency syndrome) a collection of diseases and conditions resulting from the destruction of the immune system

I

idea diagram a diagram that shows the relationship of secondary ideas to a main idea and to one another

income money coming in, such as salary or child support

individual retirement account (IRA) a type of account used to set aside money, usually for retirement or education

inductive reasoning a type of logical thinking in which the conclusion that is reached is probably true

informal group loose association of people without stated rules

installment loan a loan that is paid back in monthly installments for a fixed period of time

interest a charge set by the lender and paid by the borrower of money

intermediate-term goals objectives that can be accomplished in one to five years

Internet a worldwide computer network that enables people to communicate electronically

interpersonal intelligence the ability to understand other people and to work cooperatively with them

intrapersonal intelligence the ability to assess yourself and use that assessment to live an effective life; self-knowledge

intrinsic motivation needs and incentives that come from within us and make us act in particular ways

J

jargon specialized words used in a particular field

Johari window a model showing the effect of mutual understanding on a relationship between two people

K

key words the words you enter when using a search engine to find information on the Internet

L

leadership a set of behaviors, beliefs, and values that enables a person to persuade others to act

leading changing aspects of another person's communication style by getting them to imitate you

liability coverage a type of insurance coverage that protects the insured against the claims of others in case the insured causes property or other damage

linguistic intelligence the ability to use language and words well

logical-mathematical intelligence the ability to think logically, mathematically, and scientifically

long-term goals objectives that can be achieved over a long period of time—more than five years

long-term memory the third stage of memory, in which material is stored for years

M

marijuana a mild hallucinogen that alters the mind in many ways

mental set an overreliance on old ways of seeing and doing things

method of loci a system using images of places that can be used to help memorize information

mind-mapping a creativity technique that involves sketching the problem or topic

mineral a chemical that is needed for life and growth

mirroring to imitate another person's behavior or expressions

mnemonics devices, such as poems or acronyms, to help people remember

money market account a type of bank account whose interest rates change with market rates

monounsaturated fat a type of fat that is liquid at room temperature and found in peanut and olive oil

motivation the needs and incentives that make us act in particular ways

muscular endurance the ability to repeat movements or to hold a position for a long time without tiring

muscular strength the ability to exert force using a muscle once

musical intelligence the ability to hear musical sounds and make music

N

net income the amount of money you actually receive after amounts are withheld for taxes and other deductions

neurons the nerve cells that make up the brain and nervous system

neurotransmitters chemical substances that pass from one neuron to another, such as dopamine and serotonin

nicotine an addictive drug found in tobacco

norm in a group, the rules by which people in particular roles are expected to behave

nutrients substances used by the body for growth, maintenance, repair, and energy

O

one-way communication a form of communication in which a sender transmits a message, a receiver gets the message, and the process is complete

open-ended question a question that requires an explanation as a response

opinion a belief based on values and assumptions that may or may not be true

P

P.Q.R. system a method of reading for information that involves three steps: previewing, questioning, and reviewing

passbook account a type of bank account with low interest

pegword method a system using numbers and words that can be used to help memorize information

perceive to see, hear, smell, taste, or become aware of something through the senses

periodicals publications, such as magazines and newspapers, that appear at regular intervals

periodicals index a directory, organized by subject, that provides citations for articles about each subject; can be in book, CD-ROM, or on-line format

personal goals objectives that relate to your personal life

personal mastery the ability to achieve specific results with consistency

physical fitness the ability to carry out daily tasks without tiring and with enough energy left to enjoy leisure activities and to handle an emergency requiring physical exertion

pie chart a diagram that shows the relationship of the parts (wedges) to the whole (pie)

pitch the level of sound on a musical scale

plain text resume an unformatted resume saved as an ASCII or plain text file; used when a resume will be scanned or otherwise input into a database

planning a thinking process in which an orderly and systematic approach to achieving an objective is devised

polyunsaturated fat a type of fat that is liquid at room temperature and found in corn, safflower, and soybean oil

positive psychology a branch of psychology that studies positive aspects of human behavior

potential the capacity for development into reality; a state of possibility

preface a short essay at the beginning of a book that often summarizes the author's point of view

prejudice a negative attitude toward people because of their membership in a group

premises information upon which reasoning is based

previewing scanning a reading selection before reading

priority a task that is important and should be done first

procrastination postponing a task that should be done now, or putting off until tomorrow what should be done today

professional goals objectives that relate to your work life

projection attributing your own unacceptable behaviors and feelings to another person

pronunciation the correctness with which words are spoken

protein a chemical substance that is part of all body cells

R

rationalize to explain or excuse an unacceptable situation in terms that make it acceptable to yourself

recall words in note taking, important words that provide cues for the main ideas

receiver in communication, the person who gets a message

reframing changing a belief that one holds in order to change the meaning

respect valuing the worth of another person

responsiveness the degree to which persons are closed or open in their dealings with others

resume a short summary of your experience and qualifications, used in job hunting

role in a group, the set of expected behaviors for a particular position

S

saturated fat a fat that is solid at room temperature and found in meat and dairy products and palm and coconut oils

search engine a computerized index that can be used to find information on a particular topic on the Internet

self-belief your confidence in and respect for your own abilities; also called *self-esteem*

self-fulfilling prophecy a belief that comes true because it is believed

sender in communication, the person who sends a message

sensory memory the first stage of memory, in which material lasts a couple of seconds and then disappears

short-term goals objectives that can be achieved in a brief period of time—a year or less

short-term memory the second stage of memory, in which material lasts about 20 seconds

simple carbohydrates simple sugars such as table sugar, corn syrup, and other sweets

situational leadership the ability to adapt leadership styles to different circumstances

spatial intelligence the ability to form and use a mental model of a three-dimensional world

standard English the English spoken by news broadcasters, actors, and others who have no regional accents

state specific the quality of being associated with a particular state of mind or place

stimulant any drug that increases brain activity and other body functions and makes the user feel more awake

stress the physical and psychological reactions to events or situations that a person has difficulty coping with

student loan a loan made to students to cover educational costs; payment is deferred until the students complete their education

substandard English English spoken with poor pronunciation, enunciation, grammar, and vocabulary

surfing the Net the process of "visiting" Web pages on the Internet by clicking on text or images that link pages

syphilis a sexually transmitted disease caused by a bacterium

T

table of contents an outline of the main ideas of a book (chapters), along with page numbers

time line a diagram that shows the sequence of historical events

trust reliance on another person

two-way communication a form of communication in which a sender transmits a message, a receiver gets the message, and the receiver responds by giving feedback

U

unsaturated fat a fat that is liquid at room temperature, such as vegetable oil

Usenet discussion forums a system of discussion groups on the Internet

V

values your deepest feelings and thoughts about yourself and life

variable expenses amounts you spend that differ from one period to another; for example, vacation expense

visualization a motivational technique in which you imagine the results of achieving a goal

vitamin a chemical that is needed for life and growth

volume the intensity or loudness of a sound

W

Web page a document on the World Wide Web, part of the Internet

Web site a collection of related Web pages on the World Wide Web; it is maintained by an individual or a group

wheel a communication pattern in which a person at the hub communicates with each person on the spokes, but the people on the spokes do not communicate directly with one another

withdrawal escaping from negative feedback

World Wide Web a part of the Internet that consists of millions of interlinked documents called Web pages

References

TO THE LIFELONG LEARNER

[1]Senge, Peter M. *The Fifth Discipline.* New York: Currency, Doubleday, 1990, p. 14.

[2]O'Malley, Brian. "The Quest of Mt. Everest." Presentation, no date.

CHAPTER 1

[1]Ingold, John. "Visions of Everest: Blind Climber Sees Himself as Adventurer, Not Hero," *Denver Post,* March 6, 2001, p. E1.

[2]McNally, David. *Even Eagles Need a Push: Learning to Soar in a Changing World.* New York: Delacorte Press, 1990, p. 153.

[3]CBS News/New York Times Poll, September 2–5, 2002. Cited on The Polling Report, Inc., Web site, <http://www.pollingreport.com/news.htm>, accessed January 16, 2003.

[4]Rosenthal, Robert, and Lenore Jacobson. *Pygmalion in the Classroom: Teacher Expectation and Pupils' Intellectual Development.* New York: Irvington, 1989, pp. 46–51.

[5]Braiker, Harriet B. "The Power of Self-talk." *Psychology Today,* December 1989, p. 24.

[6]Reprinted by permission of Pocket Books, a Division of Simon & Schuster from *Unlimited Power* by Anthony Robbins. Copyright © 1986 by Robbins Research Institute.

[7]Coombs, Patrick. *Major in Success,* 3rd ed. Berkeley, Calif.: Ten Speed Press, 2000, pp. 31–32.

CHAPTER 2

[1]Canfield, Jack. "Improving Students' Self-Esteem." *Educational Leadership,* September 1990, p. 48.

[2]Goleman, Daniel. "Hope Emerges as Key to Success in Life," *The New York Times,* December 24, 1991, pp. C1, C7.

CHAPTER 3

[1]Ferguson, Tom. "Empowerment: The Heart of Wellness." *Self-Care Journal,* May/June 1991, unpaged.

[2]Wolfe, Patricia. *Translating Brain Research into Classroom Practice.* Washington, D.C.: Association of Supervision and Curriculum Development, 1996.

[3]Hammond, John S., Ralph L. Keeney, and Howard Raiffa, *Smart Choices: A Practical Guide to Making Better Decisions.* Boston, Mass.: Harvard Business School Press, 1999, pp. 5–8.

[4]Gilbert, Randy. *Success Bound.* Mt. Jackson, Va.: Bargain Publishers, 2001, pp. 86–88.

CHAPTER 4

[1]Based on Ned Herrman's Whole Brain Model in *The Creative Brain,* 2nd ed., Lake Lure, N.C.: Brain Books, 1990.

[2]Adapted from Anthony F. Gregorc, "Learning Style Information Acquisition Preference Inventory," unpublished.

[3]Kelley, Tina. "How to Separate Good Data from Bad," *New York Times,* March 4, 1999, p. E9.

[4]Ramage, John D., John C. Bean, and June Johnson, *The Allyn & Bacon Guide to Writing,* 3rd ed., New York: Longman, 2003, p. 612.

CHAPTER 5

[1]Food and Drug Administration Health and Diet Survey. Reprinted in the *FDA Consumer,* October 1989, p. 24.

[2]U.S. Department of Agriculture and U.S. Department of Health and Human Services, *Nutrition and Your Health: Dietary Guidelines for Americans.* Washington, D.C.: Authors, 2000, p. 2.

[3]Burros, Marian. "Eating Well: The Diet Pendulum Swings Again," *New York Times,* August 14, 2002.

[4]U.S. Census Bureau, *Statistical Abstract of the United States 2001.* Table 197, Percent of U.S. Adults Who Were Overweight and Percent Who Were Obese: 1998, p. 126.

CHAPTER 6

[1]Maugh, Thomas H., II. "Teens Quickly Hooked on Smoking," *Denver Post,* August 29, 2002, p. 2A.

[2]"Smokers Costly to Society," *Denver Post,* April 12, 2002, pp. 1A, 11A.

[3]Centers for Disease Control and Prevention, National Center for Health Statistics, *2001 National Health Interview Survey.* Data Table for Figure 8.1, Prevalence of Current Smoking among Adults Aged 18 Years and Over: United States, 1997–2001 <http://www.cdc.gov/nchs about/major/nhis/released200202/figures08_1-8_4.htm>, accessed February 12, 2003.

[4]Centers for Disease Control and Prevention, National Center for Health Statistics, *Health, United States, 2002.* Table 67. Alcohol Consumption by Persons 18 Years of Age and Over, According to Sex, Age, Race, and Hispanic Origin: United States, Selected Years 1997–2000 <http://www.cdc.nchs/data/hus/tables/2002/02hus067.pdf>, accessed February 12, 2003.

[5]Wechsler, H., J. E. Lee, M. Kuo, and H. Lee. "College Binge Drinking in the 1990s: A Continuing Problem," *Journal of American College Health,* Vol. 48, 2000, pp. 199–210.

CHAPTER 7

[1]Adapted from David W. Merrill, and Roger Reid. *Personal Styles and Effective Performance.* Radnor, Pa.: Chilton, 1981.

[2]Adapted from W. J. Reddin, *Managerial Effectiveness.* New York: McGraw-Hill, 1970.

[3]Carducci, Bernardo. *Shyness: A Bold New Approach.* New York: HarperPerennial, 2001.

CHAPTER 8

[1]Harris, Tom W. "Listen Carefully." *Nation's Business,* June 1989, p. 78.

[2]Zuker, Elaina. *The Seven Secrets of Influence.* New York: McGraw-Hill, 1991, p. 143.

CHAPTER 9

[1]Krotz, Joanna L. "Cell Phone Etiquette: 10 Do's and Don'ts." Microsoft bCentral, January 3, 2001 <http://www.bcentral.com/articles/krotz/165.asp>, accessed August 27, 2003.

[2]Arredondo, Lani. *How to Present Like a Pro.* New York: McGraw-Hill, 1991, pp. 16–22.

CHAPTER 10

[1]Luft, Joseph. *Group Processes: An Introduction to Group Dynamics.* With permission by Mayfield Publishing, Mountain View, Calif., © 1984, 1970, 1969 by Joseph Luft.

CHAPTER 11

[1]Asch, Solomon E. "Studies of Independence and Conformity: A Minority of One against a Unanimous Majority." *Psychological Monographs,* Vol. 9, 1956, p. 416.

[2]Adapted from W. J. Reddin. "What Kind of Executive?" *Journal of the Institute of Directors,* December 1966, pp. 448–453; and W. J. Reddin, *Managerial Effectiveness.* New York: McGraw-Hill, 1970.

CHAPTER 12

[1]Papalia, Diane E., and Sally Wendkos Olds. *Psychology,* 2nd ed. New York: McGraw-Hill, 1988, p. 567.

[2]Holmes, Thomas H., and Richard H. Rahe. "The Social Readjustment Rating Scale," *Journal of Psychosomatic Research,* Vol. 11, 1967, pp. 213–218; Masuda, M. "Life Change and Illness Susceptibility," in *Stressful Life Events: Their Nature and Effects,* ed. B. S. Dohrenwend and B. P. Dohrenwend. New York: Wiley, 1974.

[3]Posen, David B. "Stress Management for Patient and Physician." *The Canadian Journal of Continuing Medical Education,* April 1995 <http://www.mentalhealth.com/mag1/p51-str.html>, accessed March 28, 2003.

[4]Ferguson, Tom. "Your Support Group," *The Self-Care Catalog,* Emeryville, Calif.: Spring 1992.

CHAPTER 13

[1]Webber, Ross A. *A Guide to Getting Things Done.* New York: Free Press, 1980, pp. 62–63.

CHAPTER 14

[1]Porter, Sylvia. *Your Own Money.* New York: Avon Books, 1983, p. 12.

[2]Wyss, B. O'Neill. "Dollars and Sense." *TWA Ambassador,* April 1991, p. 85.

CHAPTER 15

[1]Dixon, Pam. *Job Searching Online for Dummies,* 2nd ed. Foster City, Calif.: IDG Books Worldwide, 2000.

Index

Note: Page numbers followed by the letter "f" indicate figures and numbers followed by the letter "t" indicate tables.

U

Unsaturated fats, 108
Usenet discussion forums, 21

V

Values
  Benjamin Franklin's values, 9
  changing, 8
  defined, 4
  ethical, 224–225
    Your Turn 10–2: Do The Right Thing, 226
  parts of, 4, 6
  society's, 6–7
  source of, 6
  Your Turn 1–2: What Do You Value?, 7
  Your Turn 1–3: Examine Your Values, 8
Vargas, Elizabeth, 165
Variable expenses, 322
Vegetables, 114
Victims and nonvictims, 11
Visualization, 38
Vitamins, 108

Vocabulary
  building, 89
  grammar and, 201
Voice qualities, 161
Volume, 199

W

Water, 108
Web site, 21
  career planning. *See* Internet
  corporate, 369f
Weight gain, 121
Weight loss, 120
Weihenmayer, Erik, 3–4
Wheel pattern, 252
Withdrawal, 235
World Wide Web, 20–21
  evaluating information found on, 95–97

Y

Yamashita, Takuji, 254
Yun, Chan Ho, 191